The United States and Right-Wing Dictatorships, 1965–1989

Building on David Schmitz's earlier work, *Thank God They're on Our Side*, this is an examination of American policy toward right-wing dictatorships from the 1960s to the end of the Cold War. During the 1920s, American leaders developed a policy of supporting authoritarian regimes because they were seen as stable, anticommunist, and capitalist. After 1965, however, American support for these regimes became a contested issue. The Vietnam War served to undercut the logic and rationale of supporting right-wing dictators. By systematically examining U.S. support for right-wing dictatorships in Africa, Latin America, Europe, and Asia and bringing together these disparate episodes, this book examines the persistence of older attitudes, the new debates brought about by the Vietnam War, and the efforts to bring about changes and an end to automatic U.S. support for authoritarian regimes.

David F. Schmitz is the Robert Allen Skotheim Chair of History at Whitman College in Walla Walla, Washington. He is the author of *Thank God They're on Our Side: The United States and Right-Wing Dictatorships, 1921–1965*; *The Tet Offensive: Politics, War, and Public Opinion*; *Henry L. Stimson: The First Wise Man*; and *The United States and Fascist Italy, 1922–1940*.

To Polly
For enhancing it all

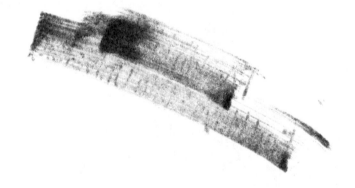

The United States and Right-Wing Dictatorships, 1965–1989

DAVID F. SCHMITZ

Whitman College

CAMBRIDGE UNIVERSITY PRESS

CAMBRIDGE UNIVERSITY PRESS
Cambridge, New York, Melbourne, Madrid, Cape Town, Singapore, São Paulo

Cambridge University Press
40 West 20th Street, New York, NY 10011-4211, USA

www.cambridge.org
Information on this title: www.cambridge.org/9780521861335

First published 2006

Printed in the United States of America

A catalog record for this publication is available from the British Library.

Library of Congress Cataloging in Publication Data

Schmitz, David F.
The United States and right-wing dictatorships, 1965–1989 / David F. Schmitz.
  p. cm.
Includes bibliographical references and index.
ISBN 0-521-86133-0 (hardback) – ISBN 0-521-67853-6 (pbk.)
1. United States – Foreign relations – 1945–1989.   2. Dictators – History – 20th century.
3. Right-wing extremists – History – 20th century.   4. Totalitarianism – History –
20th century.   I. Title.
E840.S355   2006
327.73′009′045 – dc22   2005023060

ISBN-13   978-0-521-86133-5 hardback
ISBN-10   0-521-86133-0 hardback

ISBN-13   978-0-521-67853-7 paperback
ISBN-10   0-521-67853-6 paperback

Contents

Acknowledgments

First and foremost, I want to thank my wife, Polly, for her love and support, without which this book would not have been finished. She enhances all of my work and my life.

Whitman College provided generous support that allowed me to travel to various archives to conduct research. Moreover, through the Lewis B. Perry Summer Research Scholarship Program I was able to work with Vanessa Walker, Erin Gettling, Eugene Hansen, and Mark Lanning as research assistants; they helped in locating documents at the National Archives, the presidential libraries, Seely Mudd Library at Princeton University, and Penrose Library at Whitman College. In 2002, a National Endowment for the Humanities Summer Stipend provided needed assistance.

I thank all of the archivists and librarians at the presidential libraries, the National Archives, and the university libraries that I visited for all of their assistance, aid, and advice. Without fail, I encountered dedicated professionals who went out of their way to help make my work possible. The staff at Penrose Library deserves a special thanks for all of the assistance they provided in helping me locate necessary materials. Kathy Guizar of Image Management assisted me with the cover photograph.

I owe an enormous debt to Lewis Bateman, senior editor at Cambridge University Press, for his continued support and expert advice. He provided wise guidance on revisions and numerous suggestions to make this a better work. Ciara McLaughlin, senior editorial assistant, provided professional assistance in preparing the work for publication.

Part of Chapter 4 was published as "Senator Frank Church, the Ford Administration, and the Challenges of Post-Vietnam Foreign Policy" in *Peace and Change* 21, no. 4 (1996); and part of Chapter 5 appeared as "Jimmy Carter and the Foreign Policy of Human Rights," with Vanessa Walker, in *Diplomatic History* 28, no. 1 (2004). I wish to thank the publishers and editors of both journals for permission to republish that material here.

In addition to their work as research assistants, Vanessa Walker and Erin Gettling read the entire manuscript and made excellent suggestions for improvements; Vanessa's collaboration on Jimmy Carter was a high point in the writing of this book. Amy Portwood and Bruce Magnusson read Chapter 1 and shared their expertise on Africa and American foreign policy. Amy, who is a great friend and colleague, also shared some of her research on the United States and the Congo from her dissertation. Brad Simpson generously shared some documents on John Kennedy's policy toward Indonesia, and his work has greatly influenced my thinking on that subject. My colleagues in the History Department at Whitman College read an early draft of Chapter 2 during our First Friday sessions and provided valuable feedback and suggestions. Markham McIntyre assisted me with the bibliography.

Fred Logevall read an early draft of the first three chapters and provided excellent suggestions for changes and improvements. Michael Krenn remains a trusted colleague whose advice and ideas always influence my thinking for the better. Bill Walker's close reading of the manuscript challenged me to rethink and sharpen some components of my analysis. T. Christopher Jespersen read early drafts of the manuscript, and then the completed work, and as always was a challenging critic and source of good ideas. They are all true friends for their criticisms and support. I cannot fully express my gratitude, but I can take full responsibility for any remaining mistakes of fact or interpretation. I cannot finish any work without acknowledging my debt to Lloyd Gardner as a mentor and friend. His teaching and scholarship, as always, informed my work.

Richard and Carla Scudellari were ideal hosts during research trips, and I want to thank them again for their friendship. The support of my family has been a constant over the years, and I am grateful to all of them, especially my mother, Mary Schmitz, who is always ready and willing to discuss my work and ideas, and my sister Terry and her husband, Kevin, for allowing me a place to stay when I return to Long Island on research and other trips. My children, Nicole and Kincaid, are sources of wonder, joy, and needed interruptions.

Finally, as I began, I dedicate this book to Polly.

Introduction

Since its founding, the United States has been philosophically dedicated to supporting liberal democracy and the rule of law. This commitment is found in the most important documents and treaties of the nation, including the Declaration of Independence, the Constitution, and the United Nations Universal Declaration of Human Rights, and has been proclaimed by presidents, secretaries of state, and other policymakers from the time of George Washington to the present day. In addition, throughout its history the United States has been an expansive nation territorially, economically, and culturally. As a result, the American desire to promote democracy has created a conflict between American values and ideals and American security and material interests.

During the 1920s, in an effort to resolve this dilemma, American leaders developed and institutionalized the logic, rationale, and ideological basis for the United States to support right-wing dictatorships in the name of freedom. As my book *Thank God They're on Our Side: The United States and Right-Wing Dictatorships, 1921–1965*, demonstrated, the result was a policy of support for right-wing dictatorships that promised stability, protected American trade and investments, and aligned these dictatorships with Washington against the enemies of the United States.[1] World War II challenged the idea that supporting authoritarian regimes enhanced American interests and led to a temporary abandonment of this policy.[2] The wartime opposition to fascism and the triumph of the Allies made the promotion of democracy a paramount concern as the postwar period promised a vindication of American values and institutions. From these ideas emerged the remarkable achievements in postwar West Germany, Japan, and Italy of establishing democratic governments and the

---

[1] Schmitz, *Thank God They're on Our Side.*

[2] I use the terms "right-wing dictatorship" and "authoritarian regime" interchangeably throughout the text, just as American policymakers did in their discussions of such regimes. Also following the usage of U.S. officials, both are defined as any antidemocratic regime that is not socialist or communist.

rebuilding of the economies of Western Europe and Japan. Yet the apparent change was not universal as the continued support of certain dictators indicated. American officials now distinguished between a regime such as Hitler's that threatened peace and those, such as Anastasio Somoza García's in Nicaragua, that apparently did not. Thus, policymakers adopted a pragmatic rationale for defending dictatorships they favored, and moral judgments were invoked only when the government opposed a regime rather than to provide a consistent principle to guide policy and base decisions.

With the emergence of the Cold War, expediency again overcame the American commitment to democracy as the United States came to prefer "stable" right-wing regimes in the Third World over indigenous radicalism and what it saw as dangerously unstable democratic governments. The pronouncement of the Truman Doctrine in March 1947 and the adoption of containment as the global policy of the United States brought about the change. President Harry S. Truman announced that the United States faced a global contest between two competing and incompatible ways of life, democracy and totalitarian communism. It was now a bipolar world. In that context, it did not matter that many of the regimes the United States came to support were not democratic, or had overthrown constitutional governments. If it was now a contest between only two ways of life; nations had to fit into one category or the other. Right-wing dictatorships became part of the free world no matter what the composition of their governments, and the United States gained friendly, albeit brutal and corrupt, allies, who backed American policies in the struggle with the Soviet Union.

As the Truman administration created the post–World War II national security state to carry out the global struggle against the Soviet Union, advocates of containment defended their actions by arguing that the United States, because of its position as the leading democratic nation in the world, had an obligation to defend freedom. Reaching back to the republican ideology of the American Revolution, Manifest Destiny, and notions of American exceptionalism, policymakers asserted that it was the duty and destiny of the United States to assume the burden of world leadership in order to defend liberty and the nation against communism, just as it had done in defeating Nazi Germany and imperial Japan. This World War II narrative served to frame all American actions in terms of defending the "free world" against Soviet totalitarianism.[3] As Michael Hogan has demonstrated, in constructing this understanding and pursuing the Cold War, officials in the Truman administration worried about the possible danger of undercutting freedom at home and destroying the values and institutions that the policy of containment was supposed to save.[4]

[3] See Hunt, *Ideology and U.S. Foreign Policy*, and Stephanson, *Manifest Destiny*, for the development of these ideas in the nineteenth century, and Fousek, *To Lead the Free World*, for the creation of what Fousek terms the ideology of "American nationalist globalism" during the Truman administration.
[4] Hogan, *A Cross of Iron*.

There was another contradiction that also had to be confronted, the apparent need to support nondemocratic but anticommunist regimes. Policymakers were aware of the paradox that supporting right-wing dictatorships contradicted the narrative they used to criticize the Soviet Union and carry out a global policy of containment. Yet, because the United States was seen as a unique nation, and its use of power benign and for the benefit of others, it could justify its actions as being necessary aberrations in the long-term defense of freedom. Thus, the Truman administration revived the pre–World War II rationale for supporting right-wing dictatorships. Based upon a paternalistic racism that categorized non–Western European peoples as inferior, vulnerable to radical ideas, and therefore in need of a firm government to maintain order and block communism, authoritarian regimes were viewed as the only way most Third World nations could undergo economic improvements that would allow for the development of more "mature" populations without succumbing to communism or radical nationalism. While this attitude undermined the avowed rectitude of American leaders, democracy was not seen as a viable option for newly independent nations or the countries of Latin America. Strong dictators, therefore, were seen as bulwarks against political instability and channels for modernization. Hence policymakers believed that support for authoritarian regimes protected liberalism internationally by preventing unstable areas from falling prey to Bolshevism while allowing time for nations to develop a middle class and democratic political institutions. Through nation building, dictators would be the instruments of the creation of strong and eventually free societies.

The administration also introduced an important new variable into the basic assumptions of American policy toward right-wing dictatorships. A distinction was now drawn between authoritarian dictators on the right and totalitarian dictators on the left. Autocratic regimes were seen as traditional and natural dictatorships for their societies, while totalitarian regimes were classified as imposed autocratic rule plus state control over the economy. In this understanding of the world, there was little room for moral arguments against right-wing dictators. They would be wedged into the free world, no matter what their record of abuses, as nations capable of being set on the road to democracy. No such hope was held out for communist nations. Moreover, the administration believed that whenever right-wing dictatorships were overturned, the resulting governments were weak and unstable, making those nations susceptible to communist subversion. The United States, it concluded, had to support right-wing dictators in order to provide stability, protect American economic interests, ensure American security, and promote liberalism.

American leaders remained aware of the contradictions in this policy and its shortcomings. For example, President John Kennedy and his advisors worried that right-wing dictators were proving to be ineffective bulwarks against communism and were creating political backlashes against the United States, as was the case in Cuba. Authoritarian rulers upset political stability as much as they ensured it by frustrating their populations' desires for change and democracy, and they nurtured support for left-wing and communist opposition to their rule. The problem was how to break the dependence on right-wing dictators for maintaining order, how to promote change without losing control of the political situation and unleashing revolutionary movements. The president provided an excellent example of this dilemma in 1961 when discussing the Dominican Republic. "There are three possibilities," Kennedy said, "in descending order of preference: a decent democratic regime, a continuation of the Trujillo regime or a Castro regime. We ought to aim at the first, but we really cannot renounce the second until we are sure that we can avoid the third."[5] With the growing crisis in Vietnam and revolutionary challenges in other parts of the world, the Kennedy and Johnson administrations found no answer to this problem and opted to continue to support right-wing dictators as necessary to maintain order in nations that were too politically immature for self-government, to block the spread of communism, and to preserve American access to the resources of the Third World.

After 1965, however, American policy toward right-wing dictators became a contested issue as the Vietnam War served to undercut much of the logic and rationale used to justify both American Cold War policy and support of authoritarian regimes, and brought to the fore the contradictions in American policy. The debates over and changes in American policy toward right-wing dictatorships from the mid-1960s to the end of the Cold War are the subject of this study. While the persistence of older attitudes and approaches continued to guide American policy into the 1970s, the shattering of the Cold War consensus brought forth a sustained criticism of American assistance to various right-wing dictators and an alternative approach under President Jimmy Carter. In the 1980s, President Ronald Reagan's reassertion of the verities of the Cold War and the logic and rationale that had been used to justify friendships with authoritarian regimes since the 1920s led to tense struggles and efforts to counter Reagan's policies in Central America, South Africa, and the Philippines.

Scholars have examined American support of specific dictatorships, but no comprehensive study of how American policy toward right-wing dictatorships changed in the wake of the Vietnam War exists. *Friendly Tyrants*, edited by Daniel Pipes and Adam Garfinkle, contains twenty-three case studies examining American policy and anticommunist right-wing dictatorships. American backing of these dictators is never questioned. Focusing on periods of upheaval and crisis management, mainly in the 1970s and 1980s, the book seeks to discover patterns that "could be put to practical use in managing current troubles and preventing future ones," and to answer the question, "how does one gauge when an authoritarian regime may be susceptible to an overthrow that will damage U.S. interests?"[6] Whether or not instability is endemic to such regimes and relationships is never addressed. A follow-up volume by Garfinkle and coauthors, *The Devil and Uncle Sam*, is designed as a guide for policymakers to use in conducting relations with right-wing dictators. The authors conclude

---

[5] Schlesinger, *A Thousand Days*, 769.
[6] Pipes and Garfinkle, eds., *Friendly Tryrants*, ix, 4.

that United States policy toward authoritarian regimes "has been reasonably effective in achieving a proper balance of realism and idealism, and that balance has stood us in good stead most of the time."[7] This study challenges the conclusion that American support for right-wing dictatorships has served the nation well.

Since the end of the Cold War, a triumphalist interpretation of American foreign policy has emerged that claims that the United States won the contest with the Soviet Union because of its values and its promotion of liberalism and democracy. Most notably, Tony Smith's *America's Mission* examines U.S. efforts to promote democratic governments throughout the twentieth century and argues that the promotion of democracy was "the central ambition of American foreign policy during the twentieth century." He claims that this policy was the main mechanism the United States used to further and protect American national interests abroad, and that the U.S. victory in the Cold War was attributable to the correctness of this approach and a validation of the superiority of its values: democracy, free enterprise, and liberal internationalism. Smith concludes that President Ronald Reagan's steadfast promotion of democracy abroad meant that "by 1992 democracy stood unchallenged as the only form of mass politics that offered itself as a model worldwide."[8] To make this case, Smith has to ignore much of the history of United States relations with right-wing dictatorships and interventions in the Third World to overthrow governments that the United States has opposed. American support for right-wing dictatorships demonstrates that the promotion of democracy was not a consistent, central goal of the United States, and the history of supporting authoritarian regimes cannot be dismissed or ignored in evaluating American foreign policy since 1965.[9]

This study examines the logic, rationale, and ideological justifications used by American officials for continued U.S. support of right-wing dictatorships, and the challenges that emerged after the Vietnam War that made supporting right-wing dictatorships a contested issue. The central concern is how American officials understood the problem in terms of an overall policy and in relation to specific countries, and how that shaped their decision making about various nations. Here, the more nuanced approaches to containment that détente was based on, and that reflected the reality of the Sino-Soviet split, did not influence policy as anticommunism remained a blanket position for supporting various brutal regimes in the Third World. American officials consciously and purposefully supported authoritarian regimes in the pursuit of American interests, and

---

[7] Garfinkle et al., *The Devil and Uncle Sam*, 17.

[8] Smith, *America's Mission*, 3–4, 267.

[9] I use the date 1965 as the starting point of this study for two reasons. First, while the analysis of the Congo goes back to the late 1950s to establish the context, and while Lumumba was overthrown in 1960, Mobutu does not come to power and establish his dictatorship until 1965. Second, the first volume of my analysis of United States foreign policy and right-wing dictatorships, *Thank God They're on Our Side*, ended with 1965, and this study picks up the examination chronologically at this point.

often employed covert operations and other undemocratic means to accomplish this end.

Given the large number of dictatorships in the world, the focus of this study is on American policy and the decision making in Washington, and not on bilateral relations. Moreover, as the book covers six different presidencies over three decades, and policies toward nations on five continents, it is not possible to discuss with the same depth local events that more specialized works on U.S. policy toward individual nations or regions provide.[10] Similarly, while covert operations played a large role in United States policy toward many of the nations discussed, and are noted where appropriate, there is no attempt to provide a detailed analysis and description of these activities. The concern of this work is not with the actual role of the CIA in various nations such as Indonesia, Greece, and Chile, but with why the United States supported military dictatorships in these countries. The use of such undemocratic and secretive means, however, does further demonstrate that American policy was not primarily based upon the promotion of democracy abroad.

Throughout the 1960s, support for right-wing dictators continued to shape American policy toward the Third World, with the policy expanded to encompass the newly independent nations of Africa. American officials, employing the too-familiar racial categories that marred foreign policy making, worried that the people of Africa were unprepared for and unable to maintain democratic regimes. Washington, therefore, feared that these new countries would be beset with political instability and upheavals that would threaten Western interests and open the continent up to communist appeals. In response, the United States supported strongmen and military leaders who it believed would impose order while serving to block revolutionary nationalism and communism. Most notably, the United States helped to overthrow the government of Patrice Lumumba in the Congo and in 1965 came to support the establishment of the dictatorship of Joseph Mobutu. That same year, the Johnson administration supported the overthrow of Sukarno in Indonesia and the coming to power of Suharto after the bloody massacre of hundreds of thousands of people. Two years later, when the Greek colonels overthrew the democratically elected government in Athens and established a military dictatorship, Washington again rationalized its support as necessary to maintain order, prevent the spread of communism, and protect vital American economic and security interests.

The Vietnam War, however, changed the political climate in the nation and raised new debates and questions concerning American foreign policy. America's longest war and the battles over executive power that emerged at its conclusion provided an opportune time for a reevaluation of the policies that had led to that protracted, painful, and divisive conflict, and brought forth multiple challenges to the policy of containment and support for right-wing dictators. Critics noted that in addition to the immorality of supporting

---

[10] Interested readers should consult the notes in specific sections and the bibliography for these studies.

authoritarian regimes, the policy, while providing short-term gains and benefits for the United States, created long-term instability and political backlash against the United States in various nations of the world. Right-wing dictators consistently resisted reforms urged upon them by the United States, created politically polarized societies that destroyed the political center, and fostered radical political movements that brought to power the kinds of regimes the United States most opposed and had originally sought to prevent. Moreover, the policy damaged the credibility and reputation of the United States by aligning it with some of the most oppressive and violent governments in the world.

It was the United States' role in General Augusto Pinochet's 1973 coup in Chile, and President Richard Nixon's support for his regime, that brought forth sustained criticism of American support for right-wing dictators and marked the beginning of change. Rather than acquiesce to the president's actions, Congress moved to investigate the American role in the coup and placed restrictions on American aid and support for the Chilean junta. The establishment of the Senate Select Committee on Intelligence (the Church Committee) in 1975–76 provided a central focus for investigations into American covert operations, attempts to overthrow foreign governments, assassination efforts, and support for right-wing dictators. For many Americans, these hearings provided convincing evidence that the policy of supporting right-wing dictatorships was both morally flawed and worked against the long-term interests of the United States. The committee chair, Senator Frank Church, spoke for many when he argued during the bicentennial year of 1976 that it was time to once again have American foreign policy conform to the country's historic ideals and the fundamental belief in freedom and popular government. Critics called for the United States to reorient its moral compass and to find methods other than covert activity and support for brutal dictators, such as supporting self-determination and the protection of human rights, to promote American interests in the world. In the process, these hearings broadened the range of legitimate dissent and changed the discourse on American policy toward right-wing dictatorships.

These criticisms paved the way for President Jimmy Carter's efforts to forge a post-Vietnam foreign policy that rejected the central axioms of the Cold War and the containment doctrine, and emphasized human rights. During the Carter years, new voices were heard and approaches made regarding American policy toward right-wing dictators. Carter sought to implement a post–Cold War policy that emphasized supporting American ideals and principles as a more effective means to combat communism and protect the nation's interests in the Third World. The president understood the difficulties and potential problems inherent in shaping and implementing a policy based upon human rights, was aware of the limits of moral suasion, and did not believe that change could occur overnight. Moreover, he realized that he would have to support certain allies despite their despotic rule owing to national security concerns. These realizations opened Carter up to criticism from the left that he was not doing enough, fast enough, to promote human rights and led to charges that the changes he promised were more rhetorical than real. Carter, nonetheless, stayed with his policy despite its shortcomings as he remained convinced that the old approach was morally bankrupt, had damaged America's position and credibility throughout the world, and needed to be changed. When the regimes of the shah of Iran and Anastasio Somoza collapsed in 1979, Carter saw this as the inevitable result of their authoritarian rule and refused to abandon his policy and intervene to save these two dictators.

Advocates of the old policy of supporting right-wing dictators, however, blamed Carter, rather than the widespread popular discontent in these nations, for the overthrow of these two long-term allies of the United States, and the debate over American policy was renewed. The most vocal and influential critic was a future ambassador to the United Nations, Jeane Kirkpatrick, who staunchly defended supporting authoritarian regimes as the best means to preserve American interests in the Third World by resurrecting the distinction between authoritarian and totalitarian regimes. Upon his election in 1980, Ronald Reagan adopted Kirkpatrick's arguments. Once again, American policy was to support right-wing dictators throughout the world in the name of anticommunism, stability, and trade. Under the Reagan Doctrine, the president promised to promote democracy by supporting freedom fighters around the world while protecting American friends in the Third World.

Yet it would be impossible for Reagan to restore the policy of the pre-Vietnam years. In his efforts to support the brutal military regime in El Salvador, the racist apartheid government in South Africa, and the Marcos dictatorship in the Philippines, Reagan faced significant opposition from both Congress and the American public that forced him to retreat from his efforts to provide unconditional support to authoritarian regimes. When crises emerged in these nations, questions were raised concerning the efficacy and the morality of the policy, and about the wisdom of continued American support for unpopular, corrupt, and brutal leaders. In addition, employing the language of freedom and democracy in support of his renewed Cold War policies left Reagan open to charges of hypocrisy. While there was little that was new in Kirkpatrick's analysis or Reagan's policy, it was rare to have such bold public statements of the ideas and assumptions behind American policy. This openness laid bare the contradictions between the U.S. claims that opposition to the Soviet Union and communist regimes was based on their denial of political rights to their citizens, and Washington's support for governments that were equally undemocratic, guilty of human rights abuses, and denied basic civil liberties to their populations. Critics were able to use the same concepts in their efforts to oppose Reagan's support for right-wing dictatorships, and by his second term the president had to retreat from the Reagan Doctrine. As the policy became a domestic political issue, support for right-wing dictators just because they were anticommunist and promised to support the United States was no longer automatic. The central contradictions and tensions inherent in supporting right-wing dictators in the name of freedom finally made the policy untenable as an overall approach, fundamentally altering a policy that had shaped American diplomacy since the 1920s.

No Acceptable Alternative

Mobutu in the Congo

In April 1965, Assistant Secretary of State for African Affairs G. Mennen Williams declared that "the Congo, along with Cuba and Vietnam, has been a top U.S. foreign policy headache for 5 years."[1] Yet by 1968 the State Department was able to report that "the Congo has gone off the list of critical foreign policy headaches" and that relations between the United States and the Congo were "excellent."[2] What accounted for this quick turnaround and new state of affairs was the November 1965 coup by General Joseph Mobutu (later Sese Seko Mobutu), and the United States' support for his action and the military dictatorship he established.

That the Congo would be a major problem equal to those of Vietnam and Cuba in the mid-1960s is, at first glance, surprising. Since the end of the slave trade and the European scramble for Africa at the end of the nineteenth century, the United States had minimal contact with and paid little attention to developments in what most Americans still referred to as the "dark continent." Rather, Washington dealt with sub-Saharan Africa through the colonial powers, supporting their rule and policies. At the end of the 1950s, however, a new challenge faced American foreign policymakers: the decolonization of Africa. After World War II, the rising tide of nationalism abroad, increasing Cold War tensions around the world, the emerging civil rights movement at home, and the granting of independence to African states made it impossible for Washington to continue to follow the lead of the Europeans and allow the colonial powers to dictate American policy. The new problems Washington faced in Africa were manifested in the Congo in the wake of its independence from Belgium in 1960. In the process, the Eisenhower, Kennedy, and Johnson administrations all faced the persistent dilemma central to U.S. support of right-wing dictatorships. While American policymakers supported the nationalist aspirations

---

[1] Williams, "Congo Realities and United States Policy," *Department of State Bulletin*, 24 May 1965, 793.

[2] Administrative History of the Department of State, Vol. 1, Chapter 5: "Congo," Box 2, LBJL.

and quest for independence of the nations of Africa, they were convinced that black Africans were not yet ready for self-rule and worried that "premature independence" would mean unstable governments threatened by communist movements and trying to rule populations that were susceptible to radical ideas. American leaders, therefore, feared that the newly independent states of Africa were vulnerable to communist influence and in need of authoritarian rulers to maintain order, foster economic development, and serve as the conduits for the modernization of their societies.

American foreign policy toward the Third World was fundamentally shaped by the persistent belief that nonwhite people were politically immature and childlike and therefore incapable of self-rule. This led the United States to support pro-Western dictators who would provide stability, support for American Cold War policies, and a favorable atmosphere for American business. Thus, Africa was easily fit into the existing bipolar Cold War framework and policy toward right-wing dictatorships. From the beginning, the United States reacted to the Congo's independence as a crisis. The Congo's size, its geographic position in Central Africa bordering on nine other nations, and its vast mineral wealth made it one of the most important nations in sub-Saharan Africa. Eisenhower, who saw African nationalism as "a torrent overruning everything in its path, including, frequently, the best interests of those concerned,"[3] believed that the government headed by Prime Minister Patrice Lumumba was communist-leaning if not communist-dominated and pursued efforts to oust him from power. The removal of Lumumba from office and his assassination, however, did not end the unrest in the Congo. The Kennedy and Johnson administrations, in order to avoid direct American intervention, supported the sending of United Nations and Belgian troops to establish order.

Yet these efforts failed to bring a permanent solution, and rebellions again broke out when the foreign forces were withdrawn in 1964. American leaders continued to fear that unrest in the Congo would lead to a communist triumph throughout Central Africa. With the American commitment to Vietnam escalating, Washington turned to the Congo's military and General Mobutu to provide stability and a bulwark against communism in the largest and wealthiest nation in Central Africa. Mobutu, who had been recruited by the Central Intelligence Agency in 1960 and had ousted Lumumba from power that same year, was seen as the right type of leader for the Congo. He would bring stability, prevent communism from expanding in the region, and allow for continued Western access to the Congo's raw materials. Mobutu's taking of power on 24 November 1965 was seen by American officials as a necessary antidote to the unrest and rebellions that threatened the nation, and he was hailed as the savior of the Congo from chaos and communism. For over thirty years, Mobutu would enjoy Washington's support while he ran the nation as his personal fiefdom, amassed a fortune, and bankrupted and divided the country.

[3] Eisenhower, *Waging Peace*, 573.

Modernization and Authoritarianism

The dominant American attitudes toward Africa were established in the late nineteenth and early twentieth centuries. Most Americans came to see it as "a place dark and primitive, 'tribes' living in jungles ... wild beasts dominating the landscape: a place without history, largely unchanged and untamed, and certainly uncivilized." It was believed to be a continent in need of outside guidance and assistance that benefitted from European colonial rule. This image was created through the stories and adventures of such men as Henry Morton Stanley and Theodore Roosevelt. In his travelogues describing his journey to find the missionary David Livingstone, Stanley popularized the view of Africa as the "dark continent" populated by people who were four thousand years behind the improvements of the West. He compared Africans to American Indians in their backwardness and their need for outside control, and claimed that they "possess beyond doubt all the vices of a people still fixed deeply in barbarism." Yet "they understand to the full what and how low such a state is," and could be led to civilization over time by the patient leadership of their European colonial rulers.[4]

Roosevelt presented a similar image of Africa as a continent of primitive people in need of Western assistance. Writing about the African safari he embarked upon in 1909, the former president characterized many of the people as "ape-like naked savages, who dwell in the woods and prey on creatures not much wilder or lower than themselves." He found that the "low culture of many of the savage tribes ... substantially reproduces the conditions of life in Europe as it was ... ages before the dawn of anything that could be called civilization." Self-rule by Africans, therefore, "would mean idleness, famine, and endless internecine warfare. They cannot," Roosevelt opined, "govern themselves from within; therefore they must be governed from without; and their need is met in highest fashion by firm and just control, of the kind that on the whole they are now getting."[5]

World War II and the emerging civil rights movement served to undercut the legitimacy of leaders and opinion makers publicly using such language and employing racial hierarchies to defend their policies. Yet by the time the nations of Africa began to gain their independence from Europe, little had changed in American policymakers' attitudes toward the continent except the way these ideas were expressed. The formulation of modernization theory during the 1950s allowed these racist ideas to continue to guide American thinking. They were just recast into new and acceptable categories that maintained older ideas, and built upon the confidence of American leaders in the superiority of Western ideas and values and the right of the United States to dictate proper governments and behavior in the Third World. Instead of discussing the racial characteristics

---

[4] Hickey and Wylie, *An Enchanting Darkness*, 1, 13; the titles of Stanley's best-selling books included *Through the Dark Continent* and *In the Darkest Africa*.

[5] Ibid., 14–46.

of a people or nation, modernization theory allowed policymakers to rank nations in terms of their "objective" developmental status, political systems, and cultural institutions in order to determine their needs and problems.

Modernization theory was based on the idea that economic development followed discernable paths in Western Europe and the United States, and that these could be transferred to other nations. Nations, it was argued, went through stages of growth along a continuum from traditional societies to industrialized ones. What was necessary to bring about economic growth was the transfer of Western value systems and economic institutions to the Third World. Once economic development occurred, "modern"(i.e., Western) ideas and institutions would spread into the social and political realms. This would guarantee stability and order while simultaneously blocking the spread of communism. Modernization theory and economic development apparently resolved the dilemma of promoting democracy versus opposing communism and supporting right-wing dictators. With the right programs and guidance, the support of authoritarian regimes was essential to protect Third World nations from communism while they went through the difficult transition from a traditional to a modern society. Indeed, dictators were seen as a necessary part of the process until economic growth could foster a stability grounded in a middle class and based on Western values and institutions.[6]

As one of the leading modernization theorists, member of Kennedy's national security staff, and national security advisor to President Johnson, Walt Whitman Rostow, argued, the revolutionary process of modernization in the Third World was when these nations were most in danger of falling to communism. The "weak transitional governments that one is likely to find during this modernization process are highly vulnerable to subversion." The communists were the "scavengers of the modernization process" who knew that once the "momentum takes hold in an underdeveloped area – and the fundamental social problems inherited from the traditional society are solved – their chances to seize power decline." Communism, Rostow declared, "is best understood as a disease of the transition to modernization." Dictatorships, therefore, were necessary in the Third World until the modernization process had developed enough to allow "these societies [to] choose their own version of what we would recognize as a democratic, open society."[7]

As an indication of the new significance of Africa, Eisenhower sent Vice President Richard Nixon on a three-week tour of the continent in March 1957. Nixon led the U.S. delegation to the ceremonies marking the independence of Ghana. His trip was also designed to help prepare an American policy toward Africa as states began to gain independence from European colonial rule. Upon his return, Nixon told Eisenhower that Africa represented the new area of

---

[6] See Rostow, *Stages of Economic Growth*; Park, *Latin American Underdevelopment*; Hunt, *Ideology and U.S. Foreign Policy*; and Latham, *Modernization as Ideology*.

[7] Rostow, "Guerilla Warfare in the Underdeveloped Areas," *Department of State Bulletin*, 7 August 1961, 234–47.

conflict "between the forces of freedom and international communism,"[8] and that Africa "could well prove to be the decisive factor" in the Cold War.[9]

Also in March, the United States and Great Britain jointly approved a study, "Communist Influence in Africa," that stipulated that the "battle for the next ten years would lie on the continent of Africa." Secretary of State John Foster Dulles agreed with this assessment and noted that "we would be in serious trouble if Africa were lost to the Free World." As evidence, Dulles noted his concern that Ghana planned to establish full diplomatic relations with the USSR, a development that would "provide the Soviet Union with a perfect opportunity to move into the West Coast of Africa."[10]

In addition, Dulles stated that the greatest concern of the United States was the "premature independence" of African states. He believed "that there should be an evolutionary trend toward independence but that attainment of it should be qualified by the ability of the people of an area to sustain the responsibility." The United States hoped that some nations would be wise enough to see that they were not ready for self-rule and "would retain their relationships with the mother countries." Otherwise, "it was possible that independence might be followed by a Communist takeover." It was clear to the secretary of state that the granting of independence to the nations of Africa "would undoubtedly be followed by Communist efforts to take over the new country," since it was Soviet policy to break loose all dependent areas "from the countries with which they were associated and thereafter amalgamating them within the Soviet Union."[11]

The notion that most of the new states in Africa were gaining "premature independence" was the guiding principle of Eisenhower's policy. As early as 1953, Assistant Secretary of State Henry Byroade set out the administration's position that while the United States supported self-determination, it was worried about "premature independence" for people unprepared to rule effectively and stave off the "new imperialism" of the Soviet Union.[12] In testifying before the Senate Foreign Relations Committee in 1958, Assistant Secretary of State C. Burke Elbrick noted that the administration was concerned about the end of European rule in Africa because "premature independence and irresponsible nationalism may present grave dangers to dependent people."[13]

To better prepare to meet this challenge, the State Department created a new Bureau of African Affairs, and in August 1957 the administration adopted NSC 5719/1, "U.S. Policy toward Africa South of the Sahara prior to Calendar Year 1960," as American policy. The United States sought first and foremost to support its European allies' interests in Africa and to prevent any communist gains in Africa. It was concerned that sub-Saharan Africa "develop in

---

[8] Mahoney, *JFK: Ordeal in Africa*, 35.

[9] Noer, *Cold War and Black Liberation*, 49.

[10] *FRUS 1955–1957*, 18: 53–4.

[11] Ibid., 55–6.

[12] Noer, *Cold War and Black Liberation*, 45.

[13] Mahoney, *JFK: Ordeal in Africa*, 35.

an orderly manner towards self-government and independence in cooperation
with the European powers now in control of large areas of the continent. We
hope that this transition will take place in a manner which will preserve the
essential ties which bind Europe and Africa – which are fundamentally com-
plementary areas," since Africa depends on Europe for goods and capital, and
Europe needs African minerals as well as markets. "The United States, therefore, believes it to be generally desirable that close and mutually advantageous
economic relationships between the European powers and Africa should continue after the colonial period has passed." It also wished to avoid the turning
of nationalist aspirations "to the advantage of extremist elements, particularly
Communists."[14]

The problem confronting the United States, the Eisenhower administration
believed, was that "the African is still immature and unsophisticated with
respect to his attitudes towards the issues that divide the world today." As NSC
5719/1 declared, "premature independence would be as harmful to our interests in Africa as would be a continuation of nineteenth century colonialism"
because of the communist threat. While the report noted that, up to this time,
"Communism has not been a major problem" in Africa, "its potential influence
was a matter of growing concern." The United States needed to counter Soviet
efforts while working with pro-Western nationalists.[15]

During the National Security Council discussion of NSC 5719, the only
major concern raised regarding the report's analysis was that it tended to, in the
words of Vice President Nixon, "underestimate the seriousness of the Communist threat in Africa." The communists, he predicted, would "clothe themselves
in Islamic, racist, anti-racist, or nationalist clothing. The potential danger of
Communist penetration," he believed, was "very great, because the Communists were always in a position to support and take advantage of extremist
elements, where the United States could not do so." The new secretary of state,
Christian Herter, agreed with Nixon, noting that he found the report "too optimistic" and suggesting the "addition of language which would indicate that the
potential Communist threat to Africa was greater than the actual threat at the
present time." This change was made, and the final version of NSC 5719/1 was
approved.[16]

In May 1959, responding to the rising tide of nationalism in the Third World
and the coming of many newly independent states, the State Department prepared a study, "Political Implications of Afro-Asian Military Takeovers," that
looked at the question of the stability of newly independent states and the "short
and long-range policy implications for the U.S." of the trend toward military
governments in these nations. The overall premise of the document was that
"political and economic authoritarianism prevails throughout the underdeveloped world in general and represents the predominant environment in which

[14] *FRUS 1955–1957*, 18: 76–7.
[15] Ibid., 79–81.
[16] Ibid., 73–4.

the U.S. must associate its interests with those of the emergent and developing societies." The United States, it was noted, would prefer "benevolent and experienced civilian politicians who have a broad popular base and are held to some form of accountability by a parliament or organized opposition." That, however, was not the case, and the United States would have to subordinate its ideals "to the practical and the possible for many years to come." Thus, there was no need to challenge the existing policy of supporting right-wing dictators, a policy that was seen as simply practical and inevitable.[17]

Indeed, the State Department asserted that military takeovers provided "certain short-run advantages to the United States." Authoritarian governments were better able to withstand communist pressures and generally represented what the United States saw as the best segments of their societies. Most important, they were seen as conduits to modernization and the necessary progression toward the development of newly independent societies. Reflecting the influence of modernization theory, the report asserted that "our experience with the more highly developed Latin American States indicates that authoritarianism *is required* to lead backward societies through their socio-economic revolutions." Moreover, if the "break-through occurs under non-Communist authoritarianism, trends toward democratic values emerge with the development of a literate middle class." Right-wing dictators would "remain the norm ... for a long period. The trend toward military authoritarianism will accelerate as developmental problems become more acute and the facades of democracy left by the colonial powers prove inadequate to immediate tasks." The question was what the United States could do to take advantage of this situation. The key was working with the local elites to encourage them to "modernize their societies by some 'middle way' between private enterprise and Communism, thus preserving the residue of human rights and dignity essential to the growth of democratic values."[18]

The State Department found three additional reasons why the United States "must support military regimes" at this point in the development of Third World nations. First, real security threats from communism existed. In that context, the "officer groups are often the most pro-Western, disciplined, and educated institution-in-being on which backward societies can draw in time of crisis." Second, military intervention in government "will continue to be necessary to supplant ineptness, corruption or slippage toward Communism." Finally, military guidance was necessary because it would take decades for the newly independent nations "to develop those institutions which establish in more advanced countries civilian control of the military." In these circumstances, the

---

[17] "Political Implications of Afro-Asian Military Takeovers," May 1959, Policy Subseries, NSC Series, Box 19, OSANSA, DDEL; "Briefing Note for the NSC Meeting 18 June 1959," 27 May 1959, with "Summary of Conclusion: Political Implications of Afro-Asian Military Takeovers," 410th Meeting of the NSC, 18 June 1959, AWF, NSC Series, DDEL.

[18] "Political Implications of Afro-Asian Military Takeovers," May 1959, Policy Subseries, NSC Series, Box 19, OSANSA, DDEL (emphasis added).

"essential test...should be whether a particular military regime responsibly confronts the problems facing it – security and developmental progress – and, in so doing, successfully resists Communists techniques."[19]

The report outlined the fundamental dilemmas in this policy, the potential long-range threats, and the possibility that supporting right-wing dictators could damage American prestige:

It is of course essential in the Cold War to seek to promote stability in the under-developed countries...where instability may invite Communism. A new, authoritarian regime, though less "democratic" than its predecessor, may possess much more stability and may well lay the ground for ultimate return to a more firmly based "democracy." These are compelling reasons for our maintaining relations with regimes in power. On the other hand, to become identified with an authoritarian regime and its policies makes us a target for anti-regime propaganda...and creates the impression both inside and outside of the country concerned that we approve of authoritarianism and repression so long as our self-interest is thereby satisfied. This impression once created tends to isolate us from whatever progressive forces may exist in a given country, and it discredits our sincere dedication to the principles of freedom, democracy, economic progress and development, and respect for human dignity.

In addition, there was no guarantee that authoritarian leaders would success-fully lead their respective nations forward. No doubt influenced by the over-throw of Fulgencio Batista by Fidel Castro in Cuba, the department warned that a failure to achieve "developmental revolutions...encourages a parallel trend toward 'second stage revolutions,' e.g. revolutions engendered by the dissatisfaction or stifling of opposition groups (labor, students, intelligentsia, dissident younger officer groups)." It was possible that the "incidence of polit-ical authoritarianism...weakens the fiber of democratic values and points the way toward an easier acceptance of economic controls which tend toward Com-munist controls." A developing society could "be lost to Communism short of military aggression and by failure to manage the developmental revolution."[20]

Yet the risks were worth taking, and the dangers to stability, orderly develop-ment, and American interests could be minimized. "In the bi-polar world of the Cold War, our refusal to deal with a military or authoritarian regime...could lead almost necessarily to the establishment of that regime's friendly relations with the Soviet Bloc." More optimistically, the State Department believed that a "happy medium from the standpoint of U.S. interests" could be reached that would consist of a "military regime 'civilianized' to the greatest extent pos-sible and headed by a military leader who saw security and development in perspective and thereby evidenced political leadership of the type required in a developing society." It was the task of the United States to discover "techniques whereby Western values can be grafted on modernizing indigenous developmen-tal systems." All of this could be done with no loss of prestige to the United States. "Our image," the State Department concluded, "will depend basically

[19] Ibid.
[20] Ibid.

on the example of our own democracy at work, our unequivocal support for the independence and development of emergent nations, and our assisting the regime in power to satisfy popular aspirations." The best course was to have strong leadership that the United States could assist and influence. All of this made the continuation of support for right-wing dictators both necessary and attractive to American leaders.[21]

On June 18, the National Security Council (NSC) discussed the analysis presented by the report and approved the policy recommendations. Eisenhower praised the report as the "finest" ever presented to the NSC, and noted "that it seemed to him likely that the trend toward military takeovers in the underdeveloped countries of Asia and Africa was almost certainly going to continue." Given that reality, "we must do our best to orient the potential military leaders of these countries in a pro-Western rather than a pro-Communist direction." The process, the president continued, would take time and would not immediately bring about democratic governments. Eisenhower was wary of the prospects for the success of democracy throughout the Third World, since he believed that most non-Western people were incapable of democratic government. He claimed, for example, that "if you go and live with those Arabs you will find that they simply cannot understand our ideas of freedom or human dignity. They have lived so long under dictatorships of one form or another, how can we expect them to run successfully a free government?" Given this, the president believed it was a choice between pro-Western military dictators and communist ones.[22]

Secretary of Defense Neil McElroy noted that "military leadership has basically represented a conservative element in the societies of newly independent countries," and that "while in some instances, the military can be troublesome, it remained true that in these backward societies, it was desirable to encourage the military to stabilize a conservative system." Undersecretary of State Douglas Dillon pointed out that it would be incorrect to claim that the department was endorsing a permanent continuation of military regimes in the Third World. Rather, it insisted that "in the short range, parliamentary democracy simply will not work in these countries as it works in the U.S. Accordingly," Dillon continued, "our best bet was to try to civilianize these military regimes as far as possible in the interest of the ultimate victory of democratic government."[23]

Eisenhower supported Dillon's point by noting that it was absolutely necessary "that before these colonies did become free countries their citizens should be trained for freedom. It was indeed pretty difficult if such colonies became independent before they had trained any of their people in the art of government." To make his point, the president alluded to what he termed the "paradoxical situation in Nicaragua." After years of dictatorship under Anastasio Somoza, his son had "permitted and encouraged the development of a number

[21] Ibid.
[22] 410th Meeting of the NSC, 18 June 1959, AWF, NSC Series, DDEL.
[23] Ibid.

of freedoms in Nicaragua such as freedom of speech, freedom of the press, and the like. For his pains Luis Somoza was now confronted by a revolution against his relatively mild authoritarian regime." The NSC concluded that it was essential for the United States to train the "young people of these backward countries so that they could develop the requisite sense of responsibility." The State Department was instructed to continue to monitor these issues, and was told that the conclusions of the report would be used in making policy and "preparing recommendations with regard to the Afro-Asian area."[24]

The same ideas guided the Kennedy administration's thinking on these questions. The Policy Planning Council noted in May 1962 that "because of the structural and social upheavals which generally accompany the modernization process, all developing nations are susceptible to Communist subversion and insurgency to varying degrees ... until each nation develops firm national unity and regular progress." While the goal of U.S. policy was to "promote the evolution of social and political systems which are increasingly based on the consent of the governed, capable of providing an environment of regular material progress and expanding social justice, while maintaining their national independence," there was "no simple formula – such as self-determination – [that] will apply." To insure both stability and independence – that is, noncommunist governments – the military had to play a central role.[25]

This meant that the United States would "sometimes have to accommodate [itself] to less desirable situations" and would not always be able to work with progressive democratic forces. In nations still at the "stage of traditional society, e.g., many African countries" that had been granted premature independence, it was necessary to adopt policies "designed to avoid the kind of chaos which accompanied the Belgian withdrawal from responsibility in the Congo."[26] Washington had to rely on the military as the "ultimate guarantors of internal security" because the "officer corps are generally the best organized pro-Western, non-Communist groups capable of leadership and wide support within an underdeveloped society." Moreover, "they form a powerful potential group of 'modernizers,' and a conduit of contemporary Western thought and values if their full talents and knowledge of the outside world are utilized."[27]

The State Department contended that "the history of developing societies reenforces the judgment that the military are, for good or ill, an inevitable and significant element in the modernization process." The "contemporary analyses of the dynamics of modernization, which dramatize the evolutionary character of movement from a traditional to a modern democratic society," demonstrate the "inevitability of the military role" in the process, "legitimize that role to a degree," and "provide a basis for a more coherent US doctrine and policy which need not clash with our basic commitments to the democratic creed."

---

[24] Ibid.
[25] "Basic National Security Policy Planning Tasks," Draft, 7 May 1962, JCTP, Box 6, JFKL.
[26] "Basic National Security Policy, Short Version," Draft, 9 May 1962, JCTP, Box 6, JFKL.
[27] "The Role of the Military in the Underdeveloped Areas," 1 December 1962, JCTP, Box 6, JFKL.

In the Third World, military regimes provided "the best insurance against rev-olutions or political stagnation and the emergence of a counter-elite" hostile to the United States through a "benevolent authoritarianism which imparts a sense of national unity, . . . gives a role of national participation to the intelligentsia, and holds power in trust for civilians and more representative institutions." American policy, therefore, was to "support military regimes which push for-ward with development" as they "advance U.S. interests by maintaining stabil-ity, possibly introducing reforms which civilians might shirk, and symbolizing national unity through times of crisis and hardship – all essential to the devel-opment process."[28]

Both the Eisenhower and Kennedy administrations were aware of the dangers of the policy of supporting right-wing dictators. Yet the basic Cold War assump-tions of American containment policy – that American security and prosperity faced a global challenge from communism, and that it was America's duty to protect freedom around the world – meant that American leaders could see no alternative to this policy. If it was a bipolar world, all governments fell on one side of the divide or the other. Right-wing regimes were anticommunist. They were, therefore, part of the free world, no matter what the composition of their governments or their record of abuses. In the short run, the benefits of continuing to support authoritarian regimes seemed clear, and it was difficult to look beyond the immediate crises. Modernization theory promised a long-term solution as long as nations were not first lost to communism during the difficult transition from traditional to modern societies. Supporting right-wing dictators was, therefore, seen as a lesser evil than a communist takeover and, therefore, justified as being necessary in the service to a higher purpose of defending free-dom. Developments in the Congo served to convince American leaders of the wisdom of American policy toward right-wing dictators and the applicability of modernization theory.

The Removal of Lumumba

On 30 June 1960, the Congo gained its independence from Belgium. Free elec-tions held under Belgian supervision made Patrice Lumumba its first prime minister and Joseph Kasavubu its president. Belgium, in an effort to maintain control over the Congo and protect its investments, had stipulated that its offi-cers would continue to control the Congo's army (the ANC). Within a week, the army mutinied, and Belgium responded by sending in paratroopers. The crisis quickly deepened when on July 11 Moise Tshombe, a political rival of Lumumba's and Kasavubu's, announced, with Belgium's approval, the inde-pendence of the Katanga province, the richest in the Congo. Belgian troops protected the breakaway province by disarming the ANC. The nation was beset with rebellion and in danger of breaking into pieces. Lumumba appealed to the United States for troops, but his request was rejected by the Eisenhower

---

[28] Ibid.

administration. He then turned to the United Nations, which agreed in mid-July to send troops under the control of the UN to maintain order. These forces, however, had a limited mandate; they were not sent to aid Lumumba in his effort to end the rebellion in Katanga and bring the breakaway province back into the Congo. Rather, they were sent to impose order and stop the fighting until a negotiated settlement could be arranged.

The United States supported the UN's action as a necessary step to block communist expansion into the Congo and the states on its border, and to maintain the territorial integrity of the nation. American officials were sympathetic to the Belgian desire to keep Katanga out of Lumumba's hands, but a breakaway province was not the preferred option. As the State Department noted, "while we of course sympathize with [Tshombe's] pro-Western orientation and are aware that Katanga contains most of the Congo's mineral and industrial wealth, we have continued to believe that the best economic answer for the Congo's future must be based on a continuing Katanga contribution to the central Government."[29] For the next four years, Washington would depend upon the United Nations and Belgium to maintain stability in the Congo and protect Western interests. In order to accomplish this, the United States paid 42 percent of the UN peacekeeping costs in addition to the other aid it provided to the Congo.[30]

The Eisenhower administration saw the growing crisis as a communist effort to gain control of the Congo. Eisenhower worried that "chaos [would] run wild among hopeful, expectant peoples," and that the United States "could not afford to see turmoil in an area where the Communists would be only too delighted to take an advantage." The Congo was particularly vulnerable, he believed, because its people lacked the skills of government without which "political stability was almost impossible." This situation was made worse by the raised expectations of a "restless and militant population in a state of gross ignorance – even by African standards." In his memoirs, Eisenhower noted that the crisis in the Congo was caused by "[Soviet Premier Nikita] Khrushchev's attempts at subversion with an eye to Communist takeover."[31] The director of the CIA, Allen Dulles, told the National Security Council on July 21 that U.S. policy had to be made on the assumption that Lumumba had been "bought by the Communists."[32] Regarding the various machinations of the Congo's

[29] Department of State, "The Congo," December 1960, NSF:CF, Box 86, LBJL.

[30] Administrative History of the Department of State, Vol. 1, Chapter 5: "Congo," Box 2, LBJL. There is an extensive literature on the U.S. response to the 1960–61 crisis in the Congo, the overthrow of Lumumba, and his assassination. On American policy, see Noer, *Cold War and Black Liberation*; Mahoney, *JFK: Ordeal in Africa*; Kalb, *The Congo Cables*; Weissman, *American Foreign Policy in the Congo, 1960–1964*; Schatzberg, *Mobutu or Chaos?*; and Kelly, *America's Tyrant*. Concerning the assassination of Lumumba, see United States Congress, Senate Select Committee to Study Government Operations with Respect to Intelligence Activities (hereafter Church Committee), *Alleged Assassination Plots Involving Foreign Leaders*.

[31] Eisenhower, *Waging Peace*, 572–3, 576.

[32] Church Committee, *Alleged Assassination Plots Involving Foreign Leaders*, 57.

leaders and the actions of the troops loyal to Lumumba's government, the American ambassador to the Congo, Claire Timberlake, wrote Washington that they "removed any lingering trace of the fiction that we are dealing with a civilized people or a responsible government in the Congo." Lumumba and all of his close associates, the ambassador claimed, were "anti-white" and carrying forward "the Communist plan."[33] The *New York Times* opined that the communist threat to Africa was similar to the Nazi threat in Europe and had to be met. "Just as Hitler did in Europe, so Khrushchev in Africa today is encouraging civil strife, disintegration and chaos and in the process is threatening to shatter the world's great effort to reach international stability."[34]

These views were reinforced during Lumumba's visit to the United States on July 27–29. Lumumba came seeking even greater support in the United Nations and hoping to obtain direct American aid to his government. Eisenhower decided not to return to Washington to meet Lumumba, leaving it to Secretary of State Herter and Undersecretary of State Dillon to hear his request for assistance in removing Belgian troops from the Congo and for the granting of loans to the Congo. Dillon recalled that he thought Lumumba was "just not a rational being," and that he seemed to be "gripped by this fervor that I can only characterize as messianic."[35] The secretary of state was cautious in his response, noting only that at this point the United States preferred to rely on the United Nations to aid the Congo. Lumumba further alienated American officials when he ended his visit by telling a Soviet reporter that he wanted to thank the Soviet Union as the "only great power which supported the people of the Congo in their struggle from the very outset."[36]

The National Security Council met on August 1 to discuss Lumumba's actions and the situation in the Congo. It concluded that there was an immediate danger of Soviet intervention and that the United States had to be ready "to take appropriate military action to prevent or defeat Soviet military intervention in the Congo."[37] That same day, Herter cabled the United States embassy in Brussels that in the wake of Lumumba's visit, the evidence proved that "he will not rpt not prove satisfactory. US will therefore continue search for more trustworthy elements in Congo who might be susceptible to support as part of program of reinsurance against Lumumba."[38]

The Eisenhower administration believed that it was only a matter of time before Lumumba delivered the Congo to the Soviet Union. Ambassador Timberlake informed Washington that he believed that "the Commie design" for the takeover of the Congo "now seems suddenly clear." Lumumba was to drive all the Europeans out of the country, allowing the government to "nationalize

---

[33] "Analytical Chronology of the Congo Crisis," 28, 25, Bureau of African Affairs, NSF, Box 27, JFKL.

[34] *New York Times*, 16 September 1960, 30.

[35] Church Committee, *Alleged Assassination Plots Involving Foreign Leaders*, 53.

[36] Kalb, *The Congo Cables*, 37.

[37] "Analytical Chronology of the Congo Crisis," 29–30, NSF, Box 27, JFKL.

[38] Kalb, *The Congo Cables*, 38.

their property," and then "invite Commie bloc experts in to keep business and industry going." The Soviets had captured "Lumumba and his followers like they took Castro in Cuba." This was easy for Moscow to do because the "Congolese are totally disorganized, they are political children and only pitiful few have faintest idea where Lumumba is taking them."[39] The CIA station chief in the Congo, Lawrence Devlin, sent a similar warning to Dulles. He reported that the "Embassy and Station believe Congo experiencing classic communist effort takeover government." Devlin continued that "whether or not Lumumba actually commie or just playing commie game to assist his solidifying power, anti-West forces rapidly increasing power [in the] Congo and there may be little time left in which to take action to avoid another Cuba."[40] For his part, Dulles believed that Lumumba was "a person who was a Castro or worse."[41] In order to prevent the feared communist takeover, Eisenhower authorized the CIA to engineer a coup to remove Lumumba from power and assassinate him.[42]

The political situation in the Congo continued to spiral downward throughout the summer and reached a crisis stage in early September. Lumumba saw himself as increasingly isolated. UN forces provided protection but no assistance against Tshombe, and he was unable to gain direct support for his government from the United States to counter Belgium. In August, therefore, Lumumba turned to the Soviet Union for aid. Moscow responded by sending supplies, advisors, and technicians to assist Lumumba's government.

Eisenhower called this a "Soviet invasion," and American efforts to oust Lumumba were increased.[43] On September 5, President Kasavubu, at the urging of American officials, announced that he was removing Lumumba from office. Lumumba responded by announcing that he was dismissing Kasavubu from office. The question now became which leader could command the support of the army. The answer came on September 12, when Mobutu, then the commander-in-chief of the armed forces, engineered a coup that toppled Lumumba and placed himself and Kasavubu in control. It was believed that Mobutu, who was on the CIA payroll, would bring a "measure of stability" to the Congo and prevent Lumumba from creating a communist state.[44] Lumumba was able to find safety under the protection of Ghanian troops, who were part of the UN mission and refused to allow him to be arrested. When Mobutu then placed his forces around the UN troops, this became a form of house arrest that lasted until November.

The United States, while still officially working through the United Nations in the Congo, saw Lumumba's presence in the country as a threat and continued its efforts to assassinate him. The Eisenhower administration believed that

[39] *FRUS 1958–1960*, 14: 420–1, 448–9.
[40] Church Committee, *Alleged Assassination Plots Involving Foreign Leaders*, 14.
[41] Kalb, *The Congo Cables*, 29.
[42] Church Committee, *Alleged Assassination Plots Involving Foreign Leaders*.
[43] Eisenhower, *Waging Peace*, 575.
[44] Kalb, *The Congo Cables*, 92.

unless Lumumba was eliminated, there was a danger that he could once again return to power. As Dulles told the National Security Council on September 21, "Mobutu appears to be the effective power in the Congo for the moment but Lumumba was not yet disposed of and remained a grave danger as long as he was not yet disposed of."[45] The State Department concluded that a "return of Lumumba to political power would involve the Sovietization of the Congo," while his permanent removal would allow for a "rapprochement between the Katanga and the rest of the Congo" and keep the nation "oriented toward the West."[46] The various efforts to kill Lumumba were, however, unsuccessful due to the presence of the UN soldiers who were protecting him.[47]

All that changed on November 27, when Lumumba fled his refuge in a failed effort to get to Stanleyville and rally his political supporters. Mobutu, working with the CIA, captured Lumumba three days later and placed him under arrest. Still, Lumumba presented a potential threat as a symbol of opposition and a person for Congolese nationalists to rally around. American policy, therefore, remained the same as it had been since August, when Eisenhower first approved the assassination of Lumumba – that he had to be eliminated. The CIA continued to work closely with Mobutu to find a means to kill Lumumba while providing a proper cover story. In January, Mobutu decided to send Lumumba to Katanga, thus turning him over to his bitter enemy Tshombe. This was a death sentence. While the CIA did not actually kill Lumumba, it was responsible for his removal from power and his delivery into the hands of Tshombe, who did assassinate him on 17 January 1961.[48]

No New Frontier in Africa

With the coming to office of John F. Kennedy, there was talk of a new policy toward the Congo and Africa based on a greater appreciation of the nationalist aspirations of the people. Kennedy had met with African leaders throughout the campaign of 1960 and, while distancing himself from Eisenhower's policy, claimed to be genuinely interested in supporting the new states of Africa. As early as 1957, Kennedy had declared that "the sweep of nationalism is the most potent factor in foreign affairs today. We can resist it or ignore it but only for a little while; we can see it exploited by the Soviets with grave consequences; or we in this country can give it hope and leadership, and thus improve immeasurably our standing and our security."[49] Once in office, Kennedy appointed a number of liberal "Africanists," seen as sympathetic to Africa, to key positions. Most notably, he named a former governor of Michigan, G. Mennen Williams, as assistant secretary of state for Africa, Chester Bowles as undersecretary of state,

---

[45] Mahoney, *JFK: Ordeal in Africa*, 48.
[46] Department of State, "The Congo," December 1960, NSF:CF, Box 86, LBJL.
[47] Church Committee, *Alleged Assassination Plots Involving Foreign Leaders*.
[48] See Church Committee, *Alleged Assassination Plots Involving Foreign Leaders*; Kalb, *The Congo Cables*, 50–70, 175–96; and Urquhart, "The Tragedy of Lumumba."
[49] Mahoney, *JFK: Ordeal in Africa*, 22.

and Adlai Stevenson as ambassador to the United Nations. All were known as supporters of African independence.[50]

Yet the Cold War and Washington's desire for stability, anticommunism, and its need for access to raw materials still provided the context for American policy. The threat of chaos, the perceived inability of the Congolese to govern themselves, and communist expansion remained the central concerns of American leaders. The dilemma that Kennedy faced was set out in January 1961, before the death of Lumumba was confirmed, by Martin Herz, the head of the State Department's Congo desk. He noted that American policy could succeed only by supporting a dictatorship. "We dare not," Herz wrote, "accept new elections in the Congo.... We dare not accept the convocation of the Parliament.... We dare not even see Lumumba included in a coalition government for fear that he could come to dominate. For a country that subscribes to the democratic creed, this is a remarkable predicament."[51] With the disastrous outcome of the Bay of Pigs invasion, increasing tensions with the Soviet Union over Berlin, and a growing crisis in Vietnam, Kennedy was reluctant to back his bold rhetoric with much action and sought to preserve the status quo.

In addition, older attitudes toward the Congo persisted within the government and worked against any real change in policy. Secretary of State Dean Rusk saw all the trouble in the Congo as stemming from Soviet behavior. "In the Congo," he told the American Historical Association, "amidst the confusion which followed the end of colonialism, the Communists were rigorously seeking to establish a central African base." The Soviets sought "to exploit the inevitable turbulence which accompanies the revolutionary movement toward modernization." Moscow's goal was "not national liberation but entrapment within the Communist bloc." Rusk continued by noting that establishing democratic government was a complex and difficult task that took time and "requires a citizenry which assumes substantial individual responsibility for the fate of the community." The first objective of the United States, therefore, was "to preserve the independence of the modernization process."[52] The secretary of state feared that this "Soviet onslaught" was still a danger, a threat which demanded that the United States find a means to stability and integration in the Congo or face "civil war and the ensuing chaos on which the Communists have capitalized in other parts of the world." Continued support of the United Nations was, therefore, crucial as the alternative "would have been violence and chaos and a ready made opportunity for Soviet exploitation."[53]

Reflecting the attitudes of the many within the State Department who opposed the new appointments on Africa, one official complained that "the

---

[50] Noer, *Cold War and Black Liberation*, 62–3.

[51] Mahoney, *JFK: Ordeal in Africa*, 34.

[52] Rusk, "Some Issues of Contemporary History," *Department of State Bulletin*, 15 January 1962, 85–6.

[53] Rusk, "United States Policy in the Congo," *Department of State Bulletin*, 5 February 1962, 216–17.

trouble with Bowles and Williams was that when they saw a band of black baboons beating tom-toms they saw George Washingtons."[54] Roger Hilsman, the director of the State Department's Bureau of Intelligence and Research, informed Rusk that the problem of instability in the Congo could not easily be solved because the "main protagonists simply have not absorbed many European political concepts," and concluded that the *nature of Congolese politics is unlikely to change rapidly, and the enormous difficulties the Congolese are now facing in governing themselves will probably last a generation or more.*"[55] When the administration evaluated the prospects for new initiatives in the Congo at the end of 1962, the question of removing the United Nations forces and "turning the matter over to the Africans was raised." This possibility was quickly dismissed with the statement that the "Africans cannot handle it, and this would open the Congo to eventual Communist takeover."[56]

Even the Africanists presented a similar understanding of events in the Congo. Speaking in October 1961 in defense of American policy, Williams claimed that the Soviets had failed "to reap the whirlwind they had sown," and that in its effort to "prey on the confusion and disorder it promotes," the Soviet Union had miscalculated in the Congo.[57] The next year, Stevenson noted that "it is all too easy to imagine a new Communist empire in Africa and Asia, moving in on the heels of the withdrawing Europeans." The lesson of the Congo was that the "Soviets placed their bets on chaos." They counted on the Congo, "a newborn nation – not well equipped for independence – erupting in violence and civil chaos." Prompt United Nations and U.S. action had thwarted this plan, but the need for order was still paramount for American policy.[58] As Williams stated in a November 1962 summary of American policy, the lack of a quick response in the Congo "unquestionably . . . would have led to continued chaos and the strong likelihood that a Communist foothold would have been established in the middle of Africa."[59]

In the wake of the murder of Lumumba, a semblance of stability prevailed in the Congo. Mobutu, who had already broken relations with the Soviet Union, turned power back over to Kasavubu, who appointed a series of prime ministers in an effort to create internal unity. In January 1963, the United Nations was finally able to bring an end to the Katanga secession, a move fully supported by the United States. While Mobutu did not directly govern the Congo, he was still in the eyes of the United States the most important figure in the Congo and

---

[54] Noer, *Cold War and Black Liberation*, 82.

[55] Hilsman to Rusk, "Congo: Prospects for National Reunification," 31 August 1962, NSF, Box 28A, JFKL (emphasis in the original).

[56] Memorandum for the President, "New Policy on the Congo," 13 December 1962, NSF, Box 28A, JFKL.

[57] Williams, "The Lessons of the Congo," *Department of State Bulletin*, 23 October 1961, 668–9.

[58] Stevenson, "Five Goals of U.S. Foreign Policy," *Department of State Bulletin*, 15 October 1962, 554.

[59] Williams, "The Urgent Need for Congo Reconciliation," *Department of State Bulletin*, 26 November 1962, 803–4.

remained on the payroll of the CIA. His stature was attested to when in May 1963 the U.S. Department of the Army flew him in to visit the United States, tour American military bases, and meet with President Kennedy. The trip was part of an effort by the Kennedy administration to better train and equip the army of the Congo so that it could maintain stability once the United Nations forces were withdrawn. During their meeting, Mobutu assured the president that with the proper amount of aid and advice, he could preserve order in his nation, and that he hoped to send Congolese soldiers to the United States for some of this training. Kennedy, for his part, thanked Mobutu for his cooperation and efforts on behalf of his nation. Moreover, the president declared: "General, if it hadn't been for you, the whole thing would have collapsed and the Communists would have taken over." Indeed, Kennedy went so far as to tell Mobutu that nobody, anywhere, had done more than he had to combat communism.[60]

Machiavelli in the Congo

With the removal of United Nations forces in June 1964, rebellions and internecine battles again broke out, and the Johnson administration grew increasingly concerned over the warfare and instability in the Congo. Rusk wrote the president as early as February 1964 that "there will be a serious security situation in the Congo following the withdrawal of United Nations forces" given the potential secession by Congolese "long associated with both the Soviets and Chinese." The United States would have to continue to support Belgium, the nation with primary responsibility for aiding the government of the Congo and providing stability, while increasing its own military aid to the nation.[61] On the eve of the UN pullout in June, the CIA reported that the Congo was "headed for a period of increasing instability and possibly a total breakdown of governmental authority." Faced with open rebellions, the CIA found that the "notoriously incompetent Congo National Army (ANC)" offered "little hope as an instrument for preserving order." This would mean greater reliance on Belgium for military assistance, a situation that would create the impression that the radicals' claim that Belgium maintained a neocolonial control of the Congo was correct, thereby breeding new resentments and instability.[62]

The rebellions, it was believed, were led by the left-wing Committee of National Liberation (CNL), which the CIA noted was in contact with the Chinese communists, who were providing it with material support. The CNL leadership was characterized as a "motley collection of some 150–200 self-exiled left-wing politicians, Congolese students returned from the USSR, and deserters from the ANC." While the Congo had been held in the Western camp,

---

[60] Mahoney, *JFK: Ordeal in Africa*, 228–9.

[61] Rusk to Johnson, "Training of the Congolese Army (ANC)," 15 February 1965, NSF:CF, Box 81, LBJL.

[62] "The Security Situation in the Congo," 17 June 1964, NSF:CF, Box 81, LBJL; see also Department of State, Bureau of Intelligence and Research, "An Outline Guide to Communist Activities in Africa," 15 May 1964, NSF:CF, Box 76, LBJL.

the government was unpopular due to rampant corruption, and the ANC was "noted for its pillaging and raping and is hated and feared." In order to keep the security situation from further deteriorating, the Congo needed the "presence of African or of Belgian troops" in the short term. This would provide the necessary time for the better training of the ANC "to make the army a dependable instrument of central authority."[63] It remained American policy, the State Department reported, to have Belgium take the lead in providing the actual fighting forces in the Congo as the "United States had no desire to replace the former metropole as the leading foreign influence for stability and economic development, nor was it feasible for us to do so."[64]

The danger was heightened by the administration's larger concern with communism throughout Africa. In 1964 and 1965, there was an increasing worry and a number of special reports concerning communist, and particularly Chinese, efforts to foment revolutions throughout sub-Saharan Africa. The State Department saw the "communist strategy" as an effort to work with radical nationalist parties to cause unrest that would "hasten the disengagement of Africa from the West" through "a campaign against 'neo-colonialism' in independent Africa." There was a "relatively high" danger of successful communist subversion in Africa "over the next 2–5 years when relatively large numbers of communist-trained personnel will have returned and when Africa's weak regimes will be put to their severest test."[65]

The CIA concluded at the end of 1964 that "despite the generally good order in which colonial governments withdrew, Communist influence in Africa had recently grown markedly" because "it was not in the nature of things that these fledgling states would soon produce efficient, stable governments." It characterized the countries of Africa as "politically primitive states" where the "Communist line of 'neocolonialism' quickly gained acceptance . . . when the fruits of independence proved elusive." The prospects for the communists were aided by the "primitive conditions which exist in much of the continent," where "quick change and sheer chaos are often just over the horizon" and political elites "are often moved by whim or even occult considerations rather than by rational calculations in conducting national affairs." A communist success in one nation would lead to what President Eisenhower called a domino effect, because the "susceptibility to a 'band-wagon' psychology and a proclivity to be on the winning side is peculiarly important in Africa."[66]

In July, after the removal of the UN troops, Kasavubu established a government of national unity by inviting Tshombe to serve as prime minister. This move, however, failed to preserve order, and in August rebel forces captured Stanleyville in the eastern Congo. The situation was seen as critical in

---

[63] "The Security Situation in the Congo," 17 June 1964, NSF:CF, Box 81, LBJL: see also "Belgium's Continuing Problems with the Congo," 26 June 1964, NSF:CF, Box 81, LBJL.

[64] Administrative History of the Department of State, Vol. 1, Chapter 5: "Congo," Box 2, LBJL.

[65] Department of State, Bureau of Intelligence and Research, "An Outline Guide to Communist Activities in Africa," 15 May 1964, NSF:CF, Box 76, LBJL.

[66] CIA, "Communist Potentialities in Tropical Africa," 1 December 1964, NSF:CF, Box 76, LBJL; see also "Chinese Communist Activities in Africa," 30 April 1965, NSF:CF, Box 76, LBJL.

Washington. With the ever-growing crisis in Vietnam taking up more of the administration's time and energy, it became even more urgent that stability be established in the Congo short of an American intervention. Both the National Security Council and the State Department, fearing a collapse of the government that would lead to a communist takeover, advised Johnson that immediate military action was necessary. The NSC reported on August 6 that all of the eastern Congo could fall and that the "entire Central Government may collapse in next several weeks." This meant that there was a "real danger Communists will be able to exploit" the crisis and gain power. It was urgent that a "small security force (ideally white, at a minimum white-led and, if really good, as few as 1000)" be sent to protect the government.[67] Undersecretary of State for Political Affairs Averell Harriman, recalled that China had announced at the beginning of the year that "Africa was ripe for revolution," and that the evidence suggested "that the Chinese planned that the first such revolution was to take place in the Congo" because of its strategic location in the middle of the continent. The aim, as Harriman saw it, "was to destroy central authority in the Congo and create chaos from which only the Communists could benefit."[68]

The National Security Council met on August 11 to discuss the Congo and what actions the president should take. Harriman and John McCone of the CIA opened the meeting, stressing that the Chinese communists were the cause of the present trouble and that the United States had to take action. Secretary of State Rusk argued that "while present trouble is tribal unrest and rebel bands moving freely...we must assume that if disintegration continues the Communists will take over," and recommended that the United States support the introduction of Belgian troops into the Congo to crush the insurgents. Secretary of Defense Robert McNamara agreed with Rusk, but noted that if "the Europeans fail to accept responsibility, we should not continue to carry the burden alone in the Congo." President Johnson demurred from this and stated that the United States "may have to continue our role regardless of what others do," although he emphatically pointed out that this should be the last resort. Johnson concluded the meeting by observing "that time is running out and the Congo must be saved."[69]

The president ordered increased U.S. military aid to the government, including logistical and air support, CIA-trained anti-Castro Cubans to pilot American supply planes, aid to the white mercenaries employed by the Tshombe government, and air transport for any European troops sent to the Congo. These moves served to stop the losses of the central government but did not resolve the crisis. In September, rebel forces declared their independence as a "people's republic," and the next month took American officials, missionaries, and American and Belgian citizens hostages in their effort to prevent government

---

[67] Brubeck to Johnson, "Congo," 6 August 1964, NSF:CF, Box 81, LBJL; see also Harriman to Bundy, 11 August 1964, and Bundy to Johnson, 11 August 1964, both at NSF:CF, Box 81, LBJL.

[68] Memorandum of conversation, "Events in the Congo," 13 August 1964, NSF:CF, Box 82, LBJL.

[69] NSC Meeting, 11 August 1964, NSF:NSC Meetings, Box 1, LBJL.

attacks and solidify their independence. Plans were drawn up with Belgium for an assault to free the hostages and put an end to the rebellion. On November 24, U.S. aircraft delivered some 600 Belgian paratroopers into Stanleyville. Thirty European hostages were killed along with two American missionaries during the operation, while all of the personnel of the U.S. consulate and over 1,500 other hostages were evacuated by American planes. Belgian troops, in coordination with the ANC, were able to drive the rebel forces from the city, and their resistance collapsed by January, with the leadership going into exile.[70]

The military defeat of the rebellion in the eastern Congo led to a brief period of optimism about the Congo in early 1965. The National Security Council concluded in February that *"things are looking up on the Congo*, though we're far from out of the woods." Most notably, the rebel forces were suffering from "defection, low morale and divided leadership," while Tshombe and the Belgians had reached an economic accord settling the colonial debt and providing the Congo with an ownership interest in certain Belgian companies.[71] The key now was to provide a "political umbrella" to cut off aid to the rebels in order to "bring the level of instability within ranges the Congolese can manage and we can accept."[72]

These concerns were shared by the public as well. As C. L. Sulzberger wrote in the *New York Times*, the Congo was "the most urgent problem facing United States foreign policy," including Vietnam. The Johnson administration faced "a choice between chaos, and Communist ascendancy, or East-West military intervention in Africa's heart." The situation was "alarming and cannot be allowed to drift." Should U.S. efforts to bring stability fail, "all Africa will be torn open. Either the Congo will dissolve or outright international war will explode in the heart of darkness, dragging in a continent if not a world."[73]

By the summer, most of the optimism inside the government was gone. While the rebellions remained in check, political instability continued, fueled by a power struggle between Kasavubu and Tshombe. With the two leaders caught up in their battle for power, in many areas of the nation the central government was failing to assert its authority to eliminate the remaining bands of rebels that still operated in the countryside, and it was ignoring economic problems that plagued the various regions of the nation. The CIA reported that the "budget is out of balance, provincial corruption is unabated, and trained

---

[70] Bundy to Johnson, 16 November 1964, NSF:CF, Box 83, LBJL; Department of State, Director of Intelligence and Research, "Dragon Rouge: African Reactions and Other Estimates," 18 November 1964, NSF:CF, Box 83, LBJL; Department of State, "A Chronology of Significant Events in the Congo since 1960," NSF:CF, Box 86, LBJL; Administrative History of the Department of State, Vol. 1., Chapter 5: "Congo," Box 2, LBJL.

[71] Komer to Bundy, 7 February 1965, NSF:CF, Box 85, LBJL (emphasis in the original); see also Department of State, "A Chronology of Significant Events in the Congo since 1960," NSF:CF, Box 86, LBJL.

[72] Saunders to Bundy, 24 March 1965, NSF:CF Box 85, LBJL.

[73] *New York Times*, 21 December 1964.

administrators are as scarce as ever." Moreover, "unless the political leaders turn their attention from infighting to solving the problems which caused the rebellion in the first place, the now relatively dormant insurrection may eventually reawaken." In the short term, "the mercenaries can keep the lid on any rebel activity." Eventually, however, as "economic and political conditions remain in disorder, the Congolese tribesmen may again decide to kick over the traces."[74]

While the administration wished that Kasavubu and Tshombe would continue to share power, that prospect grew increasingly dim. In October, Kasavubu ousted Tshombe from office and plunged the Congo into another political crisis. This outcome was unacceptable to the Johnson administration for a number of reasons. First, it believed that Kasavubu wanted power no matter what the cost, was willing to manipulate tribal politics to hold onto it, and "just isn't sensitive to the kind of leverage we have."[75] Second, this new situation threatened to "tear the Congo wide open again," with new dangers of secession, civil war, and chaos providing an opening to communism. Robert Komer of the NSC wrote Harriman that he believed it was necessary for the State Department to "start contingency planning *now*. . . . Otherwise we're at the mercy of the Congolese."[76] Johnson, with his attention now focused on the sending of American forces to Vietnam and the escalation of the war, did not want to see another area of the world become a crisis. Given this, the United States again turned to Mobutu to protect its interests in the Congo.

American officials in the Congo, who were in constant contact with Mobutu during this crisis, urged him to seize power and assured him of American support when he took power. After meeting with American officials, particularly CIA station chief Devlin, Mobutu ousted Kasavubu on 25 November 1965 and took over in a bloodless coup.[77] The Johnson administration welcomed Mobutu's seizure of power as the only means to prevent chaos in the Congo and saw no alternative to supporting his rule. While some officials shared the view of Belgian Foreign Minister Paul Henri Spaak that Mobutu's coup was the "best thing that could possibly have happened; it remains to be seen whether it is also a good thing,"[78] Washington did all it could to ensure Mobutu's success. It provided diplomatic support, aid, military supplies and weapons, and intelligence. Indeed, once in power, the United States was determined that Mobutu would stay in control of the Congo. For example, in July 1966 the United States alerted Mobutu to a possible attempt by Tshombe to overthrow him, allowing

[74] Intelligence Memorandum, "Situation in the Congo," 26 August 1965, NSF:CF, Box 85, LBJL; see also Intelligence Memorandum, "Situation in the Congo," 1 July 1965, NSF:CF, Box 85, LBJL.

[75] Saunders to Bundy, 16 October 1965, NSF:CF, Box 85, LBJL; see also Intelligence Memorandum, "Situation in the Congo," 26 August 1965, NSF:CF, Box 85, LBJL.

[76] Komer to Harriman, 21 October 1965, NSF:CF, Box 85, LBJL (emphasis in the original); see also Komer to Bundy, 22 November 1965, NSF:CF, Box 85, LBJL.

[77] Weissman, "CIA Covert Action in Zaire and Angola."

[78] Intelligence Memorandum, "The Situation in the Congo," 24 February 1966, NSF:CF, Box 85, LBJL.

Mobutu to take precautionary steps to stop the rebellion before it started. The next year, when the white mercenary forces still working for the ANC rebelled in an effort to return Tshombe to power, President Johnson sent three American C-130 transport planes and other supplies and support to Mobutu to help him crush the uprising. The National Security Council agreed that U.S. support was necessary to prevent the overthrow of Mobutu's government and to "reassure Mobutu that his pro-Western policy was correct."[79]

In the first full analyzes of Mobutu's government, the CIA provided a cautiously optimistic appraisal of his ability to maintain stability and improve conditions within the country. It found "a few glimmers of hope for the Congo" since the coup. Mobutu had "largely silenced the civilian politicians" and was "making a sincere effort to combat some of the country's basic ills," and the ANC was "making slow but steady progress" against the remaining rebels. The CIA favorably compared Mobutu's government to previous administrations, and noted that it was "one of the most solidly Western oriented since independence" in the Congo. Still, enormous problems remained, and "the outlook for the Congo is still bleak." It would take "stronger authority" from the government to make "significant progress toward unifying and integrating the Congo."[80]

Yet the longer Mobutu was in power, the more positive the evaluation of him and his rule became. By 1967, most of the worrying about Mobutu was gone, and he was being praised by the Johnson administration for bringing stability, preventing chaos and communism in his nation, and providing protection and opportunity for foreign investment. In assessing American policy, the National Security Council concluded that "it was correct for us to send in our C-130 planes as proof of our support" for Mobutu. The United States "had put in a half billion dollars in aid in the last few years" to stabilize his regime. The NSC concluded that the United States "must keep Mobutu in power because there is no acceptable alternative to him."[81]

A special report on "Mobutu and the Congo" prepared by the CIA began by noting that "although the Congo still faces hard times, its future looks brighter at present than at any time since independence. Opposition elements have been effectively subdued, bringing to the country a degree of political stability." Moreover, the central government was exercising its authority throughout the nation, and the economic decline that had beset the nation since independence had been halted. "A great deal of the credit for this progress," the report concluded, "is due to President Joseph Mobutu, who, with careful and skillful exercise of power...has brought the Congo to its present pacified position."

---

[79] Hamilton to Rostow, 13 July 1966, NSF:CF, Box 85, LBJL; Rostow, "Talking Points on C-130's to the Congo," 10 July 1967, NSF:CF, Box 86, LBJL; see also Rostow to Johnson, 6 July 1967, 12 July 1967, 13 July 1967, 14 July 1967, all at NSF:CF, Box 86, LBJL.

[80] Special Report, "The Congo since the Mobutu Coup," 11 February 1966, and Intelligence Memorandum, "The Situation in the Congo," 24 February 1966, NSF:CF, Box 85, LBJL.

[81] NSC Meeting, 13 July 1967, NSF:NSC Meeting, Box 2, LBJL.

His achievements in governing came from his combination of "African traditions of chieftainship liberally interspersed with ideas from his favorite political
theorist, Machiavelli."[82]

Not only was Mobutu seen as effective at maintaining order, but the report
also found that his dictatorship was popular. In the nineteen months since seizing power, "he has risen tremendously in public esteem." The analysis approv-
ingly reported Mobutu's assessment "that the Congolese – whom he describes
as but one generation removed from the villages – expect a strong chief who
must be the unquestioned authority and the sole source of power. The Congolese, he says, are used to tutelage from their years under both tribal and
Belgian rule, and are more comfortable when told exactly what is expected
of them." Mobutu, therefore, believes that Western concepts of government
"are strange and, in the final analysis, unattractive to the Congolese." Indeed,
Mobutu's "Machiavellian approach to cementing his power has drawn admiration from almost everyone, and most Congolese respect him for his power
and for effectively bringing a degree of order to the country." He was using
the ANC to quell rebellions and "discipline errant politicians," thereby leaving
no organized group to oppose him. His source of power was the military, but
the report found that he was a civilianized military leader, and that from his
"preindependence experience as a journalist and student he retains elements of
a nonmilitary outlook." He had, therefore, "brought into his regime elements
of young, university-trained intellectuals and has given them high-level advisory
and coordinative positions."[83]

Mobutu, it was believed, was emerging as a leader of the new Africa. Because
of the size and strategic position of his nation, the Congo "should be one of the
greatest powers in Africa." Mobutu represented "a true African nationalist"
who understood the need not only for economic independence but also for
cooperation and trade with the West. This led him to work to end Belgian domination of the economy while simultaneously recognizing the "necessity of keeping Belgian technicians and hence of conceding many rights to the Belgians."[84]
Furthermore, Mobutu was cooperating with Western institutions, such as the
International Monetary Fund, on economic reforms through a "politically
courageous" 67 percent devaluation of the currency, limits on government
spending and wages, and "an almost complete liberalization of imports."
The "overall success of the economic stabilization program" was allowing for
increased investment and trade.[85] His major contribution, therefore, "has been
to pacify the country" to make it safe for business activity. "If political stability
continues, the Congolese leaders and foreign business interests can exert their
energies toward improving the general economy."[86]

---

[82] Special Report, "Mobutu and the Congo," 23 June 1967, NSF:CF, Box 86, LBJL.
[83] Ibid.
[84] Ibid.
[85] Administrative History of the Department of State, Vol. 1, Chapter 5: "Congo," Box 2, LBJL.
[86] Special Report, "Mobutu and the Congo," 23 June 1967, NSF:CF, Box 86, LBJL.

All of these views were confirmed during Vice President Hubert Humphrey's visit to the Congo in January 1968. A National Intelligence Estimate prepared in advance for Humphrey's visit noted that Mobutu had security issues well in hand and that relations with his regime were excellent. Mobutu saw the "Vice President's visit as an opportunity to show the Congo as a progressive, orderly country, deserving of more assistance from the US."[87] Upon his return, Humphrey reported to President Johnson that "a new Congo" was emerging under the leadership of Mobutu. He praised Mobutu as a moderate with "a statesmanlike attitude," and as a sound nationalist who had brought peace and stability to the Congo. The vice president found Mobutu to be a popular leader, noting enthusiastic crowds throughout the capital as they drove together, and he made no negative comments about his dictatorial rule. Rather, Humphrey recommended that the United States build upon its close relationship with Mobutu by providing greater military aid and that it promote American investment in the Congo by organizing "a major campaign to expand American enterprise" there. "Now that unity and peace" were secured, Humphrey believed that the United States should do all it could "to stimulate the constructive development of this important country during the coming years." With its copper and diamond mines, and its agricultural potential, the Congo, the vice president believed, had the potential to become "to Africa what Brazil is to Latin America."[88]

It was not that American officials were unaware of the nature of the Mobutu regime or how he maintained power. As the CIA reported, Mobutu ruled the Congo as a dictatorship. The regime was "characterized by a heavy concentration of authority in the hands of the President," and it was clear that "Mobutu shares power with no one." His base of power remained the ANC, "an organization that is feared and generally hated." The army, therefore, was "both the main bulwark of the regime and the greatest potential threat to it." Yet the only concern American leaders expressed was over the possibility of Mobutu's departure. The administration believed that if Mobutu were somehow ousted from power, it "would probably result in prolonged political turmoil and a sharp decline in internal security." It would "destroy the relative stability and order now prevalent.... Moreover, because of the highly personal autocratic type of rule employed by Mobutu, the whole structure of government would be shaken."[89] This was a scenario it did not want to risk. While relations with the Congo would still require attention, American objectives "had nonetheless been achieved."[90]

---

[87] NIE, "Security Conditions in Certain African Countries," 21 December 1967, NSF:NIE, LBJL.

[88] Humphrey to Johnson, 12 January 1968, NSF:CF, Box 77, LBJL.

[89] National Intelligence Estimate, "Prospects for the Congo," 27 September 1968, NSF:NIE, Box 8–9, LBJL.

[90] Administrative History of the Department of State, Vol. 1, Chapter 5: "Congo," Box 2, LBJL.

No Acceptable Alternative

American officials simply could not see, again as the NSC put it, an "acceptable alternative" to Mobutu, casting the choice as a dichotomy between Mobutu and chaos. Most notably, Mobutu was credited with foiling a communist effort to gain a foothold in Central Africa that had the potential to disrupt the whole continent. The State Department's review of the events of 1964–65 concluded that the Soviet Union and China had brought the Cold War to the Congo by sending "large amounts" of military supplies to the rebels in the Congo. China had "hailed the 'excellent revolutionary situation' in the Congo and expressed hope that it would follow the pattern of the war in South Viet-Nam," while a defector from a Chinese embassy in Africa "attributed to Mao Tse Tung the saying, 'If we can hold the Congo, we will take the whole of Africa.'"[91] In addition, Mobutu had brought stability to the Congo; he was a reliable ally with whom "the US enjoys a high degree of prestige and influence" owing to "massive aid provided over the years and on a...long working association of US officials with Mobutu";[92] and he was providing the conditions for improved economic investment and trade. Given American policymakers' belief in the African nations' incapacity for self-government, he was seen in Washington as the right type of authoritarian military leader, a figure who was necessary for the Congo to protect the nation from communism while it went through the process of modernization in the wake of colonial rule. In addition, Mobutu was seen as a model for leadership and stability in other African countries.

As the Johnson administration's final evaluation of its relationship with Mobutu made clear, he met all of the requirements of American policy. The general provided order in the Congo; the maintenance "of its national independence and territorial integrity; strengthening of cooperation with the United States and other friendly non-Communist states;...improvement of internal security; and a reasonable increase in the rate of economic and social development." Nowhere on this list was a concern for freedom, human rights, or democratic institutions and processes. U.S. support for Mobutu's dictatorship "helped the Congo to reach a level of political and economic stability which [sic] orderly economic growth." Relations were characterized as "excellent," and optimism was expressed about the Congo's ability under Mobutu to maintain stability and economic growth. Moreover, by using covert action and supporting a dictator, the United States had been able, "with a minimum of expense and political and military involvement, but with continuing well-received counsel," to achieve all of its goals.[93] The Congo was stable, and led by an anticommunist, pro-Western dictator who supported American policies in the Cold War and promised to protect Western trade and investments.

---

[91] Ibid.

[92] National Intelligence Estimate, "Prospects for the Congo," 27 September 1968 NSF:NIE, Box 8–9, LBJL.

[93] Administrative History of the Department of State, Vol. 1, Chapter 5: "Congo," Box 2, LBJL.

In the middle of the Vietnam War, the purported benefits that Mobutu's regime provided were welcomed by the Johnson administration and served to confirm the correctness of supporting right-wing dictators. When instability and perceived threats of communist takeovers appeared in Indonesia and Greece, the administration again supported right-wing military takeovers that promised stability, anticommunism, and the protection of U.S. economic interests. But with the war in Vietnam becoming a divisive issue at home, questions were raised concerning the correctness of both the policy of containment and the support of right-wing dictators. The contradictions of American policy, protecting freedom by supporting dictators, were becoming apparent. Still, as Washington saw it, the alternative of communist takeovers was much worse. Greece would provide the first, albeit limited, domestic challenge to the policy of backing authoritarian regimes and would serve as an indicator of a shift that the Vietnam War would forge concerning American foreign policy.

2

Degrading Freedom

The Johnson Administration and Right-Wing Dictatorships

While confronting the crisis in the Congo and the escalation of the war in Vietnam, the Johnson administration simultaneously faced what it saw as the clear danger of communist takeovers in Indonesia and Greece. In both cases, American officials worried that instability, political immaturity, and misguided anti-American sentiment would lead a strategically and economically important nation to fall into the communist camp. The administration saw the military in Indonesia and Greece as the best alternative to this perceived threat and, therefore, welcomed their overthrow of the existing governments and their establishment of military dictatorships. The embrace of General Suharto in 1965–66 occurred without any opposition or much public notice in the United States as the rapid escalation of the war in Vietnam dominated America's concerns. The Vietnam War, however, would bring forth the first questioning of American containment policy and challenges to the policy of supporting authoritarian regimes. The political challenges to this policy were first manifested in 1967 in response to the Johnson administration's support of the colonels' coup and the overthrow of democracy in Greece.

American policymakers had worried since the late 1950s about the direction President Sukarno was taking Indonesia, but the situation became acute after 1963 as the Indonesian Communist Party (PKI) gained greater influence and Sukarno pulled Indonesia out of the United Nations, increased his criticisms of U.S. policy in Vietnam, confronted Great Britain in Malaysia, and aligned Indonesia with the People's Republic of China. Johnson, with his attention more and more taken up by the war in Vietnam, moved cautiously in the hope of preventing a final break with Djakarta. The president sent personal representatives to try to find ways to end the growing rift between the two countries, and to make clear to Sukarno Washington's concern about the increasing power of the PKI. The administration also cut some aid programs as a means to apply pressure, and maintained contacts with pro-Western leaders of the Indonesian army.

The crisis reached its peak on 1 October 1965, when the communist-led September 30 Movement captured and killed six army generals in a failed coup attempt. In response, General Suharto took control of the government and began, in the State Department's words, "a wholesale roundup and slaughter of Communist Party members." The general also began to change the direction of Indonesian foreign and domestic policies in support of the United States and to protect private investments, and forced Sukarno out of the presidency in March 1966. The Johnson administration welcomed all of Suharto's actions and extended support to his government, convinced that events in Indonesia again justified American support for right-wing dictators. Indeed, the State Department found that "Indonesia's transition from a nation moving steadily toward Communist control to a responsible member of the free community is one of the major success stories of recent years."[1] Moreover, the administration believed that the events in Indonesia validated its policy in Vietnam. The demonstration of American resolve, it concluded, had provided protection to the anticommunist forces in Indonesia and thereby prevented a crucial domino from falling to communism.

Support for right-wing dictators had always been based, in part, on anti-Bolshevism and since the 1940s had been seen as a necessary aspect of the larger policy to contain communism. The overriding Cold War consensus was based on the assumption that communism was monolithic, directed by the Soviet Union, aggressive, inherently expansive, and hostile to all Western interests. Communism was, therefore, a mortal enemy of the United States, an evil that had to be combated on a global scale in a bipolar world. Thus, the United States was justified in supporting right-wing dictators because the alternative – "international communism" – was not only worse but a direct threat to American national security and to worldwide freedom.

As the war in Vietnam escalated after 1965, however, opposition to American policy began to develop in different segments of American society. These opponents questioned the morality of the American effort in South Vietnam and whether the use of force there was in the national interest. Most importantly, they began to challenge the fundamental assumptions of containment, arguing that the conflict in Vietnam was a revolution and civil war sparked by nationalism and anticolonialism, and not part of a plan by the communist world to dominate Southeast Asia. The Saigon regime, rather than being an outpost on the frontier of the free world's fight against international communism, was seen by critics as a corrupt and unpopular dictatorship that lacked legitimacy and support. If communism was not monolithic, if it was not a bipolar world, then the policy of supporting such a regime became a matter of debate. Once the policy of containment was questioned, other aspects of the American foreign policy that had gone without examination because of the Cold War consensus were also open to criticism. Those who began to rethink their views on American policy in Vietnam would also begin to challenge the logic and rationale of American support for right-wing dictatorships.

---

[1] Administrative History of the Department of State, Vol. 1, Chapter 7: "Indonesia," Box 3, LBJL.

The Johnson administration would struggle to find the proper response to the Greek colonels' seizure of power in Athens in 1967 as the policy of supporting right-wing dictators was publicly challenged for the first time. Although United States officials wished the Greek colonels had not seized power without coordinating their actions with King Constantine, the Johnson administration supported the junta because it was seen as providing a necessary stability for Greece while preventing a communist takeover. American officials believed that Andreas Papandreou represented a threat to Greece and the southern flank of the North Atlantic Treaty Organization (NATO) because he challenged the role of the monarchy in Greek society and was perceived as working closely with communist groups in pursuit of his political goals. Yet the coup and American support of the colonels were criticized by segments of the media, intellectuals, and some Greek-Americans. The policy was seen as a violation of American principles and linked by critics to the Vietnam War as another example of the misguided policies of the nation that were harming rather than protecting the national interest. What was becoming clear was that the Vietnam War would fundamentally alter all discussions of American foreign policy and lead to challenges to the policy of supporting right-wing dictators.

A Captive of the Communists

Since 1949, when Indonesia gained its independence from the Netherlands, American officials had worried about the direction in which President Sukarno would take the country. Indonesia, one of the largest and most populous nations in the world, possesses abundant raw materials, such as oil and rubber, that provide the potential for great wealth and power. In addition, it sits astride the key shipping lanes of Southeast Asia, making it a strategically important country. For all these reasons, the United States had pressured the Netherlands to make concessions and grant independence to Indonesia in order to avoid having the Dutch continue to resist and possibly drive Sukarno and the nationalists toward communism.[2]

By the 1950s, however, relations between Washington and Djakarta had become tense. Sukarno declared his neutrality in the Cold War and emerged as one of the leaders of the nonaligned movement. In April 1955, he hosted the Bandung Conference, which supported decolonization and greater Third World control over its resources, and called on the world to focus on issues other than the Cold War between the United States and the Soviet Union. Domestically, he used the PKI, the third largest communist party in the world, as a political counter to the pro-Western Indonesian army. The Eisenhower administration opposed neutralism, with Secretary of State John Foster Dulles going so far as to call it immoral, seeing all nations that did not align with the United States as aiding communism. This Manichean worldview led Eisenhower in 1957 to approve

[2] McMahon, *Colonialism and Cold War*.

a CIA effort to overthrow Sukarno.[3] The coup attempt failed, and Sukarno tightened his grip on power through the elimination of most political parties (except the PKI) and other opposition groups, by instituting what he called "guided democracy," while opposing American foreign policy, particularly in Vietnam.

Relations between Washington and Djakarta briefly improved in 1962, when the United States helped negotiate a settlement to the dispute over West New Guinea between the Indonesians and the Dutch, and American officials hoped that "Sukarno would turn his attention inward and concentrate on improving his nation's shattered economy." Sukarno, however, rejected the economic stabilization program the United States had developed along with European nations and international financial institutions. He saw it as part of an effort, along with the creation of Malaysia, by the imperialist nations to surround Indonesia and destroy its independence and unity. On 16 September 1963, mobs of Indonesian students attacked the British and Malaysian embassies in the capital and two days later burned the British embassy, raising the fear of war between Great Britain and Indonesia. That fall, Sukarno indicated his willingness to confront not only Great Britain but also the United States directly when he compared Indonesia to Cuba. Both, he declared, were the center of opposition to imperialism in their respective regions of the world. Moreover, he criticized American policy in Vietnam and predicted victory for the National Liberation Front over the United States. Domestically, the State Department concluded that Sukarno was coming to rely even more on the PKI for support and that communism was "to be given the major place in the power structure and anti-Communism was considered subversive."[4]

These developments caused enormous concern in Washington, but it was not clear to the Johnson administration how to respond to the rapidly deteriorating relationship with Indonesia. As a CIA analysis in early 1964 explained, Sukarno was a formidable opponent. He was a national hero and symbol of independence; a "mass leader of extraordinary skill;" an "intuitive politician who readily grasps the strengths and weaknesses" of the groups he is dealing with; a leader who held power "by carefully balancing the strength of the Communist Party against that of the army" and who was able to count on the support of those who disagree with him "because they are convinced that he is a cohesive force essential to preserving national unity." He therefore had "no political rivals," and his power was greater than ever before. All of this also made Sukarno extremely dangerous because of his reliance on the communists, whom he saw as "nationalists first and Communists second." This allowed the PKI, the CIA concluded, to increase its membership, prestige, and power as it prepared eventually to take power.[5]

[3] Kahin and Kahin, *Subversion as Foreign Policy.*
[4] Administrative History of the Department of State, Vol. 1, Chapter 7: "Indonesia," Box 3, LBJL.
[5] CIA Special Report, "The Power Position of Indonesia's President Sukarno," 7 February 1964, NSF:CF, Box 246, LBJL.

The immediate question in light of Indonesia's opposition to Malaysia was that of continued aid to Djakarta. Congress was putting pressure on the administration to support Great Britain and cut American assistance to Sukarno's government. As the State Department noted, however, U.S. aid to Indonesia was "designed, first, to strengthen anti-Communist elements for the battle that will follow Sukarno's departure, and, second, to give us a foot-in-the-door influence on Sukarno's policies."[6] Given these goals, the administration had to decide whether it was better to terminate assistance or to continue it. All of this, as the State Department noted, created a delicate problem. "Indonesia is not a Communist country, and to treat it as one would be likely to drive it in that direction." Yet it was the primary target of "the Communist Bloc" and "its number one recipient of military and economic aid in the past three years." The United States, therefore, needed to maintain some contact with the Indonesian government and "to the greatest extent possible influence the course of its policies in order to prevent further Indonesian drift toward the Communist Bloc." American assistance was directed at "restraining the present regime and supporting the basis of a non-Communist alternative in Indonesia." In particular, the "non-Communist groups, such as the officers of the Armed Forces and police, and a growing corps of economic and political leaders look to United States assistance and depend upon it. The continuation of assistance to support the position of these people is essential to our interests."[7]

National Security Advisor McGeorge Bundy noted that there were two related considerations. It was agreed that the United States "should have a cool and firm policy of increasing opposition to Sukarno." But that was not the same as terminating all assistance to Indonesia. The main justification for cutting off aid was that "nobody likes Sukarno, and with good reason." In policy terms, it "might show Sukarno consequences of 'confrontation' with Malaysia." Yet Bundy argued that it was better to continue sending limited aid. "The programs we have planned are there now because we think them 'essential to our national interest.' They are not there because we like Sukarno, but because we are contending for the long-range future of a country of 100 million with great resources in a strategic location." In addition, a cessation of aid "could trigger a violent reaction from Sukarno ... [and] could cost us half a billion of private investments." He compared the situation to relations with Egypt in 1956. The "Aswan Dam case," Bundy argued, "should remind us that neutrals are ready to seize on *our* acts to justify *their* outrages – and to some extent they get away with it."[8]

What concerned the United States was not that Sukarno was a dictator, but that he was the wrong kind of dictator. At the National Security Council meeting on 7 January 1964, it was agreed that aid should be continued, but

---

[6] Rusk to Johnson, "Aid to Indonesia," 6 January 1964, NSF:CF, Box 246, LBJL.
[7] Department of State, "Background Statement," 21 December 1963, NSF:NSAM, Box 2, LBJL.
[8] Bundy, "Memorandum on Indonesia," 7 January 1964, NSF:CF, Box 246, LBJL (emphasis in the original).

limited, and that it had to be made clear that such assistance was by no means a sign of support for the Indonesian leader. Secretary of State Dean Rusk noted that "the stakes are very high. More is involved in Indonesia, with it [sic] 100 million people, than is at stake in Viet Nam." There was the danger that cutting off all American aid might push Sukarno to respond by "confiscating extensive U.S. investments in Indonesia." That could lead to a "showdown" in which Sukarno "might ask help from China and even Russia." Moreover, all of America's allies, most notably the British and Australians, opposed a break with Sukarno. Undersecretary of State Averill Harriman argued that continued support was essential "for keeping a foot in the door." If aid was stopped, Sukarno could turn completely to the communist world. "If the Indonesians turn against us and seize U.S. investments," Harriman warned, "the Chinese Communists might get the U.S. oil companies, thereby altering the strategic balance in the area."[9]

President Johnson, who had once wondered "whether the closer we get to Sukarno the more difficult he becomes,"[10] noted that "it was very difficult to say that aid to Indonesia under present circumstances is in the national interest." Still, he agreed to continue limited aid in the hope that "the immediate problem caused by Sukarno's confrontation policy" could be solved through negotiations. In addition, he agreed with Bundy's suggestion that he send "to Djakarta a tough man who would tell Sukarno that the President did not intend to continue assistance unless Sukarno halted the confrontation effort," and that this person should be Attorney General Robert Kennedy.[11]

The Kennedy mission was "designed to make clear to Sukarno the consequences for US-Indonesian relations if Sukarno continued his policies toward Malaysia" and to seek a negotiated settlement of the problem. While all sides pledged that they desired to end the conflict in the conference room and not on the battlefield, no solution was found, and tensions remained high throughout the year.[12] Nonetheless, the Johnson administration decided to continue existing economic and military aid programs. It remained the administration's position that the current assistance programs were an important part of "U.S. short-run political interests, and that their elimination is not especially desirable." The administration also assumed that the elimination of the aid programs "would have little or no effect in tempering Sukarno's ... activities against Malaysia" and still might provoke a seizure of American properties.[13] The goal remained to keep Sukarno from going completely over to the communists while preventing the use of force against Malaysia. As Johnson told congressional leaders, "if we cut off all assistance, Sukarno will probably turn to the Russians."[14]

[9] National Security Council Meeting, 7 January 1964, NSF:NSC Meetings, Box 1, LBJL.
[10] Memorandum of Conversation, 18 December 1963, NSF:CF, Box 246, LBJL.
[11] National Security Council Meeting, 7 January 1964, NSF:NSC Meetings, Box 1, LBJL.
[12] Administrative History of the Department of State, Vol. 1, Chapter 7: "Indonesia," Box 3, LBJL.
[13] Forrestal to Bundy, 8 May 1964, NSF:CF, Box 246, LBJL.
[14] National Security Council Meeting, 3 April 1964, NSF:NSC Meetings, Box 1, LBJL.

In August, fears that Sukarno was becoming a captive of the communists were raised to new heights in Washington. On August 10, just days after the Gulf of Tonkin incident and U.S. air strikes against North Vietnam, Indonesia officially recognized the Hanoi government. Seven days later, in his annual independence day speech, Sukarno attacked the United States, denounced the "American attack on North Vietnam," and declared that all non-Asians must leave all of Asia, noting specifically that South Korea and South Vietnam were "not yet free."[15] That same day, Indonesia landed a small force on Malaysia, which came close to sparking a British retaliation.

Sukarno's actions confirmed the administration's view of his "accelerated swing to the left during the past 18 months" and its fear that Sukarno was "well on his way to becoming a captive of the Communists." The CIA concluded that his speech "charts a course – both international and domestic – which is close to the immediate objectives of the Indonesian Communist Party," and that Sukarno and the communists had the same long-range goal – to "get the US out of Southeast Asia." Moreover, he had given in to a basic communist demand for land reform, announcing that "eventually there will be no imperialist capital operating on Indonesian soil." While "Sukarno has deliberately chosen, on his own, to stand internationally with the anti-Western Asian world, it appeared that Sukarno was no longer able to keep the communists in check" and "has allowed too much influence to slip into Communist hands."[16]

Pressure again rose to break relations with Sukarno, with congressional calls for a final cessation of aid, and there was a good deal of anger within the administration toward Sukarno. Still, administration officials could foresee no new benefits from cutting off the remaining aid and did not want to break relations with Indonesia. Rather, they continued to hold to the position that it was necessary to maintain a "foot in the door for the long term stakes" and to maintain "our relationship with the Indo military if at all possible." Given that, the National Security Council concluded that "any fast motion toward a cut-off would be a foolish waste of 15 years's investment. Far better to play it cool . . . and to make a fast pitch to our real pals, the Indo military." It reported to the president that the "case for not giving Sukarno new grounds to react is a powerful one." The United States had maintained its aid programs "on the basic premise that if he swung too far left we'd lose the third largest country in Asia – whose strategic location and 100 million people make it a far greater prize than Vietnam." To leave no openings would multiply the odds that Sukarno would "end up the prisoner of his powerful CP."[17]

[15] Central Intelligence Agency, "Sukarno's Independence Day Speech," 20 August 1964, NSF:CF, Box 246, LBJL.
[16] Ibid.; see also Rusk to Johnson, "Assistance Program for Indonesia," 30 August 1964, NSF:CF, Box 246, LBJL.
[17] Thompson to Bundy, 25 August 1964, NSF:CF, Box 246, LBJL; Komer to Johnson, 19 August 1964, NSF:CF, Box 246, LBJL.

Bundy told the president that Sukarno's "far more overtly anti-US line" did make the withholding of aid appear essential. At the same time, however, there were a number of reasons that the sharp downward curve in relations "makes it all the more important not to burn all our bridges to Indonesia." The first of these was the war in Vietnam. That commitment meant that the United States could "ill afford a major crisis with Indonesia too just now." Second, it was necessary to maintain links to the Indonesian military, which was "still the chief hope of blocking a Communist takeover." Third, there was the small chance that Sukarno would pull back from the growing conflict on his own, "and we want to keep dangling the prospect of renewed aid." Finally, it was important that the United States not "be the ones who trigger a major attack on U.S. investments there."[18]

Relations continued to decline throughout the fall and winter of 1964, leading to an increased certainty in Washington that Sukarno would deliver Indonesia, whether intentionally or not, to communist control. Beginning in September, United States consulates and United States Information Service (USIS) centers were periodically attacked and American officials harassed by crowds of Indonesians during anti-American demonstrations, leading to the eventual closing of all USIS centers in the country. In December, protestors went so far as to enter the U.S. embassy compound in Djakarta. Most American businesses were forced to work with a "supervisory team" of Indonesians to direct their operations. Moreover, the Indonesian Parliament denounced United States policies in Southeast Asia and called upon other nations to oppose American "imperialism." Embassy protests for the most part went unanswered, and American officials "ceased to have meaningful contact with top government authorities."[19]

These actions inside Indonesia, along with Sukarno's goal of removing Western influence in Southeast Asia, convinced the administration that Sukarno was moving "toward leftist totalitarianism" and was "likely ultimately to bring Indonesia under Communist control." In addition, Sukarno was working to curb the power of the army. The communists, the CIA reported, still needed Sukarno in power for the time being "to protect it while it consolidates its gains." If Sukarno held power for "a few more years, it is likely that he will eventually preside over a modified Communist regime" and that when he dies, the PKI "can make a bid for power with good chances of success."[20] Sukarno, it concluded, "apparently believes that long-run trends are working to weaken US/Western influence in Southeast Asia," and that Djakarta and Beijing will divide the spoils. When he did die, Sukarno's legacy would be "international outlawry, economic near-chaos, and weakened resistance to Communist domination." No one, however, predicted that Sukarno would start a war over

---

[18] Bundy to Johnson, "Assistance Program for Indonesia," 31 August 1964, NSF:CF, Box 246, LBJL.

[19] Administrative History of the Department of State, Vol. 1, Chapter 7: "Indonesia," Box 3, LBJL.

[20] Special Report, "Sukarno and the Communists," 23 October 1964, NSF:CF, Box 246, LBJL.

Malaysia or seek a military conflict with the West, nor was a communist takeover "imminent." This left space for continued efforts to improve relations while at the same time calling for "especial US intelligence and planning attention."[21] This meant working with the "Council of Generals" formed in January 1965 to "discuss the deteriorating political situation and what the army should do about it."[22]

On 18 March 1965, Undersecretary of State George Ball sent an ominous message to President Johnson that began: "Our relations with Indonesia are on the verge of falling apart. Sukarno is turning more and more toward the Communist PKI." What caused this new alarm was the Indonesian government's taking over of the management of American rubber plants and the danger "of an imminent seizure of the American oil companies." Ball and Rusk recommended that Johnson send Ellsworth Bunker as his personal representative to evaluate the situation, meet with Sukarno "to try to get a commitment from [him] to take a more moderate course," and make recommendations upon his return regarding future American policy.[23] Bunker was selected because of his prestige in Indonesia after having negotiated the settlement over West New Guinea. This was seen as a last effort to "arrest Indonesia's apparent drift into the Communist camp."[24]

Bunker left for Djakarta on 31 March 1965, spending two weeks meeting with top Indonesian leaders and United States officials. The mission, however, yielded little beyond platitudes concerning friendship and cooperation. Bunker reported to Johnson that relations with Indonesia "are unlikely to improve in the near future." Sukarno's opposition to American policy was due to U.S. support for Malaysia, Washington's policy in Vietnam, and the presence of U.S. military bases in the region. In addition, Sukarno saw himself as the leader of the "Afro-Asian nations in a struggle of the NEFOS (New Emerging Forces) against the OLDEFOS (Old Established Forces)" to rid the Third World of neocolonialism. "The U.S. as the most powerful leader of the developed countries is identified as enemy No. 1." All of this was fueled by "Sukarno's proclaimed Marxism and his avowed intention of doing away with capitalism in the process of socializing Indonesia" and by "the influence of the PKI . . . which looks to Peking for inspiration and whose avowed purpose is to drive the U.S. out of Indonesia."[25]

The only hopeful sign in the situation was the position of the Indonesian army. "U.S. policy," Bunker stated, "should be directed toward creating conditions which will give the [military] the most favorable conditions for confrontation." The United States, therefore, "should seek to retain a continued presence in Indonesia" and "maintain as much contact with as many other elements in

[21] "Principle Problems and Prospects in Indonesia," 26 January 1965, NSF:CF, Box 246, LBJL.

[22] CIA, *Indonesia – 1965: The Coup that Backfired*, 190–1.

[23] Ball to Johnson, "Proposed Mission for Ellsworth Bunker to Indonesia," 18 March 1965, NSF:CF, Box 247, LBJL.

[24] Thompson to Johnson, "Your Meeting with Ambassador Bunker," 24 March 1965, NSF:CF, Box 247, LBJL.

[25] Bunker to Johnson, 23 April 1965, NSF:CF, Box 247, LBJL.

Indonesia" outside of the government as possible. The Sukarno era would come to an end soon, and "the forces that will succeed him are already lining up and fighting for position," mainly the PKI and the army. "The army would seem in the best position to exert a commanding influence if the Sukarno regime were to end tomorrow." The question was how long it could maintain this position, given Sukarno's increasing reliance on the communists.[26]

Throughout the summer of 1965, the disagreements between Washington and Djakarta grew ever more tense. When the newly appointed American ambassador, Marshall Green, presented his credentials in July, "Sukarno delivered an unprecedented undiplomatic diatribe against the United States and its policies," and the ambassador was met by government-supported protesters at his residence. On independence day, Sukarno again denounced the United States and made clear his support for China and North Vietnam against the West.[27] Ambassador Green's first report emphasized that "*Sukarno is deliberately promoting Communism's cause in Indonesia.*" The final move to a complete alignment with the PKI was "being done at as rapid a pace as seems prudent without creating excessive dissidence of coalition of more conservative elements." In light of this, and Sukarno's consistent hostility to U.S. foreign policy, it was "time to come to challenge old assumptions, to look at facts anew and to re-examine our posture toward Indonesia."[28]

Ball wrote Johnson that relations "may well be past the point of no return." Sukarno's efforts to lead the "new emerging forces" against what he saw as the remaining manifestations of colonialism made any reconciliation almost impossible. "Any further efforts," therefore, "to appeal to Sukarno's megalomania would most likely only reinforce his view that the US needs him more than he needs us." The policy of trying to work with Sukarno and using economic aid to gain influence had failed. As Ball noted, "I think we have played this line out." Cutting off assistance would not necessarily mean "turning the country over to the Communists. On the contrary, it is more likely to mean a sharpened confrontation between the Communist Party and anti-Communists in the country."[29]

The administration decided it was time to put direct pressure on Sukarno, and a tougher line toward Djakarta was shown by American officials in an effort to enhance the position of the military. Members of the National Security Council, Vice President Hubert Humphrey, and Secretary of State Rusk all held separate meetings with Indonesian Ambassador Lambertus Palar to protest Indonesia's actions and to impress upon him the cost of U.S. opposition. Chester Cooper and James Thompson of the NSC stressed that "mature nations" do not use violence against another country's diplomatic installations, no matter

[26] Ibid.
[27] Administrative History of the Department of State, Vol. 1, Chapter 7: "Indonesia," Box 3, LBJL.
[28] *FRUS*, 1964–68, Vol. 26, 278–80 (emphasis in the original).
[29] Ball to Johnson, "Deteriorating Situation in Indonesia," no date [August 1965], NSF:CF, Box 247, LBJL.

how serious the disagreements, and they rejected the "simplistic categories" of "New Emerging Forces" and "Old Established Forces" for "analyzing a profoundly complex world."[30] They did not explain how the bipolar analysis of the world by the United States – between the free world and the communistic bloc – was any different.

In his meeting with Humphrey, Palar attempted to explain the views and actions of the Sukarno government. He began by noting that parliamentary democracy had failed in Indonesia because the "Indonesian electorate was not sufficiently educated" and because some leaders had taken advantage of this for personal gain. What Indonesia needed "first and foremost" was "a stable government." Sukarno's relationship with the PKI was one of necessity, because the communists were a fact in the world and were "here to stay." The Indonesian government, therefore, was trying to integrate "communism into the Indonesian society rather than having Indonesian society integrated into communism." Moreover, in the long run "nationalism will emerge stronger than communism in Indonesia," making communism "only a short term concern for the Indonesians." Finally, he contended that it was U.S. foreign policy that had "pushed us in the direction of the Chinese" to counter American actions in Vietnam and elsewhere in the region.[31]

Humphrey did not disagree with Palar's characterization of the Indonesian people or the need to abandon representative government. The United States saw the period prior to 1957 as "an unsuccessful experiment with parliamentary democracy," a view that was consistent with its rationale for supporting right-wing dictators throughout the world.[32] The vice president did, however, express concern about the direction of the Indonesian government and about the fact that "American property and personnel have been subjected to physical harassment," and he defended American foreign policy. Humphrey dismissed the idea that United States policy posed a threat to anyone but the communist nations. It was the United States' stated policy to protect freedom, and that was why it was "making such a firm commitment to the freedom of South Vietnam."[33]

In late August, Ball convened "an impromptu meeting" of a half-dozen officials to discuss Indonesia. The undersecretary asked whether it was true that given its size and location "Indonesia was objectively at least on par with the whole of Indochina," and whether "a far-left, if not a totally communist, takeover there . . . [was] only a matter of time?" The group agreed with Ball's assessment. Given this, Ball wanted to know what could be done. The group was pessimistic that the United States could counter this trend, with the CIA representative claiming the agency "did not have good assets in Indonesia."[34]

---

[30] Thompson, "Memorandum for the Record," 12 August 1965, NSF:CF, Box 247, LBJL.

[31] Memorandum of Conversation, "U.S.-Indonesian Relations," 26 August 1965, NSF:CF, Box 247, LBJL.

[32] Bunker to Johnson, 23 April 1965, NSF:CF, Box 247, LBJL.

[33] Memorandum of Conversation, "U.S.-Indonesian Relations," 26 August 1965, NSF:CF, Box 247, LBJL.

[34] *FRUS*, 1964–68, Vol. 26, 288.

Events overran any U.S. planning when on 1 October 1965 the "September 30 Movement," claiming to block an attempted coup by the army, captured and killed six top generals. Led by Lieutenant Colonel Untung, the commander of Sukarno's palace guard, and acting with the apparent knowledge of Sukarno, the 30 September group announced that it had organized to "save President Sukarno" from a planned attack by the military on October 5. The movement, however, failed to capture either General Nasution, the minister of defense, or General Suharto, the commander of the Strategic Reserve. Suharto quickly assumed command of the army and led a counter-coup, taking control of the government only hours after the initial attacks and consolidating his power over the next few days.[35]

An Effective Anti-Communist

While it was difficult during the first hours and days to know precisely what had happened in Djakarta, Washington welcomed Suharto's move and quickly indicated its support for his government. The CIA reported the day after the coup that Suharto was an anticommunist who since 1961 had taken "an active part in the army 'steering committee' in efforts to map anti-Communist strategy."[36] Ball noted that with the army taking over, there was a chance it might "keep going and clean up the PKI – this is the most optimistic expectation but it is unclear at the moment."[37] Ambassador Green noted that he was encouraging army officials to act decisively against the communists. With the discovery of the murdered bodies of the generals, "momentum is now at peak," and it was "now or never" for the army "to pin blame for recent events on [the] Communist Party and its allies" and take control.[38] The embassy reported that the "PKI and pro-Communist elements [were] very much on [the] defensive." This might embolden the army "at long last to act effectively against Communists." It was important that the U.S. covertly "indicate clearly to key people in [the] army . . . our desire to be of assistance . . . while at the same time conveying to them our assumption that we should avoid appearance of involvement or interference in any way." The State Department agreed, concerned only about "whether [the] Army can maintain momentum [of] its offensive against PKI."[39]

The obstacle to full action by the army, as the administration saw it, was Sukarno. With the failure of the coup, Sukarno had set out to portray the events of October 1 as a "political problem" that he, and not the army, should

---

35 Ibid., 300–1; Intelligence Memorandum, "Indonesia – Major General Suharto," 2 October 1965, NSF:CF, Box 247, LBJL; see also Scott, "The United States and the Overthrow of Sukarno, 1965–1967."

36 Intelligence Memorandum, "Indonesia – Major General Suharto," 2 October 1965, NSF:CF, Box 247, LBJL.

37 *FRUS*, 1964–68, Vol. 26, 302–3.

38 Green, "Implications of the September 30 Affair in Indonesia," 5 October 1965, NSF:CF, Box 247, LBJL.

39 *FRUS*, 1964–68, Vol. 26, 307–9.

settle. Both the embassy in Djakarta and officials in Washington believed that Sukarno was trying to reassert his own power and needed, therefore, to protect the Communist Party to return to the status quo. The army was in control for the time being, but Sukarno's prestige remained great and his exact knowledge about and role in the September 30 Movement unclear.

Suharto was, therefore, the critical person. He emerged from the events "as a strong military leader and apparently a firm anti-Communist" who had demonstrated the willingness to directly blame the communists for the killing of the army generals and to criticize Sukarno. "Should Sukarno move too rapidly in favor of the left," he could drive the wedge between himself and the army deeper and "promote a stronger public and political anti-Communist stand by the army."[40] Meanwhile, the embassy reported that the army was keeping up "the momentum of its drive against the PKI," while George Ball informed Senator William Fulbright that Suharto was "disobeying Sukarno" and that the communists "would have to go underground."[41]

The full extent of the army's campaign to eliminate the PKI soon became clear. In the following weeks Suharto's regime carried out "a wholesale roundup and slaughter of Communist Party members," killing or arresting most of the PKI's leadership.[42] Estimates of how many were killed range from over 100,000 to a million, with the most reliable studies placing the number killed as at least 500,000, with another 750,000 arrested.[43] "In terms of the numbers killed," the CIA stated in 1968, "the anti-PKI massacres in Indonesia rank as one of the worst mass murders of the 20th century, along with the Soviet purges of the 1930's, the Nazi mass murders during the Second World War, and the Maoist bloodbath of the early 1950's."[44]

While the exact nature and level of American involvement in the army's actions remains impossible to determine owing to the CIA's unwillingness to declassify documents relating to these events, American officials were in contact with the army throughout this period, and provided intelligence information and lists of communists to the Indonesian army. Moreover, Washington certainly welcomed Suharto's actions.[45] McGeorge Bundy reported to Johnson that the events since October 1 had been "a striking vindication of U.S. policy towards [Indonesia] in recent years: a policy of keeping our hand in the game for

---

[40] Green, "Implications of the September 30 Affair in Indonesia," 5 October 1965, NSF:CF, Box 247, LBJL; Intelligence Memorandum, "The Upheaval in Indonesia," 6 October 1965, NSF:CF, Box 247, LBJL.

[41] "Indonesia Working Group – Situation Report No. 14," 9 October 1965, NSF:CF, Box 247, LBJL; *FRUS*, 1964–68, Vol. 26, 319.

[42] Administrative History of the Department of State, Vol. 1, Chapter 7: "Indonesia," Box 3, LBJL.

[43] Kahin and Kahin, *Subversion as Foreign Policy*, 228; see also Cribb, ed., *The Indonesia Killings of 1965–1966*.

[44] CIA, *Indonesia – 1965: The Coup that Backfired*, 71.

[45] For discussions of the extent of the embassy in Djakarta's knowledge of the massacre and its role in supplying names to the army, see *FRUS*, 1964–68, Vol. 26, 338–40, 386–7. See also Reed, "U.S. Agents 'Drew Up Indonesian Hit List.'"

the long-term stakes despite recurrent pressure to pull out." He found "very promising the forces set free by the defeat of the September 30th plot," and reported that the army was "showing considerable courage" and that the population was "with the Army to an extraordinary degree so far."[46] In November, Green reported to the State Department that the army was training and arming Muslim youth groups and others to help in attacks on the PKI, and that "local commanders have free hand to take direct action against PKI and they are doing so." Moreover, the "Army is not thinking purely in military terms or intending [to] turn [the] political future of Indonesia over to civilian elements." It would not immediately replace Sukarno, as it was moving "in typically Indonesian, if not Javanese fashion . . . [of] extreme patience and slow moving time framework," but he would remain in power in name only. It was "made clear" to the army "that Embassy and the USG[overnment were] generally sympathetic with and admiring of what the army [was] doing," and that it could expect American support.[47] The State Department concluded that the policy of maintaining an official presence in Indonesia despite Sukarno's attacks "meant that we were able promptly to have contact with Indonesia's new leaders and give them encouragement."[48]

What the Indonesian army sought was weapons and communications equipment to facilitate its attacks on the PKI. The CIA reported that Washington had long "wondered when and if the Indonesian Army would ever move to halt the erosion of non-Communist political strength in Indonesia." Now that it was acting and asking for help "to crush the PKI," the United States "should avoid being too cynical about its motives and its self-interest, or too hesitant about the propriety of extending such assistance *provided* we can do so covertly."[49] The administration approved the shipment of weapons to the army "to arm Moslem and nationalist youth in Central Java against the PKI" as part of the overall campaign "to eliminate the PKI," and sent communications equipment to increase "their effectiveness in combating the Communists' efforts to eliminate non-Communist influence favorable to us in their Government."[50]

Suharto was consistently praised as "a strong, efficient and decisive officer" with a "reputation for skill and determination," and as an "effective anti-Communist" leader. He was the "pivotal military and political figure" whose decisive action against the communists was eliminating their influence in Indonesia. After October 1, Suharto had shown himself "capable of thrusting aside the 'Sukarno mystique' which has hitherto hampered independent action by all elements in Indonesia." The CIA concluded that while he paid "lip service to Sukarno's efforts to arrange a political settlement," Suharto had ignored them, blamed the PKI for the coup, and expanded his anti-Communist

[46] Bundy to Johnson, 22 October 1965, NSF: Memos to the President, Box 5, LBJL.
[47] *FRUS*, 1964–68, Vol. 26, 353–6.
[48] Administrative History of the Department of State, Vol. 1, Chapter 7: "Indonesia," Box 3, LBJL.
[49] Ibid., 361–3.
[50] Kahin and Kahin, *Subversion as Foreign Policy*, 230; *FRUS*, 1964–68, Vol. 26, 368–71.

campaign. "Regardless of whether the army really believed that the PKI was solely responsible" for the failed coup, "it is presenting this as its case and is acting accordingly."[51] Suharto's immediate objective was "the destruction of the PKI as an effective political and military force." In the longer term, he sought "the continuation of nation building, the preservation of Indonesia as a united nation, and its development as a strong one." The army, it was reported, saw itself as better equipped than any civilians to lead the nation, and was determined to hold onto power. Moreover, "some army leaders undoubtedly view Communism as an ideology which is essentially evil, totalitarian, and alien to the 'Indonesian way of life.'"[52]

By the end of 1965, the administration was confident that both Sukarno's power and communism had been crushed in Indonesia, and that Suharto would provide the necessary stability and leadership to ensure a good relationship between Washington and Djakarta. Ambassador Green reported on December 22 that "Indo politics has continued to move in [the] 'right' direction." The PKI was "no longer a significant political force," and the army had consolidated its hold on power. Indonesia, Green declared, was "now in the midst of basic political revolution." Sukarno had failed in his "bid to get full authority back in his own hands," leaving Suharto in control. The "old foreign policy has been discredited," and "Indonesia's close alignment with Communist China is shattered." Moreover, Indonesia was "starting to do normal business with us again," providing payments for damages done under Sukarno to U.S. property and seeking to work closely with the United States. "As we approach 1966," Green concluded, problems remained as the United States sought to work with the new government, but relations "will be infinitely more healthy and more promising than what we had before Oct. 1."[53]

Officials in Washington agreed. "The era of Sukarno's dominance has ended," the CIA reported to the National Security Council. In the previous three months, his prestige had been eroded to the point where "he is less the father and political hub of the country and more the petulant old man." His "advice is being ignored" as Suharto charts his own course. More importantly, "the army has virtually destroyed the PKI" and taken control of the country. The country had appeared in September 1965 to be on the road to a communist takeover and "leftist totalitarianism," but that trend was now "almost completely reversed ... by the army's prompt and forceful reaction."[54]

On 11 March 1966, Suharto forced Sukarno to transfer all government authority to himself. He quickly moved to consolidate his power by outlawing

---

[51] Intelligence Memorandum, "General Suharto of Indonesia," 8 November 1965, NSF:CF, Box 247, LBJL.

[52] Intelligence Memorandum, "The Indonesian Army: Objectives and Problems," 12 November 1965, NSF:CF, Box 247, LBJL; Intelligence Memorandum, "Indonesian Army Attitudes toward Communism," 22 November 1965, NSF:CF, Box 248, LBJL.

[53] *FRUS*, 1964–68, Vol. 26, 388–90.

[54] Intelligence Memorandum, "The Changed Political Scene in Indonesia," 3 January 1966, NSF:CF, Box 248, LBJL.

the Communist Party and purging all of those thought to be loyal to Sukarno. These actions cleared the way for direct American aid to the military government. The army had previously refused any public support from the United States because it would be used by Sukarno in an effort to portray the military as being controlled by Washington. The United States had, therefore, maintained what the administration called "a low profile" policy because it feared that "anything the United States says or does about Indonesia is subject to distortion and misinterpretation." It should wait until Indonesia, as Ambassador Green told President Johnson, finally "set its house in order" to begin sending anything more than the small amounts of covert aid already provided.[55] The National Security Council noted that the United States now had to begin "backing up success" by preparing to meet Indonesia's aid requests. "It is hard to overestimate," the NSC reported to Johnson, "the potential significance of the army's apparent victory over Sukarno." Indonesia had been "well on the way to becoming another expansionist Communist state" that would have threatened the "whole Western position in mainland Southeast Asia." Now the situation "has been sharply reversed." The United States needed to "follow through skillfully and consolidate such successes" by sending aid.[56] The president agreed, and an emergency shipment of 50,000 tons of rice was sent at the end of March as a first step "on the road back to cooperative relations" now that Sukarno was out of power.[57]

The administration worked throughout the rest of the spring and summer to increase its support for Indonesia. Vice President Humphrey told Johnson that Suharto and the other leaders of the new government wanted "to be friends of the United States" and were "interested in encouraging U.S. private investment." The key decisions on aid, however, were "not as much economic as political. It involves a basic political decision as to our willingness to cement a close political relationship with the present Government by providing economic assistance at a time of dire need."[58] In what the new national security advisor, Walt Whitman Rostow, termed "an excellent summary," the State Department reported to Johnson that Suharto's government had "moved with surprising speed... to start on the long process of putting together the almost totally shattered Indonesian economy." Suharto was ending the confrontation over Malaysia and moving "to restore normal working relations with all western countries and with Japan... and has virtually broken relations with Communist China." It was critical that the United States help the current regime to "prevent the resurgence of some form of extremism and, over time, play a useful part in the area." The policy of quiet support remained sound, "particularly in light of the wholesale killings that have accompanied the transition (even though it is perfectly clear that a Communist takeover would have been

---

[55] Memorandum of Conversation, 15 February 1966, NSF:CF, Box 248, LBJL.
[56] *FRUS*, 1964–68, Vol. 26, 419.
[57] Ibid., 425–8.
[58] Humphrey to Johnson, 13 May 1966, WHCF, NSF: Confidential File, Box 9, LBJL.

at least as bloody)," but it was necessary to point out "that we take a favorable view of the new regime," and the United States should continue to make it "clear that we are ready at the right time to begin making limited material contributions to help the new leaders get established." To that end, the State Department developed plans for further U.S. emergency assistance, multilateral debt rescheduling, long-term assistance plans, and small-scale military assistance programs for training and keeping "personal ties with key military figures of the future."[59]

On 4 August 1966, the National Security Council met to discuss Indonesia and how the United States planned "to make the most of this favorable development in Asia."[60] In its background paper for the meeting, the State Department set out the case for support for Suharto's regime and increased American assistance to Djakarta. Suharto was praised for quickly ending the coup attempt of 1 October 1965, which was "the beginning of one of the most dramatic political reversals in recent history," and for launching a political revolution in Indonesia. "A major nation, which was moving rapidly toward a domestic Communist takeover and was intimately associated with Communist China, within three months destroyed the Communist threat and altered significantly its domestic and foreign orientation." The most important political changes were "the destruction of the Indonesian Communist Party" and the "systematic reduction of the powers of President Sukarno," rendering him a mere figurehead. The administration was fully aware that Suharto's political revolution was built upon a massacre of the military's opponents and on rule by fear. "The Army," the State Department noted, "hunted down and executed the principle Communist leaders," and worked with other groups "on a systematic campaign of extermination of Communist Party cadres." It concluded that "while the exact figure will never be known, an estimated 300,000 were killed."[61]

There was, however, no commentary on this wholesale killing, and it never came up during the NSC meeting. Rather, the report went on to portray the military as popular, particularly with students who were "fed up with Sukarno, his empty slogans, and the economic chaos and bankruptcy he has brought on the nation." The military was seen as pursuing a foreign policy that was improving relations with the United States and the West, and as tackling the economic problems of the nation in a constructive manner. It has a "highly motivated, well trained, professionally competent officer corps," many of whom had been trained in the United States. Suharto, therefore, met all of the requirements for American support. He had crushed the Communist Party, kept Indonesia "out of the orbit of Communist China," and provided stability; and he was

---

[59] Rostow to Johnson, 8 June 1966, NSF:CF, Box 248, LBJL; the State Department paper on Indonesia is attached.

[60] Rostow to Johnson, 3 August 1966, NSF: NSC Meeting File, Box 2, LBJL.

[61] *FRUS*, 1964–68, Vol. 26, 449–57.

developing an effective government that could develop Indonesia's vast economic potential.[62]

All of this justified the "private encouragement" and small amounts of aid so far given to "Indonesia's anti-Communist revolution." Up to now, the department noted, American policy had been to provide assistance to Indonesia as necessary to assist the government with the "process of political consolidation" without calling any attention to American support. Indonesia was not "an economic infant, but a sick giant with [an] historically proven capacity for quick economic recuperation." American aid was necessary to help Suharto consolidate the gains made in the previous ten months. The United States, therefore, should be ready to increase the levels of short-term economic assistance to Djakarta while providing training to the military and civilian personnel and support for longer-range economic development to ensure stability and multilateral aid.[63]

Johnson began the National Security Council discussion by reminding the members of the "recent dramatic change in Indonesia's internal political situation and its foreign policy orientation." Just the previous year, the president noted, the NSC had met to discuss cutting off American aid because Indonesia "was then rapidly moving toward becoming an out-and-out Communist state." Secretary of State Rusk reported that there was a new confidence in Asia because of the American effort in Vietnam and the political changes in Indonesia. The key was to make sure "the Indonesian changes were going to stick." The main problems were economic, and the United States had to "be ready to move quickly and effectively" when the Indonesians asked for assistance. He estimated that it would take about $50 million in the first year to allow the government to meet its debt problems and bring about stability. The president concurred and approved the recommendations of the State Department along with plans to coordinate greater multilateral support for Indonesia. Johnson's only concern was whether there was any chance of a comeback by Sukarno. Both Rusk and CIA Director Richard Helms assured him that the new government was firmly in control.[64] Indonesian Foreign Minister Adam Malik came to Washington the next month to meet with various administration officials, including President Johnson, and to work out the details of American aid.[65]

In addition to welcoming Suharto's regime, the Johnson administration also believed that the political change in Djakarta justified American policy in Vietnam. The State Department and CIA produced reports in May 1966 that gave credit to American resolve and the escalation of the war in Vietnam for the defeat of communism in Indonesia. While the State Department noted that "there is no evidence that the US presence in Vietnam encouraged

---

[62] Ibid.
[63] Ibid.
[64] NSC Meeting, 4 August 1966, NSF:NSC Meetings, Box 2, LBJL.
[65] *FRUS*, 1964–68, Vol. 26, 470–6.

anti-Communists to take action," it nonetheless claimed that "the circumstances prevailing in Indonesia at that time might have been considerably different if the U.S. had been forced out of Southeast Asia and the Chinese Communists had become the dominant power of the region." Similarly, the CIA conceded that it had "searched in vain for evidence that the US display of determination in Vietnam directly influenced the outcome of the Indonesian crisis in any significant way." Still, it concluded that "events in Indonesia might have developed differently if the US had withdrawn from Southeast Asia, leaving the way open for the spread of Chinese Communist influence." It further claimed that – again with "no evidence for this – that US determination in Vietnam did indirectly have some influence in shaping events in Indonesia" because without the American escalation in Vietnam, it would already have been "in Communist hands by 1 October 1965." In this situation, and without American forces standing between China and Indonesia, "it is possible that Sukarno might by that date already have accelerated his political program" to such an extent that the army leaders would have been forced to concede all power to him.[66]

By the next month, the qualifying comments about the lack of evidence were dropped from these claims. The State Department reported to Johnson that "unquestionably the fact that we were standing firm in Viet-Nam reinforced the courage of the anti-Communist leaders" in Indonesia, and that "without our evident determination, they would have been very much less likely to have acted." In addition, the success of the Suharto regime was unlikely "without our continued firmness in Viet-Nam and in the area," and the administration should "claim credit" to this extent for what happened in Indonesia.[67] A later State Department summary claimed that "the US presence in Southeast Asia enabled Indonesia's non-Communists to attack the PKI without fear of intervention by Communist China. The fact that we stood in Viet-Nam between Indonesia and China gave Indonesia's new leadership greater flexibility in responding to the PKI bid for power."[68]

The National Security Council met in August 1967 to review American aid policies to Indonesia over the previous year and to consider additional military support. In opening the meeting, Johnson noted the "great importance of Indonesia" to the United States. The State Department reported that "our problems were those of progress" and that American aid should be increased to $100 million in the next year and should include more military equipment. Secretary of Defense Robert McNamara agreed, noting that Indonesia "should have high priority" for materials and training. Johnson supported the increased levels of support, stating that he "would like to see Indonesia become a

---

[66] Department of State, "The Vietnam Conflict and Indonesian Developments," 13 May 1966; Intelligence Memorandum, "The Indonesian Crisis and US Determination in Vietnam," 13 May 1966, both NSF:CF, Box 248, LBJL.

[67] Rostow to Johnson, 8 June 1966, NSF:CF, Box 248, LBJL.

[68] Administrative History of the Department of State, Vol. 1, Chapter 7: "Indonesia," Box 3, LBJL.

'showcase'" for development. "It has great potential," he continued, and was "one of the few places in the world that has moved in our direction."[69]

That fall, Suharto and Johnson exchanged letters. The general wrote to thank the United States for its support and "effective assistance" in meeting the needs of the Indonesian economy. This was allowing Indonesia to put "our own house in order." Johnson responded by congratulating Suharto on his "resolute leadership" of Indonesia, and on the "solid achievements of your stabilization effort in the past year." The president continued by noting that he was aware that it was the second anniversary "of a dramatic turning point in the history of Asia. The courage with which you and your people faced those crucial days in October, 1965, is still evident in your bold and farsighted efforts to reconstruct a shattered economy." Johnson assured Suharto of the "respect and support of free peoples" that he had earned, and of continuing American aid to his government.[70]

In a demonstration of American support, Vice President Humphrey visited Indonesia on 6–7 November 1967 to hold talks with Suharto and to provide assurances of continued American assistance. Upon leaving Djakarta, the vice president praised Suharto for the "policies and efforts that are being pursued by Indonesia to create economic stability" and reaffirmed American support for his regime. Humphrey reported to the NSC that Suharto was "an honest, hard-working man who benefitted from his training at Fort Leavenworth" and that other "Indonesian military leaders are now showing the great benefit of their military training in the United States." The stakes in Indonesia, he continued, were as high as those in Japan and India, making American support paramount. Further, the vice president noted that Suharto believed that "if the United States fails in Vietnam, all hope for a free Southeast Asia would be lost." When asked whether the U.S. "stand in Vietnam" had an impact on Indonesia, Humphrey responded that while the change was brought about by the Indonesians themselves, "our presence in Southeast Asia gave confidence to the Indonesians to destroy the Communist Party." In response to Johnson asking for his comment, Rusk noted that the United States was working with many nations and international organizations to supply the assistance needed by Indonesia.[71] Later that month, Johnson sent a note to Rostow stating: "I want to do everything I can for Indonesia – as quickly as I can."[72]

Suharto's bloody elimination of the Communist Party, enforced stability, and pro-Western economic and foreign policies earned him American praise and support. In the Johnson administration's final assessments of its policy toward Indonesia, all mention of the massacre of hundreds of thousands of people was absent. Rather, the army's destruction of the Communist Party and seizure of

---

[69] NSC Meeting, 9 August 1967, NSF:NSC Meetings, Box 2, LBJL.
[70] Suharto to Johnson, 18 September 1967; Johnson to Suharto, 5 October 1967, both NSF:CF, Box 249, LBJL.
[71] *FRUS*, 1964–68, Vol. 26, 536.
[72] Johnson to Rostow, 21 November 1967, NSF:CF, Box 249, LBJL.

control were described as being done "with caution and deliberation," and Suharto's regime as being "moderate." He had replaced "Sukarno's politics of emotion and policies of adventure" with "a pragmatic approach to Indonesia's problems."[73] According to the State Department, the general "proved to be a leader of sound instincts and one truly dedicated to improving the position of his people." The report concluded that American influence "was significant and sometimes crucial for Indonesia's well-being."[74] Moreover, the Johnson administration had embraced Suharto's dictatorship at the same time that it was escalating the war in Vietnam. The two actions became directly linked in the administration's view, and the events in Indonesia were seen as justifying the American commitment to South Vietnam. With the public's attention focused on the Vietnam War, support for Suharto's dictatorship went largely unnoticed. Yet the continued escalation of the war brought forth the first significant critics of the primary assumptions of American containment policy and, subsequently, the first questioning of the logic and rationale of U.S. support of right-wing dictatorships.

Cracks in the Consensus

In the late 1940s and 1950s, a remarkable consensus concerning foreign policy had emerged in the United States. In the wake of World War II and the coming of the Cold War, Americans came to agree that the Soviet Union was an aggressive, expansive nation that threatened the nations around it and the interests of the United States, that communism was a monolithic threat directed by Moscow, and that its challenge could not be met through negotiations. Morever, communism was a totalitarian and evil system of government, a bitter and implacable foe of freedom and American values that sought nothing less than world conquest. Thus, just as it had been during World War II and the fight against Nazi Germany, imperial Japan, and fascist Italy, the United States was threatened by an enemy that was the antithesis of its values and a danger to its self-interest.

By 1947, the United States was taking an increasingly hard line toward the Soviet Union. Soviet actions in Eastern Europe and the Middle East came to be seen as aggressive moves that threatened American interests and efforts to establish postwar peace and prosperity. George Kennan provided the ideological coherence for American Cold War policy. The United States, as he explained it, faced "a political force committed fanatically to the belief that with US there can be no permanent *modus vivendi*, that it is desirable and necessary that the internal harmony of our society be disrupted, our traditional way of life destroyed, the international authority of our state be broken." The Soviet Union, he argued, was motivated by a combination of traditional Russian desires to expand and by its Marxist ideology that taught there could be no cooperation with capitalist states. Moscow, however, had no legitimate

---

[73] *FRUS*, 1964–68, Vol. 26, 564–76.
[74] Administrative History of the Department of State, Vol. 1, Chapter 7: "Indonesia," Box 3, LBJL.

grievances, and there was no reason or room for compromise. Like the Nazis at Munich, the Soviets would take advantage of all sincere efforts at peace. A policy of opposition and containment was the only logical course.[75]

The British decision that they could no longer afford to pay for the Greek civil war led the Truman administration to publicly announce its new policy. Rather than viewing the conflict as a division within Greek society over the direction of that society, American policymakers interpreted it as part of a Soviet effort to expand. Invoking an early version of the domino theory, Acting Secretary of State Dean Acheson compared the situation in Greece to a barrel of apples infected by one rotten one. He told congressional leaders that if Greece fell to communism, it "would infect Iran and all to the east. It would also carry infection to Africa through Asia Minor and Egypt, and to Europe through Italy and France." Events in Greece, therefore, posed a grave threat to the United States that had to be met.[76]

In March, President Harry Truman set out the Truman Doctrine. The central theme of his speech was that there was a global contest between two competing and incompatible ways of life: democracy and totalitarian communism. The president announced "that it must be the policy of the United States to support free peoples who are resisting attempted subjugation by armed minorities or outside pressures." He asked for aid to Greece and Turkey to prevent the imposition of "totalitarian regimes" on nations under attack by the Soviet Union. If the United States faltered in its leadership, the president warned, "we may endanger the peace of the world – and we shall surely endanger the welfare of this Nation."[77] American foreign policy was, therefore, based on a bipolar worldview of inherent conflict between the United States and the Soviet Union. The world was divided into the free world and the communist bloc, a contest of good versus evil, and it was the duty of the United States, as the most powerful nation and leader of the free world, to defend other nations and the values of freedom, justice, and democracy from the Soviet Union and its allies. This paradigm meant that any right-wing dictatorship was a part of the free world, no matter how brutal the government, as long as it was anticommunist, provided stability, and supported U.S. Cold War policies.

All of these assumptions guided U.S. policy in Vietnam. The growing American commitment to Vietnam throughout the 1950s and 1960s was justified by the policy of containment. Communism was aggressive, expansive, and monolithic. South Vietnam, American officials believed, was being attacked by North Vietnam, which was acting in the interests of Communist China and the Soviet Union. The lesson of World War II was that you could not repeat the mistake of Munich by appeasing aggressors. Moreover, if South Vietnam fell to communism, as Eisenhower had explained using his domino theory, it would lead to the loss "of Burma, of Thailand, of the Philippines, and eventually Australia

[75] *FRUS*, 1946, Vol. 6, 699–707; X [Kennan], "The Sources of Soviet Conduct."
[76] Acheson, *Present at the Creation*, 219.
[77] *Public Papers of the Presidents: Truman, 1947*, 176–80.

and New Zealand."[78] Escalation of the war, therefore, was in the defense of America's national interest in the global struggle against communism, a struggle that was necessary to protect American values against communist regimes that were immoral, brutal, and totalitarian.

In April 1965, Lyndon Johnson invoked all of these reasons as he explained to the nation why the United States had escalated the fighting and why the country needed to "hazard its ease, its interest, and its power" for the sake of the South Vietnamese. "We fight," the president began, "because we must fight if we are to live in a world where every country can shape its own destiny, and only in such a world will our own freedom be finally secure." North Vietnam, he argued, "has attacked the independent nation of South Viet-Nam" with the objective of conquest. "Over this war – and all Asia – is another reality: the deepening shadow of Communist China. The leaders in Hanoi are urged on by Peking." The Vietnam War, therefore, was "part of a wider pattern of aggressive purposes" that had to be met by the United States. A retreat from Vietnam would not bring peace. "The battle would be renewed in one country and then another. The central lesson of our time is that the appetite of aggression is never satisfied." To leave Vietnam, he concluded, would result in "increased unrest and instability, and even wider war."[79]

Johnson's decision to send troops to Vietnam in July 1965 had widespread public support as a necessary action to uphold the policy of containment and to stop the spread of communism. Reflecting the consensus in American society on foreign policy, *Life* supported the president, noting that "it is wiser and takes less bloodshed to stop a bid for world tyranny early rather than late. It is also wise as well as moral to fulfill a promise to defend a victim of attack. . . . In this sense our Vietnam policy is a moral policy, and most Americans fortunately see it that way." The editors of *Time* wrote that Vietnam was "the crucial test of American policy and will" and declared that the war was "The Right War at the Right Time."[80]

Critics would come to challenge all of these claims regarding the Vietnam War and in the process begin to question the fundamental tenets of American foreign policy. The antiwar movement developed two fundamental and interrelated critiques of the war: that there was no threat to the national interest in Vietnam, and that U.S. policy and actions violated the country's professed ideals and values. Under the first category, dissenters rejected the seemingly sacrosanct logic of containment and argued that there was no such thing as monolithic communism, that the domino theory was not a realistic understanding of the complexities of revolutionary movements and social change, and that it was not a bipolar world. Vietnam, therefore, was not a pawn of China – just as China was not an extension of the Soviet Union – but a nation with a long history of conflict with its neighbor to the north. Instead of serving as an example of

[78] *Public Papers of the Presidents: Eisenhower, 1954*, 382–3.
[79] *Public Papers of the Presidents: Johnson, 1965*, 394–8.
[80] Quoted in Anderson, *The Movement and the Sixties*, 136–7.

communist aggression, Vietnam was better understood as a nation in the midst of a revolution and civil war that had indigenous roots in the struggle against French colonialism. The logic of containment, therefore, did not apply, and no fundamental American interests were at stake.

In addition, critics came to see the war as immoral and damaging to American values and institutions. The United States was supporting a military dictatorship in Saigon that was corrupt, ineffective, unpopular, and ruled through force alone. This made the policy self-defeating in the long run because it placed the United States in a position of supporting a government without any legitimacy and created anti-American sentiment in Vietnam and elsewhere. Finally, support for South Vietnam rendered American moral arguments against communist regimes hypocritical and violated American principles. By the end of the war, this analysis would be extended beyond Vietnam to raise questions about U.S. support for right-wing dictators around the world.

The initial protests against the Vietnam War were small, limited to a few peace and student groups and some individual members of Congress, and had little impact on the nation. In early 1966, however, the Senate Foreign Relations Committee (SFRC) held public hearings on the war. Chaired by Senator William Fulbright, these meetings provided legitimacy to the then-struggling antiwar movement and marked the beginning of a long fight over the direction of American foreign policy.

Senator Frank Church played a leading role in developing the so-called dove position on the war and raising larger questions about American foreign policy. Church argued that what was happening in Vietnam was part of a larger explosion of nationalist revolutions throughout the Third World that had followed World War II and not part of some plot by Moscow to conquer the world. The United States had to "escape the trap of becoming so preoccupied with Communism...that we dissipate our strength in a vain attempt to enforce a global guarantee against it." Church dismissed the idea that there was any danger from Russia or China in Vietnam. "As an international force under one directorate...Communism is a bust. China and Russia are bitter enemies," and the communist world "bears no resemblance to a monolithic mass." By supporting the regime in Saigon, the United States had placed itself on the wrong side of the changes sweeping the world and damaged its long-term interests and relations with the Third World. In the process, the United States had "downgrade[d] freedom by equating it with the absence of Communism; we upgrade a host of dictatorial regimes by dignifying them with membership in what we like to call the 'Free World.'" There were now many who questioned "our efforts in behalf of so many tottering governments afflicted by decadence and despotism and frequently despised by their own people."[81] Church, therefore, rejected the administration's arguments that the war was necessary to stop outside aggression in Vietnam. He saw the conflict in Vietnam

[81] Church, "How Many Dominican Republics and Vietnams Can We Take On?," *New York Times Magazine*, 28 November 1965, 44–5, 177–8.

as centered on the issues of independence and unity rather than communism, and saw no reason why a revolution could not be both nationalist and led by communists.

Secretary of State Dean Rusk provided the standard responses to these criticisms in testimony before the SFRC. In 1964, he instructed the senators that they needed to keep the "two different revolutions separate." The first was the "revolution of modernization, economic and social development, education." This type of revolution, which was occurring in South Vietnam and elsewhere, required stability, and justified American support of dictatorships. The other revolution was "the Communist world revolution ... the dynamic force that concerns us all." This characterized the revolution in North Vietnam and had to be opposed, because these were totalitarian regimes hostile to the United States and freedom. Indeed, Rusk argued that the North saw the progress the South was making, that it was "being outstripped by the south," and had attacked in order to prevent Saigon's success.[82]

During the public hearings, Church and Rusk debated these points. Church asserted that revolutions were to be expected in the Third World as nations challenged the status quo to redress long-standing ills and to oust many of the tyrants the United States supported. The question was what would be the best policy for the United States in response to the revolutionary nationalism that was so prevalent in the world. "I gather," Church asked Rusk, "that wherever a revolution occurs against an established government, and that revolution, as most will doubtlessly be, will be infiltrated with Communists, that the United States regards it in its interests to prevent the success of Communist uprising." The senator found this to be a "self-defeating" policy and suggested a more understanding approach to coping with the "phenomena of revolt in the underdeveloped world." Rusk did not budge from the axioms of the Cold War. He found a "fundamental difference between the kind of revolution which the Communists call their wars of national liberation, and the kind of revolution which is congenial to our own experience." The conflict in Vietnam stemmed from the actions of China, and this type of revolution "has nothing in common with the great American revolutionary tradition."[83]

These nascent criticisms and debates over U.S. policy in Vietnam foreshadowed the divisions that would emerge in America not just about the war but also over support for right-wing dictatorships. No longer would the executive branch have a free hand in shaping the logic and rationale behind policy or be able to extend support to new authoritarian governments without taking public opinion into consideration. The Vietnam War sparked a decade-long challenge to the fundamental tenets of American policy that would grow stronger with the continued escalation of the fighting and would culminate in the Senate Select Committee Hearings on Intelligence in 1975–76. As the Johnson administration

[82] U.S. Congress, *Executive Sessions,* 1964, 16: 195–6.
[83] Fulbright, ed., *Vietnam Hearings,* 52–4.

discovered in response to the colonels' coup in Greece, these changes were already starting to appear during the war.

Deviation in Greek Constitutional Practices

The announcement of the Truman Doctrine had led to a sustained American involvement in Greece. Washington's primary interests were Greece's strategic location and preventing a communist threat. This made the development of Greece's economy and the maintenance of domestic stability ongoing concerns in Washington. Beginning in 1947, therefore, U.S. policy was to prevent any recurrence of a political challenge from the left by supporting the monarchy and the political right. With the defeat of the left in 1949, a coalition of the military, the palace, and conservative parties dominated Greek politics. In order to implement the policy of containment and to help ensure stability, the United States continued to supply Athens with extensive aid, and Greece was admitted to the North Atlantic Treaty Organization (NATO) in the early 1950s.

Although Greece was a member of NATO and located geographically in Europe, the United States saw it as a traditional, developing nation. As in the case of its earlier good relations with the Fourth of August regime in Greece during the 1930s, and its continued support of the Iberian dictatorships of Francisco Franco in Spain and Antonio Oliveira Salazar in Portugal, Washington believed that Greece still faced the "basic problems of nation-building" and modernization that confronted Third World countries "in the transition toward new patterns of modern nationhood."[84] "Like most developing countries," the State Department concluded, "Greece found the problems of economic development tough but not insuperable." The difficulties of "political modernization," however, "were a harder nettle to grasp" as Greece was beset with "endemic problems and nagging deficiencies in this sector which ... accounted for a measure of political instability."[85] For American officials, this lack of what they saw as political maturity explained the colonels' coup of 21 April 1967 and what the State Department termed "a deviation in Greek constitutional development."[86] Indeed, this "almost inevitable retrogression in Greece's political order" was anticipated in Washington. As the State Department explained, the question "ultimately posed by the failure of the Greek political world to effect an orderly succession of government ... became not whether *force majeure* would be applied to the political situation but rather who would apply it."[87] While the colonels who overthrew the government were not the first choice of the Johnson

---

[84] Administrative History of the Department of State, Vol. 1, Chapter 4: "The Near East and South Asia," Box 2, LBJL; Schmitz, *Thank God They're on Our Side*, 97–113, 157–68.

[85] Administrative History of the Department of State, Vol. 1, Chapter 4: "Greece in Political Crisis," Box 2, LBJL.

[86] Administrative History of the Department of State, Vol. 1, Chapter 4: "The Near East and South Asia," Box 2, LBJL.

[87] Administrative History of the Department of State, Vol. 1, Chapter 4: "Greece in Political Crisis," Box 2, LBJL.

administration, because they acted without the cooperation of the king, they were preferable to the other perceived threats to Greek political life, George and Andreas Papandreou and the communists. Thus, the administration, while initially cutting off certain military supplies to express its displeasure with how the Greek colonels acted, supported the government as a necessary antidote to Greece's political instability and the potential threat of communism reaching the Mediterranean.

During the 1960s, there were two perceived threats to American goals in Greece – conflict between Greece and fellow NATO ally Turkey over Cyprus, and the election of George Papandreou as prime minister in 1963. A war between Greece and Turkey would have "damaged the United States' considerable strategic interests in those countries, weakened NATO, and presented opportunities for the Soviet Union to exploit." Thus, its prevention became a "dominant consideration in US policy formulation," and the Johnson administration intervened on seven different occasions to prevent a Turkish military intervention in Cyprus that would have triggered a Greek–Turkish war.[88]

In the eyes of American officials, the election of Papandreou in 1963 brought renewed political instability and crisis to Greece, and set off "a gradual degeneration" of the Greek political process, "which was especially marked in the 21-month period preceding the coup."[89] The political consensus that emerged in Greece during the 1950s on keeping the communists out of politics, the role of the monarchy, and Greece's participation in NATO, which had brought "relative stability" to Greece under Prime Minister Constantine Karamanlis from 1956 to 1963, was challenged by Papandreou's government and in particular by his son, Andreas Papandreou. The younger Papandreou was a former chair of the Department of Economics at the University of California, Berkeley, and the heir apparent to his father as the head of the Center Union party. He led the party's opposition to King Constantine for going beyond the bounds of a constitutional monarch and involving himself in politics and, therefore, questioned the continuation of the monarchy, called for the inclusion of all groups in the political process, and criticized the overwhelming influence of the United States in Greece.

Papandreou's two years as prime minister led to growing political tensions in Greece and, by the summer of 1965, to a direct conflict between the prime minister and the King, which led to the end of the Papandreou government. As a result, the divisions between the Greek monarchy, its conservative and military supporters, and the Center Party widened. This led to a period of what the State Department saw as "a steady decline of parliamentary life and proprieties, a rash of street demonstrations, sporadic strikes and a kaleidoscope [sic] of political combinations resulting in a succession of three more or less

---

[88] Administrative History of the Department of State, Vol. 1, Chapter 4: "The Cyprus Crisis," Box 2, LBJL.

[89] Administrative History of the Department of State, Vol. 1, Chapter 4: "Greece in Political Crisis," Box 2, LBJL.

passive governments."[90] The worry in Washington and for its allies in the Greek military was that new elections in 1967 would return the Papandreous to power.

A State Department intelligence report in November 1966 entitled "Clouds on the Greek Horizon" set out the concerns about Greece, and in particular about Andreas Papandreou, held by the Johnson administration. It was clear that the Center Union remained the most popular party, retaining the 53 percent support it had received in the last election. A Center Union victory would mean continued political stalemate and threatened "a major political upheaval." The department saw three possible political developments: a collapse of the political center; the formation of a united "rightist 'National Front' of anti-Papandreou elements" to oppose the Center Union and its increasing turn to the pro-communist United Democratic Left (EDA); or a "suspension of certain constitutional provisions and the installation of a government of the Palace's choice." In other words, the United States expected "further political fragmentation and a sharper polarization between left and right." Given this, a right-wing coup and the "imposition of an authoritarian regime as a means of restoring political order cannot be entirely excluded" as the best solution given the alternative.[91]

Andreas Papandreou was seen as the main cause of all of Greece's problems and as the reason why matters had reached such a stage. The State Department saw him as engaging in "traditional Greek demagogy" through his questioning of the role of the king in Greek politics, his attacks on American "interference" in Greece, his appeal to labor and peasants "for a more equitable distribution of national income," and his attacks on the "moneyed class." This last part was the most troubling. "In the 17 years since the suppression of the insurgency, Communism has been contained." Now it was again a problem in Greece as the conservatives saw Andreas Papandreou as "a crypto-Communist." This might force the palace to return Greece to authoritarianism. It was believed that "if the King became convinced that the elections would be won by the Center Union under the domination of Andreas Papandreou or would result in a government dependent upon EDA support," which were now seen as basically the same thing, "he would declare an emergency and install a dictatorship before the elections could take place."[92]

In the early months of 1967, the State Department noted that "an 'extralegal' intervention in the political process had been bruited" throughout official circles in Washington and Athens. These rumors of a coup were buttressed by the U.S. knowledge of "a longstanding contingency plan developed under the aegis of the General Staff and the King to prevent a Communist take-over of the country." With elections scheduled for May, the coup of 21 April 1967 did not catch Washington by surprise. Indeed, American Ambassador Philip Talbot met with the king in early April to explain "the extreme difficulty the United States would

---

[90] Ibid.
[91] Hughes to Rusk, 8 November 1966, "Clouds on the Greek Horizon," NSF:CF, Box 26, LBJL.
[92] Ibid.

have in living with a coup," owing to public opinion in the United States, and to explain that "whatever inherent risks the electoral process held for internal order," it preferred that the scheduled elections be allowed. The only thing that surprised the embassy and the administration was who carried out the coup. Thirty to forty officers, mostly colonels, apparently convinced that the senior officers would not act in time, carried out the plan of the General Staff and took control of the government. They feared that a Papandreou victory in the election would result in "cooperation between the political Center and the extreme Left, with the extreme Left holding the political balance as it had in 1936 and again in 1944." The colonels arrested the prime minister, opposition political leaders – most notably Andreas Papandreou – and over 5,000 suspected communists, suspended the parts of the constitution guaranteeing individual rights, and imposed martial law.[93]

The exact role of the United States in the coup is impossible to determine as the relevant documents remain classified. What is clear is that the Johnson administration blamed Andreas Papandreou for the breakdown of the political consensus in Greece and, therefore, for the coup itself, and came to support the Greek colonels. The State Department's Greek desk reported to the National Security Council that

> by attacking and even threatening the monarchy, by trying to set class against class, by consistently pounding on the theme of U.S. and NATO 'interference' in Greek life, Andreas Papandreou drove Greek political tensions to a pitch unequaled since the 1947–49 period. Thus, before Andreas' entry into Greek political life, it was possible for one party to turn over power to another without any question of this transfer meaning fundamental changes in the fabric of Greek life.... However, by 1967, through Andreas' repeated attacks aimed at undermining Greek institutions, the conservative element in Greek society concluded that Greece's political fabric could not withstand the implications of an Andreas Papandreou victory at the polls.

The State Department, therefore, saw Andreas Papandreou as "responsible for the conditions which prompted the dictatorship." His attacks on "the United States, NATO, the monarchy, the so-called Greek 'oligarchy' and the Army leadership are fully documented" and had convinced Greek conservatives that his "coming into power must be prevented at all costs." While there was no direct evidence that Andreas Papandreou was a communist, "there was no doubt that he frequently joined forces with them, and his slogans were frequently similar – and in some cases more extreme – to those of the crypto-Communist EDA party." Finally, it was clear "that in his political posture he was a demagogue whose irresponsibility was repeatedly demonstrated in his extremist attacks on his chosen targets."[94]

The NSC staff reported to Rostow that Papandreou "bears a large part of the responsibility for provoking this coup and also for disrupting sound post-war

---

[93] Administrative History of the Department of State, Vol. 1, Chapter 4: "Greece in Political Crisis," Box 2, LBJL.

[94] Owens to Saunders, "Andreas Papandreou," 27 April 1967, NSF:CF, Box 126, LBJL.

progress. No one says he's a Communist, but the evidence shows that he was willing to work dangerously closely [sic] with the Communists." Moreover, "he openly threatened the monarchy" and "proposed going farther and farther to the left than the prevailing powers could tolerate." His father had supposedly told the embassy in March that "he would have read Andreas out of the party if he weren't his son."[95] Rostow saw him as "the King's arch-enemy" and the main reason for the coup, and no one in the administration believed "that Greek politics can settle down until he is out of the picture."[96] The administration, therefore, considered Papandreou, and not the Greek colonels, responsible for the end of democratic government in Athens.

Still, the question of how to respond was not an easy one for the administration. On the one hand, American officials opposed Andreas Papandreou's coming to power and were sympathetic to the goals of the coup. On the other hand, they had hoped that a coup would not be necessary as they knew they would face public opposition from liberals and critics of the Vietnam War. Moreover, the NSC was concerned that the king had been left out of the planning and the new government. In deciding how to respond, the Johnson administration saw three alternatives: "to support the junta unconditionally; to cut itself off from the junta . . . ; or to assume a 'cool but correct' posture" of mild criticism in order to avoid criticism at home without upsetting stability in Greece.[97] It chose the third course.

The administration maintained a silence on events in Athens for a week as it evaluated the situation and decided how best to respond publicly. On the day of the coup, Rostow wrote Johnson that the immediate question that faced the administration was what it would say. He agreed with Secretary of State Rusk that they should "hold off on any substantive comment" for the time being "lest we encourage violence against the coup government," but noted that "at some point soon . . . we should express regret – even if softly – that democratic processes have been suspended. I fear that our posture before the Greek Americans and the Greek people will look weak-kneed if we completely avoid judgment." Rostow and Rusk still hoped that the king could gain control of the government to provide some legitimacy and thereby make it easier for Washington to provide support for the junta.[98]

The next day, Rostow noted that the "main issue is the Administration's posture before the intellectual and liberal communities in the U.S." These groups already were moving into opposition to the administration because of the Vietnam War, and could be expected to criticize any support for the Greek colonels. The problem, Rostow told Johnson, was "sharpened by the fact that

[95] Saunders to Rostow, "Andreas Papandreou," 27 April 1967, NSF:CF, Box 126, LBJL.
[96] Rostow to Johnson, 21 April 1967; Rostow to Johnson, 27 April 1967; Saunders to Rostow, 26 April 1967, all NSF:CF, Box 126, LBJL.
[97] Administrative History of the Department of State, Vol. 1, Chapter 4: "Greece in Political Crisis," Box 2, LBJL.
[98] Rostow to Johnson, "The Greek Coup as of 9 a.m." and "The Greek Situation as of 6:30 p.m." 21 April 1967, NSF:CF, Box 126, LBJL.

the most controversial political prisoner in Athens is Andreas Papandreou, who has a lot of friends in the academic community here." These friends, including the economists Walter Heller and Carl Kaysen, among others, were contacting the people they knew at high levels of the State Department asking about what was being done to protect Papandreou's safety. This compounded the problem of continuing to remain silent. As Rostow stated, "the argument for a mild statement of regret is that we will end up looking as if we support unconstitutional change of power if we remain silent." Yet, with the situation still in flux, maintaining silence so as to not upset the situation in Athens or give aid to the junta's opponents remained the preferred option. Besides, Rostow concluded, as Rusk had noted, the "pressures for an expression of view come from a small group – the personal friends of Andreas."[99]

Ensuring the safety of Papandreou was a high priority of the administration. The major problem, Hal Saunders of the National Security Council told Rostow, was "domestic concern for the safety of Andreas Papandreou." Critics were characterizing the coup as the "rape of Greek democracy," and accusing the administration of acquiescing, if not participating, in the events in Athens. Moreover, "the same people who accuse us of violating 'American principles' in VietNam will cite our silence on Greece as further evidence of our militaristic bent." These were "some of the wild protest that's in the air" Saunders concluded. "It's neither fair nor logical, but there it is." Ambassador Talbot spoke with junta leaders to get them to promise not to harm Papandreou, and within days of the coup the United States had asked the regime to release him from jail on the condition that he never return to Greece. Given that no one in Athens or Washington believed that Greece could have political stability as long as Andreas Papandreou was in Greece, his expulsion, the National Security Council noted, would "meet our domestic needs while at the same time being a gain for the government. They would probably rather shoot him but know that that would trigger an intolerable world reaction."[100] In order to make clear its desire for the release of Papandreou, the administration informed the junta on April 24 that it was suspending the shipment of major military equipment, such as planes and tanks, but that it would continue to send small arms.[101]

The main concern in Washington was not the destruction of Greek democracy. In his evaluation of the situation for the president six days after the coup, Rostow continued to focus on domestic public opinion. The national security advisor noted that the United States was "doing business with the new government." The main problem remained the jailing of Papandreou and the "active campaign here by friends...to get him out of jail. Coupled with this

[99] Rostow to Johnson, "Our Posture on the Greek Coup," 22 April 1967, NSF:CF, Box 126, LBJL.

[100] Saunders to Rostow, 26 April 1967, NSF:CF, Box 126, LBJL; see also Battle to Rusk, 23 April 1967, and Rostow to Johnson, 27 April 1967, NSF:CF, Box 126, LBJL.

[101] Administrative History of the Department of State, Vol. 1, Chapter 4: "Greece in Political Crisis," Box 2, LBJL.

is the feeling of many Greek-Americans that the King and the army are out to stifle Greek democracy." Rostow assured Johnson the United States was doing everything it could to protect Papandreou, but "the fact remains that Andreas is public enemy #1 in the eyes of this government. It saw him rushing Greece into the hands of the Communists," and it was a fair assessment that his "blunt political tactics were one of the main factors in precipitating the coup." If something happened to Papandreou, these critics are "quite likely to blame us for his death and the 'rape of Greek democracy.'"[102] As Francis Bator of the National Security Council put it, while "Papandreou was not helpful from a U.S. point of view," the administration had to be careful "since it is widely held, on the outside, that we sometimes act as if we couldn't tell the difference between Ken Galbraith and [Anastas] Mikoyan except in height."[103] The administration was willing to act to save Papandreou, but not to criticize the junta or endanger its ability to rule.

By this time, the domestic pressure on the administration to say something was too strong to delay a statement any longer. On April 28, Secretary of State Rusk told the press that the United States was closely following the situation in Greece, was "gratified that Greece will continue its strong support of NATO," and hoped that there could be an early return to parliamentary government in Athens.[104] Little over a month earlier, on the twentieth anniversary of the Truman Doctrine, President Johnson had written to King Constantine to commemorate the role the United States had played in saving Greece from aggression and totalitarianism, and rejoiced "that Greece is today free and prospering."[105] Now he vetoed Rostow's suggestion to add the sentence "We are, of course, deeply concerned by the serious implications of changing governments by force" to what the national security advisor termed the "bland" text of Rusk's statement. Johnson found these words to be too strong.[106] The administration would publicly ask for assurances of a return to constitutional rule at the earliest possible time, but would not threaten its relationship with "a staunch and strategic ally within NATO." As the State Department noted, the arms cutoff was only to signal displeasure "at the manner in which the new government had come to power," to apply pressure for the release of Papandreou, and to encourage a gradual movement toward constitutional processes. It did not mean a disapproval of the regime.[107]

The outbreak of the Six-Day War between Israel and its Arab neighbors on June 6 brought even this limited pressure on the Greek colonels into question.

---

[102] Rostow to Johnson, 27 April 1967, NSF:CF, Box 126, LBJL.

[103] Bator, "Andreas Papandreou," 27 April 1967, NSF:CF, Box 126, LBJL; Anastas Mikoyan was the former chairman of the Supreme Soviet.

[104] *Department of State Bulletin*, 15 May 1967, 750–1.

[105] *Department of State Bulletin*, 3 April 1967, 546–7.

[106] Rostow to Johnson, "Press Conference Statement on Greece," 27 April 1967, NSF: Memos to the President, Box 15, LBJL.

[107] Administrative History of the Department of State, Vol. 1, Chapter 4: "Greece in Political Crisis," Box 2, LBJL.

In reviewing American policy toward Greece two days later, Benjamin Read, the executive secretary of the National Security Council, noted that the "current crisis in the Middle East has pointed up the strategic value of Greece to NATO and the United States."[108] Rusk informed Johnson that the policy of withholding major arms as a way to put pressure on the Greek colonels to release political prisoners and "hopefully, of encouraging some return, however gradual, to more constitutional processes" was "no longer useful and that, if continued longer, may be counterproductive." The Greeks could follow the direction of the "French with their lukewarm and unhelpful posture in a NATO context." The Arab-Israeli war underlined "the importance of Greece...to U.S. interests," and necessitated a resumption of certain arms sales to the junta. "The over-all interest of foreign policy," Rusk wrote, "requires that we do so as soon as possible." While there would be criticism from Congress and intellectuals, "it will not be great and can be reasonably contained" by pointing out how Greece had emerged "as particularly important to the U.S. given the uncertainties in the Middle East and the Soviet thrust in that area." It was essential, therefore, that the United States "maintain Greece as an active and functioning member of NATO under whose umbrella the arms programs are developed."[109]

The United States had initially hoped that King Constantine would gain control of the government in April, and maintained its close ties with him throughout the remainder of the year. The king still held hopes of taking power and asked to meet Johnson in September to discuss U.S. support. The administration, however, had abandoned any effort to have the king replace the junta. The meeting was held despite the fact that it would again bring forth domestic criticism of U.S. policy. As Rostow noted, the Greek coup had "excited a large number of our Congressional liberals," who raised the question of the advisability "of sustaining our NATO relationship with Greece via military aid."[110] In preparation for the meeting, Rostow wrote Johnson that "while we don't like the coup government any more than he does we think the way for both of us to handle it is to work with it and try to nudge it back toward constitutional government." Any confrontation "would be bad for all of us" because it brought forth the prospect of civil war, and that would only help those groups that the United States and the king opposed.[111] It was important, as Rusk noted, that the United States "caution him against pushing the regime to the point of provoking a confrontation." Johnson needed to "impress upon the King the need to avoid chaos or civil war in Greece."[112] In brief, the king could no longer expect support from the United States unless he cooperated with the regime.

[108] Read to Rostow, 8 June 1967, NSF:CF, Box 126, LBJL.
[109] Rusk to Johnson, 21 July 1967, NSF:CF, Box 126, LBJL.
[110] Rostow to Johnson, 4 August 1967, NSF:CF, Box 127, LBJL.
[111] Rostow to Johnson, 8 September 1967, NSF:CF, Box 127, LBJL.
[112] Rusk to Johnson, 7 September 1967, NSF:CF, Box 127, LBJL.

A restoration of arms shipments except for aircraft and tanks, and full U.S. support for the colonels' regime, came in the wake of King Constantine's failed effort to take power in December. The State Department noted that there would be admiration for the king's "poignantly quixotic stand against the forces of darkness and bemoaning of the sad state of democracy in the country where the word and concept were created. Democracy, however, has never taken firm root in Greece," and the type of rule the king would have instituted "differed from the junta only in degree." The junta was now "indisputably the government of Greece," and "now has a clear opportunity to bring effective government to Greece." It needed to address the "need for political modernization" of a society that lacked the "willingness to subordinate political ambitions to the orderly process of effective government."[113]

Rostow believed that "the Greek junta *is* doing a good job in reforming certain basic Greek economic and bureaucratic structures."[114] It was, therefore, time to restore military shipments to the government and to provide formal "recognition" of the regime. The State Department believed that no more could be gained from the "cool and correct" approach and "that the time has come to re-establish formal contact." The two-pronged strategy of withholding formal recognition as a way to push for "progress towards constitutional government and to put us in a position with our domestic critics of not undercutting the King and not embracing the junta" was no longer applicable. The government had released Andreas Papandreou in December and made promises for the restoration of democratic government. The junta was firmly in control; its leader, Georgios Papadopoulos, was "reasonable and well-intentioned." The other reason, according to Rostow, for "re-establishing contact is the need to do business with whoever runs Greece. What worries us most is that the Cyprus issue is far from settled, and we may want to weigh in again any time."[115]

Thus, all remaining concerns for constitutional government were subordinated to the desire for stability, American security interests, and anticommunism, as the junta met all the criteria for American support. The remaining restrictions on arms sales were a symbolic act to please domestic critics rather than any real pressure. The State Department noted that "political evolution in Greece following the coup moved in consonance with the purposes of United States policy." Greece maintained good relations with the United States and "its neighbors within the framework of its prior commitments to NATO and the West," and had "proved exceptionally cooperative during the Middle East war." Within Greece, the government was working on "modernizing the political processes through a reform of its institutions." This allowed the United

---

[113] Hughes to Acting Secretary, "The Outlook for the Junta," 15 December 1967, NSF:CF, Box 127, LBJL.

[114] Rostow to Watson, 20 November 1967, NSF:CF, Box 127, LBJL (emphasis in the original).

[115] Rostow to Johnson, 19 January 1968, NSF:CF, Box 127, LBJL.

States to achieve its objectives in its policy toward Greece: "the preservation there of a strong eastward anchor to NATO and – the internal corollary of strategic considerations – a viable economy and stable political life within Greece."[116]

In the wake of the King's failed counter-coup, the *New York Times* termed the junta's government "illegal and unconstitutional" and called for a return to constitutional government.[117] This editorial led to a brief debate in the letters column of the paper over U.S. policy toward Greece and right-wing dictators. Former Secretary of State Dean Acheson, who had played such a critical role in the development of the Truman Doctrine and containment policy, defended the Greek colonels and the administration's policy of support and urged "caution in warning...against 'authoritarian government.'" The Greeks, Acheson declared, "both ancient and modern have had grave trouble when they experimented with nonauthoritarian rule," notably "instability and poor judgment." Greece made sound progress only under strong rule, and "certainly no friend of Greece would wish to see her return to the 'constitution government' of the two Panpendeous [sic], the old fool and the young rascal, under which she was headed for Kerenski-like chaos."[118]

Senators Wayne Morse and William Fulbright, both leading critics of the Vietnam War, questioned Acheson's position, and by extension the administration's. Morse was disheartened by the "amoral principles of foreign policy which Mr. Acheson espoused...in his choice of strong-armed colonels as appropriate rulers for Greece," and warned that such a policy was not in the interests of the United States. Fulbright pointed out the contradiction between Acheson's "friendly feelings for the Greek dictators" and the ideals of American foreign policy and the Truman Doctrine. Acheson, as acting secretary of state, had urged aid to Greece in 1947 in order to "pave the way for peaceful and democratic developments." Acheson had continued by noting that if U.S. efforts "were being frustrated by anti-democratic practices," it should cease its aid. Now he was asking for "tolerance for authoritarian rule" while continuing to oppose "other totalitarian regimes such as that of Ho Chi Minh in North Vietnam."[119]

This exchange on the letters page of the *New York Times* foretold the changes that were coming in the United States concerning American foreign policy. The Cold War paradigms that the administration had used to justify support of Suharto and that Secretary of State Rusk used to defend arms sales to Greece were no longer guaranteed to stifle dissent and prevent the questioning of policies. Rather, critics came to see support for the Greek colonels as part of a larger pattern of actions by the United States that had led to its involvement in the

[116] Administrative History of the Department of State, Vol. 1, Chapter 4: "Greece in Political Crisis," Box 2, LBJL.
[117] *New York Times*, 15 December 1967.
[118] *New York Times*, 20 December 1967.
[119] *New York Times*, 29 December 1967.

Vietnam War, the overthrowing of foreign governments, and support of brutal dictatorships that were antithetical to America's stated values and harmful to the national interest. As the war in Vietnam continued, the divisions within American society grew wider, leading to fundamental questions about American foreign policy and efforts to change the policy of supporting right-wing dictators. The Nixon administration's support of General Augusto Pinochet's military coup in Chile in 1973 would bring these debates to the center of American politics and lead to efforts by Congress to control the executive branch's ability to use covert action, intervene abroad, and support right-wing dictators.

3

Madmen

Richard Nixon, Henry Kissinger, and the Quest for Order

When Richard Nixon became president in January 1969, the Vietnam War overshadowed all other foreign policy questions. By 1967, the questions that had first appeared at the outset of the war had created deep divisions within the nation over the efficacy, nature, and morality of the war. In the wake of the Tet Offensive in January 1968, opposition to the war had grown, and it was seen as a mistake by over half the population. The crisis created by Tet forced President Johnson to cap escalation and withdraw from the presidential election. The growing disillusionment of the American public with the fighting led to a wider and more receptive audience for critics of American foreign policy and the nation's support of right-wing dictatorships. While there had always been some complaints about America's backing of brutal antidemocratic regimes, the wrenching nature of the Vietnam War, the divisions it brought about in American society, the disaster it had become, and the questions it raised about the nature of American policy brought about a crisis of legitimacy concerning American foreign policy. This, in turn, made the policy of support for right-wing dictators of abiding interest to the American public for the first time. Antiwar leaders not only called for an end to the war in Vietnam, they also questioned the logic of containment and the assumptions that had led to the American escalation of the war, and sought a reevaluation of America's policy toward authoritarian regimes.

Nixon and National Security Advisor Henry Kissinger, while retaining their belief in the verities of containment, knew that changes in how the United States implemented its policy were necessary. The president's strategy was to reduce the costs of the Cold War while continuing to uphold the main axioms of American Cold War policy. This was to be achieved by the Nixon Doctrine and later through détente with the Soviet Union. The Nixon Doctrine, a direct response to public disillusionment with Vietnam, upheld America's global commitment to contain communism, but called for an end to the use of American forces in the Third World, as had been done in Korea and Vietnam, as the main means to implement that policy. Instead, the United States would provide

72

material support and air power to countries threatened by subversion, but would expect those nations to provide the ground forces in their own defense. The Nixon Doctrine thus, sought to prevent revolutions by ensuring the ability of governments to impose order in their own nations and by building up the power of specific Third World allies to provide regional stability. This, in theory, would prevent future wars like the one in Vietnam. The United States would be the arsenal of containment, but not the actual enforcer unless it came into a direct conflict with the Soviet Union.

The Nixon administration's commitment to containment and stability mandated support for right-wing dictators and enforced order, leading to an even greater reliance upon authoritarian regimes to maintain regional stability in various parts of the world. Thus, with a series of selected nations, such as Indonesia, Greece, Iran, and the Congo, the United States increased its arms sales and overall support despite domestic criticism of these regimes. Moreover, containment and the establishment of order in Latin America were considered especially vital to the Nixon Doctrine and American national security. Nixon spoke of a special relationship between the United States and Latin America that was critical to the credibility of the United States as a great power able to protect its interests and preserve order. If there were instability close to the United States, it would be hard to establish order further away. Support for the authoritarian regimes in the Western Hemisphere was, therefore, essential to stability, containment, the protection of American economic interests, and national security. In this context, the election of Salvador Allende as president of Chile in 1970 was seen by Nixon and Kissinger as a threat to the United States and an international crisis. The president and national security advisor believed that Allende's election meant the establishment of a communist state in South America that threatened to spread unrest and instability to its neighbors. The administration attempted to block Allende's inauguration in 1970 through a CIA-backed military coup. When this failed, it worked to destabilize Allende's government while providing support to the Chilean military, and welcomed General Augusto Pinochet's bloody coup on 11 September 1973 and the establishment of a military dictatorship in Santiago.

The Nixon Doctrine

President Richard Nixon understood that the way in which the Vietnam War ended was crucial to both his own political fortune and the future course of the Cold War. He realized that the divisions within the United States over the war made it imperative that he somehow bring the war to an end, a goal he termed "peace with honor." Simultaneously, the president believed that adjustments had to be made in terms of the Cold War and America's global commitments. It was no longer politically or economically possible for the United States to continue to intervene in the Third World or constantly expand its commitments overseas. Withdrawal from Vietnam, in Nixon's and Kissinger's view, had to be done carefully, however, so that it was not misunderstood by the Soviet

Union as weakness or a retrenchment of the containment policy. Recognizing the need to disengage from Vietnam, and the limits of American power, led to the development of the Nixon Doctrine.

The president had set out the main outlines of his thinking and what would become the Nixon Doctrine in a 1967 article, "Asia after Viet Nam," published in *Foreign Affairs*. He began by reaffirming the American commitment to Asia and the need for containment. The threat from China, he wrote, "is clear, present, and repeatedly and insistently expressed" as its aggression by "proxy" in Vietnam made clear, and could be repeated in any of a half-dozen countries in Asia. Nixon believed that the American presence in Vietnam, however, was allowing for an "extraordinarily promising transformation" in Asia. He specifically noted the coming to power of Suharto in Indonesia as evidence of the positive impact of the war. The "U.S. presence," he claimed, had been "a vital factor" in blocking an attempted communist takeover and had saved the "greatest prize" in Southeast Asia. "It provided a shield behind which the anti-communist forces found the courage and the capacity to stage their counter-coup and . . . rescue their country from the Chinese orbit." There was no question, Nixon asserted, "that without the American commitment in Viet Nam, Asia would be a far different place today."[1]

Nonetheless, Nixon realized that the rising costs of the Vietnam War and the growing domestic opposition threatened to force the United States to withdraw unilaterally if no alternative strategy could be developed. "One of the legacies of Viet Nam," he wrote, "will be a deep reluctance on the part of the United States to become involved once again in a similar intervention on a similar basis." The war had brought political, social, and economic strains in the United States, while the bitter opposition at home "has torn the fabric of American intellectual life, and whatever the outcome of the war the tear may be a long time mending." Recognizing the end of the consensus on containment, he doubted whether "the American public or the American Congress would now support a unilateral American intervention" if another friendly nation were threatened by "an externally supported communist insurrection." This did not mean that the United States would not "respond militarily to communist threats in the less stable parts of the world," but it did mean that other nations had to "recognize that the role of the United States as world policeman is likely to be limited in the future."[2]

This meant that local governments had to take on a greater share of the costs and burdens of their own defense and containment. The United States would continue to provide military support and economic assistance, but more countries had to take responsibility for regional security. For Nixon, this was not a way out of Asia for the United States. Rather, it would allow Washington to continue to meet its commitments and stay in the area. Nor was it a call to revive the South East Asian Treaty Organization, whose usefulness had passed

---

[1] Nixon, "Asia after Viet Nam."
[2] Ibid.

because it was too dependent on the United States. It did mean, however, that other nations had to be willing to fight in their own defense without American troops. Turning to the question of what type of nations the United States should support, Nixon stated that these countries might not fit the Western ideal of democracy. Americans "must recognize that a highly sophisticated, highly advanced political system, which required many centuries to develop in the West, may not be best for other nations which . . . are still in an earlier stage of development." What mattered was stability and preventing the spread of communism.[3]

Nixon's initial decisions concerning the Vietnam War were a complex set of ideas designed to allow him to pursue an expansion of the war and to achieve victory while creating the appearance of seeking peace and a deescalation of the fighting. The former would be a policy carried out mostly in secret, while the latter was the public policy Nixon presented to the American people and the world. Part of his plan for victory rested on "the madman theory." As Nixon told his chief of staff, H. R. Haldeman, he wanted "the North Vietnamese to believe I've reached the point where I might do *anything* to stop the war. We'll just slip the word to them that, 'for God's sake, you know Nixon is obsessed about Communists. We can't restrain him when he's angry – and he had his hand on the nuclear button' – and Ho Chi Minh himself will be in Paris in two days begging for peace."[4] To make the threat credible, Nixon began the secret bombing campaign against Cambodia in March 1969 and later set a deadline of November 1 for North Vietnam to begin making concessions in the peace negotiations or face a savage attack.

In order to implement his strategy for victory, the president had to buy time politically by creating the appearance that his policy was one of peace and disengagement. Pursuing a policy called "Vietnamization," Nixon sought to turn more of the fighting over to the South Vietnamese forces while withdrawing United States troops. Vietnamization was part of Nixon's broader policy to reduce the costs of the Cold War. The United States would continue to supply money, arms, advice, intelligence, and, most importantly, air power, but would reduce its role in the daily fighting of the war. The first troops were removed from Vietnam that summer, with further withdrawals promised as the course of the fighting allowed. Nixon hoped that this approach would allow him to continue the war without facing domestic opposition from the antiwar movement or charges of abandoning Vietnam to the communists.[5]

On 25 July 1969, President Nixon, during a news conference on Guam, first set out what he would later call the Nixon Doctrine. Expanding on the idea of Vietnamization, the Nixon Doctrine reaffirmed the American commitment to Asia and the policy of containment, but stated that the goal of American policy

---

3 Ibid.
4 Haldeman, *The Ends of Power*, 83 (emphasis in the original).
5 On Nixon's Vietnam policy see Berman, *No Peace, No Honor*; and Kimball, *Nixon's Vietnam War*.

was to avoid direct American intervention and significant troop commitments abroad. The United States should provide other nations with all the support they needed to combat communism, but it should not fight for them. This was to be the principle of American "policy generally throughout the world."[6]

On November 3, during his "Silent Majority" speech, the president set out the three principles of the Nixon Doctrine. The United States would keep all of its treaty commitments, "provide a shield if a nuclear power threatens the freedom of a nation allied" with the United States "or of a nation whose survival we consider vital to our security," and in cases of other forms of aggression "furnish military and economic assistance when requested in accordance with our treaty commitments. But we shall look to the nation directly threatened to assume the primary responsibility of providing the manpower for its defense."[7]

This new policy placed a greater premium on stability than ever before and led to a complete embrace of various right-wing dictatorships around the globe. In implementing the Nixon Doctrine, the administration made clear its support for nations such as Indonesia, Greece, Iran, and the Congo, which were considered vital to providing regional stability in their areas of the world, and welcomed the leaders of most of these nations to the United States. Nixon had visited all of these countries during a world tour in 1967 and was familiar with their governments and how they had come to power. Two days after announcing the Nixon Doctrine, he arrived in Djakarta, where he praised Suharto as the leader of "one of the great and most populous democracies in all the world," one that "excites the imagination of all the peoples of the world." Nixon compared the history of Indonesia to that of the United States. Both, he noted, were former colonies that had experienced revolutions, and he claimed that the countries had faced similar problems. The United States, therefore, was "privileged" to assist Indonesia as it "admired" Suharto's policies and "the strength, the political stability, [and] the economic stability" he provided to Indonesia. The United States, Nixon told Suharto, was willing to "assist you in any way that you think is appropriate," because what happened in Indonesia "may well determine whether peace and independence survive in the Pacific and, therefore, in the world."[8]

When Suharto came to Washington in May 1970, relations between the two nations were deemed to be "excellent," and the visit was designed to strengthen ties with Djakarta and to increase American economic and military assistance to Indonesia. In particular, Nixon wanted to thank Suharto for his support regarding Cambodia and the president's decision to send American forces into that nation on April 30. During the visit, Nixon reassured the Indonesian dictator of America's support and its commitment to "Southeast Asia's military security, political stability, and economic growth." As Kissinger noted in a memorandum to the president, "what Suharto has done and is doing accords perfectly

---

[6] *Public Papers of the Presidents: Nixon, 1969*, 544–56.
[7] Ibid., 901–9.
[8] Ibid., 569–73.

with your concept of Asian responsibilities under the Nixon Doctrine." It was agreed that the United States would increase military aid from $5.8 million to $15 million over the next year while providing an expanded range of military supplies, from communications equipment to combat weapons and aircraft. In addition, Washington would continue to provide Djakarta with nonmilitary aid and food, because Indonesia's economic success was crucial to American interests in the region and necessary if "Suharto is to survive politically."[9] The amount was further increased to $18 million to allow Indonesia to buy 15,000 M-16s to replace the AK-47s it was sending to Lon Nol's government in Cambodia. This large increase was justified by Indonesia's economic recovery, Suharto's "courageous and remarkably successful stabilization program," and his willingness to support the American effort in Cambodia.[10]

The following year, the amount of military aid was again increased, to $25 million, in order to allow Indonesia to begin the purchase of more sophisticated weaponry. Indonesia, the State Department reported, continued to develop as "an important force for peaceful development in Southeast Asia," while improving its economic stability and production.[11] The State Department found that the "sound policies of the Suharto government" were leading to increased exports, particularly of oil, while controlling inflation. American economic and military aid was, therefore, having the desired impact in Indonesia by supporting a government that provided stability, support of American policies, and increased economic opportunities.[12] This was exactly what the president envisioned under the Nixon Doctrine.

As part of the Nixon Doctrine, the president set out to end the remaining restrictions on weapons sales to Greece. The Johnson administration had bridged the dilemma of wanting to support the Greek colonels while facing public opposition to its support of the military government in Athens by withholding the shipment of major arms such as planes and tanks while allowing other military aid to continue. The National Security Council informed Kissinger that Johnson had had to "take account of vociferous opposition by American liberals" to the military coup, and although he was unsympathetic to these critics, Johnson had faced the threat of a complete suspension of U.S. military aid to Greece and other cuts if the administration had not taken some steps. This had led to the present policy: "do business with the Junta but do it with some show of reluctance."[13] Thus, the "sum of actual US pressure was more symbolic than

[9] Kissinger to Nixon, 22 May 1970, and "Background – Military Assistance to Indonesia," NSC: VIP Visits, Box 919, RNPM.

[10] Presidential Determination 71–4, 5 September 1970; Kissinger to Nixon, 2 September 1970, both NSC: Presidential Determinations, Box 370, RNPM.

[11] Presidential Determination 72–3, 7 September 1971; Kissinger to Nixon, 1 September 1971; Department of State to Nixon, 14 July 1971. NSC: Presidential Determinations, Box 370, RNPP; NSDM 107, 5 May 1971, NSC: NSDM, Box 364, RNPM.

[12] Irwin to Kissinger, "Indonesia," 30 January 1971, NSC: President's Annual Review of Foreign Policy 1971, Box 327, RNPM.

[13] Saunders to Kissinger, 8 April 1969, NSC:CF, Box 593, RNPM.

real;" the United States never took any steps or exerted "enough pressure to risk jeopardizing the US-Greek alliance."[14]

Nixon, however, wanted to eliminate even the appearance of disapproval. Kissinger met with Greek Foreign Minister Panayotis Pipinelis on 11 April 1969 and informed him that the Nixon administration would change American policy by removing all restrictions and bring an end to any political pressure on the junta. The national security advisor commended Greece for its role in NATO and assured the foreign minister of American support. Pipinelis noted that he thought it was "not productive for the U.S. government to continue to press the present Government for an early return to full constitutional government," and that the United States "should help its NATO partner with military assistance regardless of its political system." Kissinger told Pipinelis that "he could report categorically that the policy of the President is for the United States not to involve itself in the political affairs of other countries," but to "concern itself only with the foreign policy of another country."[15]

The administration took up the issue of military assistance to Greece in the fall. As the National Security Council noted, the main issue was not military aid but the "political relationship it signifies." The primary "threat to Greek stability is internal disruption," and the government was prepared to fight a civil war, "even one supported by its communist neighbors, without further help from the US." What was essential was continued access to military bases and airfields in Greece and regional stability. Moreover, the "continuation of the present situation for long has within it the seeds of instability." The current policy of "symbolic suspension" will not bring about a return to representative government, but could increase the chances of political unrest in a vital allied state and bring about the worst-case scenario of alienating the military government while producing no domestic changes. Thus, the NSC concluded that a full resumption of military aid was the "best way of securing out [sic] interests" as the "present situation has in it the seeds of instability and difficulty for us in pursuing our interests."[16]

On November 14, Kissinger issued National Security Decision Memorandum 34 (NSDM 34), which set out Nixon's approval in principle of the decision to "resume normal military aid shipments, including all items which have been suspended." American Ambassador Henry Tasca was to inform Prime Minister Papadopoulos of the decision while noting that any movement toward constitutional government would ease the problems the administration would face in announcing this decision. He was then to prepare a report on Greece's needs and response to the decision in order to help blunt any criticism from Congress. Once final approval for the specific weapons and amounts was

---

[14] Memorandum for the President, "Military Supply Policy toward Greece – The Issues," 7 October 1969, NSC:CF, Box 593, RNPM.

[15] Memorandum of Conversation, 11 April 1969, NSC:CF, Box 593, RNPM.

[16] Memorandum for the President, "Military Supply Policy toward Greece – The Issues," 7 October 1969, NSC:CF, Box 593, RNPM.

announced, NSDM 34 noted that "the following public line be taken with members of the Congress and press as necessary: Overriding US security interests were the principal factor in the decision to lift the suspension. The US government will continue urging the government to move toward a constitutional situation."[17]

Four days later, Nixon met with Greek Ambassador Basil Vitsaxis. The president expressed his "admiration for Greece as well as real concern over certain internal problems," and noted that he had visited Greece in 1967 and "was aware of the antecedents of the present situation." The United States, he assured the ambassador, "could not involve itself in Greek internal affairs;" it was Greece's international relations and bilateral relations with the United States that mattered to his administration. Vitsaxis assured Nixon that the coup of 1967 had been necessary to rescue Greece from chaos and a threat from the left, but that the government intended to return Greece to a viable democracy as soon as the nation was ready. Nixon noted that the ambassador needed to "press this line not only with his diplomatic colleagues but, also, with the press." The president claimed that the press applied a double standard in its coverage. "Had a Leftist regime taken over in Greece," Nixon opined, "any suspension of civil liberties would have been defended by most of the press on the grounds that they were essential to stabilize the regime." He continued by noting that "systems of democracies differed and it was not for him to say that what we tried to make work in America was the system for Greece or any other country."[18]

Word of the decision to resume the sale of heavy military equipment soon leaked to members of Congress. Twenty-six members of the House of Representatives wrote the president to protest the decision. Their letter stated that they were "deeply concerned" that the administration would send aircraft, tanks, and ships "to a military dictatorship which has a clear record of oppression, torture, and the destruction of civil liberties." "The frightening implication" of this news, they wrote, was that the United States had given the Greek government assurances that it supports its rule and methods, and they called on the administration to "make clear its moral disapproval of the present Greek government." Rather than sending new weapons, "we urge that all United States military aid to that nation be discontinued."[19]

Such protests had no impact on the president. Tasca filed his report at the end of March 1970; final approval was given in June, and the decision was publicly announced on September 22. As desired, Tasca's report found that American policy "should be based on the assumption that the present regime in Greece is here to stay," that the policy of withholding "military equipment has proved ineffective in accelerating the return to democratic government and is indeed

---

[17] NSDM 34, "US Policy Toward Greece – Military Assistance," 14 November 1969, NSC:CF, Box 593, RNPP; see also Kissinger to Nixon, June 1970, NSC:CF, Box 593, RNPM.

[18] Memorandum of Conversation, 18 November 1969, NSC:CF, Box 593, RNPM.

[19] Bingham et. al., to Nixon, 25 November 1969, NSC:CF, Box 593, RNPM.

beginning to undermine Greece's strength," and that any further delay could create problems of instability and weaken Greece. Moreover, Tasca assured Nixon that Greece would move back toward constitutional government as soon as it was possible to do so without causing unrest or chaos. The National Security Council did note that lifting the suspension on the delivery of military weapons would pose a "major public relations problem of the Administration vis-a-vis the Congress," and that "several emotional attacks both in Congress and the press are anticipated." Nonetheless, that was not a reason to delay the resumption of arms sales.[20]

Secretary of Defense Melvin Laird visited Greece in early October to work out the details concerning the sale of weapons and to demonstrate the administration's support for Papadopoulos and his regime. In his conversations with Papadopoulos, Laird "stressed the importance to US interests in the Mediterranean of continued stability in Greece and close cooperation between the US and Greek governments," and said that "he favored full military cooperation with Greece." Reflecting his understanding of the Nixon Doctrine, the Greek leader assured the secretary of defense that "every weapon put into a Greek soldier's hand was as good as in the hands of an American soldier." A State Department intelligence note observed that Laird's visit would be interpreted "as a signal that the US has abandoned the reservations which it once held about the regime," and would add credibility to the junta's claim that it constitutes the "moral bastion against Communism in the Mediterranean." Taken with the September 22 announcement, the visit "will have the effect of convincing Greeks of whatever political persuasion that the US has at last found in Greece the kind of regime it prefers to deal with."[21]

Indeed, the administration would consistently invoke the "overriding requirements of the national security of the United States" to legally bypass congressional prohibitions on the sale of arms to Athens. Kissinger wrote Nixon that "given Greece's role in NATO, its strategic position, our important military installations there, and the Soviet presences in the Eastern Mediterranean, there is ample justification for this waiver." It would bring forth protests from Congress by opponents of the Greek junta, but "this was nothing new . . . and we long ago decided to pay that price because of our security interests in Greece."[22]

Iran was another nation to which the Nixon administration dramatically increased arms sales as part of the Nixon Doctrine. American support for the shah of Iran went back to 1953, when it had helped to install him in power in a CIA-assisted coup. The shah was seen as having saved Iran from communism, having brought stability to a key state in a volatile region of the world,

[20] "Report on Greece," 31 March 1970; Memorandum for the President, 21 May 1970, both NSC:CF, Box 593, RNPM.
[21] State Department Intelligence Note, "Greece: Secretary Laird's Visit," 19 October 1970, NSC:CF, Box 593, RNPM.
[22] Presidential Determination 72–11, 17 February 1972, NSC: Presidential Determinations, Box 370, RNPM.

and having developed a healthy economy and model of modernization while remaining a staunch ally of the United States. Nixon had first met the shah in December 1953, when he had gone to Tehran to assure the new ruler of American support for his regime and to praise him for his decisive actions and rule. By the end of the 1950s, the United States had entered into a bilateral defense agreement with Iran. Because it pursued reform and modernization from above while aligning closely with the West, the shah's authoritarian rule was extolled in Washington as a model for developing nations that U.S. leaders deemed unprepared for democracy. The shah was welcomed three times to the Eisenhower White House, and his visit in October 1969 was his ninth trip to Washington.[23]

By 1969, Nixon and Kissinger had come to fear new threats to the stability of the Middle East. The Six-Day War between Israel and its neighbors in 1967 had not settled any problems and had created further tensions through Israeli annexation of territories in the West Bank, Gaza, and the Golan Heights. Arab nationalists continued to criticize American support of Israel and the U.S. role in the region while looking to the Soviet Union for support. In addition, Great Britain announced that it was withdrawing its military forces from the Persian Gulf and its protection of the states of Kuwait, Qatar, Bahrein, and Oman. The United States saw these small, newly independent states as vulnerable to the appeals of radical Arab nationalists and as sources of regional instability. In this context, Iran took on a greater significance as an ally that supported the United States in the Cold War, one that could provide regional protection to other states, notably Saudi Arabia, and guarantee Western access to Middle Eastern oil. With the administration attempting to find an acceptable way out of the costly and unpopular war in Vietnam, Iran was seen as the ideal nation for carrying out the Nixon Doctrine in the region. Expanded Iranian military forces supported by the United States could fill the gap left by the British withdrawal while making it unnecessary to increase the direct American military presence in the area.

Increased arms sales were also seen as central to the modernization of Iran and the region. In 1963, the shah had launched the "White Revolution," a series of economic reforms from above that were designed to bring a modern industrial economy to a secularized Iran. This created the image in the United States of a "progressive" shah battling religious reactionaries and conservative forces in an effort to improve his nation. The consensus in Washington was that stability and security would allow the shah to quicken the pace of modernization, which in turn would increase domestic stability and provide a model for other nations in the region.

The Nixon administration, therefore, welcomed the shah to Washington as "a close friend" and valuable ally of the United States. He was believed to be popular at home because of his reforms, and was seen as a leader with "a breadth of vision" and "inspiring manner." The National Security Council

[23] Schmitz, *Thank God They're on Our Side*, 187–93.

praised the "White Revolution" as "an orderly path to the future" and a "peaceful revolution," a "revolution that builds rather than one that tears down," and one that had led to remarkable improvements in Iran. "This is the kind of revolution which the United States and other constructive forces in the world salute."[24] President Nixon publicly commended the shah for the "revolution in terms of social and economic and political progress" in Iran that provided an example for other nations to follow.[25] U.S. leaders cast the shah's dictatorship as the linchpin of stability in the region and subsequently ignored any criticism of his rule. Despite the growing political opposition in Iran and the use of secret police, political repression, and force by the shah to maintain his power, his dictatorship was seen as necessary for the development of Iran and for stability in the region. In the U.S. vision, the "White Revolution" represented the way that change should occur in the Third World – under the tight control of an authoritarian regime that was pro-Western and protected American interests.

In order for Iran to properly fill its role under the Nixon Doctrine, it would need a large influx of new weapons. During the 1950s and 1960s, Washington had provided $1.8 billion in military support to Tehran. From 1970 to 1975, the United States sold $12.1 billion worth of arms to the shah. Kissinger defended this dramatic increase by noting that Iran would "fill the vacuum left by British withdrawal" and provide the necessary bulwark against "Soviet intrusion and radical momentum" in the region. Moreover, this was possible "without any American resources" being used, "since the shah was willing to pay for the equipment out of his oil revenues." Given that Iran paid for all of its weapons, Nixon agreed in 1972 to allow the shah to purchase any type of military equipment he wanted short of nuclear weapons. Assistant Secretary of State for Near East and South Asian Affairs Joseph Sisco explained to Congress that these sales would allow Iran to ensure its own security and were an "essential prerequisite to a policy based on [Iran's role] of assuming primary responsibility for maintenance of stability in the area."[26]

While Africa was not as important to the United States as other areas of the world, the Nixon Doctrine was to be applied there as well. Nixon and Kissinger had little interest in Africa and held its people in low esteem. The president was known for his racist remarks concerning African Americans and Africans alike, frequently using the words "nigger," "jigs," and "jigaboos" when referring to them. Nixon once displayed his contempt for Africa by telling Kissinger that they would leave policy toward Africa in the hands of Secretary of State William Rogers. "Henry," Nixon said, "let's leave the niggers to Bill and we'll take care of the rest of the world."[27] The assistant to the president for domestic affairs,

[24] "Arrival of the Shah of Iran," 18 October 1969, NSC: VIP Visits, Box 920, RNPM.
[25] *Public Papers of the Presidents: Nixon, 1969*, 821.
[26] Rubin, *Paved with Good Intentions*, 128–30, 142; Wheeler to Nixon, 10 April 1970, and Kissinger to Nixon, 13 May 1970, NSC:CF, Box 601, RNPM.
[27] Hersh, *The Price of Power*, 110–11.

John Ehrlichman, recalled that Nixon told him that he thought blacks were less intelligent and "genetically inferior" to whites.[28] For his part, Kissinger, in a memorandum discussing the possibility of Nixon's giving a speech on Africa, noted that the essential point "will simply be to let the Africans know we have them in mind – despite the low priority of our interests in the continent." While there would be no new proposals, the speech would be "a worthwhile and important gesture" toward "countries whose pride and sensitivity run in inverse proportion to their power."[29] Still, Nixon and Kissinger worried about instability and potential communist advances in sub-Saharan Africa, and sought to make sure that American economic interests were not threatened. These concerns led Nixon to make the Congo and its dictator, Joseph Mobutu, critical to the implementation of the Nixon Doctrine in Africa and to improve relations with the racist white regimes of southern Africa.

The Nixon administration saw the Congo, in Kissinger's words, as "one of our policy successes in Africa."[30] Nixon first met Mobutu in 1967 as part of his trip around the world and was greatly impressed by the African dictator as a leader with great "drive and vitality." He fondly recounted his visit with Congo's ambassador to the United States, Justin-Marie Bomboko, in October 1969. The president noted that he believed the Congo was an important concern to the United States "owing to its strategic geographic location" and potential wealth. He stated that he saw the Congo as "the heart of Africa," and that "unless its heartbeat is strong and healthy the rest of Africa could be unhealthy." The United States, therefore, was "vitally interested in the Congo's political and economic development." To solidify relations, the president extended an offer to Mobutu to visit the United States the following year.[31]

The trip was arranged for August 1970, making Mobutu the first African head of state welcomed by the president. In addition to talks with Nixon and other members of the administration and Congress, including CIA Director Richard Helms, Mobutu spent five days in New York City meeting with American business and banking leaders, and with World Bank President Robert McNamara, to promote private investment in his country. Mobutu was welcomed as the man who had ended the civil war in the Congo, had brought stability and unity to the nation, and who was "strongly pro-Western and firmly anti-communist." Kissinger described him as "courageous, politically astute, conservative in his approach to government, and relatively honest in a country where governmental corruption is a way of life." Moreover, he was a "rational nationalist" who "recognizes in his bones that foreign private investment is essential to Congolese development."[32] Secretary of State Rogers stated that

---

[28] Lemann, *The Promised Land*, 204.
[29] Kissinger to Nixon, 30 December 1969, NSC:CF, Box 747, RNPM.
[30] Kissinger to Nixon, 29 July 1970, NSC: VIP Visits, Box 944, RNPM.
[31] Memorandum of Conversation, 10 October 1969, NSC:CF, Box 746, RNPM.
[32] Kissinger to Nixon, 29 July 1970, NSC: VIP Visits, Box 944, RNPM.

"Mobutu led his people out of chaos into a stability that holds great promise for the future."[33]

American economic and military assistance was seen "as an invaluable contribution" to the Congo's "stability and unity." The primary concerns were "political instability and communist influence" in the surrounding nations of Africa. This meant that the United States needed to "facilitate the purchase" of "transport aircraft (C-130s) to improve the mobility of the army" along with other necessary military equipment in order to maintain stability and create "a better investment climate."[34] In his welcoming remarks at the White House, Nixon praised the Congo as a young nation whose progress should serve as "an example for nations throughout the world," and advised American business leaders that the "Congo is a good investment not only because of its natural wealth but because of a wealth even more important than its natural resources,... a stable leadership." He repeated his plea for American investment in his after-dinner toast that evening, again noting "that the Congo is a good investment" owing to its "strong, vigorous people, and a leader who is able to provide the stability and the vision for progress" for his nation.[35]

In their private meeting, Nixon told Mobutu that he wanted the first state visit from an African chief of state to be from the leader of a major nation that provided a "fine example" for others to follow. The president noted how pleased he was that Mobutu was going to New York, and that he had been telling business leaders since 1967 to look at the Congo for good opportunities for investment because of its "strong leader" and stability. Mobutu, for his part, thanked the president but noted that communists continued to threaten the Congo and that "his country is not sufficiently mature to be able to contain the threats of subversion." Nixon promised the necessary military equipment to meet these challenges. He noted that he faced a problem in Congress, "which is well intentioned but believes that the answer is in economic development alone and opposes military assistance." Moreover, "many in Congress feel that the danger of Soviet and communist subversion is a myth." The president strongly disagreed, stating that in his view military aid and economic development went hand in hand. "There was no point in building up a country economically," Nixon opined, "if it were left defenseless and at the mercy of another poor but militarily strong country." He assured Mobutu that he understood the importance of providing military assistance to the Congo, that he would make sure "that emphasis was put on it," and that Kissinger would meet with him to work out the details. "The most important thing," Nixon concluded, was for the United States and the Congo to "work together and see that a country like the Congo was able to defend itself."[36]

[33] Rogers to Nixon, 28 July 1970, NSC: VIP Visits, Box 944, RNPM.
[34] Kissinger to Nixon, 29 July 1970, NSC: VIP Visits, Box 944, RNPM.
[35] *Public Papers of the Presidents: Nixon, 1969*, 644–6.
[36] Memorandum of Conversation, 4 August 1970, NSC:CF, Box 746, RNPM.

Turning to private investment, Nixon "stressed the importance of emphasizing stability when talking to businessmen and Mr. McNamara. They all knew
that the Congo is rich," he noted, "and the greatest incentive to investment
is its stability and the confidence that there will be no expropriation and no
revolution." The Congo had the opportunity to become the leader of the "free
African countries" because of its stability and its clear understanding of the
dangers presented by communism. In conclusion, the president reiterated that
he "understood the problems" facing the Congo and that the country had a
"friend" in the White House.[37] Nixon's and Mobutu's efforts paid off; there
was an increase of over $500 million in United States investments in mining
and energy alone in the Congo by 1973. This, in turn, made Mobutu "helpful
on political matters" that faced the United States in the United Nations and
Africa.[38] Given Nixon's low opinion of Africans and belief that they needed
a firm hand to guide them to political maturity, Mobutu was, in his estimation, the ideal leader for the Congo and for the implementation of the Nixon
Doctrine in Africa.

As part of his administration's reappraisal of American foreign policy, Nixon
ordered a new study of American policy toward Southern Africa, National
Security Study Memorandum 39 (NSSM 39). Completed in December 1969,
NSSM 39 set out different potential policies for the United States in dealing with
the white minority governments of South Africa and the Portuguese colonies in
Angola and Mozambique, ranging from full normalization of relations with the
white regimes to active opposition. The administration adopted the option that
called for a "broader association with both black and white states in an effort to
encourage moderation in the white states." Improved relations with the racist
governments of South Africa were justified on the assumption that "the whites
are here to stay and the only way that constructive change can come about is
through them. There is no hope for the blacks to gain political rights they seek
through violence, which will only lead to chaos and increased opportunities
for the communists." Washington, therefore, through a "selective relaxation of
our stand toward the white regimes, [could] encourage some modification in
their current racial and colonial policies." The United States would "maintain
public opposition to racial repression but relax political isolation and economic
restrictions on the white states."[39]

These improved relations with the white minority regimes were seen as
important for a number of reasons. Support for these governments was necessary to maintain stability, prevent communist advances, and protect American
security and economic interests. "If violence in the area escalates," NSSM 39
warned, "U.S. interests will be increasingly threatened." Primary among these

---

[37] Ibid.
[38] Rush to Nixon, 4 October 1973, WHCF:CF, Box 6, RNPM.
[39] "Study in Response to National Security Study Memorandum 39: Southern Africa," 9 December
1969, Presidential Directives, NSA; see also El-Khawas and Cohen, eds., *Southern Africa: The
Kissinger Study of Southern Africa*.

interests were the direct investment of $1 billion in South Africa that "yields a highly profitable return," trade, access to raw materials, South Africa's strategic location, and continued good relations with Portugal to insure access to American bases on its territory.[40]

There was one dissent to NSSM 39 and the new policy toward South Africa on the National Security Council staff. Winston Lord argued for a policy of "disengagement from the white regimes as basic American policy toward Southern Africa" on moral and domestic political grounds. This did not represent a disagreement with the overall direction of Nixon's foreign policy. On the contrary, Lord found the policy of supporting right-wing dictators and the "usual arguments for dealing with 'undemocratic' governments" to be sound. Moreover, he found that the criticisms and arguments traditionally made against "this approach are phony." Thus, he rejected the claim that opposing the white regimes would help to pressure those governments to moderate their policies, minimize violence, increase American prestige and influence in black Africa, and help to prevent communist influence.[41]

Why then, Lord asked, "should our moral indignation be translated into action in this case? Are we not – should we not be – moving in precisely the opposite direction, with regard to . . . Greece, Latin American dictatorships . . . ?" His answer was that southern Africa, "particularly South Africa, is *sui generis*," and that in this case the arguments that justified supporting other authoritarian regimes did not apply. Southern Africa was the only place in the world where the "governmental policies represent a direct affront to a very large segment, well over 10% of *our own people*." This added a domestic dimension not found in other cases. Moreover, the "policies of South Africa in particular are a quantum leap *more repulsive* than those of any other government since Nazi Germany's treatment of the Jews. Indeed, they are similar in the sense that they brutalize people solely on the basis of race." Under other authoritarian regimes, a person "at least may have a choice to conform to prevailing ideology."[42]

Lord noted that the Vietnam War had made foreign policy a domestic issue, and that improved relations with South Africa "will almost certainly be a major target of the blacks and youth and concerned whites" once the war is over.

To move closer . . . to the racist regimes of southern Africa will reverberate domestically and reinforce doubts about the commitment to racial justice in our own society. The niceties of a foreign policy that at once proclaims abhorrence of apartheid and conducts business as usual with its practitioners will be lost on those in this country who identify with the overseas oppressed. They will be lost on a younger generation which insists on matching rhetoric with action.

[40] "Study in Response to National Security Study Memorandum 39: Southern Africa," 9 December 1969, Presidential Directives, NSA.
[41] Lord to Kissinger, "U.S. Policy for Southern Africa: National Security Begins at Home," 17 October 1969, NSC:CF, Box 747, RNPM.
[42] Ibid. (emphasis in the original).

To critics it would be self-evident "that we have opted for our investments at the expense of a clear moral imperative." In a prescient analysis, Lord argued that there would be pressure on banks and businesses to divest from South Africa, student protests, and congressional pressure, not simply "an occasional flurry of liberal white editorials." "Once the Vietnam conflict winds down or terminates, the dissidents of American society will look for another issue." The war had submerged other issues such as South Africa, but it was the "next natural target." Finally, Lord noted that the United States already used moral judgments when criticizing communist regimes and that it was necessary to employ them in other situations where "the basic moral questions *are* black and white."[43]

Lord's criticisms were rejected with little discussion. As Robert Osgood wrote Kissinger, Lord's opinions were not those of the NSC or the Policy Planning Staff. Lord's view might be a "valid consideration" in the long-term, and "the development he anticipates is sufficiently likely and portentous to be taken into account in any long-range analysis of southern Africa and American policy options," but it was not practical as policy now.[44] Consistent with support for right-wing dictators elsewhere, perceived short-term interests and the desire for stability, anti-communism, and protection of American investments and trade led to continued support of right-wing dictators around the world. Nonetheless, the fact that Lord wrote a seven-page memorandum criticizing the logic and assumptions of the policy and based it on domestic political concerns indicates the impact that antiwar protests were having in forcing other views to be considered and in influencing the thinking of certain policymakers. As Lord correctly observed, the Vietnam War was changing the context of, and ending the consensus on, American foreign policy. Yet it would be policy toward Latin America, and more specifically Chile, and not South Africa, that would lead to the first direct challenges to executive power and the policy of supporting right-wing dictators.

A Special Relationship

At the outset of his administration, President Nixon was determined to change the nature of American policy toward Latin America. On 3 February 1969, he authorized National Security Study Memorandum 15 (NSSM 15), calling for a thorough review of U.S. policy, including its "posture toward internal political developments in Latin American countries, especially coups."[45] Later that month, Nixon announced that he was sending New York Governor Nelson Rockefeller to Latin America as the head of a mission to study the region and provide recommendations to the president on how the United States could

---

[43] Ibid. (emphasis in the original).
[44] Osgood to Kissinger, 21 October 1969, NSC:CF, Box 747, RNPM.
[45] NSSM 15, "Review of U.S. Policy toward Latin America," 3 February 1969, Presidential Directives #1, NSA.

"improve its policies and increase the effectiveness of its cooperation" with its neighbors.[46] In April, Nixon told the nation that the problems in the hemisphere required "a new policy" with "new programs" and "new approaches."[47] Two assumptions guided Nixon's thinking on Latin America and the need to find a new policy: first, that the "concepts and policies of the past were no longer adequate to meet the ferment and tensions present in the developing American societies" (i.e., the Alliance for Progress was to be abandoned as a failed approach), and second, that "a 'special relationship' existed – and ought to exist – between the U.S. and the other American republics."[48]

Rockefeller created a study group comprised of over thirty people from business, academia, and government, which met under the auspices of the Council on Foreign Relations, to prepare for the group's trips to Latin America and write the final report. The first meeting on April 9 focused on political questions and how Latin America could adjust to change. As the advance paper for the meeting stated, "the challenge to the Latin Americans is to mold modern nations" from societies that were a "disparate and incompatible array of social and human elements." This meant that "there is, first, the sheer requirement for domestic order." With the accelerating change in the whole region "and the lack of consensus about how to deal with change," it was understandable that there would be "the rise of authoritarian regimes." Rockefeller began the discussion by raising the question of "U.S. relations with non-democratic regimes in the hemisphere." It was agreed that the "simple distinction in American minds between civilian ('good') regimes and military ('bad') regimes is inadequate," and that this question, "as well as its corollary about whether there are modernizing and progressive military groups in some Latin American nations," was critical for Rockefeller to examine.[49] Given that authoritarian regimes were seen as a natural development in Latin America, it was not surprising that the governor's findings endorsed greater support for right-wing dictators.

Rockefeller submitted his report to the president at the end of August. It began by noting "that profound changes are occurring in the hemisphere, changes that have not been fully understood." To respond properly, the United States needed to "revive its special relationship with the nations of the hemisphere."[50] With the difficult problems presented by the Vietnam War and the divisions within the United States, the American national interest demanded that the United States maintain control over the region. "The moral and spiritual strength of the United States in the world," Rockefeller declared, along with the "political credibility of our leadership, the security of our nation, and the future of our social and economic progress are now at stake." Explicitly, the

[46] *Public Papers of the Presidents: Nixon 1969*, 107.
[47] Ibid., 281.
[48] "Current Policy and the Environment that Shaped It," 8 September 1971, NSSM 108, NSC, Box 11, RG 273.
[49] Plank, "Political Questions," 9 April 1969, and "Discussion Meeting Report," 9 April 1969, Records of Study Groups, Box 260, CFR.
[50] *Department of State Bulletin*, 8 December 1969, 501.

United States had to prevent a mainland Castro from coming to power; protect America's extensive economic interests in the region for continued trade, investment, and access to raw materials; and bring order in the face of growing instability. Failure to accomplish these goals and "maintain that special relationship would imply a failure of our capacity and responsibility as a great power." If the United States "cannot maintain a constructive relationship in the Western Hemisphere, we will hardly be able to achieve a successful order elsewhere in the world."[51]

The process of change, and demands for it, the report continued, were creating severe stresses and tensions in the region that were aggravated by the gap between heightened expectations and actual conditions in most countries. The overselling of the Alliance for Progress and calls for change during the past decade had only added to the instability in the hemisphere and made the problems harder to deal with. "The momentum of industrialization and modernization has strained the fabric of social and political structures." This had led to growing "political and social instability" and a questioning of the political legitimacy of "'accepted' systems of government." But "with the disintegration of old orders...newly-emerging domestic structures have had difficulty in establishing their legitimacy. This makes the problem of creating a system of political order in the Western Hemisphere more difficult." The result was a growing nationalism in the region "with strong anti-United States overtones," and the rise of "subversive forces working throughout the hemisphere...to exploit and exacerbate each and every situation." As a result, many nations were unsuccessful in adopting "democratic forms of government." They therefore moved "to authoritarian forms as a solution to political and social dilemmas."[52]

During the 1960s, thirteen military dictatorships had replaced constitutional governments in Latin America. Rockefeller defended the military takeovers as necessary for stability and to prevent radical change, and as legitimate because the military has "traditionally been regarded in most countries as the ultimate arbiters of the nation's welfare. The tendency of the military," he continued, "to intervene when it judges that the government in office has failed to carry out its responsibilities properly had generally been accepted in Central and South America," and "virtually all military governments in the hemisphere have assumed power to 'rescue' the country from an incompetent government, or an intolerable economic or political situation." Moreover, according to Rockefeller, the Latin American militaries were no longer a force for repression and protection of the status quo. Rather, they were "moving rapidly to the forefront as forces of social, economic and political change." Many members of the new leadership had been educated abroad, often in the United States, and were committed to the general improvement of their societies. "In short," Rockefeller proclaimed, "a new type of military man is coming to the fore and

[51] Ibid., 506–7.
[52] *Department of State Bulletin*, 8 December 1969, 501–2.

often becoming a major force for constructive social change in the American republics." The new leaders were adapting the "authoritarian tradition to the goals of social and economic progress."[53]

Potential problems existed with all these new authoritarian governments. There was, Rockefeller conceded, "always the risk that the authoritarian style will result in repression," with the expansion of "measures for security or discipline or efficiency to the point of curtailing individual liberties, beyond what is required for the restoration of order and social progress." The governments could become isolated from their populations, "with authoritarianism turning into a means to suppress rather than eliminate the buildup of social and political tension." Nonetheless, military governments were necessary for moving their nations through the difficult stages of development, with the "critical test" being whether they can successfully manage the transition to modernity and "a more pluralistic form of government which will enable individual talent and dignity to flourish." Rockefeller was confident that dictatorships were both necessary and capable of doing the job owing to the military leaders' "exposure to the fundamental achievements of the U.S. way of life."[54]

The military was necessary for another reason. Throughout Latin America, Rockefeller found it "plainly evident" that communist subversion was "a reality with alarming potential." Both Cuba's efforts to export revolution and indigenous "urban terrorism" threatened to "bring down the existing order." The opinion that communism "is no longer a serious threat in the Western Hemisphere is thoroughly wrong." With the prospects of "growing instability, extremism, and anti-U.S. nationalism," and new problems stemming from economic modernization, imposed order was seen as necessary to prevent the region from turning to radical solutions to its problems.[55] "This crossroads – this challenge to our system of democracy and to the very survival of our values and ourselves – is not rhetorical," the report concluded. "It is factual. Either we meet this challenge, or the prospect is for revolutionary changes leading we know not where." Right-wing dictatorships were, therefore, necessary to establish order, protect American interests, and prevent any spread of communism in the hemisphere.[56]

While a preference for democratic governments was noted, they were not to be expected in Latin America at this time for a number of reasons. "Democracy," the Rockefeller report stated, "is a very subtle and difficult problem for most of the other countries in the hemisphere. The authoritarian and hierarchical tradition of most of these societies does not lend itself to the particular kind of popular government we are used to." Moreover, few of the nations in Latin America had yet "achieved the sufficiently advanced economic and social

[53] Ibid., 504–5.
[54] Ibid.
[55] Ibid., 505–7.
[56] Ibid., 539.

systems required to support a consistently democratic system." That being the case, the question for Latin American countries "is less one of democracy or a lack of it, than it is simply of orderly ways of getting along." The United States, therefore, had to adopt a pragmatic approach in supporting right-wing dictators, recognizing that "diplomatic relations are merely practical conveniences and not measures of moral judgment." The same, of course, would never be said about Cuba or other communist regimes, where moral arguments were used all the time to explain American opposition, nonrecognition, and hostility. In noncommunist nations, however, the United States "should also recognize that political evolution takes time" and that its interests were best served by stability and order in the hemisphere. Washington should not back away from commitments and assistance to authoritarian regimes "because of moral disagreement" with these regimes.[57]

The National Security Council met on October 15 to discuss NSSM 15, the Rockefeller report, and a CIA assessment of the problem of security in Latin America. The CIA paper echoed the Rockefeller report's findings, citing "the growing social unrest generated by the strong pressures for change in Latin America," and found that efforts by radical groups on the left "could exacerbate the instability prevailing in some countries" by "further unsettling already somewhat unstable societies and draining away scarce resources." National Security Study Memorandum 15 was more direct, noting that the growing unrest and "rising nationalism posed a significant threat to U.S. interests, particularly when taken in conjunction with a Soviet presence and a Soviet willingness to offer itself as an alternative to Latin dependence on the U.S." The danger was that the "Soviets were likely to fan and exploit this growing Latin American sentiment for reducing dependence on the U.S.," thus bringing further instability to the region. In response, the NSC endorsed the Rockefeller report's recommendation of maintaining support for authoritarian governments as a necessary antidote to the problems confronting the United States in Latin America. Moreover, Nixon decided that the United States should continue to provide assistance to the Latin American military in order to give a "specific regional meaning" to the Nixon Doctrine. He later decided that the United States would have to increase its military support in order "to establish and maintain close relations with military leaders in the hemisphere." As the National Security Council noted, "this policy recognized that Latin American military establishments were expanding their role in the political, social and economic arenas."[58]

All of this culminated in President Nixon's October 31 speech to the annual meeting of the Inter-American Press Association, where he set out his views about and policy toward Latin American. Nixon called for a "more mature partnership" and new approaches that moved away from U.S. aid to a greater

[57] Ibid., 514–15.
[58] "Current Policy and the Environment that Shaped It," 8 September 1971, NSSM 108, NSC, Box 11, RG 273.

reliance on trade and free markets while maintaining the commitment to the inter-American system and joint security. After setting out the details of new multilateral economic initiatives, the president turned to what he termed "a sensitive subject" – what the U.S. "attitude should be toward various forms of government within the inter-American system." As a democracy, the president stated, the United States prefers that system of government and hoped that others "will share what we consider the blessings of genuine democracy" and freedom. "Nevertheless, we recognize that enormous, sometimes explosive, forces for change are operating in Latin America. These create instabilities; they bring changes in governments. On the diplomatic level," Nixon declared, "we must deal realistically with governments in the inter-American system as they are." The message was clear. Latin America's military regimes could expect full support from the Nixon White House. Cuba, however, was not included in this category, Nixon explained, because it "sponsors armed subversion in another's territory" and was, therefore, not a part of the inter-American community.[59]

As the administration prepared the "First Annual Report to the Congress on United States Foreign Policy for the 1970's," a debate arose in the National Security Council over whether it should include a statement in the final draft concerning American policy toward authoritarian regimes. The proposed section merely restated what the president had set out in October – that the United States should accept and support right-wing dictatorships. Viron Vaky wrote Kissinger that he disagreed with including this in the report. It would be interpreted "as indifference to coups and authoritarian trends, and is therefore quite likely to encourage coup plotting," to be resented by democratic governments in Latin America, and to be "greatly criticized in domestic liberal press and academic circles." He emphasized that his concern was "not with the substance of the policy – as a pragmatic policy it is reasonable enough." Rather, he wondered whether it was wise "to talk about it since one cannot do so without being misunderstood." It was "one thing to have such a policy and practice it," Vaky concluded, "and another to talk about it publicly." There was no reason to restate the policy, and "to do so will only expose the President to very serious criticism and our policy to problems we do not need to have." Kissinger concurred that it was better not to draw any more attention to the policy, and the section was deleted. While critics had failed to change the policy, their views were creating pressure on the administration and pointing toward future confrontations over American support of right-wing dictators.[60]

In December 1970, the National Security Council began a follow-up review of U.S. policy toward Latin America, National Security Study Memorandum 108. Its conclusions were similar to those of the earlier study and the Rockefeller

[59] *Public Papers of the Presidents: Nixon, 1969*, 893–901.
[60] Vaky to Kissinger, "President's Foreign Policy Message," 10 February 1970, NSF:CF, Box 325, RNPM; *Public Papers of the Presidents: Nixon, 1970*, 116–90.

report. The guiding assumptions remained that the United States had to maintain a special relationship with Latin America, that "with few exceptions, the nations of Latin America are fragile politically," and that "many are also fragile economically." The instability in these nations stemmed from the "strains and tensions created by the modernization process, frustration and a sense of inadequacy concerning their ability to achieve their aspirations for economic and social progress," and resentment toward the United States for its perceived failure to assist them. This created a political climate where there was "a readiness to experiment with radical and extremist solutions" and a growing anti-American nationalism. This had led to "a discernable trend to the left...as previously less articulate sectors in these societies have gained increased political strength."[61]

To protect American investments and prevent any further political deterioration, it was imperative that order be maintained. Support for military governments, therefore, remained central to American policy. Brazil was cited as an example of the benefits of this policy. While the government of General Humberto Castello Branco was the subject of criticism by Congress and members of the press in the United States because of the "repressive aspects of Brazil's government," the policy of supporting authoritarian regimes was nonetheless "warranted." Because Brazil was stable, provided a safe environment for investments and trade, and was actively working against communism in South America, it demonstrated why it was necessary for the United States to "make continuing efforts to reach influential sectors of Latin American society, including the military," in order to achieve its objectives in the region.[62]

In a summary of Nixon's policy, the NSC concluded that "the Alliance for Progress as a strategy for development had been oversold" and had raised unreasonable expectations that could not be met. It had, therefore, contributed to the growing instability throughout Latin America. The political unrest now present in Latin America "challenged the posture implicit in our previous policy of active promotion of democracy" under the Alliance. Moreover, the NSC found that these efforts had not "significantly discouraged the resort to authoritarian solutions, and there were countervailing indications that such actions fortified nationalist pride and intensified anti-American sentiments." Rather, "these trends thus suggested we had erred in the direction of zealousness and...had overestimated our capacity for influencing the evolution of sociopolitical institutions of others." The proper conclusion was the one drawn by the Rockefeller report and adopted by the president: the United States should support right-wing dictatorships as serving the interests of the United States, owing to their stability, anticommunism, and protection of American economic interests.[63]

---

[61] "U.S. Policy toward Latin America," 8 September 1971, NSSM 108, NSC, Box 11, RG 273.

[62] Ibid.

[63] "Current Policy and the Environment that Shaped It," 8 September 1971, NSSM 108, NSC, Box 11, RG 273.

A Grievous Defeat in Chile

Chile came to symbolize the conflicts in the Nixon administration's conception of the Nixon Doctrine and the idea of a special relationship with its neighbors to the south. Throughout the 1960s, American officials worried about the political future of Chile. Socialist leader Salvador Allende's calls for nationalizing important industries in Chile, particularly the mining and communications industries, which were dominated by U.S. corporations, frightened policymakers and led to increased American opposition, both covertly and overtly, to Allende's Popular Unity coalition. The Church Committee concluded that "covert United States involvement in Chile in the decade between 1963 and 1973 was extensive and continuous."[64] As Allende gained ground on the Christian Democratic candidate, Eduardo Frei, in the 1964 presidential campaign, the United States actively intervened to ensure Frei's victory. American officials saw Allende as a communist who threatened American interests in Chile and throughout the Western Hemisphere. The CIA reported in April that "of all the Latin American nations, Chile offers the Communists their best prospects for entering and potentially dominating a government through the electoral process." Allende had been a strong runner-up in 1958, and his election would pose a threat to "US private investment of more than $750 million."[65] Gordon Chase reported to McGeorge Bundy in March that Allende was an "extreme leftist" and that if "Allende wins and stays in power, we are in trouble. For example, he will probably nationalize the copper mines." Because the "U.S. has big stakes in copper and manufacturing of all kinds," it was important that "we should simply do what we can to get people to back Frei." At the end of the following month, Chase again alerted Bundy to the electoral dangers in Chile. "A Communist election victory in September 1964," he wrote, would be "intolerable for national security and domestic political reasons."[66] Bundy described the upcoming election as a potential "crisis" but was optimistic that it would be properly managed. The United States, through both its aid programs and covert CIA funding, spent $3 million to persuade the Chilean people to back Frei.[67]

Similar fears gripped American policymakers during the 1970 presidential campaign. In March, the 40 Committee, made up of senior administration officials that oversaw covert operations, approved funds amounting to $1 million for conducting "spoiling" operations against Allende during the election. In addition, International Telephone and Telegraph and other American corporations with large investments in Chile approached the CIA with offers to provide

---

[64] U.S. Congress, *Covert Action in Chile, 1963–1973*, 1.

[65] CIA, "Survey of Latin America," 1 April 1964, NSF:CF, Box 1, LBJL.

[66] Chase to Bundy, 19 March 1964, 30 April 1964, NSF:CF, Box 1, LBJL.

[67] Bundy to Humphrey, 31 August 1964, NSF:CF, Box 2, LBJL; U.S. Congress, *Covert Action in Chile, 1963–1973*, 1. Seymour Hersh places the figure for 1964 at $20 million. His larger number includes other aid that went to Chile through the Agency for International Development and not just the money that was sent directly to the presidential campaign; Hersh, *Price of Power*, 260.

money for covert actions. The CIA turned down the requests, agreeing instead to advise the corporations on which groups and individuals they should contact directly and support.[68] A July 1970 National Intelligence Estimate argued that an Allende victory would lead to the establishment of a Marxist-Leninist state in Chile similar to the Soviet-style governments in Eastern Europe.[69] Kissinger summarized the prevailing attitude in the administration, and the rationale for covert operations, when he argued that he had "yet to meet somebody who firmly believes that if Allende wins there is likely to be another free election [in] Chile." Rather, "there is a good chance that he will establish over a period of years some sort of communist government. In that case you would have one not on an island off the coast (Cuba) which has not a traditional relationship and impact on Latin America, but in a major Latin American country.... So I don't think we should delude ourselves on an Allende takeover and [that] Chile would not present massive problems for us."[70] Following Cold War logic, Allende's election was seen not as a legitimate action by the Chilean people, but as a "takeover" by hostile, outside forces.

On September 4, Allende won a plurality of the vote in a three-way race for the Chilean presidency. Given that no candidate won a majority, Chile's constitution required that its Congress decide the winner between the top two finishers, with the vote set for October 24. Historically, the Chilean Congress had always elected the top vote-getter, and there was no reason to assume it would not do so this time. The American ambassador to Chile, Edward Korry, cabled the State Department that "Chile voted calmly to have a Marxist-Leninist state, the first nation in the world to make this choice freely and knowingly." There was no reason to believe that the armed forces "will unleash a civil war or that any other intervening miracle will undo his victory." Korry lamented that it was a "sad fact that Chile has taken the path to communism with only a little more than a third (36 pct) of the nation approving this choice," and worried that it "will have the most profound effect on Latin America and beyond. We have suffered a grievous defeat; the consequences will be domestic and international."[71] Kissinger believed that "Allende's election was a challenge to our national interest." It would be difficult to "reconcile ourselves to a second communist state in the Western hemisphere," because, he claimed, Allende would provide a base for anti-American attacks, support for Cuba, and an eventual alliance with the Soviet Union. He also worried about a domino effect in South America, given that "Chile bordered Argentina, Peru, and Bolivia, all plagued by radical movements."[72]

---

[68] U.S. Congress, *Covert Action in Chile, 1963–1973*, 12–13, 19–23; Senate Foreign Relations Committee, "Multinational Corporations and American Foreign Policy"; see also Bundy, *A Tangled Web*, 200–1.

[69] U.S. Congress, *Covert Action in Chile, 1963–1973*, 44.

[70] Ibid., 52.

[71] Korry to State Department, 5 September 1970, "Chile and the United States," NSA Electronic Briefing Book No. 8, NSA.

[72] Kissinger, *White House Years*, 653–7.

Nixon ordered Kissinger to find some means to block Allende from taking power. On September 8, the national security advisor convened a meeting of the 40 Committee to discuss the prospects "for taking any kind of action which might successfully preclude Allende assuming the presidency." The director of the CIA, Richard Helms, observed that once in office, Allende would be difficult to dislodge, and noted that "a military golpe [sic] against Allende would have little chance of success unless undertaken soon," although he was not optimistic that one would succeed. Kissinger concurred, and ordered the embassy in Santiago to prepare a "cold-blooded assessment" of the "pros and cons and problems and prospects involved should a Chilean military coup be organized now with U.S. assistance," and of the difficulties involved in doing so.[73] The outcome was a two-pronged operation to promote a military coup in Chile as a way to block Allende's ratification as president. Track I was a propaganda campaign designed to convince Chileans of the dangers of Allende and of the damage he would do to the nation if he became president. Track II authorized the CIA to work in conjunction with the Chilean military to organize the coup. Nixon met with Helms on September 15 and ordered him "to save Chile!" The president stated that the "Allende regime in Chile was not acceptable to the United States" and asked for a plan in two days; he wanted this to be a "full-time job – best men we have" and promised $10 million for the operation. In addition, he ordered that the CIA "make the [Chilean] economy scream" so that worsening conditions would help to create support for a coup.[74]

The CIA worked furiously over the next six weeks, meeting with key military figures and moving money and weapons into Chile. The Chileans with whom it conspired were given assurances of American support even when the CIA disapproved of particular approaches they planned. Kissinger made it clear that October 24 was not a deadline for the operation. He told Thomas Karamessines, the CIA official with overall responsibility for Operation FUBELT, that "the agency should continue keeping the pressure on every Allende weak spot in sight – now, after the 24th of October, after 5 November, and into the future until such time as new marching orders are given." Karamessines cabled the CIA station chief in Chile, Henry Hecksher, the next day, informing him that "it is firm and continuing policy that Allende be overthrown by a coup." While it would be "much preferable to have this transpire prior to 24 October," that was not mandatory, as "efforts in this regard will continue vigorously beyond this date." It was "imperative that these actions be implemented clandestinely and securely so that the USG and American hand be well hidden." Thus, General

---

[73] Memorandum for the Record, "Minutes of the Meeting of the 40 Committee, 8 September 1970," 9 September 1970, Chile Declassification Project, Fourth Tranche, 13 November 2000, NSA.

[74] Helms, "Notes on Meeting with the President on Chile," 15 September 1970; Memorandum for the Record, "Genesis of Project FUBELT," 16 September 1970, NSA Electronic Briefing Book No. 8, NSA.

Roberto Viaux was informed that his plans for a coup could not succeed and should not go forward. Failure at this time would reduce the chances of a coup in the future. He was instructed to preserve his assets and wait, that the time would come for action and that he would "continue to have our support."[75]

The main impediment to a military coup was the Chilean military commander, General Rene Schneider. He opposed any political intervention by the military to block the constitutional election of Allende. "Neutralizing" Schneider, therefore, was central to all of the military plans developed. While the CIA was trying to defuse Viaux's attempt at a coup, it was also working with and supplying weapons to a group of Chilean officers led by General Camilo Valenzuela to eliminate Schneider and prompt a military takeover.[76] Viaux, however, did not stop his efforts, and on October 22 attempted to kidnap Schneider and take over the government. Schneider, however, resisted and was shot and killed in the botched effort. The attempted coup had failed to bring down the government as planned; Chileans defended the electoral process, and Allende's selection as president was ratified by the Congress.

The administration moved quickly to develop its policy toward Chile now that Allende was in power. National Security Study Memorandum 97 (NSSM 97) was developed by the Department of State and submitted to the National Security Council on the day of Allende's inauguration. Its working assumptions were that "the Allende government will seek to establish in Chile as soon as feasible an authoritarian system following Marxist principles," that it would quickly nationalize basic industries, gain control over the armed forces, and end the freedom of the press. "Allende is a Marxist," NSSM 97 declared, "and will be faithful to his Marxist goals." The main U.S. objectives were prevention of the establishment of a "Marxist regime, prevention of the regime's falling under Communist control, and prevention of its influencing the rest of Latin America to follow either as a model or through its external policies." Such an approach, NSSM 97 asserted, was vital to protect U.S. economic and security interests.[77]

The National Security Council met on November 6 to discuss NSSM 97. President Nixon began by emphasizing the Marxist nature of the Chilean government. Kissinger noted that "all of our agencies are agreed that Allende will try to create a socialist state," and the question was what would be the American response. As he noted, NSSM 97 presented four options, but these essentially amounted to two choices: "seek a modus vivendi with the Allende government" or "adopt a posture of overt and frank hostility." A compromise position was

---

[75] Memorandum of Conversation, 15 October 1970, Karamessines to Hecksher, 16 October 1970, NSA Electronic Briefing Book No. 8, NSA. Kissinger probably meant to say 3 November, the date of Allende's inauguration. See the CIA report, "Report on CIA Chilean Task Force Activities, 15 September to 3 November 1970," 18 November 1970, NSA Electronic Briefing Book No. 8, NSA, for a summary of the CIA's efforts to organize a coup and prevent Allende from becoming president.

[76] See, for example, CIA cables on the coup plots, 18 October 1970, NSA Electronic Briefing Book No. 8, NSA.

[77] NSSM 97, "Chile," 3 November 1970, NSA Electronic Briefing Book No. 8, NSA.

the possibility of taking "what is in fact a hostile posture but not from an overt stance." Secretary of State Rogers argued that "if we have to be hostile, we want to do it right and bring him down." A stance of public hostility, however, would cause problems in other parts of Latin America. It would be better to put "an economic squeeze on [Allende]," and "bring his downfall perhaps without being counterproductive." In addition, the American military should continue to work with Chile's to strengthen those ties. Secretary of Defense Laird agreed with Rogers that the administration had "to do everything we can to hurt [Allende] and bring him down, but we must retain an outward posture that is correct," maintain contact with the military, "put pressure on him economically," and prevent Allende from consolidating his power.[78]

Nixon wanted action. Chile, he said, could not get away with what it was doing, or it would give "courage to others who are sitting on the fence in Latin America." He did not want to hear worries "about what the really democratic countries in Latin America say – the game is in Brazil and Argentina." The main concern in Chile was that Allende "can consolidate himself and the picture presented to the world" by his success. "If we let the potential leaders in South America," the president continued, "think they can move like Chile...we will be in trouble." He was adamant that the key was that "no impression should be permitted in Latin America that they can get away with this, that it's safe to go this way. All over the world it's too much the fashion to kick us around." Nixon, therefore, wanted a policy that was publicly correct, but that privately applied economic pressure by the reduction of international aid, and made it clear that the United States opposed Allende and was taking action against him. The situation could not be treated as similar to the one in Yugoslavia, "where we have to get along and no change is possible. Latin America is not gone, and we want to keep it." There could be no illusions about Allende delivering Chile to communism. "If there is any way we can hurt him," Nixon ordered, "whether by government or private business – I want them to know our policy is negative." It was imperative that the United States demonstrate its opposition. The president also noted that he would "never agree with the policy of downgrading the military in Latin America. They are the power centers subject to our influence."[79]

The middle position outlined by Kissinger was adopted as American policy and set out in National Security Decision Memorandum 93. The United States would publicly take a "correct but cool" posture toward Chile, in order "to avoid giving the Allende government a basis on which to rally domestic and international support for consolidation of his regime," while seeking to

---

[78] Memorandum of Conversation, "NSC Meeting – Chile" (NSSM 97), 6 November 1970, Chile Declassification Project, Fourth Tranche, 13 November 2000, NSA; see also Helms Briefing for 6 November NSC Meeting, "Chile," 5 November 1970, National Security Archive Electronic Briefing Book No. 8, NSA .

[79] Memorandum of Conversation, "NSC meeting – Chile" (NSSM 97), 6 November 1970, Chile Declassification Project, Fourth Tranche, 13 November 2000, NSA.

"maximize pressures on the Allende government to prevent its consolidation and limit its ability to implement policies contrary to U.S. and hemisphere interests." In carrying out this policy, Washington had to make it clear to the other nations in Latin America that the United States opposed the creation "of a communist state in Chile hostile to the interests of the United States and other hemisphere nations." Furthermore, it would encourage them to adopt a similar position; "establish and maintain close relations with friendly military leaders in the hemisphere," consult closely with Brazil and Argentina to coordinate opposition to Chile; end American economic assistance; and "bring maximum feasible influence to bear in international financial institutions to limit credit or other financial assistance to Chile."[80]

As Kissinger's earlier instructions to the CIA had made clear, covert operations against Allende did not end at this juncture. Rather, they were made part of a policy triad that included the "cool but correct" public posture and economic pressure. Over $8 million was spent on covert operations between 1970 and the military coup in September 1973 that overthrew Allende's government. This money funded a range of activities intended to maximize pressure on Allende government, including propaganda, aid to opposition political parties, and support to the military.[81] In terms of economic pressure, U.S. bilateral aid to Chile was cut from $35 million in 1969 to $1.5 million in 1971, while Export-Import Bank credits went from $29 million to zero in those same years. American pressure on international financial institutions was successful; the World Bank made no new loans to Chile while Allende was president, and the multilateral Inter-American Development Bank cut its aid from $46 million in 1970 to $2.1 million in 1972. Simultaneously, the United States increased its military aid to Chile from $.5 million in 1970 to $15 million by 1973 because it desired to remain on friendly terms with Chile's military officers.[82] Relations with the Chilean military, the State Department noted, had "the highest priority in the region" during these years.[83]

During Allende's three years in office, intelligence estimates consistently reported that the White House's fear that Allende would create a communist state were wrong. The State Department argued prior to Allende's inauguration that there was no "imminent or even inevitable" danger of a communist takeover in Chile, finding the idea of "the rise of a Soviet-type regime in Chile under the leadership of the Chilean Communist Party . . . far-fetched." This was mainly due to its recognition of the split between Allende's Socialist Party and the Communist Party.[84] A year later, the State Department found no reason

[80] NSDM 93, "Policy toward Chile," 9 November 1970, NSA Electronic Briefing Book No. 8, NSA.
[81] U.S. Congress, *Covert Action in Chile, 1963–1973*, 2, 27–8.
[82] Ibid., 33–7.
[83] Meyer to Tarr, "FMS Credits for Chile," 22 February 1973, Chile Human Rights Documents, Chile Declassification Project, Department of State, Box 1, NA.
[84] Department of State, Research Study, "Chile: Is Allende the Prelude to a Communist Victory?," 1 October 1970, Box 2196, RG 59.

to change its estimation. Allende, a State Department intelligence note argued, was having difficulty consolidating his political position because of growing economic problems and political opposition. While his nationalization programs "were very popular," the State Department found no reason to fear a communist takeover as long as the divisions between the socialists and communist remained.[85]

The CIA's National Intelligence Estimates (NIEs) reached similar conclusions. As the Church Committee reported, in August 1971 an NIE on Chile stated that the consolidation of Marxist political leadership "was not inevitable." The following NIE, in June 1972, noted that the "prospects for the continuation of democracy in Chile appeared to be better than at any time since Allende's inauguration," that the "traditional political system in Chile continued to demonstrate remarkable resiliency," and that "legislative, student, and trade union elections continued to take place in normal fashion, with pro-government forces accepting the results when they were adverse." In addition, opposition parties in Congress were able to block government initiatives and pass legislation designed to curtail the president's power, and opposition news media continued to operate. The NIE predicted that Allende would be forced to slow the "pace of his revolution in order to accommodate the opposition and to preserve the gains he had already made."[86]

These reports were not welcomed by the president or the national security advisor, and they missed the reasons for Nixon's and Kissinger's hostility toward Allende. It was not the loss of democracy in Chile that they feared. Rather, as Nixon had stressed at the 6 November 1970 National Security Council meeting, it was the ideological challenge presented by Allende's reforms and the threat of a successful socialist state in Chile that could provide a model for other nations that caused concern and led to American opposition. This would rupture the president's vision of what the "special relationship" with Latin America meant – that is, American dominance, stability, and the prevention of communism. As the National Security Council stated, American objectives and interests in the Western Hemisphere were threatened by changes in the region that demanded the United States take action "to maintain and fortify the special relationship." The inability to do so would indicate "a failure of our capacity and responsibility as a great power." If the United States could not maintain its system in the Western Hemisphere, it could not expect to be able "to achieve a successful order elsewhere in the world."[87] Allende, therefore, represented more than a threat to American corporations in Chile. In the view of the Nixon White House, he threatened American global interests by challenging the whole ideological basis of American Cold War policy and American efforts

---

[85] Department of State, Intelligence Note, "Chile: Copper and Domestic Politics," 14 October 1971, Box 2193, RG 59.

[86] U.S. Congress, *Covert Action in Chile, 1963–1973*, 44–5.

[87] "Current Policy and the Environment that Shaped It," 8 September 1971, NSSM 108, NSC, Box 11, RG 273.

to contain communism worldwide. Thus, the covert operations were continued, the economic pressure was maintained, and the support for the Chilean military was increased.

Strengthening Chile

The exact role the United States played in the 11 September 1973 coup is still not fully resolved even after the recent release of over 50,000 pages of new documents from the Department of State, Central Intelligence Agency, National Security Council, and Department of Defense as part of the Clinton administration's Chile Declassification Project. What is certain is that the Nixon administration maintained close contact with the Chilean military leaders that carried out the coup and knew about the military's plans in advance. Moreover, Nixon and Kissinger welcomed the overthrow of the Allende government and extended immediate support to the Pinochet regime despite their knowledge of the killing and imprisonment of political opponents, including the execution of at least two Americans, the use of torture, and the suppression of all political liberties in Chile. Nixon, Kissinger, and later Gerald Ford all believed that supporting Pinochet was necessary to remove a communist government, to establish order in Chile, and to protect American investments and trade. In addition, backing the junta was seen as essential to maintaining American credibility as a world power that could prevent the spread of communism in Latin America and other parts of the world through the Nixon Doctrine.

On 8 September 1973, the CIA reported that the Chilean "navy is scheduled to initiate a move to overthrow the government" on September 10, that it had the support of the air force, and that General Augusto Pinochet had promised that the army would join in the coup. If the coup did not occur on September 10, the report continued, it would certainly happen that week. Two days later, the CIA station in Santiago informed Washington that the plan for that day had been postponed, and "that a coup attempt will be initiated on 11 September" that had the support of "all three branches of the armed forces and the Carabineros."[88] Also on September 8, the State Department submitted to the National Security Council a contingency planning paper in case of a military coup in Chile. It noted that the United States should support "any new government resulting from a military intervention" because it would "represent a turn toward moderation." Moreover, Washington had to be prepared to provide military and economic assistance, even though "it would lend credence to the inevitable charge that the US masterminded Allende's demise and moved with unseemly haste to identify itself with yet another Latin American military regime."[89]

---

[88] CIA Directorate of Operations Documents, 8 September 1970, Chile Declassification Project, CIA, Box 3, NA.

[89] Department of State, "Chile Contingency Paper: Possible Chilean Military Intervention," 8 September 1973, Box 2196, RG 59.

The coup was launched on September 11, with the military, headed by Pinochet, taking power within a day. Allende, rather than surrender to the military, committed suicide, and all resistance to the coup collapsed quickly. The initial reports from Chile spelled out the full extent of the killings, violence, and political repression carried out by the Pinochet regime in the days after it took power. For example, a CIA cable on September 21 reported a conversation held between American officials and leaders of the coup. It noted that the "prevailing mood among the Chilean military is to use the current opportunity to stamp out all vestiges of communism in Chile for good. Severe repression is planned." It continued by noting that the regime was rounding up large numbers of people and interning them, had killed over 300 students already, and would not relinquish power any time soon.[90] A Defense Intelligence Agency report stated that the tactics and techniques used by the Chilean military were "straight out of the Spanish Inquisition and often leave the person interrogated with visible bodily damage."[91] Summary, on-the-spot executions were carried out against those caught or suspected of resisting the military through late October. These actions and the martial law imposed in Chile were said to be justified in a report to Kissinger, now the secretary of state, by Assistant Secretary of State Jack Kubisch because the military saw itself to be "in a time of war." Thus, the "fear of civil war was an important factor in [the military's] decision to employ a heavy hand from the outset.[92]

The Nixon administration welcomed the news of the September 11 coup. While it took a formal public approach toward recognition and maintained silence on human rights abuses, it moved quickly to provide immediate assistance to Pinochet's regime. The U.S. naval attaché in Chile, Patrick Ryan, captured the mood of the American officials in his report on the coup. He termed September 11 "our D-Day" and a "day of destiny" that had overthrown Allende's Marxist government. In less than eight hours, "Allende was dead and a three year experiment in Marxism joined him in the grave." The question that will be asked "in retrospect is not 'Why the overthrow of the Allende Government by the Armed Forces' but rather 'Why the Armed Forces waited so long?'" He saw the coup as being "close to perfect." Moreover, he reported that the military knew that their job had not ended with the overthrow of Allende. It was their responsibility to ensure the stability and recovery of the nation. He concluded that Chile was now once again a "country in liberty." The military's progress might be slow, "but it will be as free men aspiring to goals which are for the benefit of Chile and not self-serving world Marxism."[93] The State

[90] CIA Directorate of Operations Documents, 21 September 1970, Chile Declassification Project, CIA, Box 3, NA.

[91] Department of Defense Intelligence Report, 5 February 1974, Chile Declassification Project, Defense Intelligence Agency, Box 1, NA.

[92] Kubisch to Kissinger, "Chilean Executions," 16 November 1973, Chile Declassification Project, Ford Library, Box 1, NA.

[93] Department of Defense, Situation Report, 1 October 1973, NSA Electronic Briefing Book No. 8, NSA.

Department did investigate the killings of the two Americans, Charles Horman and Frank Teruggi, but never pressured the junta for answers or saw any reason to allow this incident to threaten good relations with Pinochet. For example, during a meeting between Assistant Secretary of State Kubisch and the Chilean foreign minister, Kubisch raised the issue in the "context of the need to be careful to keep small issues in our relationship from making our cooperation more difficult."[94]

Less than two months after the coup, Kubisch was able to report to Kissinger that there were positive results in getting Chile debt relief and economic assistance from international financial institutions and private American and Canadian banks; that a second American credit for food purchases, worth $24 million, had been announced; and that efforts to sell two surplus destroyers to Chile had received a sympathetic hearing in consultations with the Senate.[95] By 1974, the United States was providing Chile over $116 million in various forms of economic assistance, up from only $10 million the year before, and another $16 million in military aid. That same year, Chile was able to secure loans from the World Bank and Inter-American Development Bank totaling over $111 million.[96] When the Chilean ambassador, Walter Heitmann, met with Assistant Security of State Kubisch in April 1974 to discuss the sale of F-5E fighter planes and tanks to Chile, he was assured that the weapons would be sold and that the administration was just waiting to decide how best to handle the announcement. Kubisch told Heitmann that Kissinger had made it clear that it was the United States' "intention to support the [government of Chile] in every appropriate way." The decision to sell "tanks and aircraft is not without a symbolic importance in that context."[97]

In early 1974, the American embassy in Santiago sent a number of positive assessments to the State Department concerning Chile's ruling junta. In a typical dispatch in January, it reported that the "junta has moved forcefully in various economic sectors, with positive results in increased industrial and copper production," a lowering of inflation, and an improvement of its international credit. Pinochet's regime had not wavered from its decision to maintain martial law, and was maintaining stability and order in the nation. These actions, the embassy claimed, enjoyed "the active support of a majority of Chileans and the tolerance of most of the rest." Finally, relations with the United States were "close and constructive."[98] Two months later, the new American ambassador, David Popper, reflecting the views of the administration, wrote that he had

[94] Popper to Kissinger, 11 February 1974, NSA Electronic Briefing Book No. 8, NSA.

[95] Kubisch to Kissinger, "Chilean Executions," 16 November 1973, Chile Declassification Project, Ford Library, Box 1, NA.

[96] U.S. Congress, *Covert Action in Chile, 1963–1973*, 34.

[97] Kissinger to Popper, 27 April 1974, Chile Declassification Project, Department of State, Box 4, NA; see also Lord to Kissinger, "Sale of Military Equipment to Chile," 22 March 1974, Chile Declassification Project, Department of State, Box 4, NA.

[98] Thompson to Kissinger, "The Junta after Four Months," 21 January 1974, Chile Declassification Project, Department of State, Box 2, NA.

"no doubt that in terms of United States interest the September 1973 coup was a change for the better. A hostile regime has been replaced by one which is avowedly friendly and which shares many of our own conceptions." Popper claimed that the military had seized power "in response to popular demand," and that there was a need for authoritarian measures "to avert Leftist counter-attack and to press onward with economic reconstruction." This meant that "whether we think in terms of our Latin American policies generally, our need for associates in facing up to the Communist world and the radical 'third world,' or our bilateral economic interests, we stand to gain substantially from a policy of sympathy and support for the present government." It was important, the ambassador continued, that the United States reject the position that it should follow a policy of noncooperation with the junta and pressure it on human rights. This would serve only to weaken the government and to "assist the internal and external conspiracy we expect to see developing" against Chile. Popper concluded by stating that it should be the "fundamental objective" of the United States "to assist as we can in maintaining and strengthening the present government in Chile" by providing economic and military assistance.[99]

On the one-year anniversary of the coup, Popper provided the State Department with a glowing appraisal of the junta. He noted that it was firmly in power, and that its greatest strength was that it "supplanted political and social strife, hyperinflation and an economy near chaos by internal order and a fairly effective if harsh austerity program." In a remarkable analysis of the coup, Popper wrote that it was inevitable that the military take over in Chile. Indeed, he argued that "to a considerable extent, rather than seeking power, the junta had power thrust upon it" owing to the irresponsibility of Allende's rule and the danger of communism. The ambassador, therefore, found that the coup was "welcomed by most as an appropriate response." He was careful to note that while Chile was an authoritarian society, it was not a totalitarian one. There was, therefore, little concern shown toward the massive human rights violations by the military regime. Popper glossed over the issue by claiming that Chile's release of most third-country nationals and its allowing some international observers into the nation demonstrated that progress was being made. Besides, he continued, the curfew and "the ubiquity of armed security forces are borne easily by the average citizen." Chile's greatest problem, in Popper's estimation, was not human rights but proper economic planning.[100]

The resignation of Richard Nixon in August 1974 and Gerald Ford's succession to the presidency brought no change in policy toward Chile. The new president agreed with Kissinger and the existing policy, and saw Pinochet's rule as necessary to block communism in South America, to provide stability in Chile, and to protect American investments. Yet Ford had to contend with

---

[99] Popper to Kissinger, 13 March 1974, Chile Declassification Project, Department of State, Box 3, NA.

[100] Popper to Kissinger, 11 September 1974, Chile Declassification Project, Department of State, Box 5, NA.

congressional opposition to American support of Pinochet, efforts to block arms sales to Chile, and demands for an improvement of human rights in Chile as a condition for any further U.S. aid. A summary of American policy in July 1975 by the NSC noted that Ford and Kissinger "expressed support and sympathy for [Chile's] efforts to rebuild the nation" and were working to obtain foreign economic aid for Pinochet's regime and the approval of a rescheduling of Chile's debts by America's European allies. The major problem was the "strong criticism of this policy from the Congress," where human rights advocates had forced a temporary halt to military sales and credits.[101]

As early as October 1973, Senator Edward Kennedy denounced the decision by the Nixon administration to extend economic assistance to Chile. He saw it as "the latest symbol of our willingness to embrace a dictatorial regime that came to power in a bloody coup and which continues to conduct summary executions, to burn books, to imprison persons for political reasons, and to deny the right to emigrate," and called for an end to all aid to Chile unless the government agreed to protect human rights.[102] Congressman Donald Fraser's House Subcommittee on International Organizations and the Subcommittee on Inter-American Affairs began holding hearings on human rights abuses in Chile in December 1973. The congressmen heard evidence on torture, executions, arrests without charges, and denial of basic human rights guaranteed by the United Nations Universal Declaration of Human Rights.[103]

In April 1974, the House Intelligence Subcommittee held executive hearings on covert operations in Chile during which it first learned of some of the Track I activities of the CIA, and the committee chairman, Lucien Nedzi, was briefed on Track II. On 8 September 1974, the *New York Times* published a summary of the information from those hearings, creating calls for further investigations by Congress.[104] President Ford defended the CIA's actions as steps taken "to help and assist the preservation of opposition newspapers...and to preserve opposition political parties," and claimed that these actions were "in the best interest of the people of Chile and, certainly, in our best interest."[105] In December, Congress passed the Hughes–Ryan Amendment to the Foreign Service Assistance Act, which prohibited future CIA covert operations unless the president found "that each operation is important to the national security of the United States and reports, in a timely fashion, a description and scope of each operation to the appropriate committees of Congress...."[106] That same month, Congress suspended U.S. military aid to Chile.

The ban, however, was a temporary one that expired at the end of June 1975. What the administration sought in the interim from the junta was some

[101] Low to Scowcroft, 1 July 1975, NSC: KS Files, GRFL.
[102] Sigmund, *Democracy in Chile*, 89.
[103] U.S. Congress, *Human Rights in Chile*, 3–28.
[104] *New York Times*, 8 September 1974.
[105] *Public Papers of the Presidents: Ford 1974*, 151.
[106] Johnson, *A Season of Inquiry*, 283.

indication that it was moderating its actions to make it easier for the United States to provide assistance. In preparation for National Security Advisor Brent Scowcroft's meeting with a member of the Chilean junta, Admiral José Toribio Merino, the NSC noted the importance of Chile's economy to the United States and the necessity, over congressional opposition, to continue American military aid in order to ensure stability in the region. The military government in Santiago was "more self-confident than at any time since it came to power," largely because of American support, an improving economy, and the "coming to power of a number of conservative military governments in neighboring areas." The Ford administration valued the "friendship and traditionally close ties with Chile" and wanted them to be "strengthened in the future." To these ends, the National Security Council was hopeful that Chile's expressed intention to take positive steps in the area of human rights would improve the administration's "ability to be responsive to the legitimate defense and development needs" of Chile.[107]

Ambassador Popper was brought back to Washington in July 1975 for talks on how the United States could persuade the junta to take some action that would make it easier for the administration to assist Chile. Pinochet, however, backed away from any intention to moderate Chile's position in response to outside pressure. He declared that there "will be no elections in Chile during my lifetime nor in the lifetime of my successor," and refused to allow the UN Commission on Human Rights to enter Chile. The junta had originally invited the commission to conduct investigations as a way of quieting international criticism, and this reversal had the opposite effect.[108] In a summary of American policy toward the junta up to that point, it was noted that the United States had worked hard to provide economic assistance to Chile, that it had voted against or abstained on resolutions in international organizations that condemned Chile's human rights record, and that it wanted to continue to provide weapons once it could get around the congressional restrictions. The administration refused, however, to see any sanctions as a viable means to bring about change in Chile. Strong signs of disapproval, Popper reported, "would not improve the human rights situation" and would only make economic conditions worse and thereby weaken the regime. The ambassador reiterated that "preventing the re-emergence of a Chilean Government essentially hostile to us is our chief interest and the human rights problem is secondary."[109]

Kissinger and Popper met, along with Assistant Secretary of State William Rogers, on July 18 to discuss economic aid and the resumption of weapons sales to Chile. Popper observed that the "Chileans must have some kind of

---

[107] Brownwell to Scowcroft, 9 July 1975, CF: Latin America, GRFL; see also Memorandum of Conversation, 12 July 1975, Chile Declassification Project, Ford Library, Box 1, NA.

[108] U.S. Congress, *Covert Action in Chile, 1963–1973*, 62.

[109] Bloomfield to Rogers, "Ambassador Popper's Policy Paper," 11 July 1975; Popper, "The Situation in Chile and the Prospects for US Policy," 1 July 1975, Chile Declassification Project, Department of State, Box 7, NA.

death wish" in light of their cancellation of the UN Commission on Human Rights visit, as it "had a very adverse impact on our ability to be helpful." Kissinger responded by asking, "[W]hy does Chile have to be the only country that must receive a human rights investigating body? Why doesn't [Idi] Amin receive a human rights commission" or some "other African countries where people are executed in the public square? There has to be some limit to this screaming hypocrisy." Popper explained that "the cancellation of the UN visit was tactically a bad move," but that the junta had a "paranoid . . . belief that there is a worldwide Communist conspiracy being conducted against them." "Well," Kissinger returned, "isn't it true?" [110]

Popper changed the topic to arms sales and the junta's disappointment at the delays imposed by Congress. Rogers assured the ambassador that the administration was going ahead with the delivery. Kissinger wanted to know "when the hell are they going to get the arms" promised to them? "There can be no doubt about my policy," he declared. "I want to strengthen Chile. I don't want to drive them to despair." Rogers replied that he understood that Kissinger had reached an agreement with Congressman Fraser that the weapons would be released only "if some progress were made on human rights." Kissinger adamantly denied he had made any such arrangement, noting that he had said only that he would listen to the congressman on what he thought should be done, but would not tie American policy to any conditions. "That approach always has the opposite effect. . . . I do not agree with that approach." On the contrary, Kissinger stated that he favored the delivery of military assistance to Chile and that he had told Fraser that he "wanted to assist the Chileans and then we would see what we could do to improve the situation. I did not say that first there must be human rights improvements and then we would assist the Chileans. It cannot work that way." At the end of the meeting, Kissinger noted that he was still thinking of going to Latin America. Popper asked if that included Chile, to which the secretary of state responded yes, "if those madmen do something on human rights." [111]

In an effort to get the Chilean government to provide some cosmetic signs of change, Kissinger wrote Chilean Foreign Minister Patricio Carvajal on August 5 to explain the restraints that the Ford administration faced in dealing with Congress. Kissinger noted that the United States saw the cancellation of the visit by the UN commission as a mistake as it hurt Washington's ability to assist Chile. He wanted the foreign minister to realize that anything the United States "can do to cooperate with the Government of Chile is directly affected by Chile's human rights posture." With the end of the congressional restriction on arms sales imposed in December 1974, the administration was moving ahead and sending the promised sidewinder missiles, TOW anti-tank system, and spare parts, but Kissinger warned that there would be a negative response

---

[110] Memorandum of Conversation, 18 July 1975, Chile Declassification Project, Department of State, Box 7, NA.
[111] Ibid.

from Congress and that there could be further restrictions. He suggested that allowing an international group to visit Chile and make a report on human rights conditions would probably satisfy the opposition in Congress and allow the administration to continue to provide Santiago with weapons and other forms of support.[112]

To make sure that the junta did not get the wrong impression about the administration's views and policy, Kissinger met with Carvajal in September. He opened the meeting by dismissing human rights as a concern. He told the foreign minister that he "read the Briefing Paper for this meeting and it was nothing but Human Rights. The State Department is made up of people who have a vocation for the ministry. Because there were not enough churches for them, they went into the Department of State." He continued by noting that his view on the question of human rights in Chile involved two levels. "One is that it is a total injustice. Nobody goes around making statements regarding what is going on in Kampala or the Central African Republic or hundreds of other countries." The other level was the "problem of helping your government under the present conditions, which we did not create, but which make it difficult for us." Kissinger assured Carvajal that he and the president "understand the problem" Chile confronted and that it was "not in the interest of the United States to turn Chile into another Portugal." (The Portugese military dictatorship had recently been overthrown.) It would, therefore, "help enormously if something can be done" by Chile to alleviate the pressure on the Ford administration by Congress.[113] A week later, in a meeting with the president, Kissinger continued to oppose the linking of foreign military sales with human rights conditions in Chile. Ford agreed, stating "that would be a very bad precedent."[114]

The Organization of American States held its annual meeting in June 1976 in Santiago. Secretary of State Kissinger decided to attend the meeting, knowing that his presence would lead to the criticism that his visit would "legitimize the military regime." Rogers wrote Kissinger that "Chile has taken on Spain's image in the 1940s as a symbol of right-wing tyranny. Like it or not, we are identified with the regime's origins and hence charged with some responsibility for its actions." While the United States "recognized that to an important degree Chile is the victim of a vindictive and coordinated international campaign," there were human rights violations that continued, including "arbitrary arrest, disappearance, detention without trial, [and] torture." Thus, Rogers noted, the secretary of state would have to address the question of human rights.[115]

[112] Kissinger to Carvajal, 5 August 1975, Chile Declassification Project, Department of State, Box 8, NA.
[113] Memorandum of Conversation, 29 September 1975, Chile Declassification Project, Department of State, Box 8, NA.
[114] Memorandum of Conversation, 6 October 1975, Chile Declassification Project, Ford Library, Box 1, NA.
[115] Rogers to Kissinger, 26 April 1976; Rogers to Kissinger, 26 May 1976, both Chile Declassification Project, Department of State, Box 10, NA.

Kissinger decided that he had to give a speech that discussed the question of human rights in general terms and reiterated American support for the United Nations Universal Declaration on Human Rights. At the same time, he would meet privately with Pinochet and assure him that his words were meaningless in terms of the Ford administration's policy toward Chile and were designed merely to appease public and congressional opinion in the United States. At their meeting on June 8, Kissinger told Pinochet that he and the president were "sympathetic with what you are trying to do here," and that he believed "the previous government was headed toward communism." The United States, therefore, "welcomed the overthrow of the Communist-inclined government" in Chile and wished the junta well. Pinochet, Kissinger opined, had done "a great service to the West in overthrowing Allende. Otherwise Chile would have followed Cuba. Then there would be no human rights."[116]

Yet the administration faced "massive domestic problems," especially in Congress, "over the issue of human rights." Congress was again discussing restrictions on aid to Chile. While Kissinger assured Pinochet that the administration opposed such measures, it was "a problem which complicates our relationships and the efforts of those who are friends of Chile." Turning to the speech he would deliver later that day, Kissinger told Pinochet that he could dismiss what he had to say, but that the general needed to understand his position. "In my statement," Kissinger said, "I will treat human rights in general terms, and human rights in a world context." There would be two paragraphs on Chile, where he would note that the issue of human rights had impaired relations between Chile and the United States, mostly because of congressional actions, and that he would add that he hoped Chile "will shortly remove those obstacles." Kissinger then explained that he would end that section of the speech by making a reference to Cuba and "to the hypocrisy of some who call attention to human rights as a means of intervening in governments." He could "do no less, without producing a reaction in the U.S. which would lead to legislative restrictions." Kissinger quickly sought to reassure his host again, noting that the "speech is not aimed at Chile." It was the secretary of state's opinion that Pinochet was "a victim of all left-wing groups around the world, and that your greatest sin was that you overthrew a government which was going Communist." The speech was just a way to deal with "a practical problem" that the administration had to take into account "without bringing about pressures incompatible with your dignity, and at the same time which does not lead to U.S. laws which will undermine our relationship." Kissinger concluded by reiterating that nothing he would say was designed to harm the junta. "I want you to succeed and I want to retain the possibility of aid." His speech and the meeting with Pinochet, therefore, were "designed to allow us to say to the Congress

[116] Memorandum of Conversation, 8 June 1976, Chile Declassification Project, Ford Library, Box 1, NA.

that we are talking to the Chilean government and therefore Congress need not act."[117]

Pinochet asserted that Chile was making progress in terms of human rights, held only 400 political prisoners, and had released more than that. What the secretary of state sought was some action, such as the freeing of a larger group, "that would be better for the psychological impact of the releases." The United States, Kissinger emphasized, wanted "an outcome which is not deeply embarrassing to you." Still, the administration had to be able to show something for its efforts "or we will be defeated." Pinochet noted that he was puzzled by all of this. "Russia supports their people 100%. We are behind you. You are the leader. But," the general complained, "you have a punitive system for your friends." Kissinger agreed, noting that there was "merit" in what Pinochet said, that it was unfortunate that this was the case in the wake of Vietnam and Watergate, and that it was "a curious time in the U.S." All he was doing, the secretary of state said, was making suggestions, concluding that the United States wanted "to help, not undermine you."[118]

Kissinger had gone out of his way to flatter and protect one of the most brutal regimes in the world. A month after the meeting, National Security Advisor Scowcroft wrote Ford that U.S. relations with Latin America were better than at any time in the recent past. He believed that this improvement resulted from the resumption of an active American role in hemispheric affairs and a "process of maturation" on the part of the nations to the south.[119] Kissinger and Ford continued to adhere to the logic and rationale of containment, credibility, and American interventionism in the Third World. But the Nixon Doctrine, while attempting to appease the antiwar movement through Vietnamization and the withdrawal of American forces from Vietnam, placed the administration on a collision course with critics of the verities of American Cold War policy.

In the wake of the Vietnam War, the continued embrace of right-wing dictators by the United States was no longer seen as necessary or justifiable by a large number of Americans. All the tensions concerning the protection of freedom abroad through undemocratic and military means, along with the threat to liberties at home posed by the national security state, tensions long subsumed by the policy of containment and the narrative of American duty to the world, began to emerge. As evidence of the Nixon administration's covert operations in Chile became public, there were demands that Congress investigate these actions. American Cold War policies were being questioned, and a growing opposition to American support of right-wing dictators in general and of Pinochet in particular was demonstrated when Congress again halted military sales to Chile in July 1976.

The administration's ability to shield Pinochet's regime from criticism and to maintain its policy of supporting right-wing dictators would face its greatest

---

[117] Ibid.
[118] Ibid.
[119] Scowcroft to Ford, 17 July 1976, CF: Latin America, GRFL.

challenge in the form of the Church Committee's investigations into CIA covert operations. There the questions of how best to defend freedom abroad and at home would take center stage in the nation's political debates. The contradictions inherent in Washington's backing of authoritarian regimes in the name of protecting the free world would bring forth a new framework of human rights as the best means to promote American values and protect the national interest.

4

Morality and Diplomacy

The Church Committee and Post-Vietnam Foreign Policy

On 29 April 1975, the day before the final fall of Saigon, President Gerald Ford announced the completion of the evacuation of American personnel from Vietnam. He stated that "this action closes a chapter in the American experience. I ask all Americans to close ranks, to avoid recrimination about the past, to look ahead to the many goals we share, and to work together on the great tasks that remain to be accomplished."[1] At a time when the overwhelming majority of Americans had concluded that the war was wrong and had come to question the policies leading to it, and at a time when Congress was becoming increasingly assertive in this area, Ford's effort to forestall any further debate about American foreign policy was sure to fail. By contrast, Senator Frank Church declared that the end of the Vietnam War provided "an opportune time for some reflection on America's role in the world" and a reevaluation of the policies that had led to that protracted, painful, and divisive conflict.[2]

These two positions demonstrated the fracturing of the elite consensus on American foreign policy and delineated the sharp debates over the meaning of the Vietnam War, the nature of American foreign policy, and the policy of support for right-wing dictators that were emerging in the wake of the Vietnam conflict. President Ford and Henry Kissinger sought to retain the old verities of the Cold War and to maintain executive control over foreign policy. In the process, they remained committed to a diplomacy of containment and credibility that condoned covert activity and global intervention. Critics such as Church questioned the central tenets of Cold War policymaking and called for the United States to reorient its moral compass and find methods other than force, clandestine activity, and support for authoritarian regimes to advance American interests in the world. The administration's efforts to provide increased aid to South Vietnam after the withdrawal of American forces, its actions

---

[1] *Public Papers of the Presidents: Ford 1975*, 605.
[2] Church, "A Post Vietnam Foreign Policy," Series 10.6, Box 8, Folder 13 (hereafter series/box/folder), FCP.

during the *Mayaguez* affair of May 1975, and its resistance to the Senate Select Committee on Intelligence hearings that investigated the Central Intelligence Agency's covert activities were a continuation of traditional Cold War policies. Opponents, however, found them emblematic of the worldview that had failed the nation in Vietnam.

For over a year, congressional proponents of change, led by Senator Church, and the administration confronted each other over the nature and future of American foreign policy. The opponents of the Vietnam War were frustrated by what they saw as the persistent exaggeration of the Soviet threat in the Third World in order to bolster American support of right-wing dictators, and the consequent character of American intervention abroad. The American obsession with communism had led to an interventionist foreign policy that was damaging to the national interest, with Vietnam, they believed, demonstrating that the old policies were flawed and, more importantly, destined to backfire. The Church Committee's investigations of the CIA's covert operations led to a series of revelations that, along with the fallout from the Vietnam War, challenged the classic Cold War paradigm and ensured that a fractured foreign policy consensus would not easily be repaired. Moreover, the uncovering of CIA efforts to overthrow foreign governments – most notably, democratically elected ones such as Salvador Allende's in Chile – and to assassinate certain leaders, such as Patrice Lumumba, helped to widen the range of legitimate discussion regarding foreign policy to include moral considerations and the condemnation of support for authoritarian regimes.

The Church Committee hearings did not bring about a complete transformation of American policy or create a new consensus. They did, however, change the debate regarding the objectives and methods of U.S. foreign policy. Further, the critics sought to reintroduce the nation's founding principles and ideals into the making of foreign policy, and to provide Congressional oversight of covert operations. The Church Committee, therefore, allowed competing views to be heard and different approaches to be discussed, and was a critical component in changing and broadening the legitimate discourse on American foreign policy. The debates concerning the direction of American foreign policy that culminated in 1975–76 continued to be waged throughout the rest of the Cold War as Americans fought over the legacy and meaning of the Vietnam War.

The Cooper–Church Amendment

As the opposition to the Vietnam War grew in the late 1960s and early 1970s, the critics of the war sought to bring the conflict to an end and to change the nature and direction of American foreign policy. Seeing the war as a bad policy decision and as a mistaken application of the containment doctrine to a nonvital area of the world, these critics questioned the war's necessity. Many opponents, however, had concluded by the late 1960s that the war was also a symptom of a larger problem facing the nation. They subsequently engaged in a sustained effort to change the assumptions and conduct of American foreign policy.[3]

Central to the critics' misgivings about the war was their belief that it was immoral. The struggle was primarily a nationalistic and anticolonial civil war, they argued, one in which the United States should not have intervened. They pointed out that Ho Chi Minh was regarded by most Vietnamese, in the words of Senator Church, "as the authentic architect of independence from the French, as the George Washington of Vietnam, so to speak." The "war in South Vietnam," therefore, "is their war, not ours."[4] The nature of the fighting, and the American use of its overwhelming power against Vietnam, appeared to many to be antithetical to the country's values and traditional support for self-determination. Moreover, they saw the Saigon government as a corrupt, ineffective dictatorship that was undeserving of American support. In place of force, opponents called for the withdrawal of U.S. forces and a negotiated settlement. Critics of the war saw it as destined to fail and bound to have negative consequences in terms of the loss of international support and prestige. Moreover, it was corrupting to American principles and values, and damaging to institutions at home. As Church argued, unless the United States came "to accept the fact that it is neither within the power nor the interest of the United States to preserve the status quo everywhere, our policy is doomed to failure."[5] These ideas were a direct challenge to the policy of containment and the premise that it was a bipolar world in which all areas of the globe had to be protected from monolithic communism. In rejecting the fundamental assumptions of America's Cold War policy, critics called for an acknowledgment of the limits of American power and a reorientation of American policy around moral concerns. This meant rejecting the policy of supporting right-wing dictators in the name of anticommunism, stability, and the protection of American economic interests.

The continued escalation of the war in the face of public opposition convinced many opponents that the war was not merely a policy mistake but a reflection of a larger problem: executive dominance of the foreign policy-making process that allowed the president to continue policies even when they were unpopular with the nation. This led to efforts by the opposition to control the president's freedom to conduct foreign policy and bring an end to the war through congressional action. If no action were taken, critics feared that the war would expand to all of Southeast Asia, continue indefinitely, and come to threaten constitutional government in the United States. Out of this concern would emerge in 1970 the landmark Cooper–Church amendment

---

[3] On the antiwar movement, see Levy, *The Debate over Vietnam*; DeBenedetti with Chatfield, *An American Ordeal*; Wells, *The War Within*; Small, *Johnson, Nixon and the Doves* and *Antiwarriors*; Jeffreys-Jones, *Peace Now*; Anderson, *The Movement and the Sixties*; and Hall, *Because of Their Faith*.

[4] *Washington Evening Star*, 15 March 1964.

[5] *Ramparts*, January–February 1965, 17–22; *New York Times*, 27 December 1964.

that placed the first limits on the president's ability to expand the war in Vietnam.

In June 1969, Church compared the growth of executive power and the creation of the "imperial presidency" to the Caesars' grab for power in ancient Rome, and predicted similar negative consequences for the Senate and the republic of the United States unless action were taken to restore the constitutional balance of power. In a speech entitled "Of Presidents and Caesars," Church spoke on the decline of constitutional government that had led to the excessive intervention of the United States in the Third World and to American support for right-wing dictatorships. The president reminded him of those Roman rulers who "subtly and insidiously...stole their powers away from an unsuspecting Senate." The "Senate has acquiesced, while Presidents have steadily drawn to themselves much of the power delegated to Congress by the Constitution." He noted that "as crisis has followed upon crisis in these last thirty years, the concentration of power in the hands of the President has grown ever more rapidly, while the Congress has been reduced to virtual impotence in the making of foreign policy." Church argued that the Vietnam War demanded that constitutional issues be addressed "because nothing less than the survival of Constitutional government is at stake. Our democratic processes...are being undermined by the very methods we have chosen to defend these processes against real or fancied foreign dangers."[6]

Church, therefore, along with other sympathetic senators, moved in 1969–70 to limit the executive's power and bring the war to an end. The first step, as he saw it, was for Congress to limit the area of the war in order to contain its scope. Such a move would simultaneously force a change in American policy and lead to the reassertion of the role of the Senate in the making of foreign policy.[7] It was crucial, Church surmised, that the senators who opposed the war win in their first major confrontation with the Nixon White House and effectively demonstrate the Senate's ability to limit the power of the president. A defeat caused by overreaching might divide the opposition and actually enhance Nixon's ability to continue the war.

In the fall of 1969, Church began to work with John Sherman Cooper on bipartisan measures to restrict the power of the president. Cooper was one of the first Republicans to publicly oppose the war, and he and Church complemented each other in their battles to limit the power of the presidency and bring an end to the war.[8] They were under no illusions about the Nixon administration's commitment to total victory in Vietnam. For example, on 15 May 1969, the day after Nixon's first major address on the Vietnam War, Church told a national

---

[6] Church, "Of Presidents and Caesars: The Decline of Constitutional Government in the Conduct of American Foreign Policy," 19 June 1969, 8.1/6/12, FCP; Schlesinger, *The Imperial Presidency*.

[7] Ashby and Gramer, *Fighting the Odds*, 293.

[8] On Cooper, see Schulman, *John Sherman Cooper*; for a more extensive discussion of the Cooper–Church Amendment, see Schmitz, "Of Presidents and Caesars." On other leading Senate opponents of the Vietnam War, see Woods, *Fulbright*; and Olson, *Mansfield and Vietnam*.

audience on *The Today Show* that he was disappointed. "We've waited for months for Mr. Nixon to reveal his plans for ending the war in Vietnam; he said he had one during the campaign. His statement last night was merely a restatement of the position that President Johnson had taken many times." He rejected the idea that the United States had to stay in order to honor its obligations to the South Vietnamese. "We've done everything that can be done to fulfill our commitment," Church stated. "If, by now, the Saigon Government cannot field an army in its own country against an enemy, that, after all, is no larger than they . . . then they never are going to be."[9]

Church attacked "the favored euphemism . . . 'honorable settlement'" as a mask for continued war. "It is time to stop the prideful nonsense about winning an 'honorable settlement' and avoiding a 'disguised defeat'; it is time to acknowledge the failure of our involvement in Vietnam." The only obligation that the United States government has is "to the American people." Church concluded that "national interest shows compelling reasons why we must extricate ourselves from Vietnam. A process of deterioration spreads through our society which cannot be arrested, much less reversed, until we disengage."[10]

In addition, Church criticized Nixon's policy of "Vietnamization" and the Nixon Doctrine. Church argued that "our strategy in Vietnam has failed" but that the Nixon administration has refused "to acknowledge that failure." Instead, "in recent weeks there has been increasing talk of changing the military mix in Vietnam by replacing American troops with Vietnamese. . . . This is not a formula for extricating the United States from Vietnam; it is, rather, a formula for keeping up to 300,000 American troops engaged in Vietnam indefinitely. Its purpose is not to get out, but to stay in."[11] The Nixon Doctrine was just containment under a different name, and threatened to increase the pressure for American intervention to protect the various dictatorships seen as vital to regional stability from their own populations.

It was Nixon's November 3 "Silent Majority" speech that provided the context for the introduction of the Cooper–Church amendments. That soliloquy was a response to the growing antiwar movement. Nixon used it to explain his policy, to buy time for his efforts to force a military solution on the North Vietnamese, and to attack his domestic opponents. Nixon asserted that the "great question is: How can we win America's peace?" He recited the by-then familiar arguments of containment and credibility and juxtaposed his policy of Vietnamization against the calls for "an immediate, precipitate withdrawal . . . without regard to the effects of that action." Warming to his task, Nixon concluded:

Let historians not record that when America was the most powerful nation in the world we passed on the other side of the road and allowed the last hopes for peace and freedom of millions of people to be suffocated by the forces of totalitarianism. . . . I pledged in my

---

[9] Transcript of *The Today Show*, 15 May 1969, 8.1/6/11, FCP.
[10] Church, 19 August 1969, 8.3/2/24, FCP.
[11] Church, "Vietnam: Disengagement Now," *Vital Speeches*, 36, no. 2 (1 November 1969), 34–9.

campaign ... to end the war in a way that we could win the peace. ... The more support I can have from the American people, the sooner that pledge can be redeemed; for the more divided we are at home, the less likely the enemy is to negotiate at Paris. Let us be united for peace. Let us also be united against defeat. ... North Viet-Nam cannot defeat or humiliate the United States. Only Americans can do that.[12]

This attempt to discredit the opposition incensed the antiwar movement and the leading Senate doves. "Nearly everyone now recognizes," Church stated, "that our intervention in Vietnam was in error. Two years ago, our political skies were still filled with hawks; today scarcely a hawk can be seen." Accordingly, Church took issue with the notion that the nation's credibility would be harmed by a withdrawal. By ending the war "we shall suffer no lasting injury to our power or prestige." Rather, "the termination of our war in Vietnam would represent a ... liberation for America, and even a victory of sorts – a victory of principle over pride and of intelligent self-interest over messianic delusion."[13]

While he favored a quick and complete withdrawal that was not tied to the preservation of the regime in Saigon, and while he was certain that the administration was intent on continuing the war, Church believed it was not yet politically possible to mandate a removal of American troops. Indeed, Nixon's speech was well received by the public. He had succeeded in portraying himself as a moderate pursuing a prudent course of gradual withdrawal and negotiation while protecting American security and credibility. With the president making it clear that he preferred conflict rather than compromise, Senate doves found themselves on the defensive. In search of a victory, they turned their attention to Laos.

In a three-hour executive session on December 15, the Senate debated an amendment to the Department of Defense Procurement and Development Act that would prohibit the use of American forces in Laos and Thailand. There was disagreement over the extent of the original amendment, with some doves opposing the restriction on American bombing in Laos. Church broke the dead-lock by submitting a compromise proposal blocking only the use of ground troops without congressional approval. With no opposition from the administration, the first Cooper–Church amendment easily passed by a vote of 73–17.[14] While Church realized that this measure did not significantly restrict the actions of the president, the first Cooper–Church amendment provided an important precedent that Church would build on when he concluded that the time was

[12] *Public Papers of the Presidents: Nixon, 1969*, 909.
[13] Church, "The Only Alternative: A Reply to the President on Vietnam," 10.6/8/2, FCP. This was based on a speech he had delivered in the Senate on 19 December 1969, 8.1/6/51, FCP. Another version of this speech was syndicated under the title "Vietnam: The Other Alternative," 8.3/4/10, FCP.
[14] Church, "War without End," 1 May 1970, 2.2/32/9, FCP; *New York Times*, 16 December 1969. The full amendment stated: "In line with the expressed intention of the President of the United States, none of the funds appropriated by this Act shall be used to finance the introduction of American ground combat troops into Laos or Thailand." "Significant Events Relating to the Cooper-Church Amendment," 2.2/39/9, FCP.

right for a more all-encompassing restriction of the president's ability to wage an undeclared war.

The overthrow of the government of Prince Norodom Sihanouk by the Cambodian military in mid-March, and the U.S. rush to support the new Lon Nol regime, led Church to believe that Nixon would use Lon Nol's seizure of power to extend the war into Cambodia. He therefore turned again to Cooper, and the two began drafting a bipartisan measure to ban U.S. combat troops from Cambodia. On April 12, Church and Cooper announced that they were planning to introduce legislation to "extend to Cambodia the present prohibition against introduction of American combat troops into Laos and Thailand." Church stated that the "recent events in Southeast Asia – including the ouster of Prince Sihanouk by a military junta in Cambodia, the intensification of the conflict in Laos and the extension of the ground battle into Cambodia – create dangerous pressures for deepening America's involvement." He noted that "it has been reported . . . that armed American military personnel have already crossed into Cambodian territory several times in recent days. In light of our tragic experience in Viet Nam, the United States must avoid being pulled into a wider war." Furthermore, he noted that the amendment "continues Congress' efforts to reassert its constitutional role in the formulation of foreign policy."[15]

Church feared that a "new front" in the war was opening up, a development that would place the policy of "de-escalation in the gravest jeopardy."[16] He saw the introduction of the Cooper–Church amendment as "an effort to hasten a close to the war in a safe and orderly manner, and to bring back to Congress those powers which, over the years since Franklin Roosevelt, have subtly drifted into the hand of one man, the President."[17] What Church did not know was that Nixon had already decided to invade Cambodia, a move that would set off a new round of protests and make a second Cooper–Church amendment the central issue in the battle between opponents and supporters of the war.

When Nixon announced to the nation on 30 April 1970 his decision to send troops into Cambodia, Church had already prepared a speech on the issue. On May 1, an angry Church addressed the Senate concerning American policy in Vietnam and the invasion of Cambodia. He blamed the failure to end the war and the new expansion of the fighting into a neighboring nation on the Nixon administration's refusal to "acknowledge the futility of our continued military intervention in Vietnam." The nation, Church declared, had to admit "the impossibility of sustaining at any acceptable cost an anticommunist regime in Saigon, allied with, dependent on, and supported by the United States." Church found that the "policy itself was deeply unsound, extraneous to American interests and offensive to American values."[18]

[15] Joint press release by Senators Church and Cooper, 12 April 1970, 2.2/39/9, FCP.
[16] Church, news release, 29 April 1970, 2.2/39/9, FCP.
[17] Church to Pfc. Robin Crawford, 19 June 1970, 2.2/32/10, FCP.
[18] Church, "War without End," 1 May 1970, 2.2/32/9, FCP.

While clearly troubled by the president's action, Church believed that it provided an opportunity for Congress and the people to take the initiative in Vietnam away from the executive branch, to limit the expansion of the war, and to bring the war itself to an end. As Church stated, it was time "for the Congress to draw the line against an expanded American involvement" in the war and begin to put an end to it. "If the Executive Branch will not take the initiative, the Congress and the people must." The best method was for Congress to immediately pass the Cooper–Church amendment as a way to force the withdrawal of American forces from Cambodia. "Too much blood has been lost, too much patience gone unrewarded, while the war continues to poison our society."[19] He was now convinced that enough pressure could be exerted on the Nixon administration to force it to abandon its policy of victory in Vietnam and settle for a negotiated agreement that would end the war.

In the ultimately successful battles to ward off the administration's efforts to block the Cooper–Church amendment, which decreed that no United States troops could be engaged in Cambodia without specific congressional approval after June 30, Church was the leader of the opposition's fight over the direction of the war. Church outlined the importance he attached to the amendment in a series of speeches in May 1970. Criticizing Congress for permitting the "president to exercise blank check authority," he argued that it was now faced with "another front . . . in this endless war." "This new crisis," Church argued, "presents the Congress with an historic opportunity to draw the limits on American intervention. . . . " It was time for Congress to reassert its power "so as to avoid a deepening American involvement" in Cambodia.[20] When the Cooper–Church amendment was formally introduced on May 11, Church noted that the Congress's failure to use its powers in relation to funding and declaring wars "is one for which historians may judge us harshly." Yet he quickly noted that "there is a precedent for what we are asking the Senate to do," referring to the first Cooper–Church amendment. What was new was the attempt to restrict the use of troops in a country where they were already committed. "Unquestionably," Church declared, "Congress had the power to accomplish" this objective.

In addition to the need to reassert congressional power and bring an end to the war, Church noted that the adoption of the measure was necessary to assure young Americans that the political system worked and that they should not give up on the government. That May, the alienation of American youth had come to a head with the shootings at Kent State and Jackson State Universities, and the closing of over five hundred colleges and universities across the nation. "This war," Church stated, "has already stretched the generation gap so wide that it threatens to pull the country apart." Many rejected the idea that the war in Vietnam was necessary to national security, "the safety of the American people, or the well-being of our society." "We now reap the bitter harvest," Church warned, "manifested in the angry uprising on campuses from coast to

[19] Ibid.
[20] Church, news release, 7 May 1970, 3.2/32/8, FCP.

coast.... Once the moral authority of the government is rejected on an issue so fundamental as an unacceptable war, every lesser institution of society is placed in jeopardy." It was futile, Church asserted, to "tell these young people that our 'will and character are being tested,' that we shall not be humiliated or accept our first defeat." They never believed that Vietnam was about the nation's security, and "they do not believe that a mistaken war should be won. They believe it should be stopped. That, for them, is the path of honor." It was thus all the more imperative that Congress "draw the line against an expanded American involvement in the widening war."[21]

The administration adamantly opposed the second Cooper–Church amendment. Central to its position was the claim that the restriction would interfere with the president's role as commander-in-chief, and that Congress had only the authority to limit the civilian acts of the president. Church argued that there was nothing in the amendment that prevented the president from fulfilling his duties as commander-in-chief, and noted that Nixon had supported the first Cooper–Church amendment without invoking this argument. The issue at hand was the war-making power. The purpose of the amendment, Church insisted, was to return that power to Congress, where it rightfully belonged.

In the face of a mounting challenge in the Senate and the massive protests against his policy, Nixon began to remove American forces from Cambodia. The president set the end of June as his deadline, and with that declared the Cooper–Church amendment moot.[22] On June 3, Nixon proclaimed the Cambodian invasion "the most successful operation of this long and very difficult war," and that all of the "major military objectives have been achieved."[23]

Church responded that whether or not Nixon was withdrawing American troops from Cambodia, the amendment was still necessary. Cooper–Church was not designed to "undo what's been done. Instead, it is addressed to the immediate need of preventing the United States from bogging down in Cambodia" and committing itself to the defense of another nation in Southeast Asia.[24] "The Cooper–Church amendment is the opening move" in extricating the United States from the Vietnam War by "setting the outer limits ... to American involvement in Cambodia." More importantly for Church, "its adoption would also signal that the Congress recognizes and stands willing to reassert its share of the responsibility for bringing the war to a close." Opponents of this measure "would concede all power to the Presidency. They would reduce the Congress of the United States to impotence, while making the President an autocrat supreme." Finally, the Cooper–Church amendment was vital as a rebuttal to those who believed the government cannot work.[25]

[21] Statement by Senator Church before the SFRC, 11 May 1970; see also Church's statement to the full Senate, 13 May 1970, both 2.2/32/8, FCP.

[22] Statement by Senator Church before the SFRC, 11 May 1970, 2.2/32/8, FCP.

[23] Ashby and Gramer, *Fighting the Odds*, 315.

[24] Statement of Senator Church before the SFRC, 11 May 1970, 2.2/32/8, FCP.

[25] Remarks of Senator Church in the U.S. Senate, 3 June 1970, 2.2/39/10, FCP.

On June 30, after seven weeks of debate and the defeat of all of the administration's qualifying amendments, the Senate passed Cooper–Church by a vote of 58–37. While the House of Representatives did not finally approve a modified version of the amendment until December, passage of the Cooper–Church amendment marked a milestone in the Vietnam War. It was the first time that Congress had restricted the deployment of troops during a war and voted against the wishes of a president. Moreover, it provided a means for both the Congress and the public to demonstrate the full extent of their opposition to the war. The Cooper–Church amendment was, therefore, a landmark in the history of opposition to the war, congressional initiatives to bring the fighting to an end, and efforts to control executive power in foreign policy.

That fall, Church announced on television and in speeches across the country that "The Doves Have Won."[26] He based his assertion on the fact that the two key propositions of the dove position, "a negotiated peace and the withdrawal of American troops," were now official policy. The remaining debate would be over when to withdraw, not whether to do so, and over the meaning of the war. "So the last service the doves can perform for their country," Church concluded, "is to insist that President Nixon's withdrawal program truly leads to a 'Vietnamization' of the war. It must not become a device for lowering – and then perpetuating – an American military presence in South Vietnam for the indefinite future. Our long ordeal in this mistaken war must end." Church continued, "The gathering crisis in our own land, the deepening divisions among our people, the festering, unattended problems here at home, bear far more importantly on the future of our Republic than anything we ever had at stake in Indochina." The opponents of the war needed to prevent the corruption of the nation and its institutions. Their opposition was, for Church, the "highest concept of patriotism – which is not the patriotism of conformity – but the patriotism of Senator Carl Shurz, a dissenter from an earlier period, who proclaimed: 'Our country, right or wrong. When right, to be kept right; when wrong, to be put right.'"[27]

The emerging antiwar majority in the Senate would challenge the executive on a number of foreign policy issues. Opposed to further American intervention abroad, critics believed that Vietnam should have convinced the nation that many of its old policies were flawed, indeed counterproductive. Cooper–Church paved the way for Congress to repeal the Gulf of Tonkin Resolution and to the passage of the War Powers Act. In 1973, Church cosponsored the Case–Church amendment that prohibited any reintroduction of American forces into Southeast Asia without congressional authorization. Beginning that

[26] See, for example, Church, "The Doves Have Won and Don't Know It," 6 September 1970 on CBS television, 2.2/32/15, FCP; "The Doves Have Won," 11 September 1970, speech at Mills College of Education; "The Doves Are Winning–Don't Despair," 26 September 1970, speech at Colorado State University; and "The Unsung Victory of the Doves," December 1970, 10.6/8/8, FCP.

[27] Church, "The Doves Have Won and Don't Know It," 6 September 1970, 2.2/32/15, FCP.

same year, the Idaho senator chaired the Senate Select Committee hearings on abuses of power by American multinational corporations. These investigation would eventually expand to include examinations of abuses of power by the president, the FBI, and the CIA, including covert actions to overthrow governments and assassinate foreign leaders. By 1975, Church was using his position as chair of the Special Committee to fundamentally reshape and redirect American foreign policy.

Post-Vietnam Foreign Policy

The Watergate crisis confirmed all of the critics' fears about the growth of presidential power, and made clear to them the need for a greater congressional role in the making of the nation's foreign policy and the renewal of democratic ideals as a component of American policymaking. Church doubted that Watergate could have occurred without the "moral and political perversion generated by Vietnam." American policy had come "full circle. If 'dirty tricks' were acceptable in foreign policy, why, in the view of the White House . . . were they any less so in domestic affairs?" Connecting the battles over the direction of American policy in Vietnam to the political crisis at home, Church asked: "If it showed commendable realism for the President to circumvent Congress's war and treaty powers in the interest of a war policy he believed to be right, why . . . was it any less respectable to sabotage the electoral process, in order to re-elect a President whose policies they believed to be right?"[28]

For Church, the only solution was a broader definition of "national security in all of its varied dimensions." The problem was that "over the last thirty years, the United States has expended its major energies on the foreign military and political aspects of national security, but gradually necessity gave way to habit, pride, and even arrogance." This had led "people at the apex of power . . . to manipulate and circumvent the processes of American democracy." The tragedies of Vietnam and Watergate demanded a return to democratic values as a guide to American policymaking and a "renewed idealism – not the soaring idealism which bred in us the illusion of divine mandate to set the world right, but rather a chastened, realistic, non-perfectionist idealism which will enable us to strike a balance between our highest aspirations and our human limitations."[29]

This point of view, however, clashed directly with efforts by the new president, Gerald Ford, and Henry Kissinger, whom he kept on as secretary of state, to maintain the policy of containment and to preserve executive control over the making of foreign policy. Ford had supported U.S. policy in Vietnam since entering Congress during the Truman administration. He and Kissinger were very much a part of that generation of post–World War II leaders who embraced containment and supported a global role for the United States that included covert action, support for right-wing dictators, and the use of military

---

[28] Church, "Beyond Vietnam," 6 June 1973, 10.6/8/13, FCP.
[29] Ibid.

force abroad. Most recently, Ford had opposed the ending of American military intervention in Vietnam and voted against the War Powers Act. Vietnam did not shake either the president's or his secretary of state's conviction that anticommunism, containment, support for authoritarian regimes, and executive freedom of action must be the basis of American foreign policy. The withdrawal of American forces from Vietnam, therefore, did not bring an end to American support for the Saigon government and the regime of Nguyen Van Thieu. The Ford administration continued American aid to Thieu as it sought to prop up an independent South Vietnam. These efforts led to a series of clashes with Congress that demonstrated the changed domestic opinion on the policies that had led to the Vietnam War and American support for right-wing dictators.

In the fall of 1947, based on overly optimistic appraisals of the situation in South Vietnam, the Ford administration requested $1.5 billion in military aid for South Vietnam. In a September 13 meeting with Ford, Kissinger, and Scowcroft, the American ambassador to South Vietnam, Graham Martin, assured the president that the Thieu regime was gaining greater support from the people of South Vietnam and warranted increased American aid. Martin told Ford that "if I thought it was hopeless, I would tell you. We can make it." More funds, however, were necessary. Kissinger concurred, adding that "Vietnam is enormously important in the international perception of the United States."[30] In requesting the money from Congress, Kissinger framed his arguments in the familiar language of containment and credibility. A failure to grant the assistance, he claimed, would have a "corrosive effect on our interests beyond Indochina." Congress, in a vote that marked a compromise between supporters of the administration and those who opposed any further aid to the faltering Saigon regime, approved less than half the amount sought, $700 million.[31]

In January 1975, as the overall situation rapidly deteriorated in South Vietnam, Ford asked Congress for an additional $222 million in military aid. In support of its request, the administration conducted an extensive public relations campaign designed to force congressional approval. Again, the administration stressed the importance of maintaining credibility by keeping faith with an ally and the responsibility of the nation to South Vietnam. In addition, it revived the domino theory as a viable explanation for events and a basis for policymaking. On February 25, Kissinger warned reporters at a news conference that the loss of Saigon would have a devastating impact on U.S. prestige. He stated that he was concerned about the "general ability of other countries to rely on the word of the United States." Kissinger snapped that "this has serious consequences. I know it is fashionable to sneer at the word 'domino theory.'"[32]

Kissinger and Ford often returned to these same points over the next two months. In March, the secretary of state avowed that there would be no change

---

[30] Memorandum of Conversation, 13 September 1974, Scowcroft Memorandum, KS Files, Box A1, GRFL.

[31] Herring, *America's Longest War*, 263.

[32] *Department of State Bulletin*, 17 March 1975, 328.

in the fundamental premises that underlay American foreign policy. "We cannot abandon friends in one part of the world," Kissinger asserted, "without jeopardizing the security of our friends everywhere."[33] On St. Patrick's Day, Ford echoed this point when he argued that the events unfolding in Southeast Asia, and the concerns being expressed by Thailand and the Philippines about American commitments, "tend to validate the so-called domino theory." He continued by noting that "if we have one country after another – allies of the United States – losing faith in our word . . . I think the first one to go could vitally affect the national security of the United States."[34] On April 3, Ford reiterated that "there is a great deal of credibility to the domino theory."[35]

At an April 9 meeting of the National Security Council, Kissinger criticized the CIA for downplaying the significance of the defeat of South Vietnam and the fall of the Thieu regime. Just because everyone expected it, Kissinger argued, did not make it acceptable. While he agreed that "nobody can deny the ineptitude of the South Vietnamese," it was still true that the "rapid collapse" of Saigon "and our impotent reaction will not go unnoticed. I believe that we will see the consequences although they may not come quickly or in any predictable manner." Ford concluded the meeting with the assertion that, regarding Vietnam, "our policy, going back to Presidents Truman and Eisenhower, was the right policy. We did not always implement it well, and we may have made many mistakes. But it was the right policy."[36]

These exhortations failed to sway Congress. In early March, Ford implored a group of representatives, just returned from a fact-finding mission in Vietnam, to make the requested funds available. "We have a fighting chance," he said, to maintain the Thieu regime. "If we don't move, we have no chance. It will be a blot on the conscience of the United States."[37] For the opponents of the war, however, the stain on the American conscience was the war itself and American support for the corrupt and ineffective dictators who ruled South Vietnam. The request, therefore, was defeated. In April, following a special mission by General Fred Weyand to South Vietnam, the president sought $722 million in emergency military assistance. The weight of Weyand's report was that "United States credibility as an ally is at stake."[38] Congress, however, again refused the administration's request, but did approve $300 million to be used for the evacuation of Americans and for humanitarian purposes.

With the fall of Saigon, Kissinger and Ford made it clear that the administration had no plans to reevaluate American policy. In order to ensure that U.S. credibility was not questioned, Kissinger told reporters in April that the "United States must carry out some act, somewhere in the world which shows

[33] Kissinger quoted in Church, "Post Vietnam Foreign Policy," 10.6/8/13, FCP.
[34] *Department of State Bulletin*, 7 April 1975, 434.
[35] *Department of State Bulletin*, 28 April 1975, 544.
[36] NSC Meeting, 9 April 1975, NSC Meeting Minutes, KS Files, Box A4, GRFL.
[37] Memorandum of Conversation, 5 March 1975, Scowcroft Memorandum, KS Files, Box A5, GRFL.
[38] Weyand to Ford, 4 April 1975, CF: Far East, Vietnam, KS Files, Box A1, GRFL.

its determination to be a world power."[39] That same month, he noted in a speech that "we cannot achieve credibility by rhetoric," but that "we have it within our power to take charge of our future."[40] The president stated that "our determination to strengthen our ties with allies across both great oceans and to work for peace and stability around the world requires a clear demonstration." On May 6, Ford bluntly noted that there would be no change in overall policy. "We are going to maintain our leadership on a world-wide basis, and we want our friends to know that we will stand by them, and we want our potential adversaries to know that we will stand up to them."[41] As Ford recalled his thinking at the time in his memoirs, he believed that "in the wake of our humiliating retreat from Cambodia and South Vietnam . . . our allies around the world began to question our resolve." It was his determination that "as long as I was President . . . the U.S. would not abandon its commitments overseas. . . . Rhetoric alone, I knew, would not persuade anyone that America would stand firm. They would need to see proof of our resolve."[42] For the Ford administration it was still a bipolar world, and this demanded American action. As one senior administration official told *Time* magazine in early May 1975, "it wouldn't be a bad thing if the other side goes a step or two too far in trying to kick us while we're down. It would give us a chance to kick them back hard."[43]

The Cambodian seizure of the S. S. *Mayaguez* on Monday, May 12, provided an opportunity for Ford and Kissinger to kick back and attempt to reestablish the containment policy, American credibility, and executive dominance over foreign policy. The administration, expressing concern for the safety of the ship's crew, immediately saw the event as a test of American will and its ability to act with force. Kissinger shaped the discussion at the first NSC meeting by arguing that U.S. credibility was the prime issue. As Ford recalled, Kissinger "leaned forward . . . and with great emotion stressed the broad ramifications of the incident. The issues at stake went far beyond the seizure of the ship he said: they extended to international perceptions of U.S. resolve and will. If we failed to respond to the challenge, it would be a serious blow to our prestige around the world." That meant that "at some point the United States must draw the line. This is not our idea of the best such situation. . . . But we must act upon it now, and act firmly."[44] One participant in the meeting claimed that Kissinger went so far as to state that the lives of the crew "must unfortunately be a secondary consideration," a comment Kissinger later denied.[45] What is not in question was that Kissinger insisted throughout the incident that force must be used as soon as possible and that Ford agreed.

[39] Nathan, "The *Mayaguez*, Presidential War, and Congressional Senescence," 361.
[40] *Department of State Bulletin*, 5 May 1975, 557.
[41] *New York Times*, 4 May 1975, 7 May 1975.
[42] Ford, *A Time to Heal*, 275.
[43] *Time*, 26 May 1975, 9.
[44] Ford, *A Time to Heal*, 276.
[45] *Newsweek*, 26 May 1975, 16.

Too often, the *Mayaguez* affair is treated as the last act of the Vietnam War.[46] The reliance on force rather than negotiation serves to support that view, yet it neglects the debate concerning postwar foreign policy that provided the immediate context for the decisions reached. With the shah of Iran scheduled to arrive in Washington on May 15, followed by President Suharto of Indonesia in July, a determination to demonstrate American resolve in response to the taking of the *Mayaguez* became all that more pressing to administration officials. Both of these dictators continued to be seen as vital to the maintenance of stability and the protection of American interests in key Third World areas. Kissinger wrote to Ford, in preparation for the upcoming visit, that the shah was a man of "extraordinary ability and knowledge" who was concerned about "how much he can count on the U.S. to provide the world leadership, strength, and initiatives which he has seen as crucial in the period since World War II." Further, the secretary of state continued, "contributing to his concern are the problems we have had with respect to our commitments to Cambodia [and] Vietnam … and the difficulties the Administration has had in relations with Congress as well as a fear that Congress and the American people may be moving toward isolationism." The first item on Kissinger's list of topics to discuss was to "assure the Shah of our firm determination to continue to play a positive, active role in world affairs despite the recent setbacks in some areas."[47]

Similar concerns were central to the planning for Suharto's visit. Indonesia, Kissinger told Ford, was "potentially the most stabilizing element in Southeast Asia." The NSC emphasized this point, telling the president that Suharto's "visit comes at a time when his ostensibly non-aligned but strongly anti-communist government is deeply concerned with the problem of living with a communist Indochina." Suharto "fears the U.S. – especially the Congress and public – may now be losing its special interest in Indonesia and in supporting the non-communist Southeast Asian countries against the potential threat from Hanoi." The first objective, therefore, "is to assure Suharto" that "we will meet our commitments and continue supporting our friends in Southeast Asia."[48]

After the first NSC meeting on the *Mayaguez* crisis, reconnaissance planes were dispatched to search for the ship and crew; the aircraft carrier *Coral Sea* and other vessels from the Seventh Fleet were ordered to the area; and marines based in Okinawa and the Philippines were readied for deployment. A senior State Department official told the *New York Times* that "we know what we have to do, we just have to wait until the means to do it have arrived on the scene."

---

[46] See, for example, Shawcross, *Sideshow*; and Olson, *Mansfield and Vietnam*. For other examinations of the *Mayaguez* affair, see Lamb, *Belief Systems and Decision Making in the Mayaguez Crisis*; Guilmartin, *A Very Short War*; and U.S. Comptroller General, *Seizure of the Mayaguez*.

[47] Kissinger to Ford, May 1975, "Strategy for Your Discussions with the Shah of Iran"; Briefing Memorandum for Kissinger, 9 May 1975, Savage Files, Box 3, GRFL.

[48] Kissinger to Ford, 5 July 1975; Ingersoll to Ford, 1 July 1975, VIP Visits: Indonesia, KS Files, Box A6, GRFL.

As Ford wrote in his memoirs, "everyone agreed that we had to mount some response, but the military situation was discouraging."[49] On Tuesday, May 13, two NSC meetings were held to discuss the exact nature of the military response as the administration waited for the chance to attack.

With the necessary ships and personnel in place by Wednesday afternoon, the orders for a military operation were issued. At dawn on May 15, Cambodian time, marines launched an assault on Tang Island, despite the near-certainty that the crew members had been moved to a different location. In addition, bombing attacks were launched against the mainland. Ford had rejected the minimum option of using only the marines in favour of the "maximum display: rescuing the ship and her crew and then 'punishing' Cambodia by airstrikes." As Ford later explained, "Henry and I felt that we had to do more" than just rescue the ship and crew. "We wanted them to know we meant business."[50]

After the marines landed and were quickly pinned down by heavy fire on Tang Island, Phnom Penh radio announced the release of the ship. After discussions with Scowcroft and Kissinger, Ford decided to allow the air strikes to proceed. The *Mayaguez* was boarded by marines from the destroyer *Holt* at 9:00 P.M., Washington time, on May 15, approximately the same time that the crew was being released from the mainland. The *Mayaguez* crew was picked up just before 11:00 P.M. Ford learned that the entire crew was safe about fifteen minutes later. Orders were given for the final air assaults to take place as planned. When Scowcroft asked if there was "any reason for the Pentagon not to disengage," Kissinger replied, "no, but tell them to bomb the mainland. Let's look ferocious! Otherwise they will attack us as the ship leaves."[51]

Congressional leaders were divided in their reactions to the administration's actions. Representative Thomas ("Tip") O'Neill referred to the Cambodians as "those bastards" and advised the White House that "we can't let them get away with this. They'll harass us forever." Senator James Eastland encouraged the administration to "blow the hell out of them."[52] But Senator Mike Mansfield asked Ford why he would bomb an area where he believed the crew was being held. Would not air strikes endanger their lives? Ford responded that he did not know the exact location of the crew and that "sure, it was a risk, but one I had to take."[53] Overall, Congress supported the president and celebrated the quick "victory." Mansfield, however, represented many in Congress when he complained that members were not consulted, simply informed of the action. To them, the administration's attitude was disturbingly familiar. In the end, forty-one marines died and another forty-nine were wounded in operations that had no impact upon the release of the crew.

[49] *New York Times*, 14 May 1975; Ford, *A Time to Heal*, 276.
[50] Ford, *A Time to Heal*, 279.
[51] Lamb, *Belief Systems*, 96.
[52] Congressional Conversations with Charles Leppert, May 1975, "*Mayaguez* Seizure," Friedersdorf Files, Box 14, GRFL.
[53] Ford, *A Time to Heal*, 281.

Ford's actions were, nonetheless, popular with the public. The White House recorded support for the operation running fifteen to one in favor of the president's use of force, and Ford's approval rating shot up by 11 percent.[54] Yet just a month earlier that same public had supported Congress when it refused to send greater aid to South Vietnam and to recommit the United States to the fighting in Vietnam. The views that motivated Ford and Kissinger might prove successful in rallying support in a short "crisis" that could be portrayed as an attack on the United States, but that was very different from rebuilding the pre-Vietnam foreign policy consensus. As the Church Committee hearings would demonstrate, the majority of Americans had come to reject American intervention in the Third World and support for right-wing dictators.

The Church Committee

The establishment of the Senate Select Committee on Intelligence stemmed from a series of revelations concerning the CIA in the fall of 1974. In November, the *Progressive* published an explosive story that charged that former CIA Director Richard Helms had lied to Congress about CIA covert operations during its investigations of efforts on the part of American multinational corporations to destabilize Chile.[55] Ford had recently defended the CIA's actions by arguing that the Soviet Union spent "vastly more money than we do" on intelligence and covert operations. An angry Senator Church responded to the president's reasoning by declaring, "I thought there was a difference, and the difference is what it's all about," and promised he would hold hearings.[56] In an executive session of the Senate Foreign Relations Committee, Church told Kissinger that he found American policy toward Chile to be "appalling," "utterly unprincipled," and contradictory to stated American principles, leaving "a hallow ring when we begin to apply them to other aspects of American foreign policy." The United States had helped to overthrow a democratically elected government, and Church could not see how such a policy could be "squared with our traditional expression of the right of self-determination" for other people. When criticizing the Soviet Union, for example, "we have all kinds of references to moral principles here that distinguishes this country and what it stands for" in the world and its struggle with communism. Yet in Chile, the United States had supported the establishment of a military government that "has imposed a blood bath" and allowed no opposition. It was no wonder that people could not understand or square this policy with "traditional American principles."[57]

Another sensational revelation of CIA perfidy finally prompted the Senate to begin a formal investigation. On December 22, Seymour Hersh charged that

[54] Ibid., 284.
[55] Miller, "Criminal Negligence."
[56] Ashby and Gramer, *Fighting the Odds*, 469–70.
[57] Executive Session, SFRC, 19 September 1974, Wolthuis Files, Box 2, GRFL.

the CIA had been illegally investigating domestic groups and individuals. The Ford administration attempted to thwart a congressional probe by setting up a commission headed by Vice President Nelson Rockefeller to look into these and other charges. In the wake of the Vietnam War and Watergate, though, an executive inquiry was not trusted by most members of the Senate, and it voted overwhelmingly to establish the Select Committee on Intelligence Activities, to be chaired by Frank Church.[58]

Church decided that Chile would be the case study that the committee would use in its examination of covert activities. The American effort to block Salvadore Allende's election and the subsequent U.S. role in his overthrow had convinced Church and others that the United States had completely lost its moral compass. Chile, Church stated, "contained all of the elements...that are normally associated with covert operations" and "contained the most dramatic examples of abuse conflicting with our professed principles as a Nation and interfering with the right of the Chilean people to choose their own government by peaceful means in accordance with their own constitutional processes."[59] Obtaining the documents needed to demonstrate this, however, was another matter. The administration was not disposed to look favorably upon Senator Church's requests for information that he could use to strengthen a critique of American foreign policy and change the direction of U.S. relations with the Third World. When Church and other members of the committee met with Ford and Kissinger on 5 March 1975, it was clear that the administration was determined to provide as little assistance as possible. Although Church assured the president that the committee would respect legitimate security concerns, Ford believed that the committee's investigation could jeopardize American security and credibility, and lectured Church that "we are a great power and it is important the we be perceived as such." Intelligence, he stated, needs to be "to a certain extent...cloaked in mystery and held in awe." Kissinger added that "asking for information is one thing, but going through the files is another. The covert action files are very sensitive."[60]

As the investigation proceeded, Church managed to control leaks and maintain a spirit of bipartisanship. The spring and summer were, however, full of rumors and reports of assassination attempts and coups against such foreign leaders as Fidel Castro of Cuba, Rafael Trujillo of the Dominican Republic, Ngo Dinh Diem of South Vietnam, and Allende. Matters came to a head that fall when the Church Committee began its public hearings and made plans to publish its findings. Kissinger and others claimed that the hearing would adversely affect national security and damage the nation's intelligence-gathering activities, and warned the president that they would hamper his ability to conduct

---

[58] Johnson, *A Season of Inquiry*, 5–15.

[59] U. S.Congress, *Hearings on Covert Action*, 63–4.

[60] Johnson, *A Season of Inquiry*, 30; Memorandum, 5 March 1975, Friedersdorf Files, Box 7, GRFL.

foreign policy.[61] Moreover, the administration was furious when it learned that the committee intended to publish not only findings and suggestions, but also documents and official records. Claiming "executive privilege," the Ford White House sought to block the publication of any documents and to discredit the committee's work. In a memorandum approved by the president, a White House aide, Jack Marsh, contended that the documents in question "were highly classified and unsanitized." The president had "provided the documents on the express assumption that they would be used by the Committee in a responsible manner."[62] Kissinger and other senior staff agreed that the publication of the reports "will be extremely damaging to the United States" and will have "an appalling and shattering impact in the international community. Without question, it would do the gravest damage to our ability to play a positive role of leadership in world affairs . . . [and] would deal a serious blow to our foreign policy from which we could recover only with difficulty."[63]

Ford wrote Church at the end of October 1975 to urge the committee "not to make public the report on the subject of assassinations." The president asserted that any public disclosure of such allegations would "result in serious harm to the national interest and may endanger individuals." Church's response revealed the fundamental differences between the administration and the critics of American Cold War policies. In the senator's view, "the national interest is better served by letting the American people know the truth and complete story. A basic tenet of our democracy is that the people must be told of the mistakes of their government so that they may have the opportunity to correct them." Concerning the nation's reputation abroad, Church wrote Ford that he believed that other people would admire the United States "for keeping faith with our democratic ideals [more] than they will condemn us for the misconduct itself."[64]

On 9 November 1975, Church appeared on *Face the Nation* to respond to the Ford administration's claims that a report and the publishing of documents would harm the national interest. The administration, Church declared, needed to acknowledge the "wrongdoing of the CIA" rather than try to cover it up, and should be willing to accept the necessary changes to prevent any further actions that violated American laws and principles. Ford and Kissinger opposed the committee's investigation because it was bringing to light "the anatomy of this secret world" of covert activity and some of the "most unfortunate episodes in our history." Church was sorry that such events had ever taken place and that the committee had to exist to investigate them, "but it was our duty to do

[61] Memorandum, 18 September 1975, Rockefeller, Kissinger, and others to the president, Box 5, ND6, WHCF, GRFL.

[62] Memorandum, Marsh to Cheney, 29 October 1975, Cheney Files, Box 7, GRFL; see also Marsh to Ford, 1 November 1975, and Memorandum, Connor to Marsh, 14 November 1975, Presidential Handwriting Files, Box 31, GRFL.

[63] Memorandum; Marsh to Cheney; 29 October 1975, Cheney Files, Box 7; GRFL.

[64] Ford to Church, 31 October 1975; Church to Ford, 4 November 1975, 10.6/1/21, FCP.

it." The government belonged to the people, not the president, and "the people are entitled to know what their government had done that's been wrong as well as right." As for the questions of credibility, American self-esteem, and the potential damage to American relations with specific nations, Church thought the premise of each question was wrong. "After all," he asked, "what are we talking about here? Agencies of the government that are licensed to undertake [the] murder" of leaders who cannot possibly harm the security of the United States? "Is the President of the United States going to be a glorified godfather?" "The greatest strength of this nation," Church contended, "is that it has the capacity to look at what's gone wrong, look at the sins of the past, look at the wrongdoing in government, to expose what had to be exposed, and then to correct it." This made the United States "different from other countries," and this was what gave it influence in the world. People in other countries "admire us more for standing up to our democratic ideals than they have ever loathed us for whatever mistakes we've made," and "people who don't understand that ought not to be sitting in the seats of power."[65]

The administration's efforts to control the documents were not surprising, but the contretemps masked the larger issue at stake: the direction of American foreign policy. The investigations confirmed that the United States was involved in the overthrow of governments in Iran, Guatemala, the Congo, and Chile, among other nations, and had attempted to assassinate foreign rulers. As the Church Committee reports made clear, U.S. policy was still based upon the same assumptions that had led the nation into the Vietnam War, assumptions that justified the toppling of governments the United States opposed and supporting authoritarian regimes.[66]

For Church, American opposition to Allende was groundless, and he dismissed the claim that Chile was a danger to U.S. national security. As the report on Chile made clear, Kissinger's claims that the election of Allende would bring an end to constitutional democracy in that nation were wrong, and were contradicted by American intelligence reports. Allende was not creating a Soviet-style communist state, and the democratic process continued to work under his government. It was the United States and the groups it supported that threatened and ended democracy in Chile.[67] The same could be said for Iran, Guatemala, the Congo, and many other nations where the United States had opposed democratically elected governments and helped to replace them with right-wing dictators who were more to its liking.

What most bothered Church and the other critics was that American leaders had purposefully carried out actions that violated the announced principles and stated ideals of the nation and possibly subverted the Constitution. As evidence,

[65] *Face the Nation*, 9 November 1975, Nessen Files, Box 64, GRFL.
[66] U.S. Congress, *Covert Action in Chile: 1963–1973*; U.S. Congress, *Alleged Assassination Plots Involving Foreign Leaders*; U.S. Congress, *Final Report*.
[67] U.S. Congress, *Covert Action in Chile, 1963–1973*, 44–5, 51–6.

the committee highlighted the 1954 Doolittle Report. President Eisenhower had appointed General James Doolittle to conduct a study of the CIA and the need for covert activity. The Doolittle Report concluded:

It is now clear that we are facing an implacable enemy whose avowed objective is world domination by whatever means and at whatever cost. There are no rules in such a game. Hitherto acceptable norms do not apply. If the United States is to survive, long-standing American concepts of "fair play" must be reconsidered. We must develop effective espionage and counterespionage services and must learn to subvert, sabotage and destroy our enemies by more clever, more sophisticated, and more effective methods than those used against us. It may become necessary that the American people be made acquainted with, understand and support this fundamentally repugnant philosophy.[68]

Opponents found the adoption of this attitude to be the central flaw of American policy, which had led to the overthrow of duly elected governments, attempts to assassinate foreign leaders, and the support of right-wing of dictators who violated all of America's stated values in the name of anticommunism and stability. They believed that moral considerations were vital when making foreign policy decisions and that the public had to be kept informed to ensure that American actions represented the desires of the public and had its support.

The Church Committee concluded that the covert operations in Chile and elsewhere had come at high costs to the United States. Covert action almost inevitably became known and caused damage to the nation as the United States was seen as hypocritical, contradicting its own claims about the proper behavior of a nation in the world and its own values, and acting in violation of "its treaty commitments and principles of long standing." Even if the operations could be kept secret for long periods of time, there were other costs. Most notably, success often turned to failure. In addition to the questionable morality of supporting right-wing dictators, the policy, though providing short-term benefits, usually led to larger problems for the United States in the long run, mainly long-term instability. Dictatorships created political polarization, blocked any effective avenue for reform, destroyed the center, and created a backlash of anti-American sentiment that opened the door to radical nationalist movements that brought to power the very forms of government the United States most opposed and had originally sought to prevent. In the end, the type of "institutions that the United States most favored" were discredited by American actions.[69]

"The most important costs," in the opinion of the committee, "even of covert actions which remain secret, are those to American ideals of relations among nations and of constitutional government." The credibility and legitimate concerns and purposes of the United States were called into question, and the perceptions of America by others were colored by the "pervasiveness of covert action." In difficult times, and with many competing interests and crisies, covert action and the support of right-wing dictators seemed to bring simpler and

---

[68] U.S. Congress, *Final Report*, 52–3.
[69] U.S. Congress, *Covert Action in Chile, 1963–1973*, 54–5.

quicker solutions to complex problems. In the process, however, they only post-poned addressing the fundamental issues and kept the United States committed to a bipolar worldview that did not represent the reality of developments in the Third World. "Given the costs of covert action, it should be resorted to only to counter severe threats to the national security of the United States. It is far from clear that that was the case in Chile."[70] As the Church Committee concluded: "The United States must not adopt the tactics of the enemy.... Crisis makes it tempting to ignore the wise restraints that make men free. But each time we do so, each time the means we use are wrong, our inner strength, the strength which makes us free, is lessened."[71]

The Church Committee's final conclusions centered on the need for bet-ter statutory guidelines for the intelligence community and control over the "excessive, and at times self-defeating use of covert action" through better con-gressional oversight and "lawful disclosure of unneeded or unlawful secrets." Specifically, the committee sought a ban on assassinations and the subversion of democratically elected governments, combined with routine reviews of covert operations by Congress. There was no blanket prohibition against covert oper-ations. The committee recognized a need to use such methods, but only "when no other means will suffice to meet extraordinary circumstances involving grave threats to national security."[72] Ford sought to prevent drastic reforms by sub-mitting his own list of restrictions to Congress. Executive Order 11905 prohib-ited the undertaking of assassination efforts and other already illegal actions and recognized the principle of congressional oversight. The Senate and House, in turn, established new intelligence committees along the lines recommended by the Church Committee.

The committee's hearings and findings had an immediate impact on Amer-ican foreign policy. The collapse of the Salazar dictatorship in Lisbon led to a crisis in Angola as Portugal moved to grant it independence. The United States, seeking to ensure a pro-Western government, began in 1974 to fund two differ-ent noncommunist groups, the National Union for the Total Independence of Angola (UNITA) and the Front for the National Liberation of Angola (FNLA). By the time Angola gained its independence in November 1975, the United States had sent over $50 million in arms to these two groups, in addition to using the Mobutu government and South Africa to provide logistical support and other assistance. The situation was well tailored to raise the hackles of veteran cold warriors. Upon gaining independence, Angola descended into civil war, with the Soviet Union and Cuba now supporting the largest and most pow-erful faction, the Popular Movement for the Liberation of Angola (MPLA).[73]

---

[70] Ibid., 55–6.
[71] U.S. Congress, *Alleged Assassination Plots Involving Foreign Leaders*.
[72] The Church Committee's recommendations are summarized in the *Congressional Quarterly Almanac* 32, 304–7; see also U.S. Congress, *Final Report*.
[73] *New York Times*, 14 December 1975, and 19 December 1975; *Newsweek*, 22 December 1975, 38; see also Gleijeses, *Conflicting Missions*.

Ford increased covert aid to $32 million and sought increased funding from Congress for the American-backed forces as he sought to prevent a MPLA victory. The administration justified its actions as a necessary step to block Soviet expansion into Africa and to demonstrate to America's friends that they could count on support from Washington.[74]

Critics, however, worried that the administration was starting down a slippery slope of escalation and commitments in Africa similar to the incremental increases that had led to Vietnam, that any involvement in Angola would get the United States bogged down in a Vietnam-like situation in Africa and damage American relations with the rest of the continent. Nathaniel Davis, the State Department officer in charge of African affairs, urged negotiations to resolve the matter. When it became clear that the administration was determined to seek a military solution, he resigned in protest because he believed the administration was backing a group that could never win, creating a situation that would lead to a wider war that would include neighboring states, and publicly aligning the United States with the racist South African regime. The latter point was seen by opponents of the administration as a particularly devastating development for relations with the Third World.[75]

Davis's resignation caused widespread concern in Congress, and in December 1975 the Senate voted to block military expenditures in Angola. Ford complained that the Soviets had to be countered and wondered how the Senate could "take the position that the Soviet Union can act with impunity many thousands of miles away ... while we refuse any assistance to the majority of the local people who ask only for military equipment to defend themselves." Kissinger stressed that American credibility was on the line and that it was important that America's friends know that they had Washington's support.[76] In January 1976, prior to a House vote to authorize funds for Angola, Ford appealed to Speaker Carl Albert to support the measure because "resistance to Soviet expansion by military means must be a fundamental element of U.S. foreign policy." A failure to act "would inevitably lead our friends and supporters to conclusions about our steadfastness and resolve."[77]

The House, however, joined the Senate in rejecting the administration's request. Ford claimed that Congress "had lost its nerve." Kissinger believed that the votes demonstrated that "Congress is in a mood of destructiveness."[78] Opponents countered that Angola was locked in a civil war in which the United States had no role. Moreover, the MPLA was no more a Soviet puppet than the National Liberation Front had been in Vietnam. To intervene

---

[74] Davis, "The Angola Decision of 1975."

[75] *New York Times*, 14 December 1975, and 20 December 1975; Davis, "The Angola Decision of 1975."

[76] *Newsweek*, 29 December 1975, 7, and 19 January 1976, 29; Minutes, GOP Leadership Meeting, 10 December 1975, Wolthuis Files, Box 2, GRFL.

[77] Ford, *A Time to Heal*, 345–6, 358–9.

[78] Ford, *A Time to Heal*, 358–9; Memorandum of Conversation, "U.S.–Chilean Relations," 8 June 1976, Chile Declassification Project, Ford Library, Box 1, NA.

would lead only to an escalating commitment to a dictatorship without popular support that would further discredit the United States. Recent disclosure of illicit covert actions and the memory of Vietnam were too much for the administration to overcome. Congress and the American public wanted change and refused to commit national resources to places where most people did not find vital American interests threatened or to support authoritarian regimes.

The administration, however, remained committed to supporting right-wing dictators owing to its desire for stability, anticommunist regimes, and the protection of American economic interests, as was demonstrated in its efforts to maintain close relations with Indonesia. When Suharto arrived in Washington in July 1975, Ford and Kissinger went to great lengths to reassure the Indonesian dictator of American support. Ford began the meeting by stating that he was "just as concerned about our good relations with Indonesia" as ever, and that the United States was "firmly committed and interested in Southeast Asia. The events in Indochina have in no way diminished our interest or commitment in the area." Ford praised Suharto for bringing stability and economic progress to Indonesia, and promised closer American cooperation with and aid to his government. Suharto responded that he had "no fear that the United States will abandon its responsibility toward peace in the Southeast Asian region," praised the American effort in Vietnam, and thanked Ford for all the support he had received.[79]

Suharto turned the conversation to Indonesian military needs and the question of East Timor. He sought assurances that the Nixon Doctrine was still American policy and that the United States would continue to assist and support those countries facing potential insurgencies or external threats from communism. With the North's victory in Vietnam, Suharto believed that they were "running against time because the Communists are working very hard" throughout Southeast Asia. "Especially at this moment," the general stated, "intelligence and territorial operations are very important" in order to detect communist activity when it first arose and to build up the ability of nations to resist these attacks. Ford agreed to a joint commission to study Indonesia's needs, both military and economic, and to determine what increases in American weapons and loans would be necessary.[80]

The overthrow of Portugal's military dictatorship in 1974 had led to unrest in its colony of East Timor. Suharto made it clear that Indonesia did not believe it was possible for East Timor to become an independent nation and that the only solution was to have it "integrate into Indonesia." The problem was further compounded, he claimed, by the fact that "those who want independence are those who are communist influenced." Neither Ford nor Kissinger expressed any concern over this proposed solution to the issue.[81] The next

[79] Memorandum of Conversation, 5 July 1975, KS Files, Box 13, GRFL.
[80] Ibid.
[81] Ibid.

month, Kissinger told his staff that it was "quite clear that the Indonesians are going to take over [East Timor] sooner or later."[82]

Ford visited Indonesia in December 1975 on his way back to the United States from China. His trip was designed, as Kissinger wrote Ford, as "a dramatic reaffirmation of the significance we attach to our relations with Indonesia, the largest and most important non-Communist Southeast Asian state and a significant Third World country." The meeting in July had succeeded in convincing Suharto of "the steadiness of our commitment to our friends in Asia and our close ties with Indonesia in particular." In the post-Vietnam era, the secretary of state continued, U.S. interests in Indonesia were more important than ever to maintaining regional stability and containing the expansion of communism. "The speed with which Indochina fell upset Suharto's calculations that Indonesia would have an extended grace period to develop its internal strength before confronting a communist threat from the north." The Indonesian dictator, therefore, needed further reassurances "as to the constancy of US policy" toward Southeast Asia and U.S. support for his regime, and recognition of Indonesia's security concerns. In particular, Kissinger noted that the United States had to explain that it recognized "the problem that Timor poses for Indonesia" and its "willingness to see a merger of the territory with Indonesia take place with the assent of the inhabitants of Timor" because it was the "reasonable solution." A State Department briefing paper noted that Indonesia feared that East Timor's "backwardness and lack of economic viability would open it to pervasive outside – especially Chinese – influence which could spread into Indonesia."[83]

In their meeting on December 6, the president once again told Suharto that the United States would maintain its commitments in the region and support Indonesia. The Indonesian general raised the issue of East Timor, claiming that Portugal could no longer control the situation in its colony. He told Ford and Kissinger that, for the sake of Indonesia's security and that of the area, "we want your understanding if we deem it necessary to take rapid or drastic action." The president replied that the United States "will understand and will not press you on the issue," and gave the green light for an Indonesian invasion. "We understand the problem you have," Ford stated, "and the intentions you have." Kissinger raised the point that the use of U.S. arms could create a problem, because Congress had explicitly prohibited their use for any purpose other than self-defense. The secretary of state noted, however, that "it depends on how we construe it; whether it is in self defense or is a foreign operation." It would, however, be better if Indonesia waited until he and the president were back in Washington before acting, because they would be better "able to influence the reaction in America" if the attack occurred after their return.

---

[82] Staff Meeting, 12 August 1975, "East Timor Revisited," National Security Archive Electronic Briefing Book No. 62, Document 2, NSA.

[83] Kissinger to Ford and State Department Briefing Paper, 21 November 1975, "East Timor Revisited," National Security Archive Electronic Briefing Book No. 62, Documents 3 and 3A, NSA.

What was most important, Kissinger declared, was "that whatever you do succeeds quickly," adding that whenever they acted, he and Ford would "try to handle [it] in the best way possible."[84] Three days later, Ford told Republican congressional leaders that he "was very impressed with Suharto and his ability to hold 3000 islands together. He too is very anti-communist." He added that President Ferdinand Marcos of the Philippines "was also very impressive." While he "did do away with some parts of the Philippines democracy," he was an excellent ally and his actions "did help the economy." These nations "are very anti-communist and want the U.S. active in the Pacific." It was, therefore, important to maintain their confidence in American power and support.[85]

Ford and Kissinger approved of the invasion of East Timor by Indonesia knowing that it raised questions of legality over the use of American weapons, that the attack would be followed by repression against opponents of Indonesia's action, and that it violated any sense of self-determination in East Timor. These were costs that the administration was willing to pay to maintain its good relations with Indonesia and to demonstrate America's continued support of right-wing dictators. Having received the go-ahead from the United States, Indonesia invaded East Timor the day after Ford's meeting with Suharto, beginning a twenty-five-year occupation and war that resulted in the deaths of 60,000 to 100,000 East Timorese in the first year and over 200,000 people altogether.[86] The brutal occupation of East Timor by Indonesia ended only with Suharto's fall from power and the introduction of an international peacekeeping force in 1999.

Fragmented Consensus

The break-up of the foreign policy consensus on containment led to criticism of the administration's policy because it ignored human rights and morality in the making of foreign policy. Congress cut off arms shipments to Indonesia, and full relations were ultimately restored, in Kissinger's words, "not very willingly," but "illegally and beautifully."[87] It was not just the opponents of the Vietnam War, however, who came to question American support for right-wing dictators. The revelations and criticisms of American covert operations and support for nondemocratic governments led to a broader discussion of the question. Most notably, in October 1975, William Bundy, the brother of the former national security advisor to presidents Kennedy and Johnson, McGeorge Bundy, who had begun his government service under President Truman, held senior foreign policy positions in the Defense and State Departments under Presidents Kennedy and Johnson, and was now the editor of the journal of the Council

[84] Ford–Suharto Meeting," 6 December 1975, KS Files, Box A3, GRFL.
[85] Minutes, GOP Leadership Meeting, 10 December 1975, Wolthuis Files, Box 2, GRFL.
[86] "East Timor Revisited," National Security Archive Electronic Briefing Book No. 62, NSA.
[87] Transcript of Staff Meeting, 17 June 1976, "East Timor Revisited," National Security Archive Electronic Briefing Book No. 62, Document 6, NSA.

on Foreign Relations, *Foreign Affairs*, published in its pages an article on "Dictatorships and American Foreign Policy." It was the first time the issue had been taken up directly in a public forum by a member of the foreign policy establishment.

Bundy began by identifying what he saw as the three basic objectives of American foreign policy: physical security against attack, the creation of "an international environment in which the United States can survive and prosper," and the use of U.S. influence to encourage "the spread of more representative and responsive governments in the world." Invoking the traditional narrative of America's past, Bundy opined that the United States "has always been 'the City on the Hill,' from which should radiate a new conception of how men could live together and govern themselves." The question for Bundy was how well the nation balanced these goals with each other, particularly the last one, which he found unique to the United States.[88]

Skipping quickly over the first 170 years of the nation's history, and the origins of the logic and rationale behind U.S. support for right-wing dictatorships, Bundy noted that World War II had made opposition to "totalitarian and expansionist dictatorships a cornerstone of American policy." The development of the Cold War, however, had led to a dilemma for American foreign policy, what Bundy termed the "ambiguities," of supporting nondemocratic nations in the name of freedom. From General Francisco Franco in Spain, to Syngman Rhee in South Korea and Ngo Dinh Diem in South Vietnam, "one after another of our 'free world' allies came under governments of an increasingly repressive and dictatorial character." The problem was compounded in Iran and Guatemala, where "the real or fancied threat of communist political action led to decisive covert interventions in support of regimes not distinguished by truly democratic practices."[89]

At the height of the Cold War in the 1950s and 1960s, "these ambiguities hardly troubled an America engrossed in what she saw as a major job of preserving the national independence of new nations and protecting them from being taken over not only by an external power but by totalitarian methods of government against which there could be no later democratic recourse." As Bundy noted, a coherent and logical set of rationales were developed that justified the support of right-wing dictators, arguments that he found "were not without some weight" and that were accepted by conservatives and liberals alike. "After all, it was argued, almost none of these nations had any historical experience with democracy. Their various cultures and traditions had usually been authoritarian, and the practical problems of economic progress and effective organization were a peculiarly difficult test of embryonic democratic structures." Bundy had nicely summarized the central arguments used since the 1920s to defend American policy. Authoritarian regimes, so the claim went, were to be expected in certain areas of the world and were not as bad

[88] Bundy, "Dictatorships and American Foreign Policy," 51.
[89] Ibid., 54–6.

as totalitarian ones. Moreover, right-wing dictatorships could still be influenced by the United States and, following the logic of modernization theory, could still evolve into democratic governments, while there was no hope for political change in nations governed by totalitarian (i.e., communist) regimes. There was one other reason, as Bundy noted, why presidents and their advisors often supported right-wing dictators. By definition, "democracies are hard and wearying, sometimes even exasperating to deal with; dictatorships, on the other hand, can deliver what they promise in personal conversation – unless, of course, they happen to be deceiving massively."[90]

The Vietnam War, Bundy conceded, had created a crisis concerning the policy of supporting right-wing dictators. American efforts at nation building in South Vietnam had culminated in the Thieu dictatorship, "another of the negatives of that ghastly national experience." In addition, the war had distorted American priorities and values, and the "sense of unhappiness over compromises on the issue of dictatorship became one of the contributing factors in a growing feeling that America had become overextended." President Johnson, in part to make sure that the sacrifices in Vietnam were not in vain, had come to believe that supporting the Greek colonels was necessary to maintain Greece's freedom from communism, and in the process had "tarnished one of the early American postwar successes." The policy of supporting authoritarian regimes had reached its nadir, Bundy believed, under Richard Nixon, whose actions now made it necessary to question the decision to support right-wing dictators. Nixon had "managed to get on strained terms with almost every democratic government in the world, while condoning and cultivating dictatorial regimes both in great and lesser powers." This could be seen in America's unnecessary complete support for the Greek colonels and, most tragically, in Chile, where Nixon, Ford, and Kissinger had "compounded the tactical error of using the CIA by embracing the present military regime, which is repulsive by any normal American standard."[91]

These developments, Bundy concluded, had caused problems "both of policy and posture" for the United States. The clear impression left abroad was "that the United States no longer cares much about how nations are governed, that it might be guided (as in Chile) by the most dubious generalizations of the cold-war era, while at the same time shedding the ideals that by and large did have a substantial effect on American conduct even at the height of that embattled period." The damage was even greater at home. What Bundy termed the "revolt in Congress during the past year on foreign policy issues" had at its root "a deep and widespread feeling" in the nation "that the Realpolitik of President Nixon and Secretary Kissinger was neglecting something fairly basic to historic American foreign policy and to our sense of our own aspirations and standards."[92]

---

[90] Ibid., 56–7.
[91] Ibid., 57–8.
[92] Ibid., 58.

Bundy, however, was not willing to give up on the fundamental distinction between authoritarian and totalitarian regimes. He feared that the United States would now be more critical of "authoritarian regimes where there *is* still a measure of freedom, but [where] sins are visible, than we are on regimes which extinguished freedom totally long ago and so have no visible sins." He therefore called for objectivity in approaching dictatorships:

Let us judge those of the Right and those of the Left on the same scales; and let us recognize that there *are* important differences of degree: it matters whether a regime can in practice be replaced, even if only by coup techniques, or whether it has total control of its people; it matters whether there is some freedom of speech and some respect for human rights, or none of either; it matters if something real is being done for the lot of the people, even if paternalistically; it matters whether there is religious freedom, and the freedom of subgroups to express their culture.[93]

The main way in which the United States could deal with the ambiguities of supporting right-wing dictators was to recognize that American power to influence other nations resided mainly in its example. "The brief era," Bundy stated, "when we could seek to transform Germany and Japan, and where all over the world American Ambassadors were watched for their approval or disapproval is definitely over." The nations of the Third World were charting their own course between the superpowers and rejecting close alliances with either the United States or the Soviet Union. Bundy believed that there was a "democratic tide to history," but he rejected that part of modernization theory which held that it could be forced or easily achieved through specific government policies or notions such as nation building.[94]

In the end, Bundy never fully engaged the ambiguities he defined or satisfactorily resolved the problem of supporting right-wing dictatorships. For example, he asserted that the United States had to support General Park Chung Hee in South Korea "despite the deplorable excesses" of his rule because of the need to defend Japan, and that the shah of Iran and King Khalid of Saudi Arabia "are facts of life, and . . . products of their respective cultures" whose rule was vital to U.S. interests. The best that could be expected was that Washington's actions did not "alienate us from those who . . . may in time succeed them." Bundy, therefore, had no specific guidelines other than not to embrace such dictators uncritically as Ford and Kissinger were currently doing. He concluded the article by stating that the U.S. "concern for democracy, and our distaste for dictatorship, should have a much clearer weight in our total policies than they have had for some years past," because it mattered what the United States said it stood for. This meant a public posture that tilted more "in the direction of democracy and against dictatorships of any stripe." This would honor the nation's past and the upcoming bicentennial celebration of the Declaration of

93 Ibid., 58–9 (emphasis in the original).
94 Ibid., 59.

Independence.[95] How to make these judgments, the problems with the basic assumptions of Cold War policy, and how to resolve the dilemma of supporting dictatorships in the name of freedom – these questions were left unaddressed. Bundy's position was as far as most policymakers and adherents to the basic tenets of containment were willing to go in criticizing American policy and promoting change.

Nonetheless, the key tension at the center of American containment policy was now a contested issue. Those who no longer saw any value in a foreign policy that supported right-wing dictators, violated American principles, and endangered basic liberties at home sought more fundamental changes. Frank Church summarized these criticisms and views in a bicentennial speech entitled "The Erosion of Principle in American Foreign Policy: A Call for a New Morality." The proper guide to establishing a balance between security interests and morality, Church argued, could be found in the thoughts of the nation's founders. The senator noted that "an objective close to the hearts of our founders was to place the United States at the helm of moral leadership in the world." Yet since the end of World War II, the notion of leading by example had been replaced by American intervention and by support for some of the most brutal dictatorships in the world. As evidence, he listed CIA-orchestrated coups in Iran, Guatemala, and Chile; various assassination plots against foreign leaders, by three administrations; and support for dictators in Africa, Asia, and Latin America. For all its efforts, the country found itself involved in a divisive, immoral war in Vietnam and allied with nations that mocked "the professed ideals of the United States." Church asked, "If we have gained little" from these policies, "what then have we lost? I suggest we have lost – or grievously impaired – the good name of the United States from which we once drew a unique capacity to exercise matchless moral leadership." The damage stemmed from an "arrogance of power" that had led the United States into Vietnam and allowed Nixon to declare "like Caesar peering into the colonies from distant Rome" that the government of Chile was "unacceptable to the President of the United States." Church concluded that the solution was clear. American foreign policy "must be made to conform once more to our historic ideals, the . . . fundamental belief in freedom and popular government."[96] For Church, unlike Bundy, this meant distancing the United States from regimes such as South Korea's and Iran's because of their undemocratic practices and human rights violations.

Given the passions aroused by the Vietnam War and the distrust engendered by the Church Committee's investigations, it should not be surprising that no new consensus emerged concerning the direction of American foreign policy. The findings raised as many questions as they answered. Critics of U.S. foreign policy did not believe that the investigations went far enough or that the

[95] Ibid., 60.
[96] Church, "The Erosion of Principle in American Foreign Policy: A Call for a New Morality," 10.6/1/17, FCP.

restrictions produced sufficient checks on executive power. Conversely, supporters of containment and foreign intervention denounced the committee for impairing the nation's ability to act in the world and for attacking friends and allies. Such disagreements, Church believed, were to be expected, and he found the whole debate healthy for the nation and for the future of its foreign policy.

The Cooper–Church amendment marked a shift in national attitudes and the end of the Cold War consensus; it constituted a starting point for efforts to restore the proper balance in American government and to prevent despotism at home as well as abroad. Building upon a decade of mounting criticism of American imperialism and the imperial presidency, the Church Committee conducted one of the most far-reaching examinations and discussions of American foreign policy the nation had ever witnessed. Moreover, its challenge to the policy of containment, the national security state, and the imperial presidency helped to legitimize alternative views about the basis of America's policy, including questioning America's support for right-wing dictators. Vietnam had shattered the foreign policy consensus and allowed for alternative perspectives that challenged the conventional Cold War wisdom at a time when real change was possible in American foreign policy. The moral outrage of the Vietnam generation led to a challenge to the fundamental assumptions of the Cold War and the policy of supporting authoritarian regimes. These actions opened the door for Jimmy Carter's emphasis on human rights and his attempts to create a post–Cold War foreign policy.

5

A Fundamental Tenet of Foreign Policy

Jimmy Carter and Human Rights

From the first day of his presidency, Jimmy Carter set out to fundamentally alter the direction of American foreign policy. Coming to office after the disillusionment brought about by the Vietnam War, Watergate, and the Church Committee's revelations concerning American support for right-wing dictators and covert activities abroad, Carter promised to take American foreign policy in a new direction by shaping it around the principles of human rights and non-intervention. Carter faced the challenge of developing and implementing his new policy in opposition to the continuing Cold War axiom of containment of the Soviet Union. This was the central dilemma the president faced as he attempted to change American policy toward right-wing dictators. The tension between the quest for a more humane foreign policy and the old imperatives of security and stability was compounded by the economic problems that beset the United States throughout the 1970s. Carter recognized the limits these economic problems presented concerning American power and believed they made it essential that a new direction for American foreign policy be found. His human rights policy sought to create a post–Cold War foreign policy that placed American ideals first, changed the fundamental nature of American relations with the Third World, and reduced the costs of the Cold War while still protecting essential American interests.

Carter's policy built upon the changes various members of Congress and others were promoting by the mid-1970s. As Carter declared in his inaugural address, his goal was to create a lasting peace "based not on weapons of war but on international policies which reflect our own most precious values." This, he continued, was not just his goal, and would not be just his accomplishment. Rather, it reflected the desires of the American people and was an "affirmation of our nation's continuing moral strength and our belief in an undiminished, ever-expanding American dream."[1] The president, therefore, set out to restore America's moral credibility in the world by reducing "the identification of the

---

[1] *Public Papers of the Presidents: Carter, 1977*, vol. 1: 1–4.

United States with repugnant regimes," and by promoting human rights, self-determination, and nonintervention.[2] In the wake of Vietnam, Carter believed, these actions were the best means to protect American interests while diminishing the influence of the Soviet Union. As he later noted, Carter believed that "the respect for human rights is one of the most significant advantages of a free and democratic nation in the peaceful struggle for influence, and we should use that good weapon as effectively as possible."[3]

The consensus among scholars regarding Carter's foreign policy is negative. Gaddis Smith's *Morality, Reason and Power* is the most comprehensive examination and contains all of the critics' main points. Smith acknowledges that Carter attempted to implement a new approach to foreign policy based on human rights and long-term benefits to the United States rather than a narrow focus on competition with the Soviet Union. He finds that the president's policy, however, suffered from inconsistency and a perception of weakness that was exacerbated by Soviet actions around the world. In particular, the Soviet invasion of Afghanistan in 1979, Smith contends, led Carter to shift his focus away from human rights back to orthodox Cold War positions. In the end, Smith concludes, divisions within the administration, the actions of the Soviet Union, and the "impossibility of seeing clearly what needed to be done – all combined to make Carter's vision appear naïve."[4]

This interpretation does not take into account Carter's, and other top officials' in his administration, awareness of the difficulties, contradictions, potential inconsistencies, and problems inherent in a foreign policy shaped around American ideals and the principles of human rights. Indeed, these contradictions were often found in the differing views of Secretary of State Cyrus Vance and National Security Advisor Zbigniew Brzezinski. In those debates, the fundamental contradictions of American support for right-wing dictators were played out: the national security claims that containment was the best means to protect freedom clashed with a different paradigm of how American ideals should guide its foreign policy. Carter was committed to invoking traditional American values beyond just their utility in fighting communism; he wanted to construct a different framework for conducting relations with the world.

[2] Bloomfield, "The Carter Human Rights Policy: A Provisional Appraisal," 11 January 1981, 1, ZBP, Box 34, JCL.
[3] Carter, *Keeping Faith*, 149.
[4] Smith, *Morality, Reason and Power*, 247; for other assessments that find Carter's human rights policy naïve, simplistic, and inconsistent, see Muravchik, *The Uncertain Crusade*; Spencer, *The Carter Implosion*; Kaufman, *The Presidency of James Earl Carter, Jr.*; Drumbell, *The Carter Presidency*; Skidmore, *Reversing Course*; Smith, *America's Mission*; Rosati, "The Rise and Fall of America's First Post–Cold War Foreign Policy"; and Vavrina, "The Carter Human Rights Policy." For the most notable contemporary critical assessment, see Jeane Kirkpatrick, "Dictatorships and Double Standards" and "U.S. Security and Latin America." For favorable studies of Carter, see Brinkley, "The Rising Stock of Jimmy Carter"; Strong, *Working in the World*; and Hargrove, *Jimmy Carter as President*. For more complete historiographical discussions, see Stueck, "Placing Jimmy Carter's Foreign Policy"; and Schmitz and Walker, "Jimmy Carter and the Foreign Policy of Human Rights."

Thus, the president's human rights policy shaped all aspects of Carter's foreign policy. In 1977, the administration developed a comprehensive policy that met Carter's desire to change the basis of American foreign policy while still protecting vital American interests, and the implementation of this new policy dominated the first two years of Carter's presidency. In the face of multiple pressures and the crises in Iran and Nicaragua in 1978–79, Carter did compromise at times, but the president never abandoned his policy and goals even as he returned to more traditional Cold War policies in terms of relations with the Soviet Union. As the regimes of first the shah of Iran and then Anastasio Somoza were threatened, the president maintained his commitment to the essence of his human rights policy and rejected pleas for American intervention to save these two dictators and long-time allies of the United States. In his response to the crises in both nations, Carter followed the guidelines set out by his administration to implement his policy.

For critics of American support of right-wing dictators, the fall of the shah and Somoza provided further proof that the policy was inherently flawed. While it had protected American interests in the short run, support for these authoritarian regimes had destroyed the political center in these nations and led to an anti-American backlash that brought to power exactly the type of governments the United States most opposed, the fundamentalist Islamic Republic of the Ayatollah Khomeini in Iran and the communist Sandinistas in Nicaragua. Carter's efforts to redirect American foreign policy were questioned and challenged in both of these cases and in others by some who believed that he did not act decisively enough to help bring about change in the nations, and by others who continued to hold onto Cold War orthodoxy. Despite withering criticism from all sides, Carter constructed a new framework that made human rights a central element of all discussions and considerations of American foreign policy, and recast the debate over the meaning of American freedom and its role in the world.

Carter, therefore, succeeded in providing legitimacy to an alternative view of American foreign policy and opening up the discourse to more than just the concerns of the Cold War and containment. In the process, he shifted American policy toward right-wing dictators away from the support they had received for decades to a policy that took a critical stance toward such regimes and used human rights as one of the primary determinants in the decision-making process. While Carter's position was not a complete break with the past, authoritarian rulers could no longer automatically expect Washington's support, and they had to demonstrate they were enacting democratic reforms in order to continue to receive aid.

The Case for Human Rights

Carter's foreign policy of human rights marked a break with Cold War diplomacy. In the thirty years following World War II, the effort to contain communism had dominated American policy and had overridden all other concerns.

The Vietnam War, however, had prompted many to challenge the basic premises of the foreign policy consensus, including American support for right-wing dictators. By the 1970s, as the congressional investigations of covert operations in general, and in Chile in particular, had demonstrated, the disillusionment with American policy in the Third World and aid to authoritarian regimes had led to calls for a change in Cold War policies. While Richard Nixon's policy of détente was one response to this crisis, it did not question the fundamental assumptions of the containment policy, and many critics saw it as just a continuation of the Cold War under a new guise. Meanwhile, an alternative basis for foreign policy based on American values, human rights, and nonintervention was emerging in Congress.[5] As one commentator noted, "thanks to a backlash that had already developed against American support of friendly dictatorships, capped by the firestorm over Vietnam," Congress sought to tie "US economic and military assistance to the human rights dimension of recipient government behavior."[6]

In 1975, in response to the Church Committee's revelations, Congress passed the Harkin Amendment, named after Congressman Tom Harkin; the International Security Assistance and Arms Export Control Act was passed the following year. The Harkin amendment banned the continuation of economic assistance to nations consistently found to violate internationally recognized standards of human rights. It called upon the executive branch to submit written reports to Congress on human rights, defined how American assistance would be used to aid the people of various nations, and stipulated that if either house of Congress found fault with the president's position, it could cut off aid to that country through a concurrent resolution.[7]

The International Security Assistance and Arms Export Control Act stated that "a principal goal of the foreign policy of the United States is to promote the increased observance of internationally recognized human rights by all countries," and that the United States should withhold assistance from any nation whose government "engages in a consistent pattern of gross violations of internationally recognized human rights." It established the position in the State Department of the coordinator for human rights and humanitarian affairs, and required the secretary of state to provide "full and complete" reports to Congress on the human rights practices of nations receiving security assistance.[8]

Moreover, in 1975, the United States was one of thirty-five nations to sign the Helsinki Final Act, which included a section on the promotion of human

[5] At the same time, a neoconservative critique of American foreign policy emerged that made human rights a central issue. It, however, was focused mainly on criticizing the Soviet Union and its allies and on furthering Cold War objectives, and will be discussed in the next chapter.

[6] Bloomfield, "The Carter Human Rights Policy: A Provisional Appraisal," 11 January 1981, 6, ZBP, Box 34, JCL.

[7] "Guidelines on U.S. Foreign Policy for Human Rights," 2 February 1977, National Security Adviser:SF, Box 10–32, JCL.

[8] Bloomfield, "The Carter Human Rights Policy: A Provisional Appraisal," 11 January 1981, 6, ZBP, Box 34, JCL.

rights. The human rights portion was a Western European initiative that the Ford administration opposed because Kissinger did not want it to interfere with his pursuit of détente with the Soviet Union. Nonetheless, the Helsinki agreement was the first time since the signing of the United Nations Universal Declaration of Human Rights of 1948 that the United States had agreed to such provisions in an international treaty, and it provided a basis for proponents of human rights to demand a return to what they saw as the fundamental American ideals of the rights of individuals and opposition to dictatorships in the making of American foreign policy.

In combination with the experience in Vietnam, the disclosures of illicit covert actions and American support for brutal dictatorships had legitimized alternative views about America's role in the world and made possible Jimmy Carter's emphasis on human rights and his attempt to redirect American foreign policy away from the logic and policy of containment. A key theme of Carter's 1976 presidential campaign was a new direction in relations with the rest of the world, and he made morality the central organizing tenet of his message. He believed that the real strength of the United States rested in its ideals and promised to return to the values of the Founding Fathers. As Carter saw it, an enduring American principle was the opposition to tyranny and dictatorships. In his formal announcement that he was running for president, Carter asserted that "our government can and must represent the best and the highest values of those who voluntarily submit to its authority," and envisioned a world where the United States would "set a standard within the community of nations of courage, compassion, integrity, and dedication to basic human rights and freedoms."[9] What he sought, Carter stated early in his campaign, was a foreign policy "that reflects the decency and generosity and common sense of our own people."[10]

The central flaw in past American foreign policy, according to Carter, was that it too narrowly focused on the Soviet Union and did not encompass all of the nation's interests and values. He saw the United States as "strongest and most effective when morality and a commitment to freedom and democracy have been most clearly emphasized in our foreign policy."[11] As Carter stated in his first major speech on foreign policy in 1976, he saw the recent actions of the United States as weakening the moral standing of the nation. He declared that "every successful foreign policy we have had ... was successful because it reflected the best that was in us. And in every foreign policy that has failed– whether it was Vietnam, Cambodia, Chile, Angola, or the excesses of the CIA– our government forged ahead without consulting the American people, and did things that were contrary to our basic character." It was, therefore, "the responsibility of the President to restore the moral authority of this country in its conduct of foreign policy." Carter concluded that "policies that strengthen

---

[9] Carter, "Formal Announcement," in *Presidential Campaign 1976*, vol. 1, 4.
[10] Carter, "Relations Between the World's Democracies," ibid., 267.
[11] Carter, *Keeping Faith*, 142.

dictators or create refugees, policies that prolong suffering or postpone racial justice weaken that authority. Policies that encourage economic progress and social justice promote it."[12]

In accepting the Democratic nomination for president, Carter noted that there was a new mood in the nation. "We have been shaken by a tragic war and by scandals and broken promises at home." It was now time "for America to move and to speak not with boasting and belligerence but with a quiet strength, to depend in world affairs not merely on the size of an arsenal but on the nobility of ideas." Carter promised new leadership based on America's historic values, a rejection of compromises with right-wing dictatorships, and a foreign policy based upon American freedom and liberty, cooperation with Congress, and more openness with the America people. Maintaining peace and security was the foremost responsibility of any president. But, Carter opined, "peace is not the mere absence of war. Peace is the unceasing effort to preserve human rights...a combined demonstration of strength and good-will." The United States, Carter continued, "was the first nation to dedicate itself clearly to basic moral and philosophical principles: that all people are created equal and endowed with inalienable rights to life, liberty, and the pursuit of happiness." This had "created a basis for a unique role of America–that of a pioneer in shaping more decent and just relations among people and among societies. Today, two hundred years later, we must address ourselves to that role."[13]

Building upon the connection with the bicentennial of the United States, these ideas were consistent themes throughout Carter's campaign as he constructed a policy alternative to the national security state. The United States had to stand up for the values and principles set out in the Declaration of Independence and protect freedoms around the world. If it was to truly claim these rights, then the United States had to stand up for them both at home and abroad. Carter was sure that "when people are put in prison without trial and tortured and deprived of basic human rights that the President of the United States ought to have a right to express displeasure and do something about it. . . . I want our country to be the focal point for deep concern about human rights around the world."[14]

Demonstrating that his proposal to change the fundamental basis of American foreign policy was not merely campaign rhetoric, Carter announced in his inaugural address that the nation's "commitment to human rights must be absolute." He called upon the American people to "take on those moral duties which, when assumed, seem inevitably to be in our own best interest," and to let the "recent mistakes bring a resurgent commitment to the basic principles of our Nation." The best way to defend freedom and advance the national interest, Carter asserted, was to "demonstrate here that our democratic system

---

[12] Carter, "Our Foreign Relations," *Presidential Campaign 1976*, vol. 1, 111.
[13] Carter, "Our Nation's Past and Future," ibid., 347–51.
[14] Quoted in Brzezinski, *Power and Principle*, 125.

is worthy of emulation.... We will not behave in foreign places so as to violate our rules and standards here at home." The United States was "a proudly idealistic nation" whose "moral sense dictates a clearcut preference for those societies which share with us an abiding respect for individual human rights."[15] That same day, the United States Information Agency broadcast a speech that Carter had videotaped to the rest of the world. The president took this unusual step in order to reaffirm his commitment to human rights, self-determination, and nonintervention. He noted that he wished to assure other nations that the United States had "acquired a more mature perspective on the problems of the world" that "recognizes that we alone do not have all the answers to the world's problems." Still, Washington should and would take the lead in promoting human rights and peaceful resolutions to problems.[16]

Carter provided his most complete statement on behalf of a foreign policy based on human rights in his 22 May 1977 commencement address at Notre Dame University. The president declared that the United States should have a foreign policy "that is democratic, that is based on fundamental values, and that uses power and influence ... for humane purposes. We can also have a foreign policy that the American people both support and, for a change, know about and understand." Carter was convinced that continued support for repressive dictatorships was not only against American ideals but also harmful to the nation's self-interest. The United States needed to overcome its "inordinate fear of communism which once led us to embrace any dictator who joined us in that fear" and place its faith in its democratic system and principles. The basic problem with the containment policy, the president announced, was that "for too many years we've been willing to adopt the flawed and erroneous principles and tactics of our adversary, sometimes abandoning our own values for theirs. We've fought fire with fire, never thinking that fire is better quenched with water. This approach," he noted, "failed, with Vietnam the best example of its intellectual and moral poverty." The United States, he believed, had to return to its belief in self-determination and democracy. Carter announced he would follow a policy based upon a commitment to "human rights as a fundamental tenet of our foreign policy." The old policy was, according to Carter, based on an inaccurate reading of history and a misunderstanding of the development of democracies. "The great democracies are not free because we are strong and prosperous." Rather, Carter argued, "we are strong and influential and prosperous because we are free." Following a foreign policy based on human rights did not dictate a policy conducted by "rigid moral maxims." But it did demand a belief in the power of ideas and a toleration of change and diversity internationally. American policy was to be based on "a larger view of global change" rather than on the bipolar Cold War approach. It also needed to be "rooted in our moral values, which never change."[17]

[15] *Public Papers of the Presidents: Carter, 1977*, 1–4.
[16] Ibid., 4–5.
[17] Ibid., 954–62.

Developing a Post–Cold War Foreign Policy

While Carter believed that "words are action," he also acknowledged that "we live in a world that is imperfect and will always be imperfect," and that he "fully understood the limits of moral suasion."[18] Ideas need to be supported by a coherent policy designed to implement them. The administration, therefore, immediately began developing the necessary guidelines and framework to turn Carter's views into a workable policy. On 26 January 1977, Carter signed Presidential Review Memorandum 1. It called for a review of United States policy toward Latin America around the question of "what options are available to the United States policy to reflect a higher and more effective level of concern for fundamental human rights in all nations?"[19] Secretary of State Cyrus Vance sent a memorandum to all assistant secretaries noting that the president "has stressed this Administration's strong commitment to the promotion of human rights," and that in order to carry out this policy, the department needed "an overall human rights strategy and internal mechanisms for helping assure balanced decisions in this area." To this end, he asked Deputy Secretary of State Warren Christopher to establish a committee, the Interagency Group on Human Rights and Foreign Assistance, to coordinate policy, and requested the Policy Planning Staff "to formulate a broad human rights policy for my review."[20] Also that year, the position of coordinator for human rights and humanitarian affairs in the State Department, held by Patricia Derian, was upgraded to the assistant secretary level; National Security Advisor Zbigniew Brzezinski assigned Jessica Tuchman to coordinate human rights policy for the National Security Council; and each American embassy was instructed to designate a "human rights officer" from its staff.[21]

Vance's memo was accompanied by a preliminary outline for a human rights strategy and guidelines for developing a policy. The State Department recognized that the numerous differences among nations made it difficult to develop a single set of human rights positions and responses. Still, the department believed that all members should "at least ask the same questions and proceed as consistently as possible on the basis of comparable data and standards." Therefore, it set out general principles to be followed and a series of questions to be used in determining if there were violations of internationally recognized human rights as defined by the United Nations Universal Declaration of Human Rights of 1948. It was essential that the policy be developed with the long-range objective of a "gradual raising of world standards" that "recognized the complexities of issues involved" and the "impossibility of uniform, automatic responses to

---

[18] Ibid.

[19] Bloomfield, "The Carter Human Rights Policy: A Provisional Appraisal," 11 January 1981, 8, ZBP, Box 34, JCL.

[20] Vance, Memorandum for All Assistant Secretaries, "Human Rights," 2 February 1977, National Security Adviser:SF, Box 10–32, JCL.

[21] Bloomfield, "The Carter Human Rights Policy: A Provisional Appraisal," 11 January 1981, 15, ZBP, Box 34, JCL.

specific violations and consequent need for case-by-case responses." In formulating policy, the United States had to consider the nature and extent of the violations in a particular country, the "level of political development" in that nation, and the "direction of human rights trend" there. Specifically, it was essential to ask if the abuses were part of a greater pattern, what role the government played in perpetrating these actions, and whether there were any "special circumstances" that needed to be taken into consideration in "formulating policies for achieving progress on human rights." These considerations included other U.S. interests in the area, American influence in the region, the expected reaction of the government in question, possible responses by other nations, and various legal and cultural factors in the nation in question. Potential responses by the United States to human rights abuses were set out, ranging from quiet diplomacy and symbolic acts or statements of disapproval to punitive actions such as withholding aid and other means of assistance. These would be determined by the specific violations in each case – that is, whether the action to be taken was designed to help an individual victim, to "raise general human rights standards in a country," to disassociate the United States from a particular regime, or some mixture of these.[22]

The potential risks of such a policy were fully noted and broken down into three categories. First, there was the danger of being accused of impinging upon the sovereignty of other nations. This could have possible negative consequences for other American interests and might allow leaders to rally nationalist sentiment to oppose U.S. actions or provide an excuse for more severe repression. The second risk was setting back general human rights efforts if expectations were raised too high without concrete results, leading to a "loss of faith in human rights efforts." Moreover, there was the danger of a backlash if there was a major fiasco "such as replacement of [an] authoritarian regime by one more repressive following US criticism." Finally, a policy based on human rights opened the United States up to being criticized for inconsistency in the application of the policy, and to charges of a "lack of balance" or "double standard." Yet the risks of inaction were seen as greater. These dangers included the continued erosion of the political image of the United States as a supporter of freedom; injury to American interests and influence abroad, particularly among future democratic leaders in nations now ruled by dictators; and a loss of public support for American foreign policy.[23]

Finally, it was recommended that the United States start implementing the policy by selecting "a limited number of 'worst' cases – perhaps one or two in a region–on which to focus in the hope of gathering the largest possible number of allies, including milder authoritarian regimes in the 'Third World' in a common attempt to raise international standards gradually from the current 'bottom' of official murder and torture." This should begin with quiet diplomacy to point

---

[22] Draft Outline for a Human Rights Strategy for the United States" and "Guidelines for US Foreign Policy for Human Rights," 2 February 1977, National Security Adviser:SF, Box 10–32, JCL.
[23] Ibid.

out areas that needed improvement and the minimum steps necessary to avoid sanctions, and move to public criticism to add pressure and "to disassociate US clearly from a repressive regime." It was important that the United States employ a "diplomatic style that reduces symbols of US embrace of authoritarian regimes and serves to communicate various degrees of disapproval of repressive measures and appropriate degrees of detachment from repressive regimes."[24] This point is critical. Human rights policy was a framework for evaluating nations and asking questions about American policy. It was never meant to be implemented all at once, uniformly, or without regard for other concerns.

Vance had provided interim measures and a temporary framework to address the issue of human rights. The next step would be the development of a systematic and comprehensive "strategy and detailed plans to implement a more vigorous national policy to advance human rights around the world, including special implementing strategies for each geographic region to take common regional factors into account." Simultaneously, speeches would have to be made to clarify the United States position and to "establish a general US posture of concern for human rights, but which present some of the complexities involved, which avoid raising unrealistic expectations and which allay fears that we are embarked on a crusade to drastically alter or topple 100-odd governments around the world."[25]

While the Presidential Review Memorandum (PRM) was being drafted, Christopher and his staff began preparing speeches on human rights for the deputy secretary and the secretary of state to deliver. Speaking to the Senate Foreign Relations Committee on 7 March 1977, Christopher explained that the issue of human rights would no longer be separate from the rest of foreign policy, considered only after other objectives had been met. Rather, it would be "woven into the fabric of our foreign policy. If we are to do justice to our goals, we must always act with a concern to achieve practical results and with an awareness of the other demands of our diplomacy." The challenge was to reconcile the goal of a foreign policy based upon human rights with the more pragmatic aspects of international relations. This meant that the administration had to do more than just focus on gross violations of the rights of individuals – torture, murder, and imprisonment of political dissenters; rather, it had to extend its concern to basic human needs and civil and political liberties. The policy, therefore, would have to be flexible and would be executed on a "country by country basis, in each case balancing a political concern for human rights against economic or security goals."[26]

Secretary of State Vance spoke at the University of Georgia Law School on 30 April 1977. His speech was designed to meet the objective of setting out the general parameters of the human rights policy while demonstrating the complexities of the issue and lowering expectations for its goals and achievements.

[24] Ibid.
[25] Ibid.
[26] *Department of State Bulletin* 76, 289–91.

As Vance noted at the outset, "our human rights policy must be understood in order to be effective." There were, Vance declared, three main categories of human rights that concerned the United States: "the right to be free from governmental violation of the integrity of the person," such as torture or political imprisonment; the right to fulfill one's vital needs, such as the need for "food, shelter, health care, and education"; and "civil and political liberties," including freedom of thought, religion, speech, press, and assembly. Vance stated that the administration's policy was "to promote all these rights" as they were recognized by all nations through the United Nations Universal Declaration of Human Rights.[27]

Vance cautioned, however, that in pursuing a policy based on human rights it was necessary to remember "the limits of our power and of our wisdom. A sure formula for defeat of our goals would be a rigid, hubristic attempt to impose our values on others." It would be necessary to evaluate the "nature of the case that confronts us," to discern the "prospects for effective action," and to balance these concerns against other interests. Moreover, the United States would need to work with the United Nations and in cooperation with regional organizations and international financial institutions. Still, it was justifiable to expect positive results. Most immediately, Vance believed that the United States could help to bring "a rapid end to such gross violations" as torture and prolonged incarceration without charges. Other "results may be slower in coming but are no less worth pursuing. And we intend to let other countries know where we stand."[28]

The administration, Vance noted, realized that the process would be "a long journey" and that there were no illusions "that a call to the banner of human rights will bring sudden transformations in authoritarian societies." Still, "our faith in the dignity of the individual encourages us to believe that people in every society, according to their own traditions, will in time give their own expression to this fundamental aspiration." This new direction in American foreign policy was necessary, Vance concluded, because it was right; because the United States always risked, as the recent past indicated, paying a serious price when it sided with repression; and because American interests and security were "enhanced in a world that shares common freedoms." Other parts of the world had been inspired by the American Revolution and its "message of individual human freedom. That message has been our great national asset in times past. So it should be again."[29]

The Interagency Group on Human Rights and Foreign Assistance (the Christopher Group) held its first meeting on May 6, with representatives from various bureaus of the State Department, the Departments of Agriculture, Commerce, Defense, and Labor, the National Security Council, and the Export-Import Bank. In all, over forty people from various offices were in attendance.

[27] Ibid., 505–8.
[28] Ibid.
[29] Ibid.

Without a formal policy on human rights to guide the deliberations, the Christopher Group's main function was to carry out the appropriate reviews of specific aid proposals for nations as called for in congressional legislation, and not to attempt to formulate any general policy or long-term policies to promote human rights in specific nations. For various reasons, security assistance, food aid, development assistance, and actions by the International Monetary Fund and the International Fund for Agricultural Development were placed outside the review of the Christopher Group, but not excluded from overall human rights policy. This left the group to oversee the extension of loans and aid through Multilateral Development Banks, leaving the questions of overall policy and authority open.[30]

By early July, a final draft of the "Presidential Review Memorandum/NSC-28: Human Rights" was completed. Eighty-five pages long, it was distributed throughout the administration on July 8 by Warren Christopher. It stated that the primary objective of a "human rights policy is to encourage the respect that governments accord to human rights." The reasons for adopting a human rights policy were numerous. It was "based on national interest as well as our moral tradition and legal obligation." Most notably, it would fulfill the nation's moral obligations stemming from its history, heritage, and values; promote cooperation with Congress and strengthen domestic support "for our foreign policy by permitting the moral and ethical values of our people to be reflected in that policy"; carry out the laws of Congress "authorizing foreign assistance that our foreign policy promote increased observance of internationally recognized human rights by all countries"; strengthen the rule of law and the upholding of international agreements such as the Helsinki Final Act; protect American interests through the promotion of American values of individual freedom and human dignity, in contrast to totalitarianism; mark an effective means to combat communism and promote democratic forces in the Soviet Union and Eastern Europe and the development of more open societies; and substitute, "in our dealing with non-communist countries, a standard based on governmental behavior toward people for an increasingly outmoded Marxist-non-Marxist standard." All of this would "demonstrate that countries which violate basic human rights do so at a cost and, conversely, that countries with positive records or improving performance benefit tangibly and intangible [sic] from their efforts." Human rights objectives, therefore, "cannot be viewed in the abstract, and it should be obvious that pursuing them can be useful in achieving other broad or particular goals, such as greater credibility in the Third World."[31]

Consistent with all earlier documents and statements by the administration, the Presidential Review Memorandum on Human Rights derived its definitions

---

[30] Memorandum, Vance and Christopher to the President, 27 March 1978, WHCF: HR, Box HU-1, JCL; Rossiter and Smith, "Human Rights: The Carter Record, the Reagan Reaction;" Smith, *Morality*, 51.

[31] Presidential Review Memorandum/NSC-28: Human Rights, 7 July 1977 (hereafter PRM: Human Rights), 1, 8–11, Lipshutz Files, Box 19, JCL.

from the United Nations Universal Declaration of Human Rights and set out the three main categories of human rights as "the right to be free from governmental violations of the integrity of the person"; the "economic and social rights" of the individual to "food, shelter, health care, and education"; and "the right to enjoy civil and political liberties," notably freedom of thought, religion, assembly, press, and speech. The first group of violations, which included torture and cruel and inhuman treatment and punishment, arbitrary arrest, and denial of fair trail, was included in the definition without debate. The universal applicability of the second and third groups was challenged by some in the debate over policy, but these were expressly included by President Carter and remained at the center of his new policy. As the PRM noted, "a policy which subordinated these rights would not only be inconsistent with our humanitarian ideals and efforts, but would also be unacceptable in the Third World where the tendency is to view basic economic and social rights as the most important human rights of all." Any policy that ignored these "would be untrue to our heritage and basic values."[32]

The third group – civil and political rights – opened the policy up to criticism that it would be an effort to impose Western values and ideas on the non-Western world, "where they have no roots and relevance," and thus a continuation of previous paternalistic policies toward the Third World. This was rejected because "these rights have been formally espoused by virtually all governments and are of worldwide significance as a matter of practice." Moreover, there was no "inconsistency between political and civil rights on the one hand and economic development on the other." There was a need, however, "for caution to avoid giving our policy a parochial cast that appears to export American-style democracy." The PRM noted that the recent experiences "in Vietnam and elsewhere have taught us the limits of our power to influence the internal workings of other nations." The goal was the "enhancement of basic human rights in diverse societies; we do not seek to change governments" or to remake other countries in the image of the United States.[33]

A key debate was whether to give each group equal weight and consideration or to accord priority to the first group over the other two. There were good reasons to give all three equal status. Most notably, "if a priority is established it would represent a judgment that violations of the second and third groups are not as serious as those of the first group." This would be a difficult position to justify in many parts of the world, would be exploited by some regimes to their advantage, and would diminish the incentives for foreign governments to cooperate with the United States and "face up to basic economic, social and political issues represented by the second and third groups."[34]

Despite the validity of these concerns, the administration decided to give priority to the first group because it included the "most egregious and horrible

---

[32] Ibid., 1–3.
[33] Ibid., 3–4.
[34] Ibid., 5–6.

abuses of authority" deserving immediate attention and would "help direct and concentrate our efforts." Since violations of human rights in the first group were subject to "immediate curtailment – whereas violations of the second and third groups generally require more time to remedy – the opportunity to achieve tangible results in the short run may be greater with respect to the first group." Moreover, the approach would help to avoid some of the potential criticisms already noted, and make it easier to gain acceptance of the policy. Finally, the administration's strategy made sense because "in countries where the first group of rights is denied or threatened, the protection of those rights has obvious priority, since human life and fundamental human dignity is threatened." In nations where the first group of rights was generally observed, "but political and civil rights are abridged or non-existent, our policy should emphasize the promotion of those rights."[35]

Turning to the implementation of human rights policy, the PRM again noted the limits of the United States' ability to change human rights practices in other countries, even with substantial efforts on Washington's part. "Thus, our expectations must be realistic, and we must concentrate on encouraging the maximum possible *evolutionary* improvement." Although there might be exceptional cases where drastic improvements were made in a short period of time, and "certain exceptional circumstances in which we will affirmatively seek drastic improvements, e.g., our efforts to promote majority rule in Rhodesia," such gains should not be expected. The human rights policy would not be a failure if violations continued, "or are reduced in intensity or frequency very slowly or unevenly despite our best efforts." The objective was one that had "to be pursued over the long term."[36]

Still, the administration believed that it could achieve success. Stability was a slow, developing process, and real changes took time. It was believed that within the next few years, "our efforts will render many governments increasingly conscious of human rights considerations to the extent that they will, in a meaningful way, take such considerations into account in their policies." Indeed, the report claimed, "a number of governments have already begun to do so." The amount of time it would take for change would vary by country and by the nature of the human rights violations to be addressed, but the time frame for achieving expected improvements in group one would be shorter than those for the other two.[37]

In addition, it had to be kept in mind that there were "other major objectives of U.S. foreign policy that are of equal – and in some situations greater – importance" than human rights. These included the fundamental security of the nation, NATO solidarity, strategic arms limitation and other aspects of improving relations with the Soviet Union, peace in the Middle East, and normalization of relations with the People's Republic of China (PRC). Hence, there would be

[35] Ibid., 4–6.
[36] Ibid., 7–8 (emphasis in the original).
[37] Ibid.

"situations in which efforts to achieve our human rights goals will have to be modified, delayed or curtailed in deference to other important objectives." Still, it was stressed that "the clear implication of making the promotion of human rights a fundamental tenet of our foreign policy is that there will henceforth be fewer instances when promotion of human rights will be viewed as a marginal objective."[38]

In addition to such trade-offs, there were other important considerations and potential costs involved in implementing a human rights policy. The administration feared that its policy could create a backlash from other governments, thereby straining relations and worsening human rights conditions. There was also the concern that the inconsistencies inherent in any effort to implement a policy based on an abstract concept such as human rights would provoke criticism. Furthermore, unique cultural and social elements had to be distinguished from human rights violations. "Failure to recognize cultural conflicts," the document cautioned, "can damage our human rights and other objectives. We must constantly reassess our own standards to ensure that we are not confusing truly objectionable conduct with unfamiliar traditional patterns of relationship or conduct." Finally, a human rights policy dictated that military assistance to and cooperation with repressive governments be reduced or terminated. As this was done, it was expected that relations with those nations would deteriorate, and that this might "adversely affect U.S. security interests." But failure to take action would be even more costly. If the human rights policy were not fully implemented, there was sure to be "a backlash of public cynicism and Congressional impatience and distrust, which may have an inhibiting or detrimental effect on the whole range of the Administration's foreign policy."[39]

The administration was aware that all of these concerns had to be balanced in each scenario and, as noted above, that no single program, goal, or standard would be effective in promoting human rights throughout the world. There were too many factors to take into consideration to effectively legislate a mandated response to each, making a flexible policy within certain guidelines the best option. As the report noted, "there are vast differences among human rights conditions in various countries, and what may rise to the level of highly egregious in one country may not be properly so characterized in the setting of another country with different circumstances." American policy must, therefore, take such differences into account. It would be a problem if the United States were "*required* to take the same action . . . with respect to different countries, even though our own best assessment of the circumstances . . . might indicate that the mandated action would be inappropriate or that other actions should be taken instead."[40]

Although the same approach would not be effective in every situation, countries were grouped together into four categories designed to assist in analyzing

---

[38] Ibid., 12–13.
[39] Ibid., 13–16.
[40] Ibid., 25 (emphasis in the original).

and discussing policy with regards to human rights: Western democracies, communist states, Third World nations, and gross violators of human rights. In terms of the Western democracies, the administration would seek their support for its human rights policy in order to add weight to American efforts and to reinforce democratic tendencies in nations such as Greece, Portugal, and Spain that had only recently established or reestablished democratic governments. Concerning communist countries, it was necessary to "recognize that major changes in communist regimes and their human rights practices will not take place in the short-term; they are only likely to occur, if at all, gradually as the basic political and social structures of these countries change." Still, the administration believed that the United States could "positively influence trends in the long-term and encourage improvements in limited but important areas in the short-term," and that it should "emphasize implementation of the Helsinki Final Act."[41]

Because of its "pivotal importance," the Soviet Union merited special consideration apart from the other communist states. The administration acknowledged that the Soviet response to American human rights initiatives was "uniformly negative and increasingly sharp, explicitly suggesting that detente is threatened by our policy." Yet the administration believed that the objective of Soviet complaints was to reduce American public advocacy of human rights in order to decrease the "most embarrassing aspects for them," and that this did not pose a threat to other interests. Rather, Moscow would "continue to pursue its perceived interests in arms control, trade, scientific and cultural exchanges and other areas of our bilateral relations, regardless of our advocacy of human rights," because of the numerous gains and materials it received. Soviet leaders, laboring under the "inevitable strain of a massive arms race" and "a need to take increasing consumer demands into account and potential unrest in Eastern Europe," could not easily abandon détente "because of U.S. human rights advocacy." Ironically, the main problem in carrying out this policy came from domestic sources. Congressional and public demands for immediate changes in Soviet policy, particularly regarding Jewish immigration, made carrying out a policy focused on the long-term objectives of Carter's policy difficult to implement. There would be continued pressure, and possibly more legislation such as the Jackson–Vanik Amendment, which was designed to set rigid standards of human rights behavior by the Soviet Union and set automatic penalties. In the end, however, the administration believed that "security interests and human rights concerns can both be accommodated" in relations with the Soviet Union, and that it could manage the problem. Indeed, it had no choice, because a "failure to execute an appropriate human rights strategy with proper balance will detract from the political value of our human rights policy elsewhere in the world."[42]

[41] Ibid., 17–18.
[42] Ibid., 18–20.

Conversely, with regard to the People's Republic of China and the normalization of relations with that country, considerations other than human rights would take priority. There could be human rights initiatives, mainly concerning family reunification, after formal relations were established. Until then, the administration had decided not to focus on human rights in conducting relations with China. As the PRM declared, "we should recognize that with respect to human rights we will have little if any leverage with the PRC at this stage in its development."[43]

Turning to the Third World, the overall concern of the policy was to "reinforce positive human rights and democratic tendencies in the Third World, particularly in states that already have demonstrated good or improving human rights performance," and to "discourage the arbitrary use of power and promote a more equitable and humane social and economic order" in states where human rights values had yet to take root. American "relations with countries that systematically violate human rights" should be correct and in line with other interests, but not close. "The tone we set in our relations is important to the credibility and thus to the success of our overall policy objectives." To achieve success, the focus would be on the "promotion of economic and social rights." The administration believed that this would evoke the most positive responses from the various governments and people and demonstrate "a responsiveness, in human rights terms, to their most immediate goals."[44]

It was the last group of nations, the gross violators of human rights, that presented the most problems. A flexible strategy was required in order first to identify them and then to address the governments that showed "a consistent pattern of gross violations of internationally recognized human rights." On the one hand, the Harkin amendment and the International Security Assistance and Arms Export Control Act both called for a cessation of assistance to any consistent violators of human rights, but provided no guidelines for assessing which nations fell into this category. Trying to develop a single measure pointed up "the limitations in the human rights context of requiring uniform actions pursuant to a statutorily-prescribed standard of conduct." Again, the PRM emphasized that policy had to take into account the "vast differences among human rights conditions in various countries... what may rise to the level of highly egregious conduct in one country may not be properly so characterized in the setting of another country with different circumstance and a different history." That is, the determination that human rights violations were taking place did not necessarily answer the question of what action to take. On the other hand, there was the danger of the perception of inconsistency that demanded some uniform questions and consistent manner of evaluating the conditions in different nations. These were divided into three groups: the nature of the case, the potential effectiveness of any actions considered, and the impact of any

---

[43] Ibid., 20.
[44] Ibid., 21–2.

actions on other aspects of American policy. While these criteria did not provide an absolute formula for determining the appropriate action, they would serve as a guide to the implementation of effective measures to improve the human rights situation in different nations.[45]

To facilitate this, "an evaluation of the particular types of action . . . must be made in light of, and the action must be tailored to fit, the exigencies of the particular case at hand, consistent with the aims of the overall strategy for the country involved." Actions should begin with quiet diplomacy. "There would appear to be no point in starting with more drastic action that would catch an offending government by surprise." From there, it was emphasized that rewards, as well as penalties, would be an important and effective component of the policy. When used in conjunction with one another, the "carrot" and the "stick" could entice otherwise unyielding opponents into improving conditions. A wide range of tactics were available beyond quiet diplomacy, including public statements, withholding of various forms of aid, and the use of international agencies to support American policy.[46]

A more specific dilemma was posed by how to develop a policy toward friendly and allied nations, such as Iran and Nicaragua, that were guilty of various and consistent human rights violations. During the campaign and at the University of Notre Dame, Carter had criticized previous administrations for supporting authoritarian regimes in the name of national security and for forming alliances with any anticommunist government. The president was determined to "combine support for our more authoritarian allies and friends with the effective promotion of human rights within their countries. By inducing them to change their repressive policies," the United States "would enhance freedom and democracy, and help those who suffer from persecution." That could be accomplished "without replacing a rightist totalitarian regime with a leftist one of the same oppressive character."[47] In such states, the report noted, "we have considerable influence, especially where the regime does not feel overwhelmingly threatened by internal security problems," and the human rights policy "will offer reform-minded elements a viable alternative to communist rhetoric." It was also critical to remember that a "failure to express human rights concerns would give real support to the continuation of repressive regimes." Yet when these nations were linked to American security interests, there was a conflict of priorities that raised a whole new set of questions.[48]

This difficulty was combined with a further frustration noted in the conclusion of the PRM. "In inaugurating our human rights policy," the report observed, "we have been faced with the anomaly that the human rights advocates on the Hill who should be our greatest supporters have been frustrated because our actions fail to meet their optimistic expectations." They were joined

[45] Ibid., 23–31.
[46] Ibid., 31–8.
[47] Carter, *Keeping Faith*, 143.
[48] PRM: Human Rights, 76–7.

by those who sought to use human rights only as a means to hamper détente with the Soviet Union. This meant that the inevitable inconsistencies of the policy would bring criticism from both the right and the left. Notably, an "insistence on military assistance for offending regimes in which we have little security interest, especially in Latin America, will bring us under increasing fire from Congress as the year goes on unless we can produce visible results." Simultaneously, the administration expected others in Congress to use human rights "for publicly pillorying the Soviet Union and Eastern European countries." This meant that the administration, as it implemented its policy, needed to review the military aid programs and make sure that the administration bolstered its policy "with examples of the positive results" achieved.[49] The administration would not try to set an exact rule that gave priority to either human rights or security interests in dealing with right-wing dictators that were allies of the United States. Rather, it would take up the issue on a case-by-case basis, and use public praise combined with private coercion to bring about change in the human rights records of such governments. Policymakers believed that this would allow the administration to achieve its goals without threatening American security. Human rights was to be part of a framework that would, they believed, protect and promote freedom better than the policy of containment had allowed.

Presidential Directive on Human Rights

The beginning of 1978 provided an opportune time for the administration to assess its human rights policy after one year. Overall, it found progress along the lines set out in the Presidential Review Memorandum on Human Rights. Jessica Tuchman of the National Security Council asserted on 5 January 1978 that the "major accomplishment ... has been to raise this issue to the forefront of world consciousness. Virtually all world leaders are now concerned with human rights. They know that now their human rights image is a significant factor in their standing in the international community – as well as in their relations to the US." Just as "Earth Day added new words and concepts to the language ... Carter's human rights policy, just as dramatically, [has] added a new aspect to international relations." Tuchman continued by noting that while foreign governments, for obvious reasons, rarely attributed changes to U.S. pressure, nonetheless a careful analysis showed "the change of attitude of the U.S. government toward freedom" to be among the contributing factors in the improvement of human rights conditions in numerous countries, particularly in Latin America. And while in many instances the "liberalizing changes have been slight, and to an extent cosmetic ... for a released political prisoner or a writer who feels freer to write again, cosmetics are reality."[50]

---

[49] Ibid., 82–5.
[50] Tuchman to Aaron, "Assessment of Human Rights Accomplishments," 5 January 1978, WHCF:HR, Box HU-1, JCL.

In a more comprehensive evaluation prepared by Anthony Lake of the Policy Planning Staff of the State Department later that month, the overall conclusion reached was that the "human rights policy is off to a good start" but that, to no one's surprise, "problems remain." In terms of accomplishments, Lake found that given the human rights policy, "our post-Vietnam, post-Watergate image has been greatly improved," that the United States had taken the ideological initiative back from the Soviet Union, and that people who lived under oppressive regimes found the policy "especially appealing." The last point "underscores what many of us frequently forget–the US is a model for many countries; our influence transcends our political, economic, and military power and is strikingly important in ethical, cultural, and value areas." American leadership was encouraging others to take up the issue of human rights, and this increased international pressure had already led to the release of political prisoners in a dozen nations and to other improvements around the world. As a result, the report concluded, "a trend seems to have begun which could gather momentum and which already is improving the plight of individuals – including those under some still authoritarian regimes. And since individuals are what the human rights policy is primarily about, even the scattered and partial successes registered to date are important."[51]

The assessment found that there had been very little cost involved in pursuing the human rights policy up to this point. There must always be concern that "the 'destabilizing' effect of international attention to human rights may lead some authoritarian regimes to tighten domestic screws." Yet in the nations where this was a possibility, "those most effected seem to want us to continue our efforts: they apparently believe that the near-term risk is in their own long-term interest." Moreover, it was noted that the pursuit of human rights objectives, while they had yet to damage other U.S. aims, could still create conflicts with other foreign policy objectives and lead to conflicts with international organizations and allies. The greatest area of concern was in East Asia, where tensions between security issues and human rights concerns in South Korea and the Philippines needed to be closely watched. Lake observed that this "survey of all the damage our human rights advocacy might have caused to other US interests – but hasn't – is a useful reminder that other governments' concrete interest in cooperation with us is often as great as ours with them, and sometimes greater." Their needs in terms of security and economic aid allow the United States "considerable room for human rights advocacy, without serious damage to other US interests."[52]

In implementing its policy, however, Washington still had to avoid the danger of being perceived as "the self-appointed guardian of the world's morals, having shifted from an anti-communist crusade to one equally sanctimonious. If our human rights policy should come to be seen as designed to further some

---

[51] Lake to Vance, "The Human Rights Policy: An Interim Assessment," 16 January 1978, 1, 5–6, WHCF:HR, Box HU-1, JCL.
[52] Ibid., 6–10.

definition of US geopolitical interest, it would not only damage our ability to press the human rights cause, but also make us suspect on other issues." This was not yet the case. Indeed, "the human rights policy has gone far to reverse the situation where cooperation with us was based more on need than respect." But the "perception of moral arrogance" could still alter the balance.[53]

That there were inconsistencies in the application of the policy was neither surprising nor a problem. As Lake noted, "there are times when security consideration, or broader political factors, lead us to be 'softer' on some countries' human rights performance than others." Indeed, "it often is a close call just what action is most likely to produce improvement in a human rights situation." That meant that "one of the most difficult questions in the human rights business is what actions on our part are most likely to encourage a government to believe that further progress is worthwhile, without leading it to think we believe its human rights problem is solved." This was further complicated by the fact that the United States had "a good deal more leverage in Latin America" than in other regions of the world, and therefore appeared to be more active there than elsewhere. Moreover, while the administration publicly stated "that all three aspects of human rights (integrity of the person; economic rights; political rights) are equally important," Washington's loan decisions, consistent with the PRM on Human Rights, were "much tougher on governments which practice torture, arbitrary arrest and detention and other violations of the person." An effective policy, he concluded, could be implemented only on a case-by-case basis that took specific and unique factors in each nation into consideration, and avoided trying to use guidelines according to which "certain human rights violations will always receive certain treatment."[54]

In summary, Lake concluded that "the human rights policy may be the best thing this Administration has going for it. It has enormously improved America's international standing and our claim to moral leadership," helped countless numbers of individuals, and improved the political situation in many nations. Nevertheless, "any serious human rights policy will be subject to conflicting criticisms. Limiting ourselves to rhetoric and quiet diplomacy would produce (and deserve) charges of superficiality and hypocrisy," while "using material pressure (i.e., economic and military assistance) produces charges of moral arrogance." In addition, "softening our human rights advocacy in some cases to protect other American interests produces accusations of double standards," while "adjusting our tactics in order to try to be effective in different situations produces accusations of inconsistency." Some justification could be found for most of these criticisms, because "any policy as difficult and complex as this inevitably has a debit side. The balance, however, is decidedly positive, and we do not believe a major change is called for." The administration has "done a lot in a short time to inject new considerations into American foreign policy – to move beyond formal relations with other governments to a concern

---

[53] Ibid., 10.
[54] Ibid., 11–15.

with how our actions affect people living under those governments. We have done so with encouraging success, and with little if any cost."[55]

Still, the assessment concluded, the administration needed to do a better job of publicly explaining its policy "and the possibilities and limits of what we can hope to accomplish. Both the policy and its execution are far more complex than we have managed to convey." It was, of course, "in the nature of the problem that our performance will not become 'perfect.'" The State Department, therefore, "should go on the offensive to convey that message, and especially a sophisticated understanding of the obstacles we confront." To that end, Lake recommended that a presidential directive be issued "to clarify to the bureaucracy how the President views the policy, its application, and the range of instruments being used."[56]

On 17 February 1978, the Presidential Directive on Human Rights, NSC-30, was issued by Carter. It declared that "it shall be the major objective of U.S. foreign policy to promote the observance of human rights throughout the world. The policy shall be applied globally, but with due consideration to the cultural, political and historical characteristics of each nation, and to other fundamental U.S. interests with respect to the nation in question." Specifically, NSC-30 noted that it

shall be the objective of the U.S. human rights policy to reduce worldwide governmental violations of the integrity of the person (e.g., torture; cruel, inhuman or degrading treatment; arbitrary arrest or imprisonment; lengthy detention without trial, and assassination) and to enhance civil and political liberties (e.g., freedom of speech, of religion, of assembly, of movement and of the press; and the right to basic judicial protections).

It would also be a continuing United States objective to "promote basic economic and social rights (e.g., adequate food, education, shelter and health)." The promotion of human rights was to be carried out using all of the available diplomatic tools and international organizations available to the administration. Positive inducements would be preferred to sanctions as a way to encourage change, and those nations that improved their human rights conditions would receive preferential treatment and "special consideration in the allocation of U.S. foreign assistance."[57]

By the beginning of 1978, the Carter administration had successfully developed and institutionalized its policy of human rights and made it a central factor in American foreign policy decisions. Yet, as Vance and Christopher pointed out to the president, the administration had "acted with moderation in these matters." Out of more than four hundred votes on loans by International Financial Institutions, the administration voted against nine and abstained on

---

[55] Ibid., 20–1.

[56] Ibid., 21, 16.

[57] Presidential Directive/NSC-30, Human Rights, 17 February 1978, Vertical File: Presidential Directives, JCL.

fourteen loans on human rights grounds. In terms of bilateral aid, the record was equally moderate; the administration deferred on only twenty-two cases of assistance, out of hundreds of requests, based on human rights considerations. Together, these decisions concerned a total of only thirteen countries (Argentina, Benin, Central African Empire, Chile, El Salvador, Ethiopia, Guinea, Nicaragua, Paraguay, Philippines, South Korea, South Yemen, and Uruguay). All of this reflected the effort to place a "greater emphasis on 'rewards' rather than 'sanctions.'" Carter pointed out in a letter to congressional critics that this record reflected the administration's desire to first use "positive actions and normal diplomatic channels in pursuing our human rights objectives," and to direct "a greater share of our bilateral and multilateral assistance to governments that respect human rights."[58]

On 6 December 1978, speaking at a White House ceremony commemorating the thirtieth anniversary of the UN Universal Declaration of Human Rights, Carter promised that "as long as I am President, the Government of the United States will continue, throughout the world, to enhance human rights." What united the nation, the president asserted, was its peoples' "common belief in peace, in a free society, and in a common devotion to the liberties enshrined in our Constitution" that made the United States "a nation founded on an idea of human rights." In conducting policy toward dictatorships and regimes "which persist in wholesale violations of human rights, we will not hesitate to convey our outrage nor will we pretend that our relations are unaffected." Addressing his critics and the question of the effectiveness of his efforts, Carter stated that the human rights policy "has contributed to an atmosphere of change – sometimes disturbing – but which had encouraged progress in many ways and in many places." He noted the release of thousands of political prisoners, the easing of repression in many nations, and the movement toward the rule of law and democratic institutions. "To those who doubt the wisdom of our dedication," Carter declared: "Ask the victims. Ask the exiles." As Carter noted, "not a single one of those who is actually taking risks or suffering for human rights has ever asked me to desist in our support of basic human rights. From the prisons, from the camps, from the enforced exiles, we receive one message – speak up, persevere, let the voice of freedom be heard."[59]

The president reiterated that "policies regarding human rights count very much in the character of our own relations with other individual countries."[60] While Carter preferred to use rewards and positive steps rather than sanctions in carrying out these relations, the actions of some nations, such as Chile, demanded an immediate change in American policy. Because of the serious nature of the human rights abuses there, and the recent Church Committee

[58] Vance and Christopher to Carter, 27 March 1978, and Carter to Moorhead, 12 April 1978, WHCF:HR, Box HU-1, JCL.
[59] *Department of State Bulletin*, January 1979, 1–2.
[60] Ibid.

revelations about the American role in the overthrow of the Allende government and the establishment of the Pinochet regime, Chile became the first nation in Latin America where the president began to implement his policy.

Human Rights and Chile

As the discussions of the administration's human rights policy made clear, Carter was determined to change the nature of U.S. relations with Latin America. He sought to end the paternalistic, interventionist policies and support for right-wing dictators that had marked American policy throughout the twentieth century and to replace it with a focus on human rights, multilateral cooperation, and self-determination. Making Latin America the subject of his first PRM, and signing the Panama Canal Treaties in September 1977, which provided for the return of the canal zone to Panama by the end of the century, were clear signs of the different directions that Carter intended to take. In April 1977, the president set out his views on U.S.–Latin American relations in a speech to the Organization of American States (OAS). Carter noted that his policies would be guided by respect for the "individuality and the sovereignty" of all nations in the hemisphere, human rights, and economic development. Carter stated that "our values and yours requires us to combat abuses of individual freedom, including those caused by political, social, and economic injustices. Our own concerns for these values will naturally influence our relations with countries of this hemisphere and throughout the world." In stark contrast to the words of his predecessors, Carter declared that "you will find this country, the United States of America, eager to stand beside those who respect human rights and which promote democratic ideals." He indicated his desire to work closely with the OAS and other international groups to promote human rights. In a direct challenge to Chile and other military dictatorships, Carter praised the Inter-American Commission on Human Rights for its "valuable services" and noted that "it deserves increased support from all our governments." The United States, he concluded, believes "deeply in the preservation and the enhancement of human rights" and was looking forward to "coordinated and multilateral action in this field." Carter saw multilateral agencies as a critical component of his human rights policy, and as necessary to counter the perception that the policy was just another form of American intervention.[61]

Even before Carter's policy on human rights was complete, it was having a tangible impact on other nations as it created worries among the military dictators and hope for those who suffered under their rule. As a joint State–CIA intelligence report in April 1977 noted, the administration's human rights initiatives "have aroused considerable resentment" among the military regimes in Latin America, who saw themselves directly challenged. They were "angered by what they regard as US failure to understand and make allowances for their political and internal security problems." Moreover, they wanted to avoid taking any

---

[61] *Public Papers of the Presidents: Carter, 1977*, vol. 1: 611–16.

action "that could be construed as caving in to US pressure."[62] Pinochet had, however, immediately responded to the election of Carter as president by taking a series of steps to improve Chile's image on human rights. In late 1976 and early 1977, the general ordered the release of over three hundred political prisoners, changed trial procedures for those held by the military, closed two detention centers, and promised future elections and a return to democratic government. All this was done in the hope of preempting any action by the new administration, and maintaining Washington's support and the flow of aid and weapons.

Yet many issues that concerned the Carter administration about Chile remained unchanged. Before it would consider extending aid to Chile, the administration sought an end to the state of siege, restoration of due process for detainees, information on those who had disappeared, and a specific timetable for the restoration of democracy rather than a vague promise of reform sometime in the future. In addition, there was the unresolved case of the murders of Orlando Letelier, the former Chilean ambassador to the United States, and his assistant Ronni Moffitt, a U.S. citizen, in Washington, D.C., in September 1976. It was known that Chilean intelligence officers, working through Operation Condor, a coordinated effort by the Southern Cone military regimes to attack and often kill political opponents in exile, were responsible for the assassination, and that Pinochet's government was protecting them. As a result, Chile was classified as one of the "gross violators" of human rights in the world, and the Carter administration reversed the Nixon and Ford administrations' policy of support for Pinochet, voted against international loans to Chile, and cut bilateral and military aid.

In May, in an highly unusual and politically symbolic act that was designed to demonstrate Carter's new policy, the administration welcomed Eduardo Frei, the former president of Chile and leader of its Christian Democratic Party, to Washington, where he met with Vice President Walter Mondale and Brzezinski to discuss Carter's policy and the future of Chile. Frei told them that he thought "President Carter's concern for human rights will have a great impact on Chile and on all of Latin America." While the policy might create short-term problems and repression, "in the long term it is the only way," and the "position of the United States was key to the future of Chile." Brzezinski responded that the administration was not on a crusade, but that it did seek "to create a moral framework" for the conduct of relations and actions of governments. Frei agreed, and noted that what was necessary was a clear signal "that unless Chile grants at least a minimal respect for human rights, for labor association, and for other political activity," it would not find a welcome in Washington. Mondale assured Frei of the administration's commitment to human rights and the encouragement of democracy in other nations. The president was "for human rights not because we are against Communism, but because we believe in human rights." In the past, Mondale said, "we had gotten these two

---

[62] "Report – Human Rights," 20 April 1977, Chile Declassification Project, Carter Library, Box 1, NA.

objectives–anti-communism and human rights–confused, and we often intervened in a clumsy way; a good example is Chile." Mondale continued by noting that as a member of the Church Committee he had been "ashamed to learn of our behavior in Chile," and that previous covert action "imposes on us a special responsibility to deal with the situation in Chile with good sense and respect for our own values as well as Chile's."[63]

The administration made it clear, in messages from both Vance and Christopher, that Chile could not expect any American support without a greater effort to address human rights abuses and restore democracy. Assistant Secretary of State Terence Todman was sent to Chile in August to make clear American policy and outline demands for change. He was instructed to explain that while the administration saw the release of some political prisoners and the reported decline of torture and arbitrary arrests as positive steps, there was much more Chile needed to do. Specifically, there was the need to lift the state of siege, restore due process, account for all prisoners, and allow visits by groups such as the Inter-American Human Rights Commission Working Group to verify the government's claims.[64] Todman was instructed to tell Santiago that any steps the "government takes towards restoring an open, responsive, and representative process or improving the human rights situation is something which we will applaud." But he was also to note that is was "necessary to make two distinctions: between an announcement of intention and the implementation of a policy, and between real and cosmetic changes."[65]

Pinochet came to Washington for the signing of the Panama Canal Treaties and met with Carter on 6 September 1977. After discussing security issues concerning Peru and Bolivia, and nuclear nonproliferation, Carter turned to human rights. He took care to note the progress made in prisoner releases and in reforming trial procedures, and said that he did not want anything to stand in the way of restoring the traditional good relations between the United States and Chile. Carter, therefore, "hoped that the charges and allegations regarding deprivations of human rights in Chile could be answered," and invited Pinochet's response. The Chilean dictator cast the problem in Cold War terms. He claimed that Chile was still emerging from a "difficult period during which the Marxist-Leninist government had no respect for human rights" and that "the military coup was designed precisely to preserve human rights." Pinochet did acknowledge some abuses during the initial period of the junta's rule, but stated that "there are no political prisoners" in Chile, and that all those arrested received fair trials. In addition, he argued that "Chile has freedom of the press, freedom of thought and freedom of travel. Restrictions remain, but they are to keep the nation from being destroyed."[66]

[63] Memorandum of Conversation, 25 May 1977, Chile Declassification Project, Carter Library, Box 1, NA.
[64] Popper to Todman, 26 July 1977, Chile Declassification Project, Carter Library, Box 1, NA.
[65] Pastor to Brzezinski, 9 August 1977, SOF:NSA: Brzezinski, CF, Box 7, JCL.
[66] Memorandum of Conversation, 6 September 1977, Chile Declassification Project, Carter Library, Box 1, NA.

The reply that Pinochet received was drastically different from Kissinger's response a little over a year before. Carter diplomatically stated that he "had no inclination to disagree with Pinochet's assessment of the situation in Chile," but noted that "in the eyes of the world Chile still had a human rights problem." The president wondered how Pinochet thought that could be alleviated. The general responded that the problem stemmed from the fact "that Chile was the victim of a vast and successful Marxist propaganda campaign." Given this claim, Carter asked if Pinochet would allow outside observers from the UN Human Rights Commission into Chile, or two observers from the United Nations sent without publicity. The general rejected these suggestions, dismissing the UN agencies as politicized and unfair. Carter, however, was undeterred and told Pinochet that there could not be any recognition of progress on human rights in Chile "unless an independent inspection occurs."[67]

Carter again raised the issue of outside observers in a 31 October 1977 letter to Pinochet. He noted that "human rights considerations remain the major obstacle to restoration of traditionally close relations between the United States and Chile," and that there could be no improvement "without increased evidence that your government is taking steps to safeguard and promote human rights and to restore to Chile the vigorous and open democratic tradition of which all Chileans have justly been proud." To that end, the president stated that he believed that Chile had to admit independent inspectors to make a report. Without such action, restrictions on American aid and other assistance would remain in place. In a direct refutation of Pinochet's claims, Carter praised the important role that nongovernmental human rights organizations had played in advancing human rights.[68] In a lengthy response, Pinochet once again dismissed the UN Human Rights Commission as incompetent at best and as a manifestation of interference in the internal affairs of Chile.[69]

Carter tried one more time to get Pinochet to agree to host the UN Commission. He noted that the United States had cosponsored a United Nations resolution on the human rights situation in Chile because of its "concern over the welfare and freedom of the people of Chile in the light of persistent reports of gross violations of human rights." In December 1977, the UN General Assembly had voted 96 to 14 to condemn Chile for human rights violations. The president, therefore, hoped that a visit to Chile by the Human Rights Commission could be worked out. Carter then went point by point through Pinochet's criticisms of the commission and its work, dismissing each and every objection. In the process, he left no doubt that he was going to stand by his policy and position, and that Chile could not expect any improvement of relations until it made concessions.[70] In what the National Security Council described as an "icy" response, Pinochet continued to express his hostility to the United

---

[67] Ibid.

[68] Carter to Pinochet, 31 October 1977, Chile Declassification Project, Carter Library, Box 1, NA.

[69] Pinochet to Carter, 9 November 1977, Chile Declassification Project, Carter Library, Box 1, NA.

[70] Carter to Pinochet, 17 January 1978, Chile Declassification Project, Carter Library, Box 1, NA.

Nations and any visit by the Human Rights Commission. He was, the NSC noted, "bitter over what he sees as our failure to understand Chile's position and our interference in Chilean internal affairs." It was decided that the president should not respond again, as Pinochet knew full well the administration's views and had rejected them.[71]

The Carter administration continued throughout its term in office to pressure Chile on the question of human rights, and relations remained strained due to the continuation of "ugly trends in Chilean human rights behavior."[72] In May 1979, the Chilean courts denied a request by the United States to extradite the three men indicted in the murders of Letelier and Moffitt. Ambassador George Landau was instructed to inform the Pinochet government that the United States would appeal the ruling, and that if the decision were not reversed, Chile could expect further "severe" sanctions from Washington.[73] When the appeal was denied in the fall, the administration debated exactly what actions should be taken. The State Department called for even more restrictive sanctions in order to make clear American opposition to an act of terrorism inside the United States, to demonstrate how seriously the administration took this decision, and to signal the world that it would use its influence to punish those who abused human rights and engaged in terrorism. In addition, congressional opponents of American support for Pinochet demanded limits on private bank loans to Santiago and even called for breaking relations with Chile.

Members of the Department of Defense, reflecting their opposition to Carter's human rights policy and adherence to the tenets of containment, feared that further sanctions would undermine the U.S. effort to contain communism in Latin America. Secretary of Defense Harold Brown argued that further sanctions would result in instability in Chile and in the southern cone of Latin America, which was dominated by military dictatorships, and that this threatened to bring more revolutions to the hemisphere similar to the ones in Nicaragua and El Salvador. "Given the serious problems we have in Central America and the instability in the Caribbean," Brown wrote Vance, "this is scarcely an opportune time to signal a further disengagement from the Hemisphere by precipitately cutting our military representation in Chile" and aid to the regime. He argued that U.S. sanctions were increasing Soviet influence in Latin America, and that "it would be especially unfortunate if we were to present the Soviets with new opportunities in Chile by cutting our military representation even further."[74]

Robert Pastor of the National Security Council termed Brown's fear that Chile would turn to the Soviets "absolute nonsense." The argument that the

---

[71] Tarnoff to Brzezinski, 3 March 1978; Pinochet to Carter, 30 January 1978, both Chile Declassification Project, Carter Library, Box 1, NA.

[72] Dodson to Clift, 23 October 1980; Tarnoff to Clift, 22 October 1980, both WHCF:CF, Box CO-15, JCL.

[73] State to Embassy, Santiago, 24 May 1979, Records Responsive to Chilean Human Rights Abuses, 1979–1981, Carter Library, Box 63, NA.

[74] Brown to Vance, 9 October 1979, Records Responsive to Chilean Human Rights Abuses, 1979–1981, Carter Library, Box 63, NA.

southern cone "could go left is ludicrous," Pastor wrote Brzezinski. "The foundation of these governments is anti-Communism. They have nowhere to go, but us. That's why they continuously seek contact with us and approval, if possible; and that's why we have a fair amount of influence over them." Pastor, therefore, rejected the idea that American policy toward Chile or Latin America should be made in terms of the Cold War. In the same vein, Vance argued that Chile's refusal to meet the American request meant that the Pinochet regime had "condoned this act of international terrorism within the United States." This made it "essential that we make clear, both to Chile and to others throughout the world, that such actions cannot be tolerated."[75]

In November 1979, in response to Chile's "failure to investigate seriously or prosecute" those responsible for the murders of Letelier and Moffitt, the United States took a series of steps against Chile. The size of the American mission in Santiago was reduced by one-fourth; all further military sales were terminated; and all Export-Import Bank financing was suspended until positive steps were taken. Only humanitarian assistance for low-income groups was maintained.[76] A ban or limit on private loans, and the breaking of relations, were rejected. As Vance wrote Carter, "while I share the outrage of those who have suggested them, I believe steps of this sort would not serve our interests in Chile or elsewhere."[77] While Carter was unable to bring about a dramatic improvement in Chile's human rights record, the changes that did occur resulted from Santiago's concern about the position of the United States and international opinion and pressure. Most importantly, Carter's policy ended American support for Pinochet's brutal regime, and American complicity with its actions, while demonstrating that withdrawing support from Pinochet's dictatorship posed no threat to U.S. national interests. In other nations, such as Iran, where American security interests were more significant, Carter faced difficult decisions that demanded that he choose between traditional American support for right-wing dictators because of Washington's desire for stability, anticommunism, and protection of American interests and his efforts to break free of those Cold War categories and implement his human rights policy.

Thinking the Unthinkable

It was in Iran that Carter's policy would be put to its first and most difficult test, as the president's quest for human rights conflicted with long-term United States support for the shah of Iran. Carter understood that Iran posed a difficult problem, and he recognized the strategic and symbolic importance of that nation. The president believed, however, that through the right combination of public praise, support, and private efforts to bring about change he could

---

[75] Vance to Carter, 19 October 1979, Records Responsive to Chilean Human Rights Abuses, 1979–1981, Carter Library, Box 63, NA.

[76] Dodson to Clift, 23 October 1980; Tarnoff to Clift, 22 October 1980, both WHCF:CF, Box CO-15, JCL.

[77] Vance to Carter, 19 October 1979, Records Responsive to Chilean Human Rights Abuses, 1979–1981, Carter Library, Box 63, NA.

get the shah to reduce human rights violations in his country and promote political reform while protecting American interests in the region. What Carter did not realize was how much support the shah had already lost prior to his taking office. Decades of political violence and oppression, and reforms that had harmed the majority of the population while enriching the royal family and its friends, had made Iran a tinderbox ready to explode. Yet Carter would face charges that it was his policy, and not the dictatorial rule of the shah, that brought about the Iranian revolution and the overthrow of the Pahlevi dynasty.

This problem was compounded by the division within his administration between Secretary of State Vance and National Security Advisor Brzezinski, which came to a boil over how best to handle the developing crisis in Iran. Vance argued that human rights had to remain the central concern of the administration and that it needed to work with opposition groups to help ease the crisis. The secretary of state did not argue that the United States should abandon the shah, but rather that it had to find a way to create a stable government that would allow the administration to carry out its dual goals of human rights reform and the protection of American interests in Iran. Brzezinski countered that strategic issues were primary and called for complete support for the shah and the use of military force to maintain his rule.

By the middle of the 1970s, increased awareness of the human rights abuses, wasteful military spending, and the oppressive nature of the shah's rule were raising considerable questions about American support for Iran. It was widely known that the Iranian secret police, SAVAK, which had been created and trained by the CIA, routinely used torture on political opponents, spied on and harassed Iranian dissidents who lived overseas, and arrested people who were held in jail without charges or trial. Moreover, it was becoming apparent that the famed stability of Iran was the result of extensive political repression by the police and army, and not due to satisfaction with the shah's governance. By the time Carter took office and began to formulate his human rights policy, he faced a growing crisis of instability in Iran that stemmed from the shah's repressive rule and allowed no easy solutions. The question that would ultimately confront the president was what the policy of the United States regarding the shah's crumbling rule should be, and whether the United States should intervene to save this long-time ally and dictator.

As Vance recalled, all of the senior officials in the Carter administration "recognized the importance of Iran in Persian Gulf security matters," and they decided that it was in the "national interest to support the Shah so he could continue to play a constructive role in regional affairs." "Nevertheless, we were also determined to hew to our position on human rights...." Neither he nor the president "believed that the maintenance of a stable relationship with Iran precluded encouragement of improvement in its human rights policy."[78] Thus, the administration set out to provide support for the shah while at the same

---

[78] Vance, *Hard Choices*, 316–17.

time pressing upon him the need to improve conditions within his nation in order to maintain his rule.

That the shah was concerned about what Carter's presidency would mean to him was evident right away. Just days after the inauguration, the Iranian ambassador to the United States, Ardeshir Zahedi, met with Brzezinski to emphasize Iran's historic ties to the United States and the importance of maintaining good relations. Brzezinski acknowledged the importance of Iran to the United States, assured the ambassador of American support, and noted that there were no immediate issues that the administration wanted to raise with Tehran.[79] Carter also set out to assuage any fears the shah might have that his administration would end American support for his government or that Iran would become a public target of the president's human rights policy. The president wrote to the shah in early February 1977 to reaffirm the importance to the United States of good relations with Iran and to assure the shah of his personal support. Carter noted that the "particularly close ties which have existed between our two countries since World War II are supported by a broad consensus in the United States that we share many vital mutual objectives and that it is in the national interest of our country to cooperate with yours." The president continued by stating that he shared this view and that he was "determined to maintain this firm relationship." Carter did note that there would be "challenges to our common objectives" of peace, order, and stability, but absent in the letter was any reference to human rights issues or any indication of American concern about the shah's rule. Carter wanted first to build a relationship with the shah before he began to push for reform.[80]

The rapidly deteriorating situation in Iran, however, would force Carter to confront the human rights atrocities and the shah's brutality more quickly than he had originally planned. Vance was sent to Tehran on 13 May 1977 to raise the issue of human rights abuses in Iran and to clarify the administration's policy. The secretary of state echoed Carter in his assurances to the shah of American support and of Iran's importance to the United States. Yet he "emphasized that the president was committed to reaffirming the primacy of human rights as a national goal," and that this would be applied to all nations. This warning was softened by Vance's praise for the shah's rule and claims of improvements in human rights. The shah, however, was clearly worried, knowing full well that any end of repression in Iran would lead to an explosion of opposition and threaten his rule. He told Vance that he had no objections to Carter's human rights policy "as long as it was a question of general principle and not directed at him or did not threaten his country's security interests." In order to deflect any further criticism, the shah returned to his standard claim, one that had always been met with agreement by past American officials: that his oppressive policies were necessary because his regime was under attack from

---

[79] Memorandum of Conversation, 25 July 1977, SOF:NSA: Brzezinski, Box 33, JCL.
[80] Carter to shah of Iran, 7 February 1977, WHCF:CF, Box CO-31, JCL.

the communists. Furthermore, he "warned that if Iran were to slip into civil strife, only the Soviet Union would stand to gain."[81]

It was clear from Vance's meeting with the shah that the monarch was not receptive to Carter's new ideas and did not plan to cooperate with him, and that it would be difficult for the president to find the right combination of praise and pressure to influence Iran to improve its human rights record. The State Department, therefore, argued that the administration needed to move slowly and with caution in approaching the question of human rights conditions in Iran. It viewed Iran as a "conservative status quo country interested in political stability on its frontiers and in the Persian Gulf area." This meant that its interests and those of the United States in the area were identical. Concerning human rights, the department noted that the "situation in Iran does need improvement," but found that many of the charges against the government were exaggerated. Iran's critics did not "adequately take into account the historical, social, and economic conditions in Iran," the threats to the government, and the upheaval that naturally occurs in any "rapidly changing society." In addition, they failed to note the improvements the shah was making and the reforms he had recently implemented. When looked at this way, the State Department did not see a case for urgent action.[82]

Carter was willing to wait until he met personally with the shah to take up the issue again. He invited the shah for a state visit in November in order to explain his goals and objectives, and to make sure that there was no misunderstanding concerning American support for Iran or Carter's human rights policy. This visit, however, would be different from the shah's eleven previous trips to Washington. Upon his arrival at the White House, the shah was met by thousands of Iranian students and others who were there to protest his rule and U.S. support for his regime. The official welcoming ceremony was disrupted when the tear gas being used against the demonstrators blew across the south lawn, causing Carter to have to wipe his eyes while speaking. From the shah's perspective, the greeting he received inside the White House was equally unsettling.

While the official purpose of the visit was "to convince the Shah of the president's firm commitment to the U.S.-Iranian special relationship," and to discuss military and economic matters, human rights became the main issue.[83] Carter began by praising the shah's rule, which he claimed had made Iran a "stabilizing force in the world at large." The U.S. ties to Iran were "unbreakable," Carter declared.[84] The president then shifted gears and told the shah that he also knew about some of the problems in Iran related to human rights. "A growing number of your own citizens," Carter stated, "are claiming that these rights are not always honored in Iran." This was damaging to Iran's reputation

---

[81] Vance, *Hard Choices*, 318.

[82] "Briefing Material for Visit of Empress of Iran," 9 July 1977, WHCF:CF, Box CO-31, JCL.

[83] Vance, *Hard Choices*, 321–2.

[84] Rubin, *Paved with Good Intentions*, 201.

in the world, and Carter wanted to know if there was "anything that can be done to alleviate this problem by closer consultation with the dissident groups and by easing off on some of the strict police policies?" The shah declared: "No, there is nothing I can do." He remained as adamant on the issue as he had been in his meeting with Vance earlier in the year, and used the same Cold War arguments to support his position. The shah stated that he "must enforce Iranian laws, which are designed to combat communism. This is a very real and dangerous problem for Iran – and indeed, for the other countries in my area and in the Western world." The shah was willing to grant that if and when "this serious menace is removed, the laws can be changed, but that will not be soon." Besides, he continued, the complaints and disturbances in his country are caused by the "very troublemakers against whom the laws have been designed to protect our country," a tiny minority that has no support among the people of Iran.[85]

The shah expected that these arguments, which had proven so successful in Washington in the past, would continue to ensure him American support without any further questions. He, however, did not understand Carter's intention to change American foreign policy so that it was no longer based just on anticommunism, Carter's commitment to human rights and questioning of support for right-wing dictators, and, as a result, the fact that he could no longer automatically assume American support for whatever he did.

Immediately after the shah's return from Washington, a series of student demonstrations and other protests broke out in Iran. The shah responded with force and continued repression against suspected opponents of his regime. As Gary Sick of the National Security Council reported to Brzezinski, after "a student demonstration at Tehran University was forcibly broken up by riot police," the police stayed on campus and every day "indiscriminately beat up a few students to 'maintain order.'" The students were intimidated from speaking, "but there is a lot of barely concealed opinion about the need to do away with the Shah." Similar events were taking place throughout the capital, and "several well-informed American experts on Iran have told us recently that ... opposition to the Shah's regime runs deeper than one would suspect."[86]

Sick believed the use of excessive force indicated that the "Shah is truly running scared" and "was probably in no mood to let things get out of hand." This would "explain his emotional response to the President's warm words of support" during his visit. While the crackdown was hurting relations with Iran, Sick noted that it was necessary to remember that the "accepted norms of political violence in Iran are more oriental than western, and the police, if given any leeway, are likely to overreact." The political opposition in Iran tended to be extreme, and "unfortunately, the repressive tactics adopted by the authorities have not been conducive to the development of a responsible opposition. To be fair," Sick continued, "it should be noted that the Shah is aware of the

---

[85] Carter, *Keeping Faith*, 436.
[86] Sick to Brzezinski, 30 November 1977, WHCF:CF, Box CO-31, JCL.

dangers of polarization and has been taking some steps to allow more freedom of expression." Sick recommended that Brzezinski, in talking to reporters, note the "general trend toward liberalization of the political process in Iran over the past year" and the continued American support for and confidence in the regime.[87]

Assistant Secretary of State for Human Rights Patricia Derian had a different view of the matter and called for the implementation of the process set out in the administration's human rights policy. She noted that the substantial increase in the use of force by the shah against his opposition indicated that the regime was moving toward greater repressive measures. These developments had not "escaped international attention . . . and the reaction of abhorrence is increasing." Given this, "the official silence of the United States government, perceived everywhere as the Shah's closest supporter, is ever more deafening" because it "casts doubt on the President's commitment to the principle of advancement of human rights, not only in Iran but globally." Derian suggested that the American ambassador, William Sullivan, speak to the shah and indicate great U.S. concern about the government's recent actions. Private pressure was necessary because the "progress toward greater respect of fundamental human rights is jeopardized by the violence and the apparent attempts to suppress free expression of domestic criticism of the government's policies." A sincere, low-key approach was necessary now to "construct the foundation for later higher level and more public approaches should they become necessary."[88]

The State Department agreed with the embassy in Tehran that Iran had apparently decided "that it has more to fear in the long run from permitting open political debate than from domestic and international criticism of repressive measures." In response to Derian's memorandum, Sullivan was instructed to meet with government officials and express "the increasing concern" of the United States "over the reports of violence in Tehran." These events were making public support of the shah more difficult, as they contradicted the claims of progress that the United States had repeatedly supported. In addition, they were "having an increasingly adverse effect on the international reputation" of Iran. Finally, Sullivan was told to emphasize in his conversations with Iranian officials "the importance which this administration, the Congress and the American public place on supporting the internationally accepted principles of protection of human rights expressed in the U.N. Charter, the Universal Declaration of Human Rights and the U.N. Covenants of political and civil rights and social and cultural rights."[89]

Carter returned the shah's visit and traveled to Tehran on 31 December 1977. In his New Year's toast, the president went out of his way to praise the shah in the hope that he could alleviate the monarch's concerns about American support and get him to make concrete changes and concessions toward his opposition.

---

[87] Ibid.
[88] Derian to Atherton, 5 December 1977, Handwriting File, Box 67, JCL.
[89] Department to Sullivan, 5 December 1977, Handwriting File, Box 67, JCL.

Carter declared that "Iran, because of the great leadership of the Shah, is an island of stability in one of the more troubled areas of the world. This is a great tribute to you, Your Majesty, and to your leadership and to the respect and admiration and love which your people give to you." He continued by noting that there was no other nation that was closer to the United States in terms of military planning, and that there was "no leader with whom I have a deeper sense of personal gratitude and personal friendship." Carter did, however, raise the issue of human rights when he claimed that "the cause of human rights is one that . . . is shared deeply by our people and by the leaders of our two nations," but chose not to push the issue any further at that time.[90]

As 1978 began, the administration remained confident that the shah would continue to maintain control in Iran and would be able to introduce democratic reforms that would end the signs of growing turmoil in the nation. The public position of the administration, therefore, remained supportive, and its criticisms were kept secret. But as the year progressed, the situation only grew worse and brought no resolution to the dilemma of how to maintain good relations with the shah and at the same time force him to make concessions on human rights. As Carter slowly discovered, the shah was not the popular leader or successful modernizer that American officials thought he was, nor was he capable of carrying out effective reforms. In response to the ever-increasing unrest in Iran, the shah swung back and forth between reform and repression in an effort to save his regime. A downward spiral was set in motion that only encouraged the shah's opponents to take bolder steps. Simultaneously, the efforts at liberalization fueled the opposition of the religious fundamentalists led by the Ayatollah Khomeini. They saw the efforts at modernization and Western political reforms as an attack on Islam and the traditional values of Iranian society.

Neither the shah nor the Carter administration, however, took seriously the challenges to his rule until late in the year. In March 1978, the shah declared that "nobody can overthrow me. I have the support of 700,000 troops, all the workers, and most of the people. I have the power." There was no disagreement in Washington. State Department analysis and intelligence estimates continued to report that the shah fully controlled his country, and missed the signs of the coming revolution. For example, in June, Assistant Secretary of State for Near East and South Asian Affairs Harold Saunders told Congress that "we believe a large majority of Iranians thoroughly approve of the very substantial improvements that have been made in living standards and economic and social opportunities during the past three decades." Saunders, therefore saw no danger of the shah losing control.[91]

The situation reached the crisis stage in the fall of 1978. On September 8, soldiers killed between 1,000 and 2,000 people as they opened fire to break up a demonstration in Tehran. The shah declared martial law and ordered the continued use of force to prevent further protests. The president called the

---

[90] *Public Papers of the Presidents: Carter, 1977*, vol. 2: 2221–2.
[91] Rubin, *Paved with Good Intentions*, 206–10.

shah after the so-called Black Friday massacre and expressed his regret about the incident and his support for Iran's ruler. Carter, however, recommended that the shah continue to pursue liberalization as the best means to bring an end to the disturbances.[92] The president still believed that the shah could maintain his power through reform; he was bringing American pressure on him to continue to open up the political process in order to split the moderate opposition away from the radical religious leaders and leftists and broaden his political base.

Carter's faith was based on his view that the opposition was led by students and intellectuals whose goals were in line with those of the United States. He believed that "Iran's growing middle class, well-educated students, and strong religious community [were] a foundation for stability and further progress." He, therefore, continued to publicly support the shah while privately urging that he resist his military advisors' call for a brutal crackdown and continue his reforms.[93] In an October 10 press conference, Carter noted that Iran's strategic position made it a crucial nation to the United States, and that it remained "a great stabilizing force in their part of the world." He praised the shah for moving "aggressively to establish democratic principles in Iran" and for having a "progressive attitude toward social questions." He hoped that reforms could be made peacefully and that the crisis could be resolved without bloodshed, and expressed continued faith in the shah's ability to lead Iran.[94] At the end of the month, Carter again personally reassured the shah of his support and the importance of Iran to the United States. The State Department praised his "political liberalization and economic reform," and noted that the United States was confident that the "Iranian Government is capable of managing the present difficulties."[95]

This view quickly changed. On November 9, Ambassador Sullivan cabled Washington that it was now time to "think the unthinkable." That is, the United States needed to begin preparing for the collapse of the shah's regime. The growing demonstrations and the shah's violent response had convinced the ambassador that the shah could not be saved and that the United States had to act in order to prevent a complete collapse in Iran and a radical takeover of power. He recommended that the administration arrange for the shah and most of the senior military officers to leave the country, while simultaneously promoting negotiations among the moderate opposition leaders and the younger officers in the military leading to a "series of elections to provide a constituent assembly, a new constitution, and eventually a parliament." Sullivan thought such an effort had a good chance of success, and that the "religious leadership, including Khomeini, might accept such an arrangement because it would give them their essential objective, the elimination of the shah, avoid a bloodbath, and endow them with armed forces willing to maintain law and order on behalf

---

[92] Ibid., 214.
[93] Carter, *Keeping Faith*, 436; see also Vance, *Hard Choices*, 325.
[94] *Public Papers of the Presidents: Carter, 1978*, vol. 2: 1750.
[95] *New York Times*, 1 November 1978.

of the new regime." It was also, Sullivan argued, in Washington's interest to take such action because "it would avoid chaos, ensure the continued integrity of the country, preclude a radical leadership, and effectively block Soviet domination in the Persian Gulf." While this would not be as good a situation as the United States had enjoyed under the shah's rule, it would be "better than one in which an inchoate revolution would succeed and the integrity of the armed forces destroyed."[96]

As Vance noted, Sullivan's telegram "caused consternation in the White House" and fear that any steps taken by Washington "that implied that we did not expect the shah to survive would contribute to his paralysis of will and stimulate the opposition to increased violence."[97] The Carter administration was split on how to respond. Brzezinski agreed that there was now a real danger that the shah might be overthrown and urged Carter to provide him full support for a military crackdown. Vance, on the other hand, advised caution and waiting to see if the shah could still stay in power and reach his own agreement with the opposition for an orderly transition to a constitutional monarchy. The secretary of state told Sullivan that while the United States had to "offer the shah our frank advice in helping to try to put together a new civilian government," Washington "could not make the decisions for the shah."[98]

Sullivan's recommendation, Vance recalled, "laid bare deep differences between Brzezinski and me as we contemplated the possibility of the fall of the shah. Zbig appeared to see a military coup, preferably in support of the shah, as the only hope of protecting American interests. I strongly advocated a political solution with the shah remaining as constitutional monarch if possible, but without him if necessary, coupled with efforts to preserve the Iranian military as an institution." Brzezinski's "iron fist" approach, Vance believed, was "antithetical to what...the Carter administration stood for."[99] This was the division and the dilemma that the president faced in November and December of 1978.

Brzezinski saw the crisis in classic Cold War terms and urged American action to save the shah or at least preserve military rule in Iran. He believed Iran's strategic importance made it imperative that the administration provide complete support for military action. The national security advisor feared that with the collapse of the shah's regime, the Soviets would gain primacy in the Persian Gulf and other nations would come to doubt the wisdom of an alliance with the United States and to question Washington's credibility. Brzezinski thought that Vance was too "preoccupied with the goal of promoting the democratization of Iran;" he believed that any further pressure or concessions would weaken the monarchy and "simply enhance instability and eventually produce complete chaos." He rejected what he called the "quaint notion" of a coalition

---

[96] Sullivan, *Mission to Iran*, 202–3.
[97] Vance, *Hard Choices*, 329–30.
[98] Ibid.
[99] Ibid., 331.

government as the solution to a revolutionary situation driven "by homicidal hatred."[100]

Indeed, Brzezinski blamed the effort at promoting human rights for the crisis because it had weakened the shah. Immediate action was necessary to save the regime, Brzezinski believed, because "prolonged ambiguity regarding the situation in Iran would simply destroy the loyalty of the Army and produce overall fragmentation."[101] In his so-called arc of crisis speech in December, the national security advisor summarized his views and fears. He still believed that the shah could be saved, and that the United States had to support him to the hilt. If it did not, and it appeared that the United States had abandoned the shah, the whole United States position in the Middle East would be undercut, leading to growing instability throughout the area. With the "fragile social and political structures in a region of vital importance to us threatened with fragmentation... the resulting political chaos could well be filled by elements hostile to our values and sympathetic with our adversaries. This could face the West as a whole with a challenge of significant proportions."[102]

It was only now that the president fully realized the depths of the opposition to the shah and recognized that he faced the choice of trying to save his regime or not. Carter rejected Brzezinski's proposal for U.S. intervention and support for a military crackdown, as well as the fundamental assumptions it was based on. He saw the national security advisor's arguments as simply the old verities of the Cold War that had justified U.S. support for the shah's dictatorship for over two decades. He did not believe that they could provide a solution at this point. Rather, the president held to the positions he had set out during his presidential campaign and in the human rights policy developed in his first year of office. Carter, therefore, backed away from his public support of the shah, advised him to accept a constitutional monarchy as the first step in creating a new government in Iran, and stood by his policy of nonintervention and refusal to commit the United States to the protection of a right-wing dictator. On December 8, in response to a reporter's question asking him to reconcile his "statements about the Shah's concern for human rights, democracy and liberalization with the pretty well documented record" of abuses by his regime, the president indicated his doubts about the shah's rule and future. Carter started by reiterating the importance of Iran to the United States and its stabilizing role in the region. In that context, the United States had tried to help the shah to maintain order during a difficult period while implementing reforms. He acknowledged that there were human rights abuses in Iran "as measured by any objective standard," including the "incarcerations of people without formal charges and trial," abuses that the United States found unacceptable. Still, he thought that the trend had been "toward democratic principles and social liberalization," and that the shah was working toward a coalition government.

[100] Brzezinski, *Power and Principle*, 355.
[101] Ibid., 374.
[102] Rubin, *Paved with Good Intentions*, 235.

As to the question of whether the shah could continue to hold power, Carter stated, "I don't know." He hoped so, as the United States would "prefer that the Shah maintain a major role in the government." But, the president declared, "that's a decision for the Iranian people to make." Moreover, he stated that his administration had "never had any intention" and had no current or future "intention of trying to intercede in the internal political affairs of Iran."[103]

Carter now agreed with Vance that the shah could no longer rule the country, and that the best the United States could do was to get him to leave and support a transitional government while hoping the military could maintain order. When the shah appointed Shahpour Bakhtiar as prime minister on December 29, the administration noted its approval and supported Bakhtiar's demand that the monarch leave the country. On 16 January 1979, the shah left Iran, ending over twenty-five years of rule. His dictatorship had enjoyed U.S. support beginning with the initial CIA campaign to install him in power in 1953. Carter, however, had refused to be swayed by the old rationales for supporting right-wing dictators that had led to the original backing of the shah, even if his fall from power was the result. As he told the press the day after the shah's departure, the United States would not intervene in Iran to ensure a government of its own liking. Carter stated that he had "no desire... to intrude massive forces into Iran or any other country to determine the outcome of domestic political issues." The United States, he continued, "tried this once in Vietnam. It didn't work well, as you well know."[104]

One can debate whether Carter could have distanced the United States from the shah more quickly, or done more sooner to promote a change in the government. What cannot be denied is that the president changed the American policy toward right-wing dictators when he refused to intervene to save the shah. He would follow a similar course of action later that year in response to the revolution in Nicaragua against the rule of Anastasio Somoza. In the face of criticism and pressure from many sources, and foreign policy reversals in other areas, Carter maintained his commitment to the essence of his human rights policy and rejected pleas for the kind of American intervention that had previously marked relations with Central America. Human rights provided an alternative to the previous policies of military intervention and support for dictatorships that had marred U.S. relations with Latin America and created the crisis in Nicaragua.

A Unique History

Since marines were first sent to Nicaragua in 1912, the United States had sought to impose stability in that nation. Removed briefly in 1925, the marines returned again in 1926; they stayed until 1933, when they turned the task of maintaining order over to the National Guard under the direction of Anastasio

---

[103] *Public Papers of the Presidents: Carter, 1978*, vol. 2: 2172–3.
[104] *Public Papers of the Presidents: Carter, 1979*, vol. 1: 50–2.

Somoza Garcia. The elder Somoza took over all power in 1936, and he along with his two sons, Luis and Anastasio Somoza Debayle, ruled Nicaragua until 1979. The United States supported the Somoza dictatorship because it believed Nicaraguans were too politically immature for self-rule and vulnerable to radical ideas. They therefore needed a firm hand to maintain order, prevent communism, and protect American investments and trade in their nation.[105] The National Sandinista Liberation Front (FSLN) was founded in 1961, but it did not appear to American officials to pose any threat to Somoza's rule, and Nicaragua was seen as one of the most stable nations in Latin America.

In the wake of the massive December 1972 earthquake in Nicaragua, however, the Sandinistas were able to begin to challenge Somoza's rule. Somoza's blatant stealing of relief funds, and his use of force to quell the protests against his actions, brought a period of mounting unrest in Nicaragua and criticism from members of Congress about the human rights abuses of the National Guard. When the Sandinistas captured a number of government officials in 1974, Somoza launched a countrywide crackdown against the FSLN that heightened concern in Washington that a Cuban-supported communist group could take power in Nicaragua if the dictator failed to reestablish order.

By the time Carter took office in January 1977, there was a growing revolution in Nicaragua that would challenge Carter's efforts to create a new approach toward Latin America. His administration's analysis of the situation in Nicaragua brought out the central dilemma and tension in American policy: the desire to distance the United States from the Somoza dictatorship and base American policy upon human rights without aiding a communist revolution. While the administration's analysis of the problem was similar to that of its predecessors, Carter saw the dilemma as a false dichotomy and refused to base his policy solely on the choice between Somoza and communism. Rather, he sought to find a third way, based on his human rights policy and the principle of nonintervention.

Developing such a policy was complicated by the divisions within the administration and by the political pressure brought by Somoza's supporters in the United States. Brzezinski, on the one hand, saw the Sandinistas' revolution as a "challenge thrown down by the Soviet bloc" that demanded that the United States provide aid to Somoza.[106] Vance, on the other hand, argued that the roots of the revolution were domestic and stemmed from the abuses of the Somoza regime and not some outside conspiracy. The secretary of state, therefore, advised Carter to "drop the notion of a 'special relationship' which smacked of paternalism, and deal with each Latin American and Caribbean nation as a sovereign power with different problems."[107] The problem of reconciling these positions was further compounded by the domestic division within the United

---

[105] See Schmitz, *Thank God They're on Our Side*, 48-57, on the United States' establishment of the National Guard and support of Somoza.

[106] Brzezinski, *Power and Principle*, 210.

[107] Vance, *Hard Choices*, 33.

States between the strong pro-Somoza lobby in Congress and growing public awareness of and opposition to Somoza's brutal rule. Carter, consistent with his policy elsewhere, combined public support for Somoza and praise for improvements with private pressure in the hope of bringing about reform in Nicaragua that would end human rights abuses, begin the process of democratic reform, and prevent the Sandinistas from coming to power. As he implemented his policy, Carter had to defend his actions against charges that he was abandoning an ally and opening the door to communism in Central America, while he was simultaneously criticized for supporting a flagrant perpetrator of human rights violations.

Somoza initially acquiesced to Carter's pressure for reform in 1977, lifting press censorship and curtailing the activities of the National Guard. In return, the administration praised the dictator, encouraged further action, and made it clear that future U.S. aid was dependent on continued improvement. In a September 1977 assessment, the State Department noted that "our traditionally close bilateral relations have stiffened due to U.S. concern over violations of human rights in Nicaragua." While some improvements had been made, the Somoza government's record in human rights remained a matter of concern as there continued to be "numerous reliable reportings of serious human rights violations in Nicaragua." The National Guard still "at times used indiscriminate and harshly repressive tactics" in fighting the FSLN, and a state of siege was in effect, which meant the holding of prisoners without charges and military trials for those suspected of subversion or helping the Sandinistas. The administration, therefore, intended to continue to restrict the provision of aid and credits to Nicaragua until there was a "marked decrease in reported violations by the Nicaraguan National Guard" and efforts to "restore the civil liberties suspended under the state of siege."[108]

By Carter's second year in office, the Sandinista challenge to Somoza's rule in Nicaragua had reached the point of crisis and tested the administration's commitment to human rights. As the fighting between the National Guard and FSLN intensified in the spring of 1978, Carter responded by sending additional aid to Somoza. In June, Brzezinski persuaded Carter, over objections from Robert Pastor of the National Security Council and the State Department, to send Somoza a personal letter demonstrating American support for his regime. Pastor worried that Somoza would misinterpret such a letter "as a sign of favor that did not, in fact, exist." Moreover, the administration had to make sure that it did not alienate the moderate opposition in Nicaragua by appearing to support Somoza. The State Department added that Somoza often made promises but "did not have a good record of actually carrying out promised reforms, and the president's proposed letter might be premature." Carter, however, agreed to send the letter in the hope that such a move would convince Somoza to begin making the political changes that the president saw as necessary to bring about democratic reforms and to undercut the appeal of the FSLN. In his letter, Carter

[108] Tarnoff to Brzezinski, 6 September 1977, WHCF:CF, Box CO-46, JCL.

praised the recent promises Somoza had made to curtail human rights abuses, writing that the "steps toward respecting human rights you are considering are important and heartening signs; and, as they are translated into actions, will mark a major advance in answering some of the criticisms recently aimed at the Nicaraguan government."[109]

The letter turned out to be an enormous mistake by Carter. Somoza, while initially seeing the letter as a sign of support, quickly came to see it as "designed to give us a false sense of security," and Carter as "stepping up his attack against me and the government of Nicaragua."[110] Meanwhile, when the letter was published in the *Washington Post* in August, it was categorized as praising Somoza and supportive. As Brzezinski wrote Carter, the administration was unable to get its interpretation adopted by the press or Congress. "While we have tried to explain that the purpose of the letter was not to praise Somoza but to encourage him to take steps on human rights, still the dominant interpretation in the US and throughout Latin America is that it was a sign of support for Somoza."[111]

With the Sandinista attack on the National Legislative Palace in September, and the kidnaping of most of the Congress and several of Somoza's relatives, events quickly outpaced Carter's effort to slowly push Somoza to reform his government while maintaining American support, and the president was forced to choose between his human rights policy and supporting the dictator. The administration now concluded that the only way to prevent a Sandinista takeover was the removal of Somoza and the establishment of a moderate government. As Brzezinski told Carter, the State Department and the National Security Council agreed that the situation was "deteriorating rapidly and that Somoza had decided to take steps to suppress the moderate opposition, thus trying to force us to choose between him and the Sandinistas."[112] While it was important that the objective not become publicly known, "ultimately Somoza would have to go" if the United States hoped for a moderate government, and not the Sandinistas, to replace him. This course of action was "tricky not only because of the international principle of non-intervention but also because of reasons internal to the U.S. political process since Somoza has a number of very powerful political allies." The dictator was counting on this support, and "trying to create a situation where we will have to choose between Somoza or chaos."[113]

It was, therefore, agreed that the United States should promote efforts by the other nations of Central America to mediate negotiations between Somoza

[109] Strong, *Working in the World*, 86; Carter to Somoza, 30 June 1978, WHCF:HR, Box HU-1, JCL.
[110] Strong, *Working in the World*, 90.
[111] Brzezinski to Carter, 18 September 1978, WHCF:HR, Box HU1, JCL.
[112] Memorandum, Brzezinski to Carter, 4 September 1978, ZBP, Box 36, JCL.
[113] Memorandum of Conversation, "U.S. Policy to Nicaragua," 4 September 1978, ZBP, Box 36, JCL.

and moderates in the opposition to bring about a "transfer of power in Nicaragua."[114] Vance told Carter that the "unique history of our association with the Somozas...puts US prestige on the line" and made it critical that Washington distance itself from the dictator. "Somoza," Vance warned, "is determined to stay in power, and is out to destroy his legitimate opponents so as to fulfill his prophecy that he is the only alternative to chaos and communism." Moreover, the secretary of state believed that the Sandinistas were not currently strong enough to seize power, but would continue to grow in strength the longer Somoza stayed in power. Conversely, they would lose support if Somoza were replaced, allowing time for a peaceful transition of power. In any case, Vance concluded, it was now clear that "support of the status quo through Somoza will simply not serve our interests." Thus, the best means to bring an end to the crisis and the removal of Somoza through an orderly transfer of power was "mediation by Nicaragua's neighbors in Central America."[115] This would avoid charges of American intervention while preserving the current institutions of Nicaragua.

The CIA did not believe that "an internally generated compromise" was possible, and argued that the United States was the "key to a viable solution." With that in mind, Robert Pastor advised Brzezinski that the "best transitional government, and also the most widely acceptable, would be one which preserved current institutions but displaced Somoza and some of his closest lieutenants." The moderates were critical of Somoza but not of the institutions, and this would leave the National Guard intact, allowing for "sufficient capability to continue the fight against the Sandinistas." Thus, this should be the goal of the mediation process.[116] The new Special Coordination Committee (SCC) on Nicaragua met on September 12 to discuss the crisis. Made up of members from the Departments of State and Defense, the Joint Chiefs of Staff, the CIA, and the NSC, the SCC concluded "that the situation in Nicaragua was deteriorating rapidly and becoming increasingly polarized. The longer Somoza stays in power, the more support the Sandinistas will receive, the more likely we will face a choice between Somoza and the Sandinistas, and thus the fewer options we will have." All participants agreed that supporting Somoza would mean more violence and that the United States would find itself "in a downward spiral." Deputy Secretary of State Christopher outlined three options: a passive disassociation from Somoza; support for Somoza in the current crisis; or international mediation "aimed at bringing the new coalition of moderate forces into power now in an effort to control the Sandinistas." The first option would lead to a Sandinista victory, and the second option was "impractical" as it would just increase the violence and polarization. It was, therefore, the recommendation

---

[114] Memorandum, Brzezinski to Carter, 4 September 1978, ZBP, Box 36, JCL.

[115] Memorandum, Vance to Carter, 4 September 1978, ZBP, Box 36, JCL.

[116] Pastor to Brzezinski and Aaron, 7 September 1978; CIA, "Nicaragua – Factors and Figures in the Process Leading to a Transition Government," 7 September 1978, both ZBP, Box 36, JCL.

of the SCC that the administration place "U.S. prestige behind a mediation effort by others . . . to build as much international support as possible" for the removal of Somoza.[117]

Ambassador Bill Jordan was sent to Central America the following week to meet with the presidents of other Central American nations to "seek their leadership and support for international mediation." David Aaron of the White House staff and Brzezinski wrote Carter on September 15 that the "situation in Nicaragua is deteriorating very rapidly," and that the moderate opposition would no longer negotiate with Somoza. The State Department, therefore, had formally urged Somoza to "accept mediation and seek an enduring resolution of the crisis." They told Carter that the consensus of the SCC was that "Somoza is the reason why the Sandinistas are as strong as the are today," and that the dictator "must step down soon, or else the Sandinistas stand a very good chance of discrediting moderate opposition and seizing power." If, however, "Somoza were to resign and be replaced by moderates . . . with the institutions in place, we believe that the Sandinistas support would decline, their hardcore forces contained and a moderate solution enhanced." This made the international mediation effort critical in order to bring about this change right away. Jordan did not have explicit instructions to "support the removal of Somoza," but it was necessary to acknowledge that this was "the direction that all these efforts are leading," and that such "a transfer of power to moderate elements in Nicaragua in this time of crisis will not take place without American behind-the-scenes support."[118]

What is significant is that Carter did not support Somoza, or turn to direct American intervention to save his regime. Instead, the administration upheld its policy of human rights and nonintervention. Unlike previous administrations, it did not see only two alternatives, the dictator or communism. Rather, it continued to pressure Somoza and worked toward a moderate solution to the crisis. The administration concluded that any further support of Somoza would only increase the violence in the nation and further polarize the country, "with the moderates in the middle the big losers." It was critical that the United States give the broad opposition in Nicaragua what it wanted, the departure of Somoza. This would make for a better chance that "a moderate compromise . . . will have the time and elements necessary to take root and grow as a viable democratic alternative to Somoza rule or Marxist encroachments."[119] Carter, therefore, continued to urge negotiations for a transition in government while stepping up the pressure on Somoza to make concessions by lifting the state of siege, granting an amnesty bill for opponents of the regime, ending the censorship of the press, and preparing to leave office.

---

[117] SCC Meeting, 12 September 1978; Aaron to Carter, 15 September 1978, both ZBP, Box 36, JCL.

[118] Aaron to Carter, 15 September 1978, ZBP, Box 36, JCL.

[119] Memorandum, "Nicaragua – Factors and Figures in the Process Leading to a Transitional Government," 7 September 1978, ZBP, Box 36, JCL.

There were also larger regional concerns driving the administration's policy. As Pastor made clear, American support of right-wing dictators in the region meant that Nicaragua-style crises were also likely in El Salvador, Honduras, and Guatemala. Pastor noted that, like Nicaragua, each nation had "a strong, intransigent military government with little or no popular support" opposed by "revolutionary guerrilla groups which are predominantly indigenous but maintain ties with the Cubans and each other," and a "relatively weak" moderate middle. In addition, U.S. influence in all of these nations was formidable, and it "stimulates a negative and reactive nationalism among some and a 'Fanonian' immaturity among others."[120]

Prior to Carter's coming to office, "government-sanctioned counterterrorism was the rule" in all these nations. "The military governments ... felt they could serve the U.S. interest in stability in whatever way they wanted." Since the adoption of a policy of human rights, the dictators "feel inhibited from using violence or torture to suppress political opposition or to eliminate guerrilla movements." This was creating opportunities for democratic change and the moderate opposition, but also for the revolutionary movements. The support of right-wing dictators had greatly weakened this middle, making it difficult to find a moderate road toward change. The real danger in Nicaragua was that if the Sandinistas prevailed, "the democratic middle in these other countries may conclude that it is time to throw their fate in with the guerrillas against the government."[121]

Pastor identified the two central dilemmas facing the Carter administration as it sought to move away from supporting right-wing dictators to a post-Cold War policy of human rights and nonintervention. "How do we deal with the fact that the political middle is under attack from the two extremes," Pastor asked, and "what can we do to effectively promote our human rights policy" under such circumstances? Second, how does the United States reconcile the "goal of wanting to discard a century of U.S. paternalism with a need and an instinct to try to manage events rather than let them manage us?" Given the long history of U.S. intervention and support for brutal dictatorships, Pastor concluded that "Central America is a power keg of instability which could blow up and take with it Carter's Latin American policy." The same scenario that faced the administration in Nicaragua, "a choice between supporting an unpopular military dictator or intervening to prevent a Communist take-over," was present elsewhere. In order to have another alternative, the administration had to continue to develop and implement its human rights policy through the use of bilateral aid and loans and its support for the moderate, democratic forces.[122]

At the same time, the administration was being subjected to enormous criticism at home from conservative supporters of Somoza who cast the struggle in Nicaragua in Cold War terms. Led by Congressman John Murphy of New York,

[120] Pastor to Brzezinski and Aaron, 23 October 1978, SOF:NSA:CF, Box 45, JCL.
[121] Ibid.
[122] Ibid.

a longtime friend of the Nicaraguan dictator, they sought full American support for Somoza's regime. Murphy and fifty-nine of his colleagues in the House of Representatives wrote Carter in September 1978 urging the president to take all steps "to demonstrate the support of the United States Government for the Government of Nicaragua and President Anastasio Somoza, a long and consistent ally of the United States." They claimed to have "irrefutable evidence" that "amply documents the fact that the campaign of violence, urban terrorism and near civil war in Nicaragua is being carried out by a revolutionary group whose leaders have been trained in Havana and Moscow and whose goal is to make Nicaragua the new Cuba of the Western Hemisphere." If the Somoza regime fell, "the Marxist terrorists forces would be the chief beneficiaries," and the United States "would certainly lose a long-standing and loyal ally." The representatives, therefore, asked Carter "to take immediate steps to correct the misguided application of your policies by the Department of State, particularly regarding unsubstantiated and erroneous allegations against the government of Nicaragua," and to publicly express his support for Somoza "during this period of crisis."[123]

The administration, however, continued to urge negotiations for a transitional government while increasing the pressure on Somoza to lift the state of siege, grant an amnesty bill for opponents of the regime, and prepare to leave office. Somoza finally agreed to these concessions in December, but continued to hold onto power. He resisted any effort toward negotiations to establish a transitional government, and expressed the hope that the United States would now, in return for his actions, make a statement supporting him. Moreover, Somoza believed that he still could retain power without any further compromise. He told the American embassy in Managua that "although life may be unpleasant in the coming months, [his government] can resist both internal and international pressures."[124] He was confident in early 1979 that the changes urged by the United States "did not reflect the general wishes of the large mass of Nicaraguans of more modest means who were comfortable with the way things had been done in the past fifty years," and "pointed to the case of the Shah of Iran to support his thesis that too brusque a change in institutional pattern can be highly destabilizing."[125] The embassy in Managua concluded that he was not preparing to leave office. Instead, "Somoza wants the moderate third force to disappear so that the choice that is left is between the government and the communists."[126]

As the Carter administration struggled to find a moderate course in Nicaragua in early 1979, the Bureau of Human Rights cautioned that any

[123] Murphy et al. to Carter, 25 September 1978, WHCF:CF, Box CO-46, JCL.

[124] United States Embassy, Nicaragua, to Department of State, 23 December 1978, Nicaragua Collection, Box 2, NSA.

[125] United States Embassy, Nicaragua, to Department of State, 13 January 1979, Nicaragua Collection, Box 2, NSA.

[126] Embassy, Nicaragua, to Department of State, 13 January 1979, Nicaragua Collection, Box 2, NSA.

continued support of Somoza would "undermine our capacity to work for other foreign policy goals in the hemisphere, . . . raise fundamental and disturbing questions about our strength of purpose internationally," and destroy the possibility of "opening political institutions and promoting human rights" in the hemisphere. Indeed, a failure to force Somoza to leave office would "encourage just those forces likely to promote hardline military and repressive responses to the inevitably unsettled social and political conditions" of the region.[127]

As Washington feared, Somoza's intransigence on negotiations led to increased violence and a strengthening of the Sandinistas. The moderate forces were losing influence, caught as they were between the "left which is inimical to their interests" and the "much hated Somoza."[128] Thus, the administration faced two choices, "the prospect of [a] leftist government in the region or the necessity of US intervention," neither of which it wanted. As Pastor noted, "the first will be unacceptable politically in the US, and the second would toll the death of the President's Latin American policy."[129]

At the end of June 1979, the Carter administration made its final attempt to force Somoza to leave office peacefully without creating a power vacuum, hoping to remove the dictator while maintaining the power of a restructured National Guard to provide protection to the transitional government. Convinced that it was not a question of "if Somoza will fall, but when and under what circumstances," and that the moderate center was "being chewed up" by the fighting, it was agreed that the United States had to act.[130] As Christopher stated, the key remained "to persuade Somoza that his departure will not lead to a political vacuum, and that it is in his interest to assure a stable, noncommunist future for Nicaragua."[131] The United States increased its pressure on Somoza to resign. American diplomats told him that the Sandinistas were preparing for a new series of attacks on the government and that if the dictator did not leave soon, his departure would "appear to have been the result of a military defeat rather than a negotiated agreement." That scenario would spell the end of the political center as the Sandinistas would be able to claim responsibility for the removal of Somoza and a legitimate right to rule.[132]

Carter wrote Somoza again in July, reminding him that he had rejected all earlier compromises that would have avoided the current fighting and apparent Sandinista victory. He told the Nicaraguan dictator that he could not hold onto power and win militarily, and that prolonging the fighting "will only result in

[127] Memorandum, Bureau of Human Rights and Humanitarian Affairs to Bowdler, 19 January 1979, Nicaragua Collection, Box 2, NSA.
[128] Embassy, Nicaragua, to Department of State, 16 March 1979, Nicaragua Collection, Box 2, NSA.
[129] Memorandum, Pastor to Brzezinski, Aaron, and Owen, 8 June 1979, ZBP, Box 25, JCL.
[130] Presidential Review Committee, 11 June 1979, ZBP, Box 25, JCL.
[131] Christopher to All ARA Diplomatic Posts, 15 June 1979, Nicaragua Collection, Box 2, NSA.
[132] Embassy, Nicaragua, to Department of State, 13 July 1979, Nicaragua Collection, Box 2, NSA; see also Brzezinski to Carter, 23 June 1979 and 25 June 1979; Pastor to Brzezinski and Aaron, 1 July 1979, all ZBP, Box 30, JCL.

further suffering and loss of life, and in deeper radicalization of the situation."
"The only chance that remains," the president stated, "to achieve an enduring
and democratic solution is to establish a transition process . . . which will permit
moderate elements to survive and compete with extremists, which will avoid
reprisals, and which will provide a chance for an eventual freely elected regime
to emerge." The opportunity to preserve the center and shore up the moderates
"will exist only if we move quickly to end the war and begin to effect the
transition." Somoza, therefore, had to give up his power and leave the country
immediately.[133]

Realizing that he could no longer hold onto power, and finally convinced that
the United States would not save him, Somoza resigned on 17 July 1979. It was,
however, too late for an alternative to the Sandinistas, who took power three
days later. Initially, relations between the United States and Daniel Ortega's
government were cordial, and there was some hope on both sides that friendly
relations could be established. The administration reported to Congress that
despite similarities between the Nicaraguan and Cuban revolutions, the Sandinistas were an "authentic Nicaraguan phenomenon" and that "the Sandinista
movement represents a societal consensus that a radical change was needed in
Nicaragua." After years of repression and civil war, Nicaragua was in great
need of aid, and the administration indicated that it would be "generous in
its assistance and supportive of the democratic aims of the Sandinista revolution."[134] Congressman Murphy, however, led a successful effort in Congress to
block any aid to the Sandinistas, and relations between the United States and
Nicaragua quickly deteriorated.

Carter would face accusations from conservatives that his human rights policy had destabilized and undermined a critical ally and led to a communist
takeover in Nicaragua. The revolt in Nicaragua, however, was well under way
by the time Carter entered office and, barring direct American intervention,
beyond his control. The president sought a middle course that he believed
would allow him to uphold his human rights policy while protecting American
economic and strategic interests. Somoza's intransigence caused the search for a
moderate solution to fail. Some liberals, on the other hand, claimed that Carter
had stood by Somoza and his repressive regime too long. While the administration was unhappy with the outcome, Carter had maintained his commitment
to both nonintervention and human rights in the face of enormous pressures
and had not attempted to rescue Somoza's regime.

After the fall of the shah and Somoza, Carter was less willing to criticize certain dictators, and he backed away from his earlier criticisms of South Korea
and pressures on its government after a military coup in December 1979. In
addition, it is undeniable, as PRM/NSC 28 set out, that human rights was never

[133] Department of State to United States Embassy, Nicaragua, "Somoza's Departure," 14 July
1979, Nicaragua Collection, Box 2, NSA.
[134] Embassy, Nicaragua, to Department of State, 23 August 1979, Nicaragua Collection, Box 2,
NSA.

used in fashioning policy toward the People's Republic of China, and that this led to Carter's support for the murderous Khmer Rouge in Cambodia after their ouster from power by the Vietnamese.[135] Still, as Kathryn Sikkink has concluded in her study of human rights and American foreign policy, Carter's policy was effective in limiting human rights abuses in numerous nations, and it "indirectly contributed to democracy by withdrawing U.S. symbolic and material support for . . . authoritarian regimes."[136] In the process, Carter established a new framework that reshaped American policy toward right-wing dictatorships, moving away from unquestioned support to a post–Cold War policy that used human rights as an equal variable along with national security and other American interests in determining American actions.

Pressing for Democratic Values

Jimmy Carter's human rights policy led to a dramatic change in American policy toward right-wing dictatorships. In contrast to the policy of his predecessors, Carter rejected the prevailing logic that supported authoritarian governments based on anti-communism, stability, and American economic interests. Instead, he began to distance the United States from such regimes and sought to promote democratic values and institutions. The president was determined to demonstrate that the interests of the United States could be protected without embracing and propping up authoritarian rulers throughout the Third World. As the development of his human rights policy showed, Carter was well aware of the continuing national security questions and dilemmas involved in creating a foreign policy based upon human rights, and of the political limits to and criticisms of his approach, but he was convinced that American interests in the Third World would be better served by upholding American ideals and principles rather than by continuing to support right-wing dictators who violated those beliefs and created long-term instability and anti-American sentiment in their nations. Carter saw revolutions as a predictable end result of dictatorial rule and not as something the United States should try to crush. It was better to maintain political flexibility and adjust to the changing circumstances than to attempt to use covert action, counterinsurgency, and other methods to block change. The administration "saw the human rights issue as representing a major failing of [its] predecessors which had the effect of undermining international support for the United States."[137] Carter, reflecting the mood of the nation and the wishes of Congress after the Vietnam War, set out to restore the nation's moral legitimacy in the world by broadening the basis of American foreign policy beyond mere anticommunism, by promoting democratic values, and by ending the unquestioned American support for right-wing dictators.

---

[135] Clymer, "Jimmy Carter, Human Rights, and Cambodia."
[136] Sikkink, *Mixed Signals*, 123, 142–7.
[137] Bloomfield, "The Carter Human Rights Policy: A Provisional Appraisal," 11 January 1981, 10, ZBP, Box 34, JCL.

In an assessment of its policy in January 1981, the Carter administration found the "human rights policy was a definite plus for the United States in its international position" helping to repair the damaged American image brought about by the Vietnam War and covert American interventions abroad. This had been done by breaking with the bipolar, Cold War axioms that had led to the "valid goal of good relations with one or another geostrategically important" country to "become confused with unqualified support for obnoxious regimes that were cruel and abusive to their citizens, and thus failed the crucial test of looking significantly different from Communist totalitarianism."[138] The Carter White House summarized the new direction of the president's policy by noting that "instead of funneling more support to regimes which have drawn consistent international criticism for human rights abuses, we have a clear record of pressing for democratic values in those countries." This came from an understanding that it was in the best interests of the United States to "argue for political democracy, follow a humanitarian vocation, avoid the deadly embrace of despots whether of left or right, and always remember the supreme value of this nation's policy is people, not things."[139]

If the Carter administration appeared to its critics inconsistent or indecisive at certain times, this was because of the depth of its understanding of the complexity of the problems, its moderation and desire to work through diplomatic channels whenever possible, and its efforts to protect what it understood to be vital American interests while conducting a foreign policy centered on human rights. As an evaluation of Carter's human rights policy by the National Security Council put it in January 1981, the administration's promotion of human rights through private pressure and public support had led to charges of weakness and inconsistency, and it was "satisfactory neither to human rights advocates or critics."[140] Yet for all of its complexities, difficulties, and critics, the effort to develop a post–Cold War foreign policy based on human rights had significantly changed the discourse on American foreign policy, making human rights a central concern of American diplomacy. Human rights was now a fixture on the policy agenda and part of both American and world discussions of international relations. Carter's policy had provided support to those struggling against abusive and dictatorial governments; had led to the release of political prisoners in nations in Africa, Asia, Europe, and Latin America; and had forced governments to modify their behavior or risk losing American support and aid. When crises arose, the burden now rested on the critics of human rights to make the case for supporting certain dictatorships while opposing others, or for rejecting human rights as part of foreign policy considerations. In the end, this change was the most significant of the efforts Jimmy Carter made to forge a post–Cold War foreign policy for the United States.

138 Ibid., 28, 5.
139 Ibid., 48.
140 Ibid., 20.

This policy was challenged in 1980 by Ronald Reagan, who ran for president on a call for a return to the Cold War. He criticized the human rights policy as weakening the United States, and Carter for not providing greater support to the shah of Iran and Somoza. In response, Reagan promised once again to combat communism globally while supporting anticommunist regimes. As the administration acknowledged, its human rights policy had "produced some of the most notable moral and political successes" of Carter's term, but at the same time it had "generated the sharpest criticisms," and it was the policy "least likely to be followed by his immediate successor." As one administration official noted concerning the upcoming change of presidents, Carter's effort to "reduce the identification of the United States with repugnant regimes – an identification previously . . . justified by a global strategy of opposing the spread of Soviet influence and power" was to be abandoned. Support for right-wing dictators was once again to become the policy of the United States.[141] Reagan, however, would discover that the impetus for Carter's policy remained alive in the American public, making his efforts to ignore human rights violations outside the Soviet bloc and his determination to use simple anticommunism as the main criteria for policy toward the Third World a contested issue. The debate over American policy toward right-wing dictatorships was to be renewed at the outset of the Reagan presidency.

[141] Ibid., 1.

6

What Is the Alternative?

The Reagan Doctrine and Authoritarian Regimes

During the 1980 presidential campaign, Ronald Reagan criticized Jimmy Carter's foreign policy for creating a lack of respect for the United States in the world that damaged vital national interests. He blamed Carter's emphasis on human rights for the loss of Nicaragua and Iran, renewed Soviet adventurism, and the decline of American power and prestige in the world. To remedy this situation, Reagan called for a return to the policies of the Cold War. He promised to restore American strength through an arms buildup and to reverse what he saw as American losses overseas by unconditionally upholding the policy of containment and assisting right-wing dictators who promised stability and support for American policies. Reagan argued throughout the campaign that the Soviet Union was responsible for all the unrest in the world, and that it was the obligation of the United States to back its friends and allies against Moscow's efforts to overthrow their governments. Given this, any authoritarian regime, no matter how odious, would receive American aid as long as it was anticommunist and friendly to the United States.

Reagan's classic bipolar, Cold War view drew upon the neoconservative critique of American foreign policy developed during the late 1970s. The neoconservatives saw détente as a one-way street, with the Soviet Union gaining all of the advantages, and believed that the policy of human rights was directed only against American allies, while leaving the worst enemies of freedom, totalitarian communist regimes, unaffected. In support of its policy, the Reagan administration distinguished between authoritarian and totalitarian regimes. It argued that authoritarian, right-wing dictatorships were friendly to the United States and capable of evolving into democratic states, while totalitarian regimes were hostile to American interests, permanent dictatorships that could not become democratic. Using this logic, Reagan again threw American support behind right-wing dictatorships in the name of defending freedom and thwarting communist expansion.

Moreover, Reagan and the neoconservatives drew a dramatically different lesson from the Vietnam War than did the war's critics and the Carter administration. To Reagan, the Vietnam War represented a proper use of American power to uphold containment; the war had been abandoned due to misguided opposition from the American people and a lack of will among American leaders. This had led, according to the neoconservatives, to the "Vietnam Syndrome," which made the United States unwilling to use its power overseas to defend its friends and interests. They saw this hesitancy, in combination with the effort to promote human rights, as providing a green light to Soviet adventurism. In their view, from Afghanistan to Africa to Central America, Soviet communism was again expanding, taking advantage of what Reagan termed American weakness and fear of intervention. It was again time, Reagan insisted, for the United States to use its power actively in the Third World to back its friends and counter these Soviet moves.

To demonstrate American resolve and reverse what he saw as Soviet gains, the new president implemented the so-called Reagan Doctrine. Reagan vowed to go on the ideological offensive to promote democracy in the world by supporting nongovernment "freedom fighters" who were attacking communist nations in the Third World, most notably in Afghanistan and Nicaragua, and thereby rolling back perceived Soviet gains. "In the past two decades," the administration held, "Communist regimes have been created in a significant number of developing nations. In turn, indigenous anti-Communist resistance movements are challenging them." It was imperative that the United States provide "aid in their battle for freedom against Communist dictatorship." This was justified "morally, because human rights abuses are an integral part of Marxist-Leninist dictatorships," and strategically, "because these regimes threaten our own security and the security of our allies and friends."[1] The Reagan Doctrine, therefore, was designed to overcome what the president saw as the passive nature of containment and to bring about Cold War victories in the Third World.

Building on the logic that authoritarian regimes were part of the free world, Reagan provided support for friendly right-wing governments that were under attack. The president made El Salvador the first test of his policies by immediately intervening in that nation's civil war to defend its military regime. The administration ignored the human rights violations and brutality of the government, and the death squads aligned with the military government, and poured billions of dollars worth of military supplies and other resources into the nation in an effort to destroy the armed insurgency and maintain the status quo. The president's policy, however, faced broad-based opposition at home, and Reagan was forced to modify his actions in order to receive funds from Congress. This moderation included the key replacement of the secretary of state, with George Shultz replacing Alexander Haig in June 1982. Reagan found that the changed relationship between Congress and the executive branch since the Vietnam War and Watergate did not allow him a free hand to support right-wing dictators just because they were friends of the United States. In addition, using the language

---

[1] "The Reagan Doctrine," SF: FG001, Case File 390429, Box 41, RRL.

of democracy and freedom as the main weapon to attack communist regimes proved to be a double-edged sword that was taken up by Reagan's opponents against his own policies in El Salvador and elsewhere.[2]

In South Africa, Reagan sought to improve relations with the white minority government in Pretoria through the policy of "constructive engagement." He reversed Carter's efforts to use human rights and political pressure to bring an end to the apartheid system, and sought to work with white South Africans to insure security and economic stability so that, in theory, the government would begin to implement reforms and provide more freedom and rights to the majority black population. Again, Reagan was unable to bring back the old policy of unquestioned American support for right-wing dictators due to opposition at home. Most Americans could not see how supporting a repressive minority regime was part of promoting democracy, and they brought increased pressure on both the administration and American corporations doing business in South Africa to disengage from the apartheid regime.

Reagan found himself incapable of using his notable powers as an orator to convince the American public of his benign view of right-wing dictators. As a political crisis began to engulf the regime of Ferdinand Marcos in the Philippines, Reagan was unable to find a solution to keep Marcos in power. In a scenario remarkably similar to those in Iran and Nicaragua, where Reagan had criticized Carter for not supporting America's loyal friends, the president discovered the limits of American power and the unwillingness of the American people to continue to support such regimes. Lacking a means to intervene in the Philippines, and facing domestic opposition to his efforts to prop up a faltering ally, the president was forced to acquiesce to Marcos's removal from office. The Reagan Doctrine failed and had to be replaced by a policy that supported freedom and democracy.

Authoritarian versus Totalitarian Regimes

At the same time that critics of the Vietnam War were developing a new approach to America foreign policy built upon nonintervention and human rights, neoconservative thinkers were developing a defense of traditional Cold War policy. Former liberals who had supported the war in Vietnam and who rejected both détente and human rights as the basis for foreign policy, they called for a return to containment and the guiding assumptions of the Cold War. They did, however, advocate making morality a part of foreign policy by focusing on the dictatorial nature of communist regimes rather than just on Soviet power, and they criticized the Soviet Union and its allies for their failure to abide by the human rights provisions of the Helsinki accords.[3] They defended the Vietnam War, in Reagan's words, as "a noble cause"[4] in the defense of freedom

[2] See Carothers, *In the Name of Democracy*, for more discussion on this point.
[3] See Ehrman, *The Rise of Neoconservatism*, for a discussion of other neoconservative thinkers.
[4] Young, *The Vietnam Wars*, 315.

and, therefore, continued to advocate the use of American power in the Third World.

The most well-known critic of Carter's policy was the Georgetown University professor Jeane Kirkpatrick. She led the attack on Carter's policy toward Nicaragua and Iran in 1979 with the publication of her article "Dictatorships and Double Standards" in *Commentary*. Together with a second piece published in January 1981 in the same magazine, "U.S. Security and Latin America," her work set out the views of the incoming Reagan administration and constituted the most comprehensive public defense of the policy of supporting right-wing dictatorships. She argued that in the 1970s, the United States had witnessed a decline in power and prestige resulting from its failure in Vietnam and a "posture of continuous self-abasement and apology vis-a-vis the Third World." Kirkpatrick opined that the "failure of the Carter administration's foreign policy is now clear to everyone except its architects, and even they must entertain private doubts, from time to time."[5]

In particular, she blamed Carter's human rights policy for leading to the overthrow of longtime allies – most notably, Somoza in Nicaragua and the shah of Iran. Kirkpatrick argued that the United States need not apologize for its support of "moderate autocrats." Such a policy was in the national interest and not incompatible with the defense of freedom. Kirkpatrick contended that autocratic governments were to be expected in nations such as Nicaragua and Iran, and that the regimes of the Somoza family and the shah of Iran were not as bad as their opponents had claimed. For example, in discussing the Somozas, Kirkpatrick claimed that their government "was moderately competent in encouraging economic development, moderately oppressive, and moderately corrupt."[6] Moreover, Kirkpatrick emphasized that each government was a strong bulwark against communism and a good, loyal ally of the United States. Yet the "Carter administration has not only failed to prevent the undesired outcome, it actively collaborated in the replacement of moderate autocrats friendly to American interests with less friendly autocrats of extremist persuasions."[7]

Central to her argument was the concept that there was a fundamental difference between right-wing and communist dictatorships, or between what she called authoritarian and totalitarian regimes. The crucial distinction, according to Kirkpatrick, was that "traditional autocrats," such as the Somozas and the shah, "leave in place existing allocations of wealth, power, status, and other resources," and "they do not disturb the habitual rhythms of work and leisure, habitual places of residence, habitual patterns of family and personal relations. Because the miseries of traditional life are familiar, they are bearable to ordinary people who ... acquire the skills and attitudes necessary for survival in the miserable roles they are destined to fill." Almost the exact opposite was true, she claimed, for life under communist rule. Left-wing regimes established

[5] Kirkpatrick, "Dictatorships and Double Standards," 45, 34.
[6] Kirkpatrick, "U.S. Security and Latin America," 35.
[7] Kirkpatrick, "Dictatorships and Double Standards," 34.

totalitarian states that "create" the type of "social inequities, brutality, and poverty" that traditional autocrats merely "tolerate."[8]

Kirkpatrick claimed that because right-wing dictators left traditional patterns in place, "given time, propitious economic, social, and political circumstances, talented leaders, and a strong indigenous demand for representative government," their nations could evolve from autocratic societies into democracies. Totalitarian communist states could not. Indeed, by their very nature, Kirkpatrick argued, communist societies shut off any of these avenues toward development and, therefore, democratic change. Hence, right-wing dictatorships were a necessary and inevitable stage of government for Third World nations, and support by Washington not only was in the interest of the United States but also served to protect liberalism and promote democracy. She saw the people in the Third World as too politically immature for democratic government and, therefore, in need of strong rule to prevent radical ideas from taking hold. The United States, she concluded, was helping to provide the stability and economic modernization these states needed for the development of democratic institutions while serving its own interests by blocking communist expansion and protecting American trade and investments. "Democratic governments," she argued, only come into being "slowly, after extended prior experience with more limited forms of participation." Attempts to promote human rights, reform, and democratization were therefore bound to fail. "Efforts to force complex and unfamiliar political practices on societies lacking the requisite political culture ... not only fail to produce the desired outcomes; if they are undertaken at a time when the traditional regime is under attack, they actually facilitate the job of the insurgents."[9]

In addition, Kirkpatrick stated, the United States should not be surprised or bothered by the brutal tactics that autocratic regimes relied upon to rule. Both Somoza and the shah were "confronted by radical, violent opponents bent on social and political revolution. Both rulers, therefore, sometimes invoked martial law to arrest, imprison, exile, and occasionally, it was alleged, torture their opponents." Given that Nicaragua and Iran were "led by men who had not been selected by free elections," they could employ such practices because they were under "no duty to submit themselves to searching tests of popular acceptability." She saw the Carter administration as misunderstanding this essential point. "When [Carter] says that 'the Somoza regime lost the confidence of the people,' the President implies that the regime had previously rested on the confidence of 'the people,' but that situation had now changed. In fact, the Somoza regime had never rested on popular will (but instead on manipulation, force and habit), and was not being ousted by it." Yet the Carter administration had acted on "the assumption that the armed conflict of Sandinistas and Somozistas was the military equivalent of a national referendum," and this had

[8] Ibid., 44.
[9] Ibid., 37–8.

"enabled the President to imagine that it could be, and should be, settled by the people of Nicaragua."[10]

As Kirkpatrick noted, "the Carter administration's commitment to nonintervention proved stronger than strategic considerations or national pride." She claimed, however, that the administration criticized only right-wing dictatorships, and that the "principles of self-determination and non-intervention are thus both selectively applied. We seem to accept the status quo in Communist nations (in the name of 'diversity and national autonomy'), but not in nations ruled by 'right-wing dictators' or white oligarchies." This claim of an inconsistent application of the human rights policy became a standard criticism of Carter's policy and led Kirkpatrick to conclude that "what the rest of the world regarded as a stinging American defeat" in Nicaragua and Iran had come from the Soviets' ability to take advantage of Carter's efforts.[11]

Reviving the verities of the Cold War, Kirkpatrick continued by arguing that only the Soviet Union benefited from Carter's policy. What she saw as the attack on autocratic governments was costing the United States friendly allies and providing the Soviets with new bases for operations. In addition, "everywhere our friends will have noted that the U.S. cannot be counted on in times of difficulty and our enemies will have observed that American support provides no security against the forward march of history." Carter's encouragement of change and promotion of human rights meant, Kirkpatrick asserted, that the United States "ends up aligning...tacitly with Soviet clients." Given her Manichean understanding of the world, and seeing all revolutions as Soviet inspired, Kirkpatrick could see no other option but to oppose all movements for change. Indeed, she believed that American policy had done what the insurgents could not, overthrow the dictatorships. "American efforts to impose liberalization and democratization on a government confronted with violent international opposition not only failed but actually assisted the coming to power of new regimes in which ordinary people enjoy fewer freedoms and less personal security than under the previous autocracy – regimes, moreover, hostile to American interests and policies."[12]

Though Kirkpatrick's essays generated much discussion, they contained little that was new. She was only stating publicly what had been the main assumptions and arguments used by policymakers in private discussions and papers to justify American support for right-wing dictators for much of the century. As the subsequent collapse of communism in Eastern Europe in 1989 and the disintegration of the Soviet Union in 1991 demonstrated, this reasoning remained as faulty as it was during the 1920s when it was first being developed.[13] Nonetheless, Kirkpatrick's arguments were designed to allow moral arguments to be used to criticize the Soviet Union and those designated as enemies of the United

---

[10] Ibid., 35, 43.
[11] Ibid., 41, 36.
[12] Ibid., 35–6, 41.
[13] See Schmitz, *Thank God They're on Our Side*, 9–84.

States while sparing right-wing allies from similar condemnation. Her views became part of the Reagan administration's new Cold War policies, and provided a starting point for its approach toward right-wing dictators.

Reagan never abandoned the view of the Vietnam War that he set out in 1966 while governor of California. Speaking in opposition to student protests against the war, he declared that "there is no substitute for victory." It was unthinkable to him that "our young men are dying in a war with a country whose whole gross national product is less than the industrial output of Cleveland, Ohio." The United States should use its power "to level Vietnam, pave it, paint stripes on it, and make a parking lot out of it."[14] During the campaign of 1980, Reagan revived the language of the Cold War and built upon the ideas of Kirkpatrick and the other neoconservatives. He set out his understanding of world events in clear and simple terms. "Let us not delude ourselves," Reagan declared. "The Soviet Union underlies all the unrest that is going on. If they weren't engaged in this game of dominoes, there wouldn't be any hot spots in the world."[15]

Reagan repeated these ideas in his basic campaign speech as he defended the war in Vietnam and attacked its critics. It was true, Reagan declared, that the war was not fought according to General Douglas MacArthur's dictum that "there is no substitute for victory." Yet "50,000 Americans died in Southeast Asia. They were not engaged in some racist enterprise." When they made the "ultimate sacrifice to defend the people of a small, defenseless country in Southeast Asia from Communist tyranny, that, my friends, is a collective act of moral courage, not an example of moral poverty." "Isn't it time," Reagan asked, that the nation "recognized the veterans of that war were men who fought as bravely and as effectively as any American fighting men have ever fought in any war? And isn't it time we told them that never again will we allow the immorality of asking young men to fight and die in a war our Government was afraid to let them win?" If he were president, there would be "no more Vietnams" that ended in defeat.[16] He promised to end the "Vietnam Syndrome," restore American power, and protect the friends of the United States.

Contending that all the problems and unrest in the world stemmed from Soviet aggression, Reagan stated that Carter's was a "foreign policy bordering on appeasement" that allowed friendly governments to be overthrown while "a student mob can hold hostage, with impunity, diplomats and marines in the American embassy in Iran." The only way to correct this problem, as Reagan saw it, was a massive buildup of American power and a willingness to intervene in the Third World to combat revolutionary change. As for the opinions of other nations, Reagan noted that he did not "care if they like us or not. We intend to be respected throughout the world." He would, therefore, "begin the moral and military rearmament of the United States for the difficult, dangerous decade ahead." Once he was president, Reagan concluded,

[14] Johnson, *Sleepwalking through History*, 79.
[15] Steel, "Cold War, Cold Comfort," 15.
[16] *New York Times*, 29 February 1980.

"there will be no more abandonment of friends by the United States of America." Right-wing dictatorships that were allies would be supported by his administration no matter what the cost.[17] Guided by this analysis, Reagan pledged during his campaign to stop the spread of communism in Central America by opposing the Sandinista government in Nicaragua and supporting the military in El Salvador. As the Republican Party platform stated, the United States faced a danger to its interests from the "Marxist Sandinista takeover of Nicaragua and the Marxist attempts to destabilize El Salvador, Guatemala, and Honduras."[18]

After his election, Reagan demonstrated his opposition to using human rights as a criteria for judging right-wing dictatorships by naming Jeane Kirkpatrick his ambassador to the United Nations and Ernest Lefever as the head of the human rights section of the State Department. Lefever was another well-known critic of Carter's policy who had testified to a House subcommittee in 1979 that in his view "the United States should remove from the statute books all clauses that establish a human rights standard or condition that must be met by another sovereign nation," and that the United States should not be concerned about South Africa's apartheid system and worry only about how to incorporate that nation into the battle against communist expansion.[19]

Once in office, Reagan reiterated his rejection of Carter's policy and his intention to back right-wing dictatorships. To signal the change, the president hosted two military dictators, General Chun Doo Hwan of South Korea and General Roberto Eduardo Viola of Argentina, in his first months in the White House. Moreover, he lifted the ban on exports and military aid to nations such as Chile and other nations designated as gross violators of human rights by the Carter administration. In March 1981, responding to a question from Walter Cronkite on the place of human rights in American foreign policy, Reagan claimed that during the previous administration

we took countries that were pro-Western that were maybe authoritarian in government, but not totalitarian, more authoritarian than we would like, did not meet all of our principles of what constitutes human rights, and we punished them at the same time we were claiming détente with countries where there are no human rights. The Soviet Union is the greatest violator today of human rights in all the world.

With friendly allied dictators "we should look at it that we're in a better position remaining friends, to persuade them of the rightness of our view on human rights than to suddenly, as we have done in some places, pull the rug out from under them and then let a completely totalitarian takeover that denies what human rights the people had had." Cronkite followed up by asking, "doesn't that put us in the position rather of abetting the suppression of human rights for our own selfish ends... until such time as we can make those persuasive

---

[17] Ibid.
[18] Johnson, *Sleepwalking through History*, 253.
[19] *Public Papers of the Presidents: Reagan 1981*, 196.

changes?" Reagan responded: "Well, what has the choice turned out to be? The choice has turned out to be they lose all human rights because there's a totalitarian takeover."[20]

In the president's view, supporting authoritarian regimes was necessary in the name of freedom, no matter how undemocratic their rule at home. Seeing all right-wing dictators as opponents of communism and allies in a global struggle, Reagan cast them as freedom fighters on the front lines of America's battle against communism. As Reagan declared in his 1985 State of the Union message, "our mission is to nourish and defend freedom and democracy." In order to do this "we must stand by all our democratic allies," including right-wing dictators. Thus, backing right-wing regimes was linked to the Reagan Doctrine as one policy in the defense of freedom. It was critical, the president believed, that the United States "not break faith with those who are risking their lives – on every continent, from Afghanistan to Nicaragua – to defy Soviet supported aggression and secure rights which have been ours from birth. . . . Support for freedom fighters is self-defense."[21] Reagan, therefore, would attempt to restore American support for authoritarian regimes in order to promote stability, defend longtime allies, and bring about the defeat of communism in the Third World. Yet his invocation of promoting democracy abroad revealed, Kirkpatrick's views notwithstanding, the contradictions in the president's approach that would ultimately lead to changes in his policy.

A Sense of Proportion: Reagan and El Salvador

At the outset of his administration, President Reagan made El Salvador the place where he would demonstrate American resolve to support its right-wing allies and contain communism. El Salvador would become one of the primary battlefields of the new Cold War as the United States–supported Salvadoran military battled the Farabundo Marti National Liberation Front (FMLN) for the rest of the decade. Despite consistent human rights abuses by the military and the right-wing death squads, Reagan persisted in supporting the government of El Salvador in order to block what he saw as a Soviet-inspired insurgency while assuring friendly dictators around the world of Washington's support. The government in San Salvador became dependent on American aid, which totaled over $4 billion, and could not continue the war without support from Washington. The brutality of the Salvadoran military forces, however, shocked the American public and created a domestic opposition to Reagan's policy. The majority of Americans rejected the administration's analysis of the events in El Salvador, seeing it as a revolution caused by poverty and the injustices of the El Salvadoran ruling class, and demanded that American aid be tied to the protection of human rights and negotiations. This opposition forced some concessions from the administration as it sought to curb the worst excesses of the

---

[20] Ibid.
[21] *Public Papers of the Presidents: Reagan 1985*, 135.

military without harming its ability to wage war. In the end, the war brought about enormous destruction to the region, killing over seventy thousand people in El Salvador alone; and approximately one million people, making up twenty percent of the population, became refugees as a result of Reagan's failed attempt to use force to shape El Salvador to his wishes.

Since the nineteenth century, El Salvador had been dominated by the so-called forty families (the oligarchy) that controlled the politics and wealth of the nation. The consolidation of the oligarchy's rule in the 1880s displaced tens of thousands of peasants from the lands they farmed, creating a social and economic structure built on unequal land distribution and the use of force to maintain the status quo. A peasant uprising in January 1932 was brutally crushed by the government of General Maximiliano Hernández Martínez in the *matanza* (massacre) that killed thirty thousand El Salvadoreans. Fearing instability and threats to American property, and seeing the rebellion as a communist revolt, the Hoover administration supported the government's actions and began the long history of American support of El Salvador's military rulers. For the next fifty years, the military protected the interests of the oligarchy against the peasants, who lived in endemic poverty and fear.[22]

The international economic crisis of the 1970s hit El Salvador's coffee economy hard and brought political unrest to the nation. The military and allied right-wing death squads, financed by the oligarchy, launched a series of attacks on the political opposition and peasants in an effort to crush all dissent. The growing repression, however, failed to end the upheaval as the government's brutality increased the popularity of the opposition forces. Leftist guerrilla organizations appeared, demanding land reform and political change. Their strength grew throughout the decade, providing the first significant threat to the military's and oligarchy's control of the nation. The challenge to the government's rule was not limited to the rural peasants. The urban middle class, also suffering economically, sought moderate reforms to modernize the economy and open up the political process. Centered around the presidential campaign of the Christian Democratic Party (PDC) leader Jose Napoleon Duarte, the moderate opposition unified in 1972 to form the National Opposition Union (UNO). Duarte garnered the majority of the votes, only to have the election stolen by the military. Subsequently, Duarte was tortured and then expelled from the nation. This outright fraud convinced many that the military would not tolerate even moderate criticism, and that the political process could not bring about change.[23]

During the 1970s, the Catholic Church in El Salvador emerged as a leading voice of opposition to the military and its right-wing allies. Beginning with the Medellín Conference of Latin American Bishops in 1968, the church condemned

---

[22] See Montgomery, *Revolution in El Salvador*, for a good overview of this history; Anderson, *Matanza*, for the events of 1932; and Schmitz, *Thank God They're on Our Side*, 57–72, on U.S. support for the military.

[23] Montgomery, *Revolution in El Salvador*.

the "institutionalized violence" of the social structure, which systematically repressed the poor, and encouraged efforts to promote political reform. The military denounced the priests who worked with the peasants as "communists" and "subversives," and in 1977 started to assassinate priests as part of its wider repression. These attacks forced the new bishop, Oscar Romero, to defend the church and speak out about the dire conditions of the peasants and against the political repression in El Salvador.[24]

The Carter administration, as it sought to stop the worst human rights abuses and promote democratic reforms, immediately placed El Salvador in the category of gross violators of human rights and cut off military aid in March 1977. Sanctions remained in place until the fall of 1979, when a group of young officers overthrew the government and promised reforms. In early 1980, a reconstituted junta brought in Duarte and other civilians in an effort to create a more moderate government and gain support from Washington. These measures were too little, too late, to solve the problems that had built up over decades in El Salvador, and any chance of receiving significant support from the United States soon vanished. Government repression, attacks on peasants and the church, and human rights abuses continued. On 23 March 1980, Archbishop Romero denounced the junta's actions as "reforms bathed in blood," and urged soldiers to disobey their officers. The next day, he was assassinated by the death squads while presiding over a funeral.[25] In response, all opposition parties except the PDC formed the Democratic Revolutionary Front (FDR), which was designed to overthrow the government. The moderate center had moved to the left, giving up all hope of working with the military and the oligarchy. That fall, the FMLN was formed, and joined with the FDR to create a united opposition to the oligarchy and the military.

Reagan's election in November had an immediate impact on events in El Salvador. The El Salvadoran military and the death squads saw Reagan's victory as a green light to carry out any actions in their effort to defeat the newly formed FMLN and unleashed a new wave of violence against their opponents. The night after Reagan's victory, a mutilated body was found on the streets of San Salvador with a sign that declared: "With Reagan, we will eliminate the miscreants and subversives in El Salvador and Central America."[26] At the end of the month, six leaders of the FDR were assassinated by the death squads in an effort to destroy any organized political opposition to the regime. Finally, on December 2, three American nuns and a female lay worker were raped and murdered by the military for their alleged support of the FMLN. The killings were designed as a warning to others not to aid the insurgency. The Carter administration again suspended military and economic aid to El Salvador, bringing about a collapse of the ruling junta and a new military government, with Duarte

[24] LaFeber, *Inevitable Revolutions*, 218–25.
[25] Gettleman et al., *El Salvador*, 62.
[26] Armstrong and Shenk, *El Salvador*, 173–4.

as president. In response, the administration restored some economic aid to El Salvador in the hope of supporting the moderate forces that Duarte supposedly represented.[27]

The FDR and FMLN concluded, however, that there were no moderate forces in the government and that the only way to bring about change was through armed struggle. Convinced that the situation would only get worse when Reagan took power, the FMLN launched a series of attacks in late December and a general offensive in January 1981 to overthrow the government. The assault, however, failed to bring down the junta. Thus, when Reagan took office, all efforts at reform had been abandoned, and El Salvador descended into full-scale civil war.

Invoking Kirkpatrick's thesis on the benefits of supporting authoritarian regimes, the Reagan administration launched an all-out propaganda campaign to gain support for waging war in El Salvador. In February 1981, the State Department released a White Paper on El Salvador, *Communist Interference in El Salvador*, designed to prove an international communist conspiracy to overthrow the government in San Salvador. It claimed to provide "definitive evidence of the clandestine military support given by the Soviet Union, Cuba, and their Communist allies to Marxist-Leninist guerrillas now fighting to overthrow the established government of El Salvador," and to underscore the "central role played by Cuba and other Communist countries beginning in 1979 in the political unification, military direction, and arming of insurgent forces in El Salvador." The events in Central America were portrayed as "a strikingly familiar case of Soviet, Cuban, and other Communist military involvement in a politically troubled Third World country." All this was designed to make it look as if the insurgency was an illegitimate, outside invasion of El Salvador, an effort to "overthrow the established government and the imposition of a Communist regime in defiance of the will of the Salvadorean people." As the White Paper concluded, "over the past year, the insurgency in El Salvador had been progressively transformed into a textbook case of indirect armed aggression by Communist powers through Cuba."[28]

By contrast, the ruling junta in El Salvador was portrayed as a moderate, democratizing force that was working to overcome the abuses of the past and create a model Third World government. The record of El Salvador's rulers throughout the twentieth century was so bad that the White Paper could not completely ignore it. Rather, it quickly skipped over this history in a paragraph and claimed that the repression and state-sanctioned violence were now a thing of the past. The current regime, the State Department asserted, was a stable one, under the respected leadership of Duarte, "aware of the need for change," and beginning to address the most important issues such as land reform. Duarte was presented as the representative of a moderate middle who was working to end "the terrorism practiced by extremists of both the left and right," and

---

[27] Gettleman et al., *El Salvador*, 63.
[28] Department of State, *Communist Interference in El Salvador*.

as the leader of a government that "has stuck to its reform programs" and gained popular support. This argument ignored the fact that the recent killings of American nuns and others had been carried out by the forces of this very government, and was designed to place the responsibility elsewhere so as to justify American support. With all the violence now blamed on extremist forces, the administration went forward with its defense of the Duarte regime and efforts to provide it aid. "In sum, the Duarte government is working hard and with some success to deal with the serious political, and economic problems that most concern the people of El Salvador."[29] Thus, the administration invoked all of the traditional arguments for supporting a right-wing dictatorship as it claimed that American support of the ruling regime was necessary to prevent a communist takeover of El Salvador; to provide stability, thereby allowing for economic reform and democratic change; and to protect American interests.

Having characterized the revolution as a Soviet-led attack on El Salvador, the administration claimed that the danger extended beyond Central America to the United States and the whole Western world. This provided further justification for American intervention in support of Duarte's regime. Secretary of State Alexander Haig told America's NATO allies immediately before the release of the White Paper that El Salvador faced "a systematic, well-financed, sophisticated effort to impose a Communist regime" on the country by the Soviet Union that fit its pattern of aggression all over the world and presented "a threat, in our view, not just to the United States but to the West at large." The United States, therefore, had "no alternative but to act to prevent forces hostile to the U.S. and the West from overthrowing a government on our doorstep, particularly when that government offers the best hope of progress toward moderate democracy."[30]

The next month, Haig invoked the Kirkpatrick thesis to defend the administration's support of the Duarte regime. In a March 31 speech, the secretary of state argued that supporting such an authoritarian regime was in the interests of the United States and the promotion of its values. In making policy, "[W]e should distinguish between the so-called totalitarian and authoritarian regimes," Haig stated. "The authoritarian regime usually stems from a lack of political or economic development and customarily reserves for itself absolute authority in only a few politically sensitive areas." This meant, he asserted, that authoritarian regimes were "more likely to change than their totalitarian counterparts." Thus, it would be wrong to treat them in a similar manner. Moreover, totalitarian communist regimes had the worst human rights records and should be the focus of criticism. It was important, Haig lectured, that the United States "adopt a sense of proportion in dealing with the violators."[31]

In support of its policy, the administration dramatically increased American assistance to the Duarte regime. In February and March, American aid to the government increased fivefold, including $35 million in arms and over

---

[29] Ibid.
[30] Gettleman et al., *El Salvador*, 217–18.
[31] *New York Times*, 21 April 1981.

$125 million more in economic assistance. In addition, American military advisors were dispatched to train El Salvador's troops, and the administration secretly arranged for both Argentina and Panama, two other right-wing dictatorships that received renewed support from the Reagan administration, to train Salvadorean forces, give military assistance, and provide conduits for secret funds.[32] At the same time, the administration began funding anti-Sandinista forces in Honduras. Reagan claimed that this was necessary to stop the flow of arms from Nicaragua to El Salvador, and that the United States supported only this effort to interdict arms. It immediately became clear, however, that the administration had launched a covert effort to overthrow the Sandinista government.[33]

The National Security Council saw the sending of military advisors as critical to the success of Reagan's support for the El Salvadoran regime. Without American military personnel in country, there would be no "hope of preventing the overthrow of the moderates by the Marxist Left," making it "very hard to then rally our Latin neighbors to take a stand in the next case – which will be Honduras." Having even a few small U.S. training teams "would have an uplifting psychological and morale effect" on government forces and would provide the "greatest single hope for any reversal" of the regime's current losses. The NSC also claimed that the presence of advisors would improve the human rights record of the security forces as it would have a *"disciplining* effect on the Salvadorean troops. The sense of despair and fear when you are in combat alone and losing sometimes leads to acts of brutality and even barbarism." The presence of U.S. military soldiers, in theory, would bring this to an end.[34]

The White Paper and the administration's actions were quickly criticized as ideologically driven arguments and actions, based on few facts, that ignored the indigenous nature of the revolution. Moreover, the administration's policy was seen by many as placing the United States on a path similar to the one taken in Vietnam. President Reagan sought to dismiss such fears and focus the debate on the danger of communist expansion. Richard Allen, Reagan's first national security advisor, prepared a document for Reagan and other administration officials to use on "Why El Salvador Isn't Vietnam." The central point to be stressed was that "strategically, the situation in El Salvador is much different" from the one in Vietnam. El Salvador was a small nation close to the United States without a contiguous communist nation to aid it, and a country the United States had "a high cultural identity with." Finally, there was a "high degree of understanding for the situation in Central America" by the United States, in contrast to Vietnam, which "was completely foreign to us." The administration was confident that the United States could succeed in El Salvador if America acted, since all other Cuban-supported insurgencies in

[32] Haig to Reagan, 13 March 1981, "Additional Assistance for El Salvador," NSC:CF, Box 91363, RRL; Johnson, *Sleepwalking through History*, 256–60.
[33] LaFeber, *Inevitable Revolutions*, 281–2, 296–300.
[34] Schweitzer and Fontaine to Allen, 24 February 1981, "NSC Meeting 25 February," NSC:CF, Box 91363, RRL (emphasis in the original).

the hemisphere that it had opposed had failed. It claimed that the only communist success, Nicaragua, was due to the lack of U.S. action. Thus, the United
States could win the war, and "stability will return to El Salvador if the present
regime is stabilized."[35]

On March 3, the president was interviewed by *CBS News* anchorman Walter
Cronkite. In response to a question asking whether he saw any parallels between
his administration's sending military advisors and assistance to El Salvador and
the early steps of American escalation in Vietnam, the president answered no.
He asserted that what the United States was doing in El Salvador was "offering
some help against the import of the export into the Western Hemisphere of
terrorism, of disruption, and it isn't just El Salvador. This happens to be the
target at the moment. Our problem is this whole hemisphere and keeping this
sort of thing out." Three days later, in a news conference, Reagan again rejected
the comparison. The difference this time, the president stated, was that the
problem was in

our front yard, it isn't just El Salvador. What we're doing, in going to the aid of a
government that asked that aid of a neighboring country and a friendly country in our
hemisphere, is try to halt the infiltration into the Americas by terrorists, by outside
interference and those who aren't just aiming at El Salvador but, I think, are aiming at
the whole of Central and possibly later South America – and, I'm sure, eventually North
America.

The United States was seeking "to stop this destabilizing force of terrorism
and guerrilla warfare and revolution from being exported here, backed by the
Soviet Union and Cuba."[36]

The president's assurances did little to stem a growing opposition within the
nation. While there was little active support for the administration's backing
of the brutal El Salvadoran government, various religious and secular organizations mobilized to oppose American intervention in Central America, and
public opinion polls consistently showed that most Americans were against any
greater involvement by the United States.[37] In the wake of the Vietnam War,
the Church Committee revelations, and the growing awareness of human rights
considerations during the Carter years, the American public was now skeptical
of White House claims of the need for greater military support for a right-
wing dictatorship. Moreover, most Americans rejected the view that the revolution stemmed from a communist conspiracy, seeing the problems as instead
rooted in the poverty of the nation and the brutality and corruption of the
government.

The debate intensified in March, when Haig defended the administration's
policy during testimony in the House. Concerning the killing of the American
nuns and lay worker, Haig stated that "some of the investigations would lead

[35] Allen to Baker and Meese, 25 February 1981, "Why El Salvador Isn't Vietnam"; Fontaine to
    Allen, 27 February 1981, "Why Vietnam Isn't El Salvador," both NSC:CF, Box 91363, RRL.
[36] *Public Papers of the Presidents: Reagan, 1981*, 191, 207.
[37] Smith, *Resisting Reagan*, 95.

one to believe that perhaps the vehicle that the nuns were riding in may have tried to run a roadblock, or may accidently have been perceived to have been doing so, and there'd been an exchange of fire and then perhaps those who inflicted the casualties sought to cover it up." He continued by exonerating any government or military official from any role in the murders, contending that "the facts on this are not clear enough for anyone to draw a definitive conclusion." In this, he was echoing Jeane Kirkpatrick, who had said the previous December that "the nuns were not just nuns. The nuns were also political activists ... on behalf of the Frente [FMLN]." The next day in the Senate, Haig tried to back away from the implications of what he had said, that the nuns had tried to run a roadblock or that they were armed and involved in a shoot-out. Nonetheless, he stuck to his point that one of the most prominent theories as to how they were killed involved an accident at a roadblock. Opponents quickly noted that it was known that the nuns were picked up by security forces and killed hours later in a different place.[38] Privately, administration officials acknowledged they knew that the security forces committed the killings.[39] The purpose of Haig's suggestion that the American nuns were responsible for their own deaths was to confuse the issue and divert attention from the type of government the administration was supporting. Instead, it led to more questions about the administration's goals and greater scrutiny of its policy.

This opposition manifested itself in Congress, where 60 percent of the president's aid requests for El Salvador were denied in the first two years of the administration because lawmakers feared an ever-growing American commitment could lead to direct United States intervention. While no one in Congress wanted to see a FMLN victory, the opponents of the president disagreed with the administration's analysis of the crisis and, therefore, with its conclusion that military action was the solution. As Republican Senator David Durenberger noted in April 1981, members of Congress agreed with the administration that "the armed leftist opposition in El Salvador represents neither the wishes nor the best interests of the Salvadorean people." The issue "separating critics and supporters of President Reagan's policies is over how best to isolate and deal with these terrorists, through military assistance or through reforms that eliminate the grievances upon which they depend for sustenance."[40]

This debate continued throughout the year. In mid-April, it was revealed that the Treasury police had massacred at least twenty-four people in Soyapango, a working-class suburb of San Salvador, earlier that month. The government claimed that the deaths were the result of a shootout, and that "the bound and mutilated corpses were dragged in by the guerrillas while the police were caring for their wounded." No independent organization or American official believed this version, and all agreed that the Salvadorean government was responsible for most of the civilian killings. As Allen informed Reagan, "the Soyapango

---

[38] Arnson, *Crossroads*, 62–3.
[39] Allen to Reagan, 16 April 1981, NSC:CF, Box 91363, RRL.
[40] *Congressional Record*, 7 April 1981, S 3427–28.

killings, as the State Department has observed, differ only in 'scope and noto-riety' from other similar incidents committed regularly in El Salvador by the extreme right and left, and (unfortunately) government security forces – the Treasury Police in particular." Allen also informed the president that it was the Treasury police who "were almost certainly responsible for the killing of the four American churchwomen." The administration's main concern was not getting to the truth of this case, any more than it had been in the killing of the American nuns. Rather, it was concerned that these killings would "make our position in El Salvador more difficult," and with getting the embassy in San Salvador to do its "best to remind the government that disciplining the security forces is essential for continued American support" because "our effort in El Salvador will succeed or fail first in the United States and not in El Salvador."[41]

These points were reemphasized in the following days as Ambassador Dean Hinton returned to Washington for meetings with senior administration offi-cials. The National Security Council noted that it was essential that the ambas-sador make clear to the Salvadorean government that a satisfactory solution to the killings of Americans be found, "because the war in El Salvador will be won or lost in the United States." In addition, the administration worried about the "possible murder of a US newsman" covering the government's actions, not because it would be a tragedy in itself, but because it "would be a disaster for our position." It acknowledged that "there is no cohesive center" in El Salvador, and that the key to continued aid was the El Salvadoran government's ability to present a better image to the American people.[42] The reason for the admin-istration's concern became clear the following month, when over one hundred thousand people marched through Washington, D.C., and across the Potomac to the Pentagon to protest American support of the Duarte regime.

In order to bolster its position that without sustained U.S. aid to El Salvador the communist insurgents would win, and to pressure Congress to grant more funding, the administration arranged for a four-day visit to Washington in September by Duarte. The administration sought to "reassure Duarte of our firm support" for his government and to help him in the elections scheduled for the following March.[43] Haig wrote Reagan that Duarte represented the best hope for the United States in El Salvador, and that it was essential, in order to defeat the "well armed *Marxist-Leninist guerrilla movement* supported by Cuba and Nicaragua," to demonstrate "*that this Administration is commit-ted to being as helpful as possible within our budgetary constraints.*" There were, of course, "major problems with Congress," which they hoped Duarte's "presence will ameliorate." The administration was "*not winning the struggle to convince a clear majority within the Congress that the Salvadorean govern-ment deserves US assistance.*" The meetings, therefore, had to emphasize "that

[41] Allen to Reagan, 16 April 1981, "Soyapango Killings in El Salvador: Fallout," NSC:CF, Box 91363, RRL.
[42] Fontaine to Allen, 22 April 1981, NSC:CF, Box 91363, RRL.
[43] Bremer to Allen, 16 September 1981, NSC:CF, Box 91363, RRL.

the Salvadorean government is taking *firm steps to control acts of violence* against non-combatants by right-wing 'death squads' and the security forces." This, he told the president, *"would strengthen our hand with Congress."* It was equally important to strengthen Duarte's prestige at home. "Although Duarte is President of the junta, the military remains the country's dominant political force," and, Haig noted in a telling admission, *"Duarte thus far had been ineffective in confronting the military or curtailing their excesses."*[44]

The trip failed on both of its main goals, to improve the image of El Salvador in the United States and to curb the excesses of the Salvadorean military and death squads. Congress continued to reduce or reject the administration's requests for more aid, and in December 1981, in order to keep some control over American policy, required that the administration certify every six months that the human rights situation in El Salvador was improving as a condition for military aid to continue. At the very same time that Congress was making the improvement of human rights a requirement for continued aid, El Salvadoran soldiers massacred over seven hundred people in El Mozote and its surrounding villages. This story broke in both the *New York Times* and the *Washington Post* on 27 January 1982, the day before the administration submitted its certification of progress on human rights by the junta, and claimed that killings by the military and the death squads in El Salvador were declining. Raymond Bonner's front page story in the *Times* was the more detailed, reporting that peasants "said that all these [victims], their relatives and friends, had been killed by Government soldiers of the Atlacatl Battalion in a sweep in December." Bonner estimated that 733 people had been killed in the operation by these American-trained soldiers.[45] This report demonstrated that the idea of a moderate government working to control the extreme right was a fiction, and gave the lie to the claims that there was no connection between the military and the death squads.

Congress responded by sharply criticizing the president for ignoring its wishes and failing to bring about any improvements in El Salvador. The purpose of American aid was to support Duarte and the so-called moderates in the junta so that they could control the security forces. Plainly, that was not the case, and there was no evidence that the administration was making any efforts along these lines. One Democratic lawmaker opined that "if there is anything left of the English language in this city ... it is gone now, because the president has just certified that up is down and in is out and black is white. I anticipate him telling us that war is peace at any moment."[46] The Republican chair of the Senate Foreign Relations Committee, Charles Percy, raised concerns about the certification in the wake of these reports, and wondered what message it would send to El Salvador's military. Representative Michael Barnes correctly noted that "the administration is not going to stop aiding the Salvadorean military."

---

44 Haig to Reagan, 19 September 1981, NSC:CF, Box 91363, RRL (emphasis in the original).
45 *New York Times*, 27 January 1982.
46 Danner, *The Massacre at El Mozote*, 132.

What the Congress had to be concerned about was "the signal being sent by this certification...that the United States condones these abuses."[47]

The administration's position, however, was predicated on the position that Duarte was the lesser of two evils compared to communism, that the government's military action was a necessary condition to maintain order and defeat the insurgency, and that any efforts to challenge that logic was a challenge to the overall policy of defeating communism. Support for right-wing dictatorships was, therefore, an essential component of Reagan's policy. As a consequence, the administration responded to this congressional anger by denying San Salvador's responsibility for the massacre, attempting to discredit the reports, and blaming the FMLN for the killings. U.S. embassy officials responsible for investigating the charges never went to El Mozote, relying instead upon Salvadorean officials in filing their reports. On January 30, the embassy claimed there was a lack of evidence to support the charge of a massacre, and blamed the guerrillas for the deaths of any civilians in the area. "It is certain that the guerrilla forces who established a defensive position in El Mozote did nothing to remove them [the civilians] from the path of the battle." The embassy confirmed that some noncombatants did die in the area, but claimed that "no evidence could be found to confirm that government forces systematically massacred civilians in the operation zone, nor that the number of civilians killed even remotely approached number being cited in other reports circulating internationally." The Reagan administration used this report to substantiate the claim that the charges made against the regime were baseless and to denounce the press and critics of its policy as spreading propaganda for the guerrillas.[48] Moreover, in defiance of congressional opponents, Reagan signed an executive order allowing for the shipment of $55 million in defense equipment to San Salvador.

Further evidence, however, continued to appear, forcing Ambassador Hinton to conduct his own investigation. He wrote the State Department two days after the initial report that he "would be grateful if [the] department would use extreme care in describing my views on [the] alleged massacre." While he did not agree with the version of events being reported by the FMLN, "additional evidence strongly suggests that something happened that should not have happened and that it is quite possible that the Salvadorean military did commit excesses." Hinton became increasingly critical of the security forces in the next week, a position that damaged the White House's claim that the Duarte government was a moderate force positioned between the extreme left and right.[49] When President Reagan was asked on February 12 about the ambassador's complaints concerning the El Salvadoran government, Reagan held to the position that his administration was supporting a moderate regime. "We know that there have been problems from both the left and the right," he answered, which

[47] Arnson, *Crossroads*, 87.
[48] Danner, *The Massacre at El Mozote*, 195–201.
[49] Ibid., 207–8.

was why he "supported the Duarte government, which is between both of those factions, both of which have been somewhat extreme."[50]

The reports of the El Mozote massacre, and the strong congressional and public response, forced a shift in tactics by the administration to maintain its policy. Reagan turned his focus to the upcoming elections in March in El Salvador, making the issue one of a struggling democracy opposed by communism. On February 24, in a speech to the Organization of American States, the president declared that the government of El Salvador "has repeatedly urged the guerrillas to renounce violence, to join in the democratic process, an election in which the people of El Salvador could determine the government they prefer.... The guerrillas have refused. More than that, they now threaten violence and death to those who participate in such an election." Reagan continued by claiming that communist propaganda had succeeded in misleading many concerning the true nature of the conflict in El Salvador. The insurgency was not, he claimed, about overcoming oppression. "Very simply, guerrillas, armed and supported by and through Cuba, are attempting to impose a Marxist-Leninist dictatorship on the people of El Salvador as part of a larger imperialistic plan."[51] It was now necessary to support Duarte in order to preserve democracy in El Salvador.

The election, however, proved to be a disaster for Washington. The FMLN, recalling the assassinations in 1980 and noting their fear of reprisals, announced that they would not participate in the voting. While this would seemingly help the government, and while the Reagan administration threw its complete support behind Duarte in an effort to prove it was backing a moderate middle course in El Salvador, the right-wing ARENA Party, under the leadership of Roberto D'Aubisson and with the support of the military and the oligarchy, won the election. In an effort to salvage what it could, the administration was successful in preventing D'Aubisson, who was directly linked to the death squads and the murder of Archbishop Romero, from being named president, and in getting the Christian Democrats to join in a coalition government. Still, there was no doubt that this was a victory for the right as the new government put an end to land reform. In response, Congress rejected a request by the administration for a supplemental aid package to El Salvador of $35 million and reduced the overall amount of aid for 1983 by $100 million.[52]

That summer, with Haig's resignation, the administration sought to mend its fences with Congress on El Salvador. As George Shultz later noted, he faced the challenge of persuading the El Salvadoran army and "their right-wing supporters that violation of human rights by them would not be tolerated. This was no easy task." The State Department's second human rights report on El Salvador acknowledged that there were problems with the military and abuses by the security forces. The congressional conditions on aid and the

[50] *Public Papers of the Presidents: Reagan, 1982*, 174–5.
[51] Ibid., 214.
[52] Arnson, *Crossroads*, 99–100.

legal requirement that the State Department certify that progress was being made toward democracy forced an administration that had started out hostile to human rights to take these issues into account. As Shultz acknowledged, he "had to defend that certification against informed and critical questioning."[53]

Moderation did not mean that the debates were over or that there had been a full change in policy. The administration continued to support the government in El Salvador, provide military assistance and advisors, and help it to expand the war, no matter what its record of abuses. In October, when Ambassador Hinton warned the El Salvadoran government that it "must make progress in bringing the murderers of our citizens, including those who ordered the murders, to justice" or the United States, "in spite of our interests, in spite of our commitment to the struggle against communism, could be forced to deny assistance to El Salvador," the White House criticized his speech and denied that it represented American policy.[54] It even went so far in its January 1983 certification of an improvement in human rights to argue that because "human rights abuses continue" by the government, and because the "further development of democracy and the protection of human rights is not to be taken for granted," more aid from the United States was necessary.[55]

In March 1983, Reagan blamed his critics, and Congress's refusal to fund all of his requests, for the continued lack of human rights in El Salvador and a possible communist victory. In April, speaking to a joint session of Congress, the president reiterated the basic assumptions of his policy as he sought to overcome congressional limitations on spending in El Salvador. He began by attacking the FMLN for failing to participate in the elections of March 1982, claiming that their refusal reflected not their fear of attack by government forces, but their fear of being "exposed for what they really are – a small minority who want power for themselves and their backers, not democracy for the people." He continued to assert that the insurgency existed only because of the actions of Cuba and the Soviet Union, and that the "guerrillas are not embattled peasants" but professional revolutionaries. It was necessary to support El Salvador, no matter what the problems with the government, because it was under attack by the communist world. Moreover, the United States itself was under attack. "The national security of all the Americas is at stake in Central America. If we cannot defend ourselves there, we cannot expect to prevail elsewhere. Our credibility would collapse, our alliances would crumble, and the safety of our homeland would be put in jeopardy."[56] Thus, supporting the government in San Salvador, and by extension any other authoritarian regime, was in Reagan's view necessary to protect the United States. In a bipolar world as described by the president, anticommunism justified any actions taken.

---

[53] Shultz, *Turmoil and Triumph*, 129–30.
[54] Arnson, *Crossroads*, 104.
[55] Ibid., 119.
[56] *Public Papers of the Presidents: Reagan, 1983*, 374, 601–7.

These arguments were no more persuasive now than they had been over the previous two years. Senator Christopher Dodd responded for the Democrats by criticizing the president's analysis. Dodd argued that while everyone opposed a new Marxist state in Central America, the administration's approach only furthered the violence and repression in the area and increased the chances of revolutionary success. "We believe," Dodd declared, "the Administration fundamentally misunderstands the causes of the conflict in Central America" because it ignored the poverty and historical repression of the governments that had fueled the revolution. "If Central America were not racked with poverty, there would be no revolution." Yet "instead of trying to do something about the factions or factors which breed revolution, this Administration has turned to massive military buildups" as its solution. Dodd characterized this as "a formula for failure," and called for Reagan to use the influence of the United States to promote negotiations and a political settlement to the problems.[57]

The advocates of negotiation found their position strengthened by the Contadora process. The Contadora nations – Colombia, Mexico, Panama, and Venezuela – saw U.S. policy as increasing the support for the rebels in El Salvador, and the war as threatening to engulf the whole region. Their call for all five nations of Central America to enter into negotiations was agreed to in September 1983. The administration quickly moved to prevent the negotiations from taking place, pressuring El Salvador, Honduras, and Costa Rica to reject any negotiations with the Sandinistas. It saw the Contadora process as a threat to unilateral U.S. action and a challenge to its policy in Central America.

Congressional opposition, however, finally forced the administration to put pressure on the El Salvadoran government or face a complete cut-off of aid. In December 1983, Vice President George Bush informed El Salvador's president, Alvaro Magana, that his government's "cause is being undermined by the murderous violence of reactionary minorities" and that the "cowardly death-squads are just as repugnant to me, to President Reagan, to the U.S. Congress, and to the American people as the terrorists of the left." If the government could not control their activity, it would "lose the support of the American people."[58] Secretary of State Shultz delivered a similar warning the next month. "Death squads and terror have no place in a democracy," Shultz told Magana. The military had to act with discipline if the government expected continued support from Washington.[59]

Reagan, however, did not completely abandon his efforts to gain political support for his policies. In July 1983, he established a National Bipartisan Commission on Central America, chaired by Henry Kissinger. Its report in January 1984 supported the administration's interpretation of events, blaming the crisis on Soviet actions and blaming the inability of the government

---

[57] *New York Times*, 28 April 1983.
[58] Arnson, *Crossroads*, 143.
[59] Montgomery, *El Salvador*, 203.

to crush the rebellion on the lack of adequate funding from the United States. Furthermore, it rejected the idea of negotiations with the FMLN or any sharing of power with the FDR. Still, the report, over the objections of Kissinger, stated that military aid should be tied to the human rights record of the government and improvements in that area.[60] This endorsement of the president's policy and a military solution in El Salvador did little to change the political opposition the administration faced. Given this, the administration again focused on the upcoming presidential elections in El Salvador to try and save its policy.

Blocked by the Congress from fully funding his war in Central America, Reagan knew that only a Duarte victory and the appearance of controlling the death squads would allow for more military aid to El Salvador. In order to ensure this outcome, the administration covertly sent over $2 million to support Duarte in his effort to defeat D'Aubisson and the ARENA government in the March 1984 El Salvadoran elections. The results, however, were inconclusive; neither candidate was able to gain a majority of the vote, forcing a run-off election in May.[61] With massive support from Washington, including the promise of large new aid packages if the PDC won, Duarte defeated D'Aubisson. The administration hailed the results as a victory of moderation over extremism, and called on Congress to support the new government. In response, Congress passed an aid package of over $300 million for the next two years in the hope that a true centrist government would emerge that could end the human rights abuses and bring reforms to El Salvador.

In reality, all that was accomplished was a stalemate in El Salvador. Duarte continued to rely upon the military, the oligarchy, and the Reagan administration for support and for his political survival. He could not act independent of any of these groups, all of whom still sought a military solution to the crisis in El Salvador. The activities of the death squads continued unabated, and peace and reform were no closer now than they had been in 1981, when the administration began its support for the Salvadorean military. Not only was the implementation of Kirkpatrick's ideas unpopular, it had failed to bring the promised results of shoring up a pro-American dictatorship that would provide stability and a bulwark against revolutions. Rather, it had brought death and destruction to the whole region. As George Shultz noted, by the start of Reagan's second term he "was convinced that the U.S. approach was not working."[62] Similar failure awaited the administration as it threw its support behind other repressive regimes and attempted to implement the Reagan Doctrine as a means to combat communism. As it had in Central America, Reagan's policy would be met with opposition, forcing the administration to reverse its course and support democratic processes, human rights, and reform.

---

[60] U.S. National Bipartisan Commission on Central America, *Report of the National Bipartisan Commission on Central America.*

[61] Montgomery, *El Salvador*, 182–4.

[62] Shultz, *Turmoil and Triumph*, 970.

Constructive Engagement and South Africa

Chester Crocker, who would become assistant secretary of state for African affairs in 1981, set out the logic of Reagan's policy of constructive engagement toward South Africa in a 1980 article in *Foreign Affairs*. Crocker believed that there was "at present a window of opportunity" to bring about "evolutionary change" and "political liberalization" in South Africa. This could be accomplished, he argued, only through support for Pretoria and the current government. Otherwise, the only course for change would be violence, a situation that the communists were sure to exploit. By working with South Africa, however, the United States could protect a key ally in the Cold War while at the same time bringing about political change. The choice was not, Crocker asserted, between support for apartheid and sanctions against South Africa to force change. The real issue "in southern Africa in the 1980s concerns our readiness to compete with our global adversary in the politics of a changing region whose future depends on those who participate in shaping it."[63]

Crocker's analysis and the policy of constructive engagement were based on the assumption that there was a moderate–extremist split within the Afrikaner population and the ruling National Party. This was matched by an equally important split between moderates who sought peaceful change in South Africa and extremist opponents of the regime who wanted to bring about change through violence and revolution. The moderates, Crocker claimed, were led by Prime Minister P. W. Botha and were currently in control. This meant that "the long delayed prospects for political change have opened up." The new leaders of South Africa, he asserted, viewed the apartheid system as having created "an unworkable monster," both politically and economically, and wanted to work toward a more modern and rational system.[64] Indeed, Crocker went so far as to characterize Botha's coming to power as "a drawn-out coup d'etat" that promised long-term reforms.[65] In language that echoed modernization theory, Crocker argued that given South Africa's advanced economy, it was now ready to make the transition to more freedom. Terming Botha and his political allies "modernizers," Crocker asserted that they were cautious, moderate reformers who were seeking to change South Africa while forestalling a violent revolution. "The modernizers who are taking over Afrikaner nationalist politics... do not have an ideological blueprint. They have a set of attitudes – pragmatic, flexible, determined – and a concept of strategy defined as the continuing process of matching means and ends." Crocker went so far as to claim that "it would be unwise to view the South African Defense Force (SADF) as an instrument of domestic brutality or as the rogue elephant of southern Africa, crashing across borders...." Rather, the "military's purpose is to buy time for political solutions" by providing stability and protection against South Africa's extremist

---

[63] Crocker, "South Africa: Strategy for Change," 345.
[64] Ibid., 328.
[65] Ibid., 334.

opponents. The SADF had the "potential as a lobby of modernizing patriots whose growing professionalism" made it supportive of change.[66]

The goal of the United States was to foster "the emergence in South Africa of a society with which the United States can pursue its varied interests in full and friendly relationship, without constraint, embarrassment or political damage." Thus, the United States, Crocker argued, had to support the Botha government as the only means to protect American interests and promote peaceful change in South Africa, "recognizing that American interests will suffer inevitably if such change fails to occur."[67] Sanctions and economic pressure should be rejected in favor of a policy of supporting the so-called modernizers within South Africa, thus reaping the benefits of their control while preventing revolutionary upheaval. Crocker termed criticizing all aspects of the apartheid system a "trap" leading to trade and investment sanctions. Constructive engagement "does not mean waging economic warfare ... nor does it mean erecting foolish pinpricks that only erode the American position in South African and world markets." Rather, "it is in favor of sustained and orderly change."[68]

The overriding concern of the policy of constructive engagement was to allow Washington to work closely with Pretoria against communism in the region while maintaining American economic interests in South Africa. "Constructive engagement," Crocker wrote, "in the region as a whole is the only basis for Western credibility. . . . Our credibility in Moscow and Havana depends on adopting a strong line against the principle of introducing external combat forces into the region," which would further the instability in the area. "There can be no presumed communist right to exploit and militarize regional tensions, particularly in this region where important Western economic, resource and strategic interests are exposed."[69] In adopting the policy of constructive engagement, the administration could publicly present an image of opposition to and abhorrence for apartheid while doing little to bring about change. Botha would be supported owing to his anticommunism and his ability to maintain stability, protect American interests, and control the political forces in his nation demanding change.

Crocker's article was a direct criticism of Carter's condemnation of the South African regime's racist policies, and its efforts, in the wake of the Soweto uprising of June 1976 and Pretoria's violent crackdown, to use political and economic pressure to contain the regime's military attacks against its neighbors and force an end to apartheid. To Reagan, South Africa was a critical ally in the Cold War for both economic and strategic reasons, and vital to containing communist influence in the region. He therefore dismissed criticisms of providing support to Pretoria's racist regime and reversed Carter's policy of using pressure to alter the apartheid system. In March 1981, Reagan asked: "Can we

---

[66] Ibid., 337–8.
[67] Ibid., 324.
[68] Ibid., 346–7.
[69] Ibid., 346.

abandon a country that has stood beside us in every war we've ever fought, a country that strategically is essential to the free world in its production of minerals we all must have and so forth?" His answer was a resounding no. While Reagan publicly condemned the system of apartheid, he saw South Africa as a "friendly nation" that the United States should support and believed that Washington should work with Pretoria to bring about a slow, gradual change to its abhorrent system. "As long as there's a sincere and honest effort being made," it seemed to the president that the United States should be patient and provide support to the South African government.[70] Change, therefore, was to be solely white-led and on a timetable designed to protect the status quo.

With the goal of constructive engagement being to maintain domestic and regional stability in southern Africa and to allow American corporations to continue to operate there, Reagan endorsed the Sullivan principles as a proper guide to business practices. Established by Reverend Leon Sullivan, a Baptist minister in Philadelphia, the Sullivan principles were a set of standards for fair employment practices for American corporations operating in South Africa. Adherence to these rules was a middle-ground position between doing nothing to aid black South Africans and divesting completely. Thus, companies could claim to be helping blacks while continuing to operate under the laws of apartheid.

In May 1981, South African Foreign Minister Pik Botha visited Washington to meet with senior administration officials, including the president. Haig wrote Reagan that the meetings accomplished the administration's "major objective – *to establish a new relationship with South Africa based on a realistic appraisal of our mutual interests in the southern African region.*" The meetings "effectively ended the unproductive ostracism of recent years, while making clear that *a more forthcoming approach on our part must be reciprocated by them.*" In particular, the "South Africans now have a *sure sense of where we are coming from in strategic terms.*" Invoking the Reagan Doctrine and linking it directly to constructive engagement, Haig declared "they know that we are determined to *roll back Soviet influence* throughout the world."[71] With Cold War concerns the primary issue, the South African government was assured of American support.

How completely the administration had adopted the views and rationale of the South African government for the continuation of white minority rule was demonstrated during the first meeting between P. W. Botha and American Ambassador Herman Nickel. Botha began the discussion by expressing his pleasure at the "new and more constructive chapter" in the relations of the United States and South Africa and the administration's acceptance of his policies. He told Nickel that the process of change would take "a generation" and could only be done slowly. He said that "pressuring South Africa would have exactly the opposite effect from the effect intended and he expressed satisfaction that the Reagan administration appeared to have learned this lesson from

---

[70] *Public Papers of the Presidents: Reagan 1981,* 197.

[71] Haig to Reagan, 20 May 1981, Executive Secretariat, NSC, Box 91343, RRL (emphasis in the original).

the mistakes of its predecessors." The first step would be "bringing Coloreds and Asians into the new political dispensation." This was possible because the "Coloreds . . . were a 'western' people and including them would give whites a greater sense of self-confidence in dealing with the problems of the blacks." As for black South Africans, Botha described them as continuing to hold to their "traditional tribal identification" while simultaneously developing an "urban identity and common consciousness." Nonetheless, the "tribal loyalties still was very strong." Finally, Botha lamented that except for "President Reagan and his Secretary of State, the Western world had not grasped the seriousness of the Soviet threat in Africa." Nickel concurred with Botha's observations and views, positions that the administration would consistently repeat in defense of constructive engagement.[72]

Throughout his first term in office, Reagan claimed that the economic and political support he provided to South Africa were helping to bring positive change. Good relations were critical for employing what Reagan termed "quiet diplomacy" to bring about reform.[73] Reagan argued that this was the best method for working with the moderates, both white and black, in South Africa. "We think," he declared, "that there are many people in South Africa who want that system changed. And we think we are giving them encouragement in our support of that position. And we are working steadily and quietly with them and are going to continue to do that."[74] At the same time, the president vehemently opposed economic sanctions against South Africa, claiming that they would be ineffective and only hurt the people, the black majority, that he claimed that the United States was trying to help.

In response to criticisms of his policy, the president stated that "if we're going to sit down at a table and negotiate with the Russians, surely we can keep the door open and continue to negotiate with a friendly nation like South Africa."[75] Indeed, the president saw supporting Pretoria as critical to winning the struggle against communism in Africa and defeating the African National Congress, which Reagan saw as an instrument of Soviet policy, and which was calling for the immediate end to apartheid. His efforts, Reagan asserted in 1984, were bringing an end to the fighting in southern Africa and allowing peaceful change. It remained "a moral imperative that South Africa's racial policies evolve peacefully but decisively toward a system compatible with basic norms of justice, liberty, and human dignity."[76] Sanctions or political pressure, in Reagan's view, would strengthen the extremists in the National Party, embolden the African National Congress, and lead to more violence.

In a statement to the Senate Foreign Relations Committee in September 1984, Crocker also claimed that the administration's policy had brought progress in

[72] Nickel to Shultz, 29 April 1982, Executive Secretariat, NSC, Box 91340, RRL.
[73] *Public Papers of the Presidents: Reagan 1984*, 1873.
[74] *Public Papers of the Presidents: Reagan 1985*, 82.
[75] *Public Papers of the Presidents: Reagan 1981*, 197.
[76] *Public Papers of the Presidents: Reagan 1984*, 1357.

fostering real reforms in South Africa. The assistant secretary stated that he was "confident that there is a new dynamic at work in South Africa," citing "clear evidence of progress toward a more favorable climate for change." He pointed to the 1983 constitution, which created two extra parliamentary chambers for "Coloreds" and "Indians," as proof of his point. The fact that no power was shared with these groups, and that the constitution completely excluded 73 percent of the people, the majority black population who had no voting rights or representation, did not deter Crocker. He saw this as a "new willingness of the whites to support the concept of reform." Nor was this contradicted by the recent upsurge in violence, according to Crocker, as "this is a phenomenon that historically tends to occur precisely when rigid old patterns are beginning to break up." Crocker claimed that the "U.S. role is one of a catalyst" for these changes, and that in order for change to occur, it was necessary to maintain an American presence in South Africa and to "provide concrete, tangible support of those groups, institutions, and processes which are essential to change in South Africa."[77]

For all the administration's claims of progress, Reagan's policy was met by a growing opposition within the United States that saw constructive engagement as immoral and helping to perpetuate a reprehensible and violent regime. By the early 1980s, a broad-based, popular anti-apartheid movement had emerged that demanded American divestment from South Africa and an end to Washington's support of Pretoria. The movement developed out of the concerns of some in the the American civil rights movement who were seeking to extend racial justice internationally, along with others who supported efforts to change American foreign policy in the wake of the Vietnam War. Horrified by the growing violence used by the South African government to maintain power, anti-apartheid activists called for an end to American support for apartheid, and were able to make the issue of divestment by universities and corporations an important political issue while gaining increased congressional support for sanctions against South Africa. They argued that the so-called moderate–extremist split within the Nationalist Party was a myth, that white rule and apartheid were the sources of violence and instability, and that change had to include the majority of the population and had to be democratically implemented. In doing so, the movement directly challenged the administration's policy of constructive engagement and its support of the Botha government.[78]

These domestic critics were aided by international opposition to Reagan's policy. When Bishop Desmond Tutu won the Nobel Peace Prize in 1984 for his efforts to bring peaceful change in South Africa, Reagan invited him to a meeting in an attempt to link Tutu's work to his own policy of constructive engagement. Prior to the meeting, however, Bishop Tutu told the House of Representatives that Reagan's policy was "immoral, evil and totally unchristian"

---

[77] Crocker, "An Update of Constructive Engagement in South Africa," 26 September 1984, Cohen Files, Box 92241, RRL.
[78] On the anti-apartheid movement, see Massie, *Loosing the Bonds*.

because it marked a collaboration with the racist white government and had led the South African government to believe it would have U.S. support for its repression. He called upon Reagan to abandon constructive engagement, follow a policy similar to that of President Carter, condemn South African reforms as meaningless, and support disinvestment.[79] During their December 1984 meeting, Tutu told Reagan that his "policies have worsened the situation for blacks in South Africa," and called for economic sanctions. In a news conference later that day, Reagan disagreed with Tutu, claiming that the situation had not worsened, and that "sizable progress" was being made "in persuading the South African Government to make changes." Furthermore, he rejected the notion that the Botha government had become more repressive. He said he regretted the "surge of violence here and there" by the government that "has resulted in violence from the other side," but reiterated that his policy was making "solid progress" and would be continued. When asked if his policy gave credibility to the South African regime, and how he could "justify dealing with a nation that does not recognize something so basic as the concept of racial equality," Reagan responded that he thought it was "counterproductive for one country to splash itself all over the headlines, demanding that another government do something, because that other government then is put in an almost impossible political position. It can't appear to be rolling over at the demands of outsiders." Moreover, he said condemnation of American investment in South Africa and calls for economic sanctions and divestment were "based on ignorance," and that the "black tribal leaders there have openly expressed their support in American business investment" because of those companies' adherence to the Sullivan principles of nondiscrimination in hiring.[80] As Secretary of State Shultz noted, Reagan, while a proponent of democracy, was always "disposed to give the benefit of the doubt to an anti-Communist leader, even if authoritarian and dictatorial."[81]

By 1985, pressure on the administration to change its course was mounting. The divestiture movement was beginning to achieve successes, with some universities, foundations, churches, and city governments voting to withdraw their funds from businesses that continued to operate in South Africa. Moreover, Congress was debating legislation, the Comprehensive Anti-Apartheid Act (CAAA), that called for economic sanctions against South Africa. The newly elected chair of the Senate Foreign Relations Committee, Richard Lugar, became the leading sponsor of the bill, gaining support in both houses of Congress and on both sides of the aisle. Reagan made his opposition to the bill clear, and promised to veto it if passed. He continued to insist that constructive engagement was a success, and that he could acknowledge the "repugnance of apartheid" and still work with the regime in South Africa. There were many moderates, Reagan claimed, who wanted constructive change, and his policy

[79] McFarlane to Reagan, 6 December 1984, Cohen Files, Box 91876, RRL.
[80] *Public Papers of the Presidents: Reagan 1984*, 1873.
[81] Shultz, *Turmoil and Triumph*, 1115.

was "giving them encouragement in our support of that position."[82] Sanctions, therefore, were misguided because they "would only hurt the people we're trying to help."[83]

Moreover, Reagan refused to link the mounting violence to the government's policies and the continuance of apartheid, blaming instead extremists who were working outside the system. When seventeen blacks were shot to death on 21 March 1985, Reagan stated in a news conference that he was not considering a change in his policy. To characterize the killings as those of ordinary people, the president opined, with "the violence coming totally from the law and order side ignores the fact that there was rioting going on in behalf of others there." He claimed that there was "an element in South Africa that does not want a peaceful settlement of this, who want a violent settlement, who want trouble in the streets. And this is what's going on."[84]

The next month, the president refused to blame Pretoria for the increasing death toll of blacks. When asked again if it was time to change his policy of constructive engagement, Reagan claimed that constructive engagement was having the "best effect and the most effect of anything that we could do," and that "some progress has been made." The problem was not the government versus its opponents. Rather, there was "a sector that wants violence as the answer and are even violent to the others, not to the government alone." Furthermore, he declared, in the black community "you've got rival factions, and the violence is sometimes between them, fighting each other. And we've seen evidence of that, and we've seen murders." He concluded by stating that the issue was that "there is an element that wants an overthrow of the government by violence and is not just limiting its fighting to the government."[85]

The Reagan administration continued to attempt to cram the events in South Africa into a Cold War framework in order to legitimize the continuation of constructive engagement and its opposition to sanctions. The State Department wrote to National Security Advisor Robert McFarlane that American interests "in strategic and mineral-rich southern Africa are advanced if stability and progress occur; they suffer if the region becomes engulfed in hatred and violence." The Soviets had recognized this and were attempting to "exploit the region's crisis for their own purposes." Sanctions, while "morally appealing," would not work given South Africa's economic independence. An end to constructive engagement would leave southern Africa "open to the Soviets."[86] Specifically, Reagan pointed to the African National Congress as an extremist group, stating that "there is no question about the violence of the ANC and their striking and their attacks on people and their murdering and so forth." The president had no doubts as to who was responsible for this violence and

---

[82] *Public Papers of the Presidents: Reagan 1985*, 82.
[83] Ibid., 973.
[84] Ibid., 329.
[85] Ibid., 382.
[86] Platt to McFarlane, 30 July 1985, African Affairs Directorate, Box 91206, RRL.

who would benefit if he changed course. He declared that "for us to believe the Soviet Union is not, in its usual style, stirring up the pot and waiting in the wings for whatever advantage they can take – we'd be very innocent, naive, if we didn't believe that they're there ready to do that."[87]

With the violence unabated, the South African government declared a state of emergency in July and further cracked down on anti-apartheid demonstrations. Formally, the Reagan administration expressed disapproval and called for the state of emergency to be lifted. Yet the president defended his policy of continued cooperation with South Africa and excused the use of violence by Pretoria. Reagan saw the regime's moves as a "reaction to some violence that was hurtful to all of the people" and a proper response "from the law enforcement against riotous behavior." The president stated that it was necessary "to recognize sometimes when actions are taken in an effort to curb violence." In addition, he still rejected the calls for sanctions as only "harmful to the black citizens there" and to the neighboring nations that depended on South Africa for trade.[88]

On August 15, a defiant P. W. Botha lashed out at those calling for an end to apartheid and white rule. In his infamous "Rubicon speech,"[89] Botha declared that "reasonable South Africans will not accept the principle of one man, one vote in a unitary system." Real democracy, he claimed, "would lead to chaos" and had to be rejected. "I am not prepared," Botha continued, "to lead white South Africans and other minority groups on a road to abdication and suicide." The end of white rule in South Africa, he stated, would lead the nation "into factions, strife, chaos and poverty." The only alternative to his policies, he claimed, was turmoil, bloodshed, and murder. Botha characterized his opponents as people who rejected peaceful negotiations in favor of violence designed to bring about "totalitarian and tyrannical ends." He attacked foreign critics as well, calling them enemies who sought revolution over reform in order to divide and destroy South Africa.[90]

Administration officials were disappointed with the speech as they had hoped there would be a call for reforms. Still, in an effort to curb the damage and save their policy, they indicated continued support for Botha and claimed that "he tried to give as much as he could" without alienating the extremists within the National Party by offering to negotiate and providing an alternative to violence. It was important, the White House noted, to take "into account Mr. Botha's ability to make changes and not suffer politically." In a more detailed response the next day, Chester Crocker fully employed the idea of a moderate–extremist split to explain the continuation of the policy of constructive engagement in light of Botha's speech. He stated the South African leader had "made clear" within the context of the National Party that he wanted to move toward more reform and an "acceptance of the principle of participation and joint responsibility by

---

[87] *Public Papers of the Presidents: Reagan 1985*, 1012.
[88] Ibid., 973.
[89] Massie, *Loosing the Bonds*, 586–7.
[90] *New York Times*, 16 August 1985.

all South Africans in an undefined constitution," and had issued "an explicit call for negotiation on these issues." Crocker insisted that the speech was not easy for Americans to fully understand because,it was "written in the code language of a foreign culture within a polarized society."[91] President Reagan also continued to see Botha as a moderate, characterizing his regime as "a reformist administration" following a policy that was designed to encourage "the path of reform and bringing about a more perfect democracy in their country."[92] He went so far as to claim that while segregation was not yet completely eliminated, there was "a great improvement over what has ever existed before."[93]

In the wake of Botha's speech, pressure against the administration's policy quickly mounted. Opponents noted the failure of constructive engagement to bring about any significant change and the fallacy of the idea that reform could come as long as whites held all political power in South Africa. The speech undercut all of the assumptions and rationales that constructive engagement was built upon. The South African government was not seeking an end to apartheid, and U.S. support was not bringing about reform. Critics pointed out that while the social apartheid laws that prohibited intermarriage among the races and integration in public areas had been modified, the main components of political apartheid remained. In particular, the laws that divided all South Africans into racial groups, and that kept such institutions as schools and the health care system segregated, and the laws that enforced separate living areas remained intact. As long as these pillars of apartheid were in place, along with the 1983 constitution that still completely excluded the majority black pop-ulation, political power would stay in the hands of the white minority. The critical issue, the critics contended, was political freedom and not economics. The Sullivan principles were a side issue and a smokescreen to divert attention from the fundamental political question of rights and freedom for black South Africans. Opponents, therefore, saw the government's reforms as insignificant changes designed to create the illusion of progress. They noted that nonwhite South Africans were not fooled and continued to press for the full abolition of apartheid. As the protests grew, and as the South African government's efforts to control its opposition grew more violent, the anti-apartheid movement in the United States forced the Reagan administration to begin to modify its policy.[94]

On September 9, in an effort to stave off legislation calling for an economic embargo, President Reagan issued an executive order that placed limited pro-hibitions on certain kinds of trade with South Africa. He framed his action as a part of constructive engagement and continued to defend his basic assump-tions about South Africa and his policies. While imposing restrictions on the

[91] Crocker, "The U.S. and South Africa: A Framework for Progress," 16 August 1985, NSC:CF, Box 91028, RRL.
[92] *Public Papers of the Presidents: Reagan 1985*, 1011–12.
[93] Ibid., 1046.
[94] Haas, "South Africa under Apartheid."

sale of computers to police agencies, prohibiting the export of nuclear goods, and banning loans to the South African government, Reagan insisted that the aim of American policy "cannot be to punish South Africa with economic sanctions that would injure the very people we're trying to help." Rather, the United States had to continue to work with those the president saw as moderates and "recognize that the opponents of apartheid, using terrorism and violence, will bring not freedom and salvation, but greater suffering and more opportunities for expanded Soviet influence within South Africa and in the entire region." He again claimed that South Africa was beginning "a process of change," and that it was "not a totalitarian society." This allowed for protests "that would never be possible in many parts of Africa or in the Soviet Union." The president declared that he understood the importance of encouraging change, "but in doing so we must not damage the economic well-being of millions of people in South and southern Africa." He also announced that he would therefore veto any congressional bill that imposed an economic embargo, and that he had appointed an advisory committee chaired by Secretary of State George Shultz to provide recommendations on other measures that could be taken to promote peaceful change. This, Reagan asserted, would allow the United States to continue to work with the "responsible" leaders, both white and black, in South Africa to bring about change. "The problems of South Africa were not created overnight," Reagan concluded, "and will not be solved overnight."[95] Responding to a question later in the year on why he was pushing for human rights in the Soviet Union but not in South Africa, the president asserted that change was inevitable in an authoritarian state, but not in a totalitarian one. The key was "how and when" it would occur. He worried that if it came too quickly, "the people could well exchange one oppressor for another."[96]

Given this, the administration remained committed to supporting Botha and to white control in South Africa. The State Department noted in December 1985 that in the wake of Botha's "disastrous" speech, questions had arisen as to whether "P. W. Botha has the stuff it takes to pull his country through its present crisis." It recommended that the United States stick with Botha as there was no one to replace him and it was not "persuaded it would be good news" if he left power. Yet the momentum was moving against the South African government and the administration's policy and toward disinvestment and sanctions, and the "time frame for reversing the negative cycle may be the next 6–9 months." It was urgent, therefore, that the administration work with Botha "to steer a middle course" between sanctions and full support for the government in order to help South Africa obtain peaceful change through negotiations. This meant sticking with constructive engagement.[97]

[95] "Remarks of the President on Signing Executive Order Regarding South Africa," 9 September 1985; McFarlane to Reagan, 7 September 1985, "Proposed Presidential Executive Order and Letter to President Botha, both NSC:CF, Box 91026, RRL.

[96] *Public Papers of the Presidents: Reagan 1985*, 1468.

[97] Platt to McFarlane, 16 December 1985, NSC:CF, Box 91026, RRL.

To this end, Reagan wrote Botha on 4 January 1986 reaffirming his policy and his support, but calling for real negotiations to bring about political change. The president noted that he recognized the difficult challenges that Botha faced in "leading your country toward justice and full participation for all South Africans without unleashing a destructive upheaval." Reagan claimed that the South African leader had moved his nation "impressively away from the failed policies of the past," and that it pained him to see South Africa "become the object of criticism and abuse, much of it based on over-simplified or distorted notions." He assured Botha that he would continue to work against sanctions and that he wanted him "to succeed in propelling your country forward on the path of peaceful, constructive change." South Africa, the president wrote, "must remain strong and its economy must prosper for the sake of its people, Africa, and the world at large. It must not become a playing field for Soviet ambitions." Reagan encouraged Botha to work with "black moderates" to "wrest the political initiative from those who are more interested in destroying than in building" by lifting the state of emergency and beginning negotiations. Such steps "could strengthen moderates and check the actions of those who seek only chaos."[98]

Throughout early 1986, the administration defended the Reagan Doctrine against accusations of inconsistency and failure. In a message to Congress in February, the president reiterated his bipolar view of the world and the verities of the policy of containment that provided the logic and rationale for his doctrine. Reagan insisted that the United States "must actively wage the competition of political ideas – between free government and its opponents – and lend our support to those who are building the infrastructure of democracy." From Afghanistan to Nicaragua to Angola, he called for the support of so-called freedom fighters against Soviet imperialism and communist subversion. Continued backing for authoritarian regimes, therefore, had to be part of the overall campaign against communism as they provided stability and access to vital raw materials. In South Africa, Reagan asserted that his administration stood "forthrightly on the principle that the government must achieve freedom and justice for all of its citizens," and continued to hold to the view that Botha led moderate forces that would bring change. The United States, he noted, has "a major stake – as elsewhere, both moral and strategic – in encouraging a peaceful transition and avoiding a terrible civil war." He therefore rejected the approach of those who he saw as extremists, those who called for economic sanctions and an immediate end to apartheid, as serving the interests only of the Soviet Union and raising the specter of communism in South Africa. The apartheid regime, in keeping with the logic of the Reagan Doctrine, was still a defender of freedom.[99]

That same month, Crocker held what he termed "useful" meetings with Pik Botha in Geneva. In his report to Washington, the assistant secretary explained

[98] Reagan to Botha, 4 January 1986, NSC:CF, Box 91026, RRL.
[99] *Public Papers of the Presidents: Reagan 1986*, 161.

the slow pace of change in South Africa in terms of the moderate–extremist split within the government and the continued power of the right-wing whites; claimed that steady progress was being made; and reasserted the correctness of constructive engagement. Botha, he reported, wanted the United States to continue to press for reform without sanctions as the best means to aid the moderates in the government "who are pushing for change and who will need help in harsh intraparty battles yet to come." Crocker assured him of American support and continued efforts to assist the government.[100]

As pressure built up against constructive engagement and support for South Africa's racist regime, the administration stubbornly held to its analysis that Botha led a group of moderate modernizers who were opposed by extremists in both the white and black populations who, if successful, would bring about a communist South Africa. Testifying to Congress in March, Crocker stated that the administration's long-standing opposition to the ANC was based on the fact that it was an extremist group that employed a "policy of violence" and upon "that organization's ties to the Soviet Union."[101] In April, Reagan stated that "we know that there are two factions in South Africa.... One of them stubbornly is holding to continuation of the past practices. The other, and this includes President Botha, wants change and has taken a number of steps – as many as he can get away with." Botha "finds the past system repugnant and is trying to get changes as quickly as possible." At the same time, the president minimized the issues at stake, claiming that Botha's inability to pursue further reform was similar to his own problems in getting legislation passed, declaring "it's just like me dealing with the Hill up here. Sometimes he can't get all that he seeks."[102]

Time, however, was running out on constructive engagement. With the reestablishment of the state of emergency in South Africa, congressional support for economic sanctions grew, and it became clear that such a bill would pass that summer. On the tenth anniversary of the Soweto uprising, Senator Nancy Kassebaum denounced the reimposition of the state of emergency that had suspended normal laws and allowed the police "sweeping powers to arrest and detain anyone without regard to legal processes and protections." Representing those in Congress who had changed their positions and now supported the CAAA, Kassebaum declared that this action convinced her "that the situation in South Africa is now virtually beyond hope" and that the policy of constructive engagement had become "irrelevant." With no ability to promote change, and "little hope for progress," Senator Kassebaum announced that the "only action left to us is to protest in the strongest possible terms." This meant economic sanctions.[103]

---

[100] Crocker to Shultz, 13 February 1986, NSC:CF, Box 91026, RRL.
[101] *Public Papers of the Presidents: Reagan 1986*, 333–4.
[102] Ibid., 445.
[103] Kassebaum, "Statement on South Africa," 16 June 1986, African Affairs Directorate, Box 91026, RRL.

While Reagan claimed that he regretted the state of emergency, he announced his continued opposition to sanctions and his support for Botha. He stated that South Africa was now in a state of "outright civil war" that included "blacks fighting against blacks, because there's still a tribal situation involved there in that community," which demanded continued efforts to work with the current regime.[104] "We think that, first of all, that the Botha government has shown its willingness to take steps and has even expressed its desire to rid the country of apartheid. At the same time he is faced ... with a faction in his own government that disagrees and doesn't go along with what he's trying to accomplish." Reagan had no doubt that Botha was genuinely interested in change, and that it "would be truly counterproductive and disastrous ... for us, out of sheer pique or anger, to just remove ourselves and lose all contact with that government."[105] Indeed, that summer Reagan praised what he called the "dramatic change" brought to South Africa by Botha, and again attacked the ANC as a communist organization that had to be controlled.[106]

The overwhelming majority in both houses of Congress disagreed, and in August each passed laws calling for economic sanctions. As Crocker later noted, Reagan's "strident pro-Pretoria tilt disarmed those in Congress who preferred to let the executive branch conduct policy toward this complex region." Senator Lugar told Crocker in August that by its continued defense of the white minority government, the administration "had forfeited the opportunity to lead on South Africa."[107] Support for the bill in the House was so overwhelming that the vote was not recorded, while the Senate passed its bill by more than the necessary two-thirds margin needed to override a veto. As Lugar stated, Congress "sent a very strong signal of its intent to President Reagan, and asked him to move against South Africa's white racist regime more quickly and decisively than he has." The goal of the sanctions was to express American opposition to the current state of affairs and to pressure South Africa to move toward a true democracy. For that to occur, Lugar argued, Pretoria had to release its political prisoners, most notably Nelson Mandela; end the state of emergency; permit the formation of political parties; and repeal the law creating artificial black homelands so that negotiations for power sharing could begin. Failure by the government to act would lead to further violence and polarization that would only bring chaos. "We want to prevent a bloody civil war and the destruction of a nation." Unlike Reagan, Lugar and the vast majority of the members of Congress believed that only real pressure to force change could prevent that from happening.[108] As promised, Reagan vetoed the CAAA when it reached his desk in September, but Congress easily overrode the veto the following month

---

[104] *Public Papers of the Presidents: Reagan 1986*, 770.
[105] Ibid., 828–9.
[106] Massie, *Loosing the Bonds*, 616.
[107] Crocker, *High Noon in Southern Africa*, 323, 327.
[108] *New York Times*, 24 August 1986.

and the sanctions became law, bringing an end to the policy of constructive engagement.

The final blow to the logic of constructive engagement came in 1987, when Reverend Sullivan changed his position and concluded that the implementation of his principles by over 150 American corporations with facilities in South Africa had failed to promote political and social change and was having no positive impact on South African society. Sullivan now called upon American corporations to stop doing business in South Africa. This was the only way to promote change and bring an end to apartheid.

Reagan, however, continued to denounce sanctions and oppose efforts to isolate South Africa until apartheid was dismantled. Yet, as in the case of his policy toward El Salvador, the president was forced to make concessions to his opposition and found himself unable to provide the level of support he wanted to an authoritarian regime. Congress's and the American public's opposition to constructive engagement, and the sanctions they supported, along with worldwide pressure on Pretoria, discredited the president's strategy and helped send South Africa down the road to ending apartheid. At the same time that Reagan's policy toward South Africa was being reversed by Congress, he was forced to abandon another authoritarian "friend," Ferdinand Marcos in the Philippines, in response to democratic challenges in Manilla and opposition in the United States.

Adherence to Democratic Principles

American involvement in the Philippines began in 1898 during the war with Spain, when U.S. forces seized Manilla. After four years of bloody fighting, the Filipino resistance was crushed and the archipelago became an American colony. Upon granting the Philippines independence in 1946, Washington maintained close relations with Manila, helping it to defeat a communist-led insurgency in the 1950s and establishing two major American military installations on the islands, Clark Air Force Base and Subic Bay Naval Base. The Philippines was seen as a crucial member in the Southeast Asian Treaty Organization and as part of the Great Crescent of containment of communism in East Asia. Moreover, it was held up as a democratic model for other nations in the region because of its peaceful transfer of power every four years.

In September 1972, however, democratic rule came to an end with President Ferdinand Marcos's declaration of martial law. He claimed that drastic steps were necessary to meet a growing communist threat to his nation. Although Marcos was nearing the completion of his second term in office and barred from running again by the Filipino constitution, his action guaranteed that he would remain in power after his term ended in 1973. Nixon, in the midst of the final Vietnam negotiations and his reelection campaign, welcomed Marcos's move as a means to ensure stability in East Asia, protect the American bases, and uphold the Nixon Doctrine. The previous month, the American ambassador to the Philippines, Henry Byroade, had informed Marcos that he would have

American support for declaring martial law "in the event of a genuine Communist danger." The Nixon administration believed that Marcos's move was "understandable" given the "deplorable breakdown in the whole social fabric of the country." Due to the communist threat, "something had to be done and done very drastically."[109] The chief political officer in Manila, Francis T. Underhill, recalled that the administration saw the Philippines as "a hopeless mess" in need of "a strong man, a man on horseback to get the country organized and going again." Marcos was seen as that man.[110] National Security Decision Memorandum 209 set out Nixon's and Kissinger's support for Marcos and his dictatorship, stating that on the basis of continued cooperation by Marcos, economic and military assistance would be maintained in "our pursuit of fundamental U.S. interests in the Philippines and of implementation by the Marcos Administration of measures aimed at long-term stability for the Philippines."[111]

Marcos quickly set out to consolidate his power and enrich himself. By the end of the decade, he had created state-supported monopolies over most commodities produced in the Philippines and appointed his friends and supporters to run them. At the same time, he increased the size and influence of the military and used it to attack and threaten his political opposition – most notably Benigno "Ninoy" Aquino, who was jailed just after martial law was declared and held until 1980, when the Carter administration helped to secure his release. Personally, Marcos amassed a fortune estimated at over $6 billion while his corruption and policies created economic ruin for most of the nation.[112]

Marcos represented the type of Third World leader that Reagan liked and that he had criticized Carter for not supporting: an authoritarian ruler who was anticommunist, protected American economic interests, and promised stability in a crucial area of the world. Reagan first met Marcos in 1969 when he was governor of California, and he was impressed by the opulent welcome he received and the attention the Filipino leader bestowed upon him. As president-elect, Reagan met with Imelda Marcos in New York and informed her that he saw the Philippines as a "major ally" that would again receive American support.[113]

Marcos, however, was under pressure at home to ease his repressive rule and to quiet criticisms from the Catholic Church and the middle class. To that end, in January 1981, Marcos ended martial law while maintaining all of the power he had gained through his 1973 constitution and special legislation. As the American embassy in Manila reported, having governed under martial law for eight years, Marcos had "adequately institutionalized in one fashion or another – economic, military, police, media and, of course, political control" – all the power he needed to continue his dictatorship. "Marcos can have the best

---

[109] Karnow, *In Our Image*, 358–60, 380.
[110] Bonner, *Waltzing with a Dictator*, 93.
[111] Ibid., 138.
[112] *New York Times*, 9 February 1987.
[113] Bonner, *Waltzing with a Dictator*, 300.

of both worlds – he rids himself of the onus of martial law while retaining the broad powers he now holds."[114]

Once in office, Reagan referred to Marcos as his "old friend and ally" and as a quintessential anticommunist leader, and he set out to provide whatever support he could to the Filipino dictator. Vice President George Bush was sent to Manila in June 1981 to "reassure Marcos that the Reagan administration regards him as a friend."[115] Following Marcos's rigged reelection later that month, Bush declared: "We love your adherence to democratic principles and to the democratic processes. And we will not leave you in isolation to the degree we have any vibrant strength – it would be turning our backs on history if we did."[116] When Bush's statement drew the obvious criticisms, the vice president said he would "repeat it and stand by it," while White House press secretary Larry Speakes noted that "the president was aware of the statement both before it was made and after it was made and I'm sure he concurs with it."[117]

The next year, Reagan hosted Marcos on a state visit to Washington, where he set out the basis for American support. The president welcomed the Filipino dictator with words of praise for the "shared history and common ideals" of the two nations going back to World War II, when they had fought together in the "defense of freedom." Reagan declared that the "values for which we struggled – independence, liberty, democracy, justice, equality – are engraved in our constitutions." Ignoring Marcos's destruction of the 1946 constitution of the Philippines and the undemocratic nature of the new one, and the growing unrest and problems within his nation, Reagan claimed that the archipelago "can boast a record of solid economic growth over the past decade, attributable in significant part to its hospitable attitude toward free enterprise and private initiative." The United States was the Philippines' leading trade partner, and American businesses were its largest foreign investors, "reflecting their confidence in your progress and prospects for economic growth." Finally, noting his strong support for American foreign policy and anticommunism, Reagan called Marcos's "a respected voice for reason and moderation in international forums." Later that evening at a state dinner, Reagan fondly recalled his visit to Manila in 1969 and pledged to strengthen American ties with the Philippines, particularly in matters of defense and economic assistance.[118] Reagan made good on his promise in 1983, increasing the payment for the American bases in the Philippines from $500 million to $900 million annually for the next five years. As Secretary of State Shultz went to Manila to sign the agreement in June, the State Department rated relations with the Philippines "excellent."[119] While relations between Washington and Manila may have been excellent, conditions

[114] Ibid., 303.
[115] Karnow, *In Our Image*, 5, 401.
[116] Smith, *America's Mission*, 281.
[117] Bonner, *Waltzing with a Dictator*, 308.
[118] *Public Papers of the Presidents: Reagan*, 1982, 1166–7, 1172–3.
[119] Bonner, *Waltzing with a Dictator*, 338.

in the Philippines were not. Marcos's repression and economic plunder were creating social strife and a growing opposition in the form of the communist-led New People's Army (NPA). With government and military corruption rampant, and economic misery on the rise, the growing insurgency gained support throughout the nation. By 1983, unemployment or underemployment had reached forty percent, and the economy was suffering from double-digit inflation, mounting debt, and declining productivity. The Senate Foreign Relations Committee released a staff study that predicted that the power of the NPA could equal that of the Philippine army as early as 1987 unless changes were made in the way Marcos ruled.[120] Officials in the American embassy in Manila reported that the insurgency was gaining strength, and that without "new directions from the top" there would be a "continued deterioration" that could eventually bring the defeat of Marcos and a communist victory.[121] Shultz shared these concerns and worried that the "rapidly deteriorating economic and political situation" would create chaos and that the United States might be drawn in to prop up Marcos in order to protect its military bases.[122]

The political crisis that consumed the Marcos regime began on 21 August 1983, when Ninoy Aquino was assassinated by the military as he deplaned in Manila. His death gave the opposition a person and symbol to rally around and to unify behind. Over a million people took part in Aquino's funeral procession, revealing the depth of the opposition to Marcos. Over the next two and a half years, massive antigovernment demonstrations became the norm, and Marcos's hold on power slipped away. The Reagan administration now faced a crisis similar to the ones the Carter administration had confronted in Iran and Nicaragua. An unpopular and corrupt dictator who had enjoyed American support faced a military insurgency, growing middle-class opposition, and an economic crisis.

Reagan, consistent with his criticisms of Carter's policy, was unwavering in his support for Marcos. While he canceled a trip that fall to Southeast Asia that had included the Philippines, the president made it clear that it was not due to opposition to Marcos. Reagan wrote Marcos a personal letter in which he stated that he "always had confidence in your ability to handle things," and that his friendship "remains as warm and firm" as ever. Bush, speaking for the administration in October, stated that he did not believe Marcos was responsible for the killing of Aquino. "Marcos may be a lot of things, but I don't think he is a dumb guy." The United States, therefore, would "not cut away from a person who, imperfect though he may be on human rights, has worked with us." Furthermore, the administration "does not want to have another Khomeini" situation on its hands – a pro-American ruler being replaced by someone hostile to the United States.[123]

[120] Friend, "Timely Daring," 208–9, 212.
[121] Karnow, *In Our Image*, 406.
[122] Shultz, *Turmoil and Triumph*, 608–10, 625.
[123] Bonner, *Waltzing with a Dictator*, 352.

Pressure for a change in policy, however, was building in the United States. In September 1984, Representative Stephen Solarz, the chairman of the House Subcommittee on Asian and Pacific Affairs, began holding hearings on the Philippines highlighting the corruption of the Marcos regime, the increasing threat posed by the NPA, and the danger that the United States could again face as it found itself tied to a failing right-wing dictator. Within the administration, many shared Solarz's fears and began advocating a change in policy. While the president was still determined to back Marcos, the State Department now advocated putting pressure on Marcos to begin to implement reforms lest he lead the Philippines down the same road as Nicaragua. This, it believed, was the only way to maintain a friendly government and protect American interests. Another group of senior officials, led by Admiral William Crowe, then navy commander for the Pacific and soon to be chairman of the Joint Chiefs of Staff, went even further and urged Marcos's removal as the only viable policy for protecting American interests in the Philippines and stopping the growth of the NPA.

The embassy in Manila reported in June 1984 that the Communist Party of the Philippines (CPP) was operating throughout all of the islands and that the NPA was increasing the territory under its control. "Across the Philippine archipelago the CPP is moving in a ratchet-like manner to expand its influence." The government could still institute reforms and "take effective action and reverse the trend of events, but the longer it delays in beginning to deal effectively with the problem the harder this will be." The embassy concluded that without any action, "the eventual outcome – ultimate government defeat, a communist takeover of the Philippines – thus becomes a very possible scenario." The State Department estimated in September that the NPA had grown to a force of "13–15,000 armed regulars and several thousand part-time guerrillas operating in 62 of 73 provinces." The reason for its growth was Marcos and his policies. In particular, the report noted that the regime's corruption, failed economic policies, repression, and authoritarian rule were the sources of the NPA's appeal. Marcos, it concluded, had lost all legitimacy. "As in Nicaragua, a plundering of the country by the local oligarchy rather than foreign oppression or simple poverty has united the Philippine middle class, the business community, the church, and youth against the regime, while the decay of government institutions and a declining economy have sown the seeds of revolution in the countryside."[124]

Reagan, however, continued to support Marcos, making any other approach untenable as the president would not change his policy. In October, during his second presidential debate with Walter Mondale, Reagan was asked about the crisis in the Philippines and how he proposed to prevent it from becoming another Nicaragua. The president framed his response in terms of authoritarian versus totalitarian regimes and the Cold War, and defended Marcos and his

[124] Embassy to Secretary of State, 7 June 1984; "Causes of the Philippine Communist Insurgency," 18 September 1984, both Philippines Collection, NSA.

support for his regime. He stated: "I know there are things there in the Philippines that do not look good to us from the standpoint right now of democratic rights, but what is the alternative? It is a large Communist movement to take over the Philippines. They have been our friend since their inception as a nation." It was therefore necessary for the United States to stand with Marcos. "I think," Reagan continued, "we've had enough of a record of letting – under the guise of revolution – someone that we thought was little more right than we would be, letting that person go, and then winding up with totalitarianism, pure and simple, as the alternative." The United States should, therefore, "retain our friendship and help them right the wrongs we see, rather than throwing them to the wolves and then facing a Communist power in the Pacific." Reagan, ignoring the democratic opposition to Marcos, saw no alternative, declaring that the overthrow of the Marcos government would mean a government that "would be hostile to the United States."[125]

The president was determined to stick with Marcos because he saw him as the only barrier to a communist takeover. The Department of State, on the other hand, continued to believe that Marcos's rule without reforms would be detrimental to American interests, since he could not, contrary to the president's view, prevent communism in the Philippines. Rather, the longer Marcos ruled the stronger the insurgency would grow unless changes were implemented. In November, the State Department presented a new policy paper to the National Security Council designed to change the president's mind. Rejecting the view that Marcos should be removed as too extreme, it based its recommendation on the position that while Marcos "is part of the problem" confronting the United States in the Philippines, "he is also necessarily part of the solution." What was needed was enough pressure to bring about reform but at a pace that would not "destabilize" the regime. Moreover, Marcos had to "set the stage for peaceful and eventual transition to a successor government whenever that takes place."[126] This was the central dilemma that continually faced American policymakers in supporting right-wing dictators. Those calling for pressure had the same goal as Reagan, to protect American interests. The advocates of reform, however, now believed that this could be done only through the promotion of real change and democracy, while the president continued to back Marcos and his dictatorship as the only alternative to communism.

In January 1985, after two months of debate, Reagan signed a new National Security Directive that called for political pressure to be placed on Marcos for reform. The president sent a personal letter to Marcos outlining the political, economic, and military reforms the United States wanted to see implemented. Reagan called upon him to open up the political process, pursue economic policies that would bring about growth in the economy, and insist on more professional behavior by the military to cut down on the number of abuses against civilians. Reagan stated that his administration "supports strongly the

[125] *Public Papers of the Presidents: Reagan, 1984*, 1605.
[126] Bonner, *Waltzing with a Dictator*, 362–3.

efforts of you and your government, working with all Filipinos of moderate political views, to revitalize and strengthen your democratic institutions." These changes, the president believed, would make the government "more effective in combating the rising communist insurgency in the Philippines."[127]

The president explained the shift the next month in an interview with the *New York Times*. Asked if the Philippines could become another Iran, Reagan responded, "I certainly hope not," and noted that his administration was being as helpful as it could in the situation to "a long-time friend." His policy was designed to make sure "that the Philippines remain a democracy" by preventing the coming to power of the communists. "Now, we realize there is an opposition party that . . . is pledged to democracy. We also are aware that there is another element in the Philippines that has Communist support and backing." Reagan wanted to be sure that if a change in government took place, "it would be that opposition faction which is still democratic in its principles" that came to power. Too quick a change, however, could be a disaster "if, out of the friction between those two parties, the third element, the Communist element should get in, because we know their result is always totalitarian."[128]

In much the same way as he had handled the situation in South Africa, Reagan retained his faith in Marcos and now claimed that the best way to protect American interests and bring reform was to stick with his regime, and continue military and economic aid, in order to maintain influence and push for improvements. Based on this reasoning, the administration opposed congressional efforts to cut funds from the foreign aid package to the Philippines as counterproductive. The effort to pressure Marcos and bring about reform was, therefore, not serious and carried no consequences when the dictator failed to act. Moving to save his regime, Marcos, instead of implementing reforms, increased the repression and violence. The Marcos government was built upon undemocratic and repressive institutions that could not be changed without his losing control and power. As Frederick Brown, a staff member of the Senate Foreign Relations Committee, reported to Richard Lugar in August 1985, "Marcos's prime objective is to stay in power, not to promote change which could endanger him in the short term." The dictator fully understood that "U.S. demands for reform run diametrically counter" to his interests and meant the death knell for his government. Marcos, therefore, had no intention of pursuing any of the changes recommended to him, because they would weaken his regime. In addition, the Philippine dictator still believed that he could manage the crisis because he had the support of the president, and that the United States "will not dare to pull its support."[129]

Marcos was correct. Reagan was still loyal to him and convinced that he could remain in power. Marcos was pro-America, protected the U.S. bases, and was anticommunist. To the president, any alternative was worse. He feared

[127] Chanda, "A Word in Your Ear."
[128] *Public Papers of the Presidents: Reagan, 1985,* 157.
[129] Bonner, *Waltzing with a Dictator,* 379.

another Nicaragua, with the removal of an authoritarian government leading to a communist victory, either outright or after a weak democratic government had replaced Marcos. In particular, the administration saw the leading opposition figure, Corazon "Cory" Aquino, the widow of Ninoy Aquino, as soft on communism and a threat to American interests because she had discussed removing the American military bases and negotiating with the insurgents to bring about peace.[130]

Still, the president recognized that the situation in the Philippines was getting worse and that Marcos had to enact some reforms to stop the decline and the growing unrest. Shultz urged him to support reforms, telling Reagan that they were in the interest of both the Philippines and the United States.[131] To that end, Senator Paul Laxalt was sent to Manila in October to again impress upon Marcos the need for change. Laxalt assured Marcos that he retained Reagan's support, but told him that he needed to take some steps to counter his critics in the United States, and to reestablish his authority and control at home.[132] In November, Marcos responded with a surprise decision to hold elections the following February. Convinced that he would defeat a divided opposition, Marcos believed that his victory would demonstrate that his rule was legitimate and that he was instituting democratic reforms. Moreover, he reasoned, it would put his critics on the defensive while allowing him to proceed with the crushing of the NPA's insurgency. The dictator was so confident in his power that he invited foreign observers to come and monitor the polling.

To Marcos's surprise, the opposition did not splinter. Rather, at the urging of Cardinal Jaime Sin, it united behind the candidacy of Cory Aquino. In the weeks leading up to the election, Reagan made it clear whom he preferred. Speaking for the president, the White House chief of staff, Donald Regan, stated that even if Marcos were elected by "massive fraud," the administration would "have to do business with Marcos." He added that "there are a lot of governments elected by fraud."[133] The signal was clear. Reagan wanted Marcos to win and would be willing to overlook electoral abuses to ensure that outcome.[134]

When the voting was held on 7 February 1986, Marcos, as expected, attempted to rig the election through intimidation of the opposition and fraud. While independent monitors reported an Aquino victory, the official election commission held back its reports while the dictator's minions worked to tailor the vote for a Marcos triumph. American observers reported the extensive abuses back to Washington and made it clear that the only basis for a Marcos win would be a stolen election. Reagan, nonetheless, backed Marcos. On February 11, Press Secretary Speakes indicated that Marcos had won and that

---

[130] Karnow, *In Our Image*, 411–12.
[131] Shultz, *Turmoil and Triumph*, 614–15.
[132] Bonner, *Waltzing with a Dictator*, 382–3.
[133] Ibid., 403.
[134] See Shultz, *Turmoil and Triumph*, 618–19.

Aquino should "get on the team" and join Marcos to "form a government."[135] That same day, Reagan acknowledged that fraud had occurred but insisted that the really important matter was that elections had been held, providing "evidence of a strong two-party system now in the islands." Concerning the violence and fraud that had marred the election, the president attempted to lessen their importance by noting that "even elections in our own country – there are some evidences of fraud in places and areas," and that he was concerned about the "violence that was evident there and the possibility of fraud, although it could have been that all of that was occurring on both sides." When asked if the U.S. military bases in the Philippines were "of paramount importance" to U.S. policy or if he would "put the future of those bases at some risk if it meant standing up for democracy," Reagan responded that "one cannot minimize the importance of those bases," and that he did not know of anything "that's more important than the bases on the Philippines."[136]

The evidence, however, was overwhelming that the violence and fraud had been conducted by Marcos, and Reagan was forced by a domestic uproar to reverse his position. He announced that he was sending a special envoy, Philip Habib, to Manila and acknowledged on 15 February that "it has already become evident, sadly, that the elections were marred by widespread fraud and violence perpetrated largely by the ruling party. It was so extreme that the election's credibility has been called into question."[137] Reagan did not, however, call upon Marcos to resign or acknowledge his defeat, even after the Filipino dictator declared victory in the election, and Marcos's refusal to yield plunged the Philippines into a political crisis that threatened to turn into a civil war.

The crisis came to a head on Saturday, February 22, when Marcos's Chief of Staff Fidel Ramos and Defense Minister Juan Ponce Enrile shifted their support to Aquino and announced that they would lead forces against Marcos. Enrile admitted to his own role in rigging the voting and other election fraud, and stated that he wanted "the will of the people to be respected. I believe that the mandate of the people does not belong to the regime." Meanwhile, after an appeal by Cardinal Sin, hundreds of thousands of Filipino civilians took to the streets to help protect the rebel army camp. In response, the White House issued a statement calling on Marcos to find a peaceful solution to the crisis.[138]

That same day, Habib returned to Washington, reporting that Aquino had won and that Marcos had to go. Early on Sunday morning, he met with Shultz, Secretary of Defense Casper Weinberger, National Security Advisor Admiral John Poindexter, Deputy CIA Director Robert Gates, and other high-level administration officials. Shultz set out the issue confronting them as how to convince Reagan to withdraw his support from Marcos and get him to leave office before civil war broke out. Habib began by informing the group that

---

[135] Karnow, *In Our Image*, 414.

[136] *Public Papers of the Presidents: Reagan, 1986*, 188, 195, 201, 208.

[137] Ibid., 216.

[138] *Public Papers of the Presidents: Reagan, 1986*, 246; Friend, "Timely Daring," 214–15.

Marcos was politically isolated but that he refused "to realize that he faced a widespread movement to dump him." Determined to hang on, Marcos could move to put down the military rebellion and then attempt to destroy Aquino's supporters. Shultz noted that such a move would worsen the situation by leaving only Marcos's regime and the communist insurgency. In the past, the secretary of state continued, such "total shifts" had led to disasters such as Nicaragua and Iran. "We pay a heavy price for our past," Shultz added. Habib noted that "it's not Iran. There is a democratic opposition backed by the Catholic Church." All agreed that it was crucial that Marcos leave office immediately so that power could effectively be transferred to Aquino before full-scale fighting broke out. Weinberger thought it would be best to have new elections, but Gates cut him off, stating: "Let's be realistic, not legalistic. The public view is that Aquino won. So we have to think of a way to install her in power and give Marcos a fig leaf to depart. Aquino in, Marcos out." The problem was getting the president to agree.[139]

The National Security Council met that afternoon. Speaking for the president, Donald Regan defended Marcos and, referring to the example of Iran, opposed any withdrawal of United States support as potentially "opening the door to Communism" in the Philippines. Habib replied that "the Marcos era has ended" and that he had to be removed. Shultz informed the president that "nobody believes that Marcos can remain in power. He's had it." Any effort to help him remain in power would "destroy the democratic alternative to the Communists." At that point, Reagan yielded, noting that Marcos should be "asked rather than told" to leave, and that he could be granted asylum in the United States.[140] The White House issued a statement warning Marcos that any "attempt to resolve this situation by force will surely result in bloodshed and casualties, further polarize Philippine society, and cause untold damage to the relationship between our two governments." If force were used "against other elements of the Philippine military which enjoy substantial popular backing," U.S. military aid would be cut.[141]

Finally, on Monday morning, the White House issued a public statement calling for Marcos to give up his power. "Attempts to prolong the life of the present regime by violence are futile. A solution to this crisis can only be achieved through a peaceful transition to a new government."[142] Marcos, clinging to the hope that Reagan had not approved the message, called Senator Laxalt to find out if it represented the president's views or only those of the State Department and others. In addition, would Reagan approve a deal that would allow him to share power with Aquino? Laxalt, after meeting with Reagan and Shultz, called Marcos back and told him that there could be no deal but that he could come to the United States. Marcos then asked Laxalt what he should do.

[139] Karnow, *In Our Image*, 419; Shultz, *Turmoil and Triumph*, 632–4.
[140] Karnow, *In Our Image*, 420; Shultz, *Turmoil and Triumph*, 635–6.
[141] *Public Papers of the Presidents: Reagan, 1986*, 246–7.
[142] Ibid., 248.

"Cut and cut cleanly," the senator replied. "The time has come."[143] On Tuesday, February 25, Marcos left the Philippines and Cory Aquino assumed power. Reagan had been forced to do what he had criticized Carter for doing, abandon an authoritarian ally of the United States whose corrupt and brutal rule had divided his society and led to a domestic revolt.

The denouement of American policy toward Marcos demonstrated the changed nature of the debates over the policy of support for right-wing dictators. President Reagan wanted Marcos to retain power while implementing reforms at a pace that would alleviate the political crisis without destabilizing his regime. The president's support echoed the arguments made since the 1920s, that it was a choice between a friendly dictator or chaos and communism. This was the central dilemma: how to promote change and democracy without losing control over the situation. In other words, as American officials saw it, the question confronting policymakers was whether they could pressure authoritarian regimes to institute democratic reforms without aiding revolutionary nationalist or communist movements. Given the prevailing views among policymakers that the people in the Third World were unprepared for self-rule and vulnerable to communist appeals, the answer had long been no. The United States had to back right-wing dictatorships until economic development and modernization made a transition to more democratic rule possible.

By the 1980s, however, that position was untenable and, to many officials, undesirable as events demonstrated the bankruptcy of the logic and rationale used to defend authoritarian regimes. Reagan was unable to reestablish the automatic American support of any right-wing dictatorship regardless of its oppressive rule as long as it supported U.S. policy and was anticommunist. When the policy of supporting authoritarian regimes led to a series of crises and became a political issue at home, much of Congress and the public opposed Reagan's efforts and forced the president to alter his policy. No such restraints had existed prior to the 1970s, when the new human rights framework was implemented by Congress, reflecting shifts in public opinion. Reagan was able to provide aid to many brutal regimes, and his policy in Central America caused an enormous amount of destruction. These actions were now contested issues, and while the president wanted to do more, he was unable to because the parameters of an acceptable policy and the range of legitimate opposition had changed, creating sharp divisions over foreign policy.

---

[143] Bonner, *Waltzing with a Dictator*, 439–40.

Conclusion

Throughout most of the twentieth century, the United States supported right-wing dictatorships in the name of stability, trade, and anticommunism. Authoritarian regimes promised to maintain order, prevent revolution, and protect American investments and access to markets. This violation of America's political ideals was justified by the argument that non-Western European people were unprepared for self-government and that democratic governments in Third World nations would be weak and unstable, making these countries open to radical ideas and communist insurgencies that promised quick solutions to their problems. American policymakers, therefore, defended their actions by asserting that they had been taken in the name of freedom; right-wing dictatorships were necessary evils that would serve as antidotes to political unrest, bulwarks against communism, and conduits for modernization.

While American support for right-wing dictatorships was always morally questionable, racist assumptions, the desire for stability, fear of revolution, and the Cold War trumped the promotion of freedom and human rights that the United States claimed it was protecting when it came to American policy. It was only with the cracking of the Cold War consensus during the Vietnam War that the issues of democracy, human rights, and the types of government to which the United States provided aid entered into the public debates over foreign policy. The opposition to the Vietnam War, and the revelations of covert activities by the Church Committee, brought new voices into the making of American foreign policy. Proponents of change were able to invoke these values, making the debates revolve around the meaning of American freedom and foreign policy. In the process, they constructed a different framework for thinking about and implementing foreign policy, around human rights and the promotion of democracy, that is now part of all discussions and policy. Instead of their having to justify the place of moral concerns in foreign policy, it now falls to the critics of human rights to make the case for supporting dictatorships and not promoting democracy when crises emerge.

Reagan dismissed using the criterion of human rights as harmful to the national interest, and insisted that support for right-wing dictators was essential to national security. Through the Reagan Doctrine, however, the president framed much of his own policy in terms of morality and the defense of freedom. If American Cold War policies and opposition to communism were often based on moral arguments and the promotion of freedom and democracy, then the policies could be criticized when they failed to uphold those standards and principles. Reagan, therefore, could not escape the accusations of hypocrisy in his policy. Why, critics asked of the Reagan Doctrine, was it acceptable to support "freedom fighters" when they opposed a communist regime but not when people struggled to overthrow right-wing dictatorships?

Moreover, due to covert operations, the United States was often responsible for the very existence of many of the most odious rulers in the world, and its aid supported and sustained their ability to stay in power. This made the United States complicit in political repression, denial of human rights, and often violence used by governments against their own people. In the Reagan years, this was compounded by the unleashing of political violence in Central America and southern Africa that killed tens of thousands of people, created over a million refugees, and brought widespread international opposition to American policy. When popular unrest arose against authoritarian regimes and created crisis situations, exposing the myths of their popularity and effectiveness, the American public and Congress rejected the position that support for right-wing dictators in the name of stability, trade, and anticommunism always best served the national interest.

The end of the Cold War challenged many of the ideas previously used to justify American support for right-wing dictators and opposition to left-wing regimes as anticommunism no longer provided a unifying theme for American policy. The collapse of communism in Eastern Europe in 1989, the reunification of Germany in 1990, and the breakup of the Soviet Union in 1991 demonstrated the fallacy of the argument that there was a fundamental difference between authoritarian and totalitarian regimes; democracy took hold in many nations that had previously been considered totalitarian and incapable of political change. This removed one of the last rationalizations for the policy of supporting right-wing dictators as a means to protect American interests and promote American values.

Still, the conflict between American efforts to promote democracy in other nations and the need to protect other national interests remains. While the 1990s provided examples of Washington's support for the democratic process, from the Balkans to Southeast Asia, the United States has also continued to support many dictators in the name of stability and economic development. As the only superpower, the United States has found itself drawn into conflicts around the world. Some of these interventions have led it to back local efforts aimed at democracy and self-determination, while others have seen it support the status quo. The nation remains divided on these issues, and decisions most often have been made on a case–by–case basis rather than following a coherent policy.

Moreover, since 11 September 2001 the war against terrorism has become the greatest priority in American foreign policy. Under the Bush Doctrine, the United States has embarked on a policy of preemptive strikes, using America's overwhelming military superiority to attack nations, such as Iraq, that it claims are fostering terrorism and hostile to American interests. President George W. Bush, however, has to cast his policy in terms of promoting freedom, and has claimed that the overthrow of Saddam Hussein was designed to create a democratic Iraq that would provide a stable government in the region and serve as a model for other nations in the effort to combat Islamic extremists.

Yet, in order to carry out the war on terrorism and against Iraq, the administration has relied on and provided support to nations, such as Pakistan and Saudi Arabia, that are ruled by autocratic leaders, demonstrating that the ideological, economic, and racial arguments used to rationalize American support for authoritarian regimes continue to have influence and shape policy toward some nations. What is clear from an examination of American support for right-wing dictators is the policy's failure. Beyond contradicting the values and ideals of the United States, the policy has been unsuccessful as an effort to permanently secure American interests in the world, harms the development of democratic institutions, creates politically polarized societies, and helps to breed hostility to the United States. While the support for various dictators often provided short-term stability and support for the United States, these regimes became long-term problems. Designed to insure stability, prevent radical governments, and protect American economic interests, the policy tied the United States to regimes that often caused as many problems as they solved, and American officials found they often had much less leverage and ability to influence these regimes' actions than they thought. Indeed, as was demonstrated in Iran and Nicaragua, to name two recent examples and continuing problems, right-wing dictatorships created political polarization that led to instability and anti-American views among the local populations, and brought to power the exact forms of government the United States had sought to prevent.

The CIA has termed this phenomenon blowback: the unintended consequences of a policy that create a backlash of hostility toward the United States. In addition to revolution, blowback most often takes the form of anti-American sentiment and terrorist attacks against American targets and people. People in other nations admire America's vital economy, technology, and institutions. Still, they cannot understand the hypocrisy of American foreign policy. Officials in Washington proclaim their respect for human rights and their desire to promote democratic institutions. Yet the United States employs these positions only selectively in carrying out its foreign policy, criticizing certain regimes while continuing to support some of the most brutal and undemocratic governments in the world. These actions have serious consequences for the United States. As one Defense Department study in 1997 reported, "historical data show a strong correlation between U.S. involvement in international situations and an increase in terrorist attacks against the United States. In addition, the military asymmetry that denies nation states the ability to engage in overt attacks against the United States drives the use of transnational actors [that is, terrorists from one country attacking in another]."[1]

This was most evident recently in Afghanistan. During the 1980s, the United States armed and aided any group willing to fight the government in Kabul and the Soviet forces that were trying to defend its client state. The ultimate outcome was the coming to power of the Taliban, a violent, fundamentalist Islamic regime that represented the antithesis of American values. Moreover, it supported various terrorist groups, most notably Osama bin Laden's al-Qeada organization, that have waged a series of attacks against the United States and its allies. The hostility bred by American support for oppressive right-wing dictatorships will continue to harm the United States as the memories of its actions and its support for undemocratic forces continues to help shape politics in various areas of the world.

To resolve this contradiction between American interests and democratic values will take a full commitment to make the promotion of the nation's most cherished values and principles the top priority in foreign policy. Otherwise, the only certainty is that the dilemma over relations with right-wing dictators will continue, along with the negative consequences of supporting undemocratic regimes. However, a policy based on human rights to determine who the United States supports; self-determination to ensure that it is not aligned with repressive regimes; and the upholding of treaties and the rule of law so that when the nation acts, its policies have legitimacy and the full support of the American people would finally bring to a close this unhappy and tragic chapter in the history of American foreign policy.

[1] Johnson, *Blowback*, 9.

Abbreviations in Notes

AWF	Papers as President of the United States, 1953–61 (Ann Whitman Files), Dwight D. Eisenhower Papers, Dwight D. Eisenhower Presidential Library
CF	Country Files
CFR	Council on Foreign Relations, New York
CIA	Central Intelligence Agency
DDEL	Dwight D. Eisenhower Presidential Library
FCP	Frank Church Papers, Boise State University Library
FRUS	*Foreign Relations of the United States*
GRFL	Gerald R. Ford Presidential Library
HR	Human Rights
JCL	Jimmy Carter Presidential Library
JCTP	James C. Thompson Papers, John F. Kennedy Presidential Library
JFKL	John F. Kennedy Presidential Library
KS Files	Kissinger–Scowcroft Files, Gerald R. Ford Presidential Library
LBJL	Lyndon B. Johnson Presidential Library
NA	National Archives
NIE	National Intelligence Estimate
NSA	National Security Archives
NSAM	National Security Action Memorandum
NSDM	National Security Defense Memorandum
NSC	National Security Council
NSF	National Security Files
NSSM	National Security Study Memorandum
OSANSA	Office of the Special Assistant for National Security Affairs
RG59	Record Group 59: Records of the Department of State, National Archives
RG273	Record Group 273: Records of the National Security Council, National Archives

RNPM   Richard Nixon Presidential Materials, National Archives
RRL   Ronald Reagan Presidential Library
SF   Subject Files
SOF:NSA   Staff Office Files: National Security Adviser
WHCF   White House Central File
ZBP   Zbigniew Brzezinski Papers, Jimmy Carter Presidential Library

Bibliography

Primary Sources

Archives

Boise State University Library, Boise, Idaho
    Frank Church Papers

Council on Foreign Relations, New York, New York
    Records of Groups
    Records of Meetings

Jimmy Carter Presidential Library, Atlanta, Georgia
    Jimmy Carter Presidential Papers
        President's Files
        Staff Office Files
            National Security Adviser
        White House Central Files
    Robert Lipshutz Papers
    Zbigniew Brzezinski Papers

Dwight D. Eisenhower Presidential Library, Abilene, Kansas
    John Foster Dulles Papers, 1952–59
    Dwight D. Eisenhower Papers
        Papers as President of the United States, 1953–61 (Ann Whitman Files)
        White House Central Files, 1953–61
    White House Office
        Office of the Special Assistant for National Security Affairs, 1952–61
        Office of the Staff Secretary, 1952–61

Gerald R. Ford Presidential Library, Ann Arbor, Michigan
    Gerald Ford Papers
        Friedersdorf Files
        Kissinger–Scowcroft Files
        Savage Files

        White House Central Files
        Wolthuis Files

Lyndon B. Johnson Presidential Library, Austin, Texas
        Lyndon B. Johnson Presidential Papers
        National Security Files, 1963–69
        White House Central Files, 1963–69

John F. Kennedy Presidential Library, Boston, Massachusetts
        Roger Hilsman Papers
        John F. Kennedy Pre-Presidential Papers, 1946–60
        John F. Kennedy Presidential Papers, 1961–63
                National Security Files
                President's Office Files
                White House Central Files

National Archives, College Park, Maryland
        Chile Declassification Project (Chile Human Rights Documents)
                Carter Presidential Library
                Central Intelligence Agency
                Defense Intelligence Agency
                Department of Justice
                Department of State
                Federal Bureau of Investigation
                Ford Presidential Library
        Record Group 59: Records of the Department of State
        Record Group 273: Records of the National Security Council
        Richard Nixon Presidential Materials
                Henry Kissinger Office Files
                National Security Council Files
                White House Central Files

National Security Archives, Washington, D.C.
        Electronic Briefing Book No. 8: Chile
        Electronic Briefing Book No. 62: East Timor
        Nicaragua Collection
        Philippines Collection
        Presidential Directives

Ronald Reagan Presidential Library, Simi Valley, California
        Executive Secretariat, National Security Council
                National Security Council: Country Files
        Herman J. Cohen Files
        Records Declassified and Released by the National Security Council
        Subject Files
        White House Staff and Office Files: African Affairs Directorate: National Security
        Council

Public Documents and Government Publications

Beschloss, Michael R. *Taking Charge: The Johnson White House Tapes, 1963–1964.*
    New York: Simon and Schuster, 1997.

Beschloss, Michael R. *Reaching for Glory: Lyndon Johnson's Secret White House Tapes, 1964–1965*. New York: Simon and Schuster, 2001.

Central Intelligence Agency. *Indonesia – 1965: The Coup that Backfired*. Washington, DC: Central Intelligence Agency, 1968.

Congressional Record. Washington, DC: U.S. Government Printing Office.

Fulbright, J. William, ed. *The Vietnam Hearings*. New York: Random House, 1966.

Kornbluh, Peter. *The Pinochet File: A Declassified Dossier on Atrocity and Accountability*. New York: The New Press, 2003.

Mokoena, Kenneth, ed. *South Africa and the United States: A Declassified History*. New York: The New Press, 1993.

Porter, Gareth, ed. *Vietnam: A History in Documents*. New York: New American Library, 1981.

Public Papers of the Presidents. Washington, DC: U.S. Government Printing Office.

United States Comptroller General. *Seizure of the Mayaguez*. Washington, DC: U.S. Government Printing Office, 1976.

United States Congress. *Executive Sessions of the Senate Foreign Relations Committee (Historical Series)*. Washington, DC: U.S. Government Printing Office.

United States Congress. House Committee on Foreign Affairs, Subcommittees on Inter-American Affairs and International Organizations and Movements. *Human Rights in Chile*. Washington, DC: U.S. Government Printing Office, 1974.

United States Congress. House Committee on Foreign Affairs, Subcommittees on Inter-American Affairs and International Organizations and Movements. *Human Rights in Chile, Part II*. Washington, DC: U.S. Government Printing Office, 1975.

United States Congress. Senate Select Committee to Study Governmental Operations with Respect to Intelligence Activities. *Alleged Assassination Plots Involving Foreign Leaders*. New York: Norton, 1976.

United States Congress. Senate Select Committee to Study Governmental Operations with Respect to Intelligence Activities. *Covert Action in Chile, 1963–1973*. Washington, DC: U.S. Government Printing Office, 1975.

United States Congress. Senate Select Committee to Study Governmental Operations with Respect to Intelligence Activities. *Final Report*. Washington, DC: U.S. Government Printing Office, 1976.

United States Congress. Senate Select Committee to Study Governmental Operations with Respect to Intelligence Activities. *Hearings on Covert Action*. Washington, DC: U.S. Government Printing Office, 1975.

United States Congress. *The Presidential Campaign 1976*, 3 vols. Washington, DC: U.S. Government Printing Office, 1978–79.

United States Department of State. *Communist Interference in El Salvador*. Special Report No. 80 (23 February 1981). Washington DC: U.S. Government Printing Office.

United States Department of State. *Department of State Bulletin*. Washington, DC: U.S. Government Printing Office.

United States Department of State. *Foreign Relations of the United States*. Washington, DC: U.S. Government Printing Office.

United States National Bipartisan Commission on Central America. *Report of the National Bipartisan Commission on Central America*. Washington, DC: U.S. Government Printing Office, 1984.

Autobiographies and Memoirs

Acheson, Dean. *Present at the Creation: My Years in the State Department*. New York: Norton, 1969.

Brzezinski, Zbigniew. *Power and Principle: Memoirs of the National Security Adviser, 1977–1981.* New York: Farrar, Straus, Giroux, 1983.

Bush, George, and Brent Scowcroft. *A World Transformed.* New York: Knopf, 1998.

Carter, Jimmy. *Keeping Faith: Memoirs of a President.* New York: Bantam, 1982.

Davis, Nathaniel. "The Angola Decision of 1975: A Personal Memoir." *Foreign Affairs* 57 (Fall 1978): 109–24.

Eisenhower, Dwight D. *Mandate for Change, 1953–1956.* Garden City, NY: Doubleday, 1963.

Eisenhower, Dwight D. *Waging Peace, 1956–1961.* Garden City, NY: Doubleday, 1963.

Ford, Gerald R. *A Time to Heal.* New York: Harper and Row, 1979.

Haldeman, H. R. *The Ends of Power.* New York: Times Books, 1978.

Haldeman, H. R. *The Haldeman Diaries: Inside the Nixon White House.* New York: G. P. Putnam's Sons, 1994.

Johnson, Lyndon B. *The Vantage Point: Perspectives of the Presidency, 1963–1969.* New York: Holt, Rinehart and Winston, 1971.

Kissinger, Henry. *White House Years.* Boston: Little, Brown, 1979.

Kissinger, Henry. *Years of Renewal.* New York: Simon and Schuster, 1999.

Kissinger, Henry. *Years of Upheaval.* Boston: Little, Brown, 1982.

Nixon, Richard. *RN: The Memoirs of Richard Nixon.* New York: Grosset and Dunlap, 1978.

Shultz, George. *Turmoil and Triumph: My Years as Secretary of State.* New York: Charles Scribner's Sons, 1993.

Sullivan, William. *Mission to Iran.* New York: Norton, 1981.

Vance, Cyrus. *Hard Choices: Critical Years in America's Foreign Policy.* New York: Simon and Schuster, 1983.

Secondary Sources

Ambrose, Stephen E. *Nixon: Ruin and Recovery, 1973–1990.* New York: Simon and Schuster, 1991.

Ambrose, Stephen E. *Nixon: The Triumph of a Politician, 1961–1972.* New York: Simon and Schuster, 1989.

Anderson, Terry H. *The Movement and the Sixties.* New York: Oxford University Press, 1995.

Anderson, Thomas P. *Matanza: El Salvador's Communist Revolt of 1932.* Lincoln: University of Nebraska Press, 1971.

Armstrong, Robert, and Janet Shenk. *El Salvador: The Face of Revolution.* Boston: South End Press, 1982.

Arnson, Cynthia. *Crossroads: Congress, the President and Central America, 1976–1993.* University Park: Pennsylvania State University Press, 1993.

Arnson, Cynthia. *El Salvador: A Revolution Confronts the United States.* Washington, DC: Institute for Policy Studies, 1982.

Ashby, LeRoy, and Rod Gramer. *Fighting the Odds: The Life of Senator Frank Church.* Pullman: Washington State University Press, 1994.

Bailey, Samuel L. *The United States and the Development of South America, 1945–1975.* New York: New Viewpoints, 1976.

Baritz, Loren. *Backfire: A History of How American Culture Led Us into Vietnam and Made Us Fight the Way We Did.* New York: Morrow, 1985.

Barnet, Richard. *Intervention and Revolution: The United States in the Third World.* New York: New American Library, 1972.

Berman, Larry. *No Peace, No Honor: Nixon, Kissinger and Betrayal in Vietnam.* New York: Free Press, 2001.

Bill, James A. *The Eagle and the Lion: The Tragedy of American-Iranian Relations.* New Haven, CT: Yale University Press, 1988.

Bonner, Raymond. *Waltzing with a Dictator: The Marcoses and the Making of American Policy.* New York: Times Books, 1987.

Bonner, Raymond. *Weakness and Deceit: U.S. Policy and El Salvador.* New York: Times Books, 1984.

Brands, H. W. *Bound to Empire: The United States and the Philippines.* New York: Oxford University Press, 1992.

Brinkley, Douglas. "The Rising Stock of Jimmy Carter: The 'Hands On' Legacy of Our Thirty-Ninth President." *Diplomatic History* 20 (Fall 1996): 505–29.

Bundy, William. *A Tangled Web: The Making of Foreign Policy in the Nixon Presidency.* New York: Hill and Wang, 1998.

Bundy, William. "Dictatorships and American Foreign Policy." *Foreign Affairs* 54 (October 1975): 51–60.

Carothers, Thomas. *In the Name of Democracy: U.S. Policy toward Latin America in the Reagan Years.* Berkeley: University of California Press, 1991.

Chanda, Nayan. "A Word in Your Ear." *Far Eastern Economic Review* 31 (January 1985): 30–1.

Church, Frank. "How Many Dominican Republics and Vietnams Can We Take On?" *New York Times Magazine,* 28 November 1965.

Clymer, Kenton. "Jimmy Carter, Human Rights, and Cambodia." *Diplomatic History.* 27, no. 2 (April 2003): 245–78.

Cribb, Robert, ed. *The Indonesian Killings of 1965–1966: Studies from Java and Bali.* Clayton, Australia: Centre of Southeast Asian Studies, 1990.

Crocker, Chester. *High Noon in South Africa: Making Peace in a Rough Neighborhood.* New York: Norton, 1992.

Crocker, Chester. "South Africa: Strategy for Change." *Foreign Affairs* 59 (Winter 1980–81): 323–51.

Danner, Mark. *The Massacre at El Mozote: A Parable of the Cold War.* New York: Vintage, 1994.

DeBenedetti, Charles, with Charles Chatfield. *An American Ordeal: The Anti-War Movement of the Vietnam Era.* Syracuse, NY: Syracuse University Press, 1990.

Dinges, John. *The Condor Years: How Pinochet and His Allies Brought Terrorism to Three Continents.* New York: The New Press, 2004.

Drumbell, John. *The Carter Presidency: A Re-evaluation.* New York: St. Martin's Press, 1993.

Dunkerley, Jones. *The Long War: Dictatorship and Revolution in El Salvador.* London: Junction Books, 1982.

Ehrman, John. *The Rise of Neoconservatism: Intellectuals and Foreign Affairs, 1945–1994.* New Haven, CT: Yale University Press, 1995.

El-Khawas, Mohamed A., and Barry Cohen, eds. *Southern Africa: The Kissinger Study of Southern Africa.* Westport, CT: L. Hill, 1976.

Engerman, David C., et al., eds. *Staging Growth: Modernization, Development, and the Global Cold War.* Amherst: University of Massachusetts Press, 2003.

Findling, John. *Close Neighbors, Distant Friends: United States–Central American Relations.* New York: Greenwood Press, 1987.

Fink, Gary M., and Hugh David Graham, eds. *The Carter Presidency: Policy Choices in the Post–New Deal Era.* Lawrence: University Press of Kansas, 1998.

Fitzgerald, Frances. *Fire in the Lake: The Vietnamese and the Americans in Vietnam.* Boston: Little, Brown, 1972.

Fousek, John. *To Lead the Free World: American Nationalism and the Cultural Roots of the Cold War.* Chapel Hill: University of North Carolina Press, 2000.

Friend, Theodore. "Timely Daring: The United States and Ferdinand Marcos." In Pipes, Daniel, and Adam Garfinkle, eds., *Friendly Tyrants: An American Dilemma.* New York: St. Martin's Press, 1991, pp. 201–19.

Fukuyama, Francis. *The End of History and the Last Man.* New York: Free Press, 1992.

Gardner, Lloyd. *Approaching Vietnam: From World War II through Dienbienphu, 1941–1954.* New York: Norton, 1988.

Gardner, Lloyd. *Pay Any Price: Lyndon Johnson and the Wars for Vietnam.* Chicago: I. R. Dee, 1995.

Garfinkle, Adam, et al. *The Devil and Uncle Sam: A User's Guide to the Friendly Tyrants Dilemma.* New Brunswick, NJ: Transaction, 1992.

Gettleman, Marvin, et al., eds. *El Salvador: Central America in the New Cold War.* New York: Grove Press, 1981.

Gibbons, William Conrad. *The U.S. Government and the Vietnam War: Executive and Legislative Roles and Relationships, Part II, 1961–1964.* Princeton, NJ: Princeton University Press, 1986.

Gibbons, William Conrad. *The U.S. Government and the Vietnam War: Executive and Legislative Roles and Relationships, Part III, January–July 1965.* Princeton, NJ: Princeton University Press, 1989.

Gibbons, William Conrad. *The U.S. Government and the Vietnam War: Executive and Legislative Roles and Relationships, Part IV, July 1965–January 1968.* Princeton, NJ: Princeton University Press, 1995.

Gibbs, David N. *The Political Economy of Third World Intervention: Mines, Money, and U.S. Policy in the Congo Crisis.* Chicago: University of Chicago Press, 1991.

Gibbs, David N. "The United Nations, International Peacekeeping, and the Question of Impartiality: Revisiting the Congo Operation." *Journal of Modern African Studies* 38, no. 3 (2000): 359–82.

Gleijeses, Piero. *Conflicting Missions: Havana, Washington and Africa, 1959–1976.* Chapel Hill: University of North Carolina Press, 2002.

Guilmartin, John F. *A Very Short War: The Mayaguez and the Battle of Koh Tang.* College Station: Texas A&M University Press, 1995.

Haass, Richard N. "South Africa under Apartheid." In Pipes, Daniel, and Adam Garfinkle, eds., *Friendly Tyrants: An American Dilemma.* New York: St. Martin's Press, 1991, pp. 403–20.

Hall, Mitchell. *Because of Their Faith: CALCAV and Religious Opposition to the Vietnam War.* New York: Columbia University Press, 1990.

Hargrove, Erwin. *Jimmy Carter as President: Leadership and the Politics of Public Good.* Baton Rouge: Louisiana University Press, 1988.

Herring, George. *America's Longest War: The United States and Vietnam, 1950–1975.* Philadelphia: Temple University Press, 1986.

Hersh, Seymour M. *The Price of Power: Kissinger in the Nixon White House.* New York: Summit Books, 1983.

Hickey, Dennis, and Kenneth Wylie. *An Enchanting Darkness: The American Vision of Africa in the Twentieth Century.* East Lansing: Michigan State University Press, 1993.

Hogan, Michael. *A Cross of Iron: Harry S. Truman and the Origins of the National Security State, 1945–1954.* Cambridge: Cambridge University Press, 1998.

Hunt, Michael. *Ideology and U.S. Foreign Policy*. New Haven, CT: Yale University Press, 1987.

Jeffreys-Jones, Rhodri. *Peace Now! American Society and the Ending of the Vietnam War*. New Haven, CT: Yale University Press, 1999.

Johnson, Chalmers. *Blowback: The Costs and Consequences of American Empire*. New York: Metropolitan Books, 2000.

Johnson, Chalmers. *The Sorrows of Empire: Militarism, Secrecy, and the End of the Republic*. New York: Metropolitan Books, 2004.

Johnson, Haynes. *Sleepwalking through History: America in the Reagan Years*. New York: Norton, 1991.

Johnson, John J. *Latin America in Caricature*. Austin: University of Texas Press, 1980.

Johnson, Loch. *A Season of Inquiry: The Senate Intelligence Investigation*. Lexington: University Press of Kentucky, 1985.

Kahin, Audrey R. and George McT. *Subversion as Foreign Policy: The Secret Eisenhower and Dulles Debacle in Indonesia*. New York: New Press, 1995.

Kahin, George McT. *Intervention: How America Became Involved in Vietnam*. New York: Knopf, 1986.

Kalb, Madeleine G. *The Congo Cables: The Cold War in Africa–From Eisenhower to Kennedy*. New York: Macmillan, 1982.

Karnow, Stanley. *In Our Image: America's Empire in the Philippines*. New York: Random House, 1989.

Karnow, Stanley. *Vietnam: A History*. New York: Viking Press, 1983.

Kaufman, Burton I. *The Presidency of James Earl Carter, Jr.* Lawrence: University Press of Kansas, 1993.

Kelly, Sean. *America's Tyrant: The CIA and Mobutu of Zaire*. Washington, DC: American University Press, 1993.

Kimball, Jeffrey P. *Nixon's Vietnam War*. Lawrence: University Press of Kansas, 1998.

Kirkpatrick, Jeane. "Dictatorships and Double Standards." *Commentary*, November 1979, 34–45.

Kirkpatrick, Jeane. *Dictatorships and Double Standards: Rationalism and Reason in Politics*. New York: Simon and Schuster, 1982.

Kirkpatrick, Jeane. "U.S. Security and Latin America." *Commentary*, January 1981, 29–40.

Kousoulos, Dimitrios George. *Modern Greece: Profile of a Nation*. New York: Scribner, 1974.

Krenn, Michael L. *Black Diplomacy: African Americans and the State Department, 1945–1969*. Armonk, NY: M. E. Sharpe, 1999.

Krenn, Michael L. "Their Proper Share: The Changing Role of Racism in U.S. Foreign Policy since World War One." *Nature, Society, and Thought* 4 (1991): 57–79.

Krenn, Michael L., ed. *Race and United States Foreign Policy during the Cold War*. New York: Garland, 1998.

Kwitny, Jonathan. *Endless Enemies: The Making of an Unfriendly World*. New York: Congdon and Weed, 1984.

LaFeber, Walter. *Inevitable Revolutions: The United States in Central America*, 2nd ed. New York: Norton, 1993.

Lamb, Christopher. *Belief Systems and Decision Making in the Mayaguez Crisis*. Gainesville: University of Florida Press, 1989.

Langley, Lester D. *The United States and the Caribbean in the Twentieth Century*, rev. ed. Athens: University of Georgia Press, 1985.

Latham, Michael E. *Modernization as Ideology: American Social Science and "Nation Building" in the Kennedy Era.* Chapel Hill: University of North Carolina Press, 2000.

Lemann, Nicholas. *The Promised Land: The Great Black Migration and How It Changed America.* New York: Knopf, 1991.

Levy, David. *The Debate over Vietnam.* Baltimore: Johns Hopkins University Press, 1991.

Little, Douglas. *American Orientalism: The United States and the Middle East since 1945.* Chapel Hill: University of North Carolina Press, 2002.

Mahoney, Richard D. *JFK: Ordeal in Africa.* New York: Oxford University Press, 1983.

Massie, Robert. *Loosing the Bonds: The United States and South Africa in the Apartheid Years.* New York: Doubleday, 1997.

McMahon, Robert J. *Colonialism and Cold War: The United States and the Struggle for Indonesian Independence, 1945–1949.* Ithaca, NY: Cornell University Press, 1981.

Miller, Judith. "Criminal Negligence: Congress, Chile, and the CIA." *Progressive,* November 1974, 15–19.

Montgomery, Tommie Sue. *Revolution in El Salvador: Origins and Evolution.* Boulder, CO: Westview Press, 1982.

Muravchik, Joshua. *The Uncertain Crusade: Jimmy Carter and the Dilemmas of Human Rights Policy.* Lanham, MD: Hamilton Press, 1988.

Nathan, James A. "The *Mayaguez*, Presidential War, and Congressional Senescence." *Intellect,* February 1976, 360–2.

Newsom, David D., ed. *The Diplomacy of Human Rights.* Lanham, MD: University Press of America, 1986.

Nixon, Richard. "Asia after Viet Nam." *Foreign Affairs* 46 (October 1967): 111–25.

Noer, Thomas. *Cold War and Black Liberation: The United States and White Rule in Africa, 1948–1968.* Columbia: University of Missouri Press, 1985.

Olson, Gregory Allen. *Mansfield and Vietnam: A Study in Rhetorical Adaptation.* East Lansing: Michigan State University Press, 1995.

Park, James William. *Latin American Underdevelopment: A History of Perspectives in the United States, 1870–1975.* Baton Rouge: Louisiana State University Press, 1995.

Pastor, Robert. *Condemned to Repetition: The United States and Nicaragua.* Princeton, NJ: Princeton University Press, 1987.

Paterson, Thomas G. *Meeting the Communist Threat: Truman to Reagan.* New York: Oxford University Press, 1988.

Pipes, Daniel, and Adam Garfinkle, eds. *Friendly Tyrants: An American Dilemma.* New York: St. Martin's Press, 1991.

Powers, Thomas. *The Man Who Kept the Secrets: Richard Helms and the CIA.* New York: Knopf, 1979.

Rabe, Stephen G. *The Most Dangerous Area in the World: John F. Kennedy Confronts Communist Revolution in Latin America.* Chapel Hill: University of North Carolina Press, 1999.

Reed, Christopher. "U.S. Agents 'Drew Up Indonesian Hit List.'" *London Guardian,* 22 May 1990.

Rosati, Jerel. "The Rise and Fall of America's First Post–Cold War Foreign Policy." In Rosenbaum, Herbert D., and Alexej Ugrinsky, eds., *Jimmy Carter: Foreign Policy and Post-Presidential Years.* Westport, CT: Greenwood Press, 1994, pp. 35–52.

Rosenbaum, Herbert D., and Alexej Ugrinsky, eds. *Jimmy Carter: Foreign Policy and Post-Presidential Years.* Westport, CT: Greenwood Press, 1994.

Rossiter, Caleb, and Anne-Marie Smith. "Human Rights: The Carter Record, the Reagan Reaction." *International Policy Report*, September 1984, pp. 1–27

Rostow, W. W. *The Stages of Economic Growth: A Non-Communist Manifesto*, 3rd ed. New York: Cambridge University Press, 1991.

Roubatis, Yiannis P. *Tangled Web: The U.S. in Greece, 1947–1967*. New York: Pella, 1987.

Rousseas, Stephen. *The Death of a Democracy: Greece and the American Conscience.* New York, Grove Press, 1967.

Rubin, Barry M. *Paved with Good Intentions: The American Experience and Iran*. New York: Oxford University Press, 1980.

Schatzberg, Michael G. *Mobutu or Chaos? The United States and Zaire, 1960–1990.* Lanham, MD: University Press of America, 1991.

Schlesinger, Arthur M., Jr. *A Thousand Days: John F. Kennedy in the White House.* Boston: Houghton Mifflin, 1965.

Schlesinger, Arthur M., Jr. *The Imperial Presidency.* Boston: Houghton Mifflin, 1973.

Schmitz, David F. "Congress Must Draw the Line: Senator Frank Church and the Opposition to the Vietnam War and the Imperial Presidency." In Woods, Randall B., eds., *Vietnam and the American Political Tradition: The Politics of Dissent*. New York: Cambridge University Press, 2003, pp. 127–48.

Schmitz, David F. "'Of Presidents and Caesars': Senator Frank Church and the Cooper-Church Amendment." In Schmitz, David F., and T. Christopher Jespersen, eds., *Architects of the American Century: Individuals and Institutions in Twentieth Century U.S. Foreign Policymaking.* Chicago: Imprint Publications, 2000, pp. 144–60.

Schmitz, David F. "Senator Frank Church, the Ford Administration, and the Challenges of Post-Vietnam Foreign Policy." *Peace and Change* 21, no. 4 (October 1996): 438–63.

Schmitz, David F. *Thank God They're on Our Side: The United States and Right-Wing Dictatorships, 1921–1965.* Chapel Hill: University of North Carolina Press, 1999.

Schmitz, David F., and T. Christopher Jespersen, eds. *Architects of the American Century: Individuals and Institutions in Twentieth Century U.S. Foreign Policymaking.* Chicago: Imprint Publications, 2000.

Schmitz, David F., and Vanessa Walker. "Jimmy Carter and the Foreign Policy of Human Rights: The Development of a Post–Cold War Foreign Policy." *Diplomatic History*, 18, no. 1 (January 2004): 113–43.

Schulman, Robert. *John Sherman Cooper: The Global Kentuckian.* Lexington: University Press of Kentucky, 1976.

Scott, Peter Dale. "The United States and the Overthrow of Sukarno, 1965–1967." *Pacific Affairs* 58, no. 2 (1985): 239–64.

Shawcross, William. *Sideshow: Kissinger, Nixon and the Destruction of Cambodia.* New York: Simon and Schuster, 1979.

Sheehan, Neil. *A Bright Shining Lie: John Paul Vann and America in Vietnam.* New York: Random House, 1988.

Sherrard, Philip, and John Kennedy Campbell. *Modern Greece.* New York: Praeger, 1968.

Sigmund, Paul E. *The United States and Democracy in Chile.* Baltimore: Johns Hopkins University Press, 1993.

Sikkink, Kathryn. *Mixed Signals: U.S. Human Rights Policy and Latin America.* Ithaca, NY: Cornell University Press, 2004.

Simpson, Bradley R. "Modernizing Indonesia: United States–Indonesian Relations, 1961–1967." Ph.D. dissertation, Northwestern University, 2003.

Skidmore, David. *Reversing Course: Carter's Foreign Policy, Domestic Politics and the Failure of Reform.* Nashville, TN: Vanderbilt University Press, 1996.

Small, Melvin. *Antiwarriors: The Vietnam War and the Battle for America's Hearts and Minds.* Wilmington, NC: Scholarly Resources, 2002.

Small, Melvin. *Johnson, Nixon and the Doves.* New Brunswick, NJ: Rutgers University Press, 1988.

Smith, Christian. *Resisting Reagan: The U.S. Central America Peace Movement.* Chicago: University of Chicago Press, 1996.

Smith, Gaddis. *Morality, Reason and Power: American Diplomacy in the Carter Years.* New York: Hill and Wang, 1986.

Smith, Gaddis. *The Last Years of the Monroe Doctrine, 1945–1993.* New York: Hill and Wang, 1994.

Smith, Tony. *America's Mission: The United States and the Worldwide Struggle for Democracy in the Twentieth Century.* Princeton, NJ: Princeton University Press, 1994.

Spencer, Donald. *The Carter Implosion: Jimmy Carter and the Amateur Style of Diplomacy.* New York: Praeger, 1988.

Stanley, Henry M. *In the Darkest Africa: The Quest, Rescue and Retreat of Emin, Governor of Equitoria.* New York: Scribner, 1890.

Stanley, Henry M. *Through the Dark Continent.* New York: Harper and Brothers, 1879.

Steel, Ronald. "Cold War, Cold Comfort." *The New Republic,* 11 April 1981, 15–17.

Stephanson, Anders. *Manifest Destiny: American Expansion and the Empire of Right.* New York: Hill and Wang, 1995.

Steuck, William. "Placing Jimmy Carter's Foreign Policy." In Fink, Gary M., and Hugh David Graham, eds., *The Carter Presidency: Policy Choices in the Post–New Deal Era.* Lawrence: University Press of Kansas, 1998, pp. 244–66.

Stockwell, John. *In Search of Enemies: A CIA Story.* New York: Norton, 1978.

Strong, Robert. *Working in the World: Jimmy Carter and the Making of American Foreign Policy.* Baton Rouge: Louisiana State University Press, 2000.

Tomes, Robert P. *Apocalypse Then: American Intellectuals and the Vietnam War, 1954–1975.* New York: New York University Press, 1998.

Urquahart, Brian. "The Tragedy of Lumumba." *New York Review of Books,* 4 October 2001, 4–7.

Vavrina, Vernon J. "The Carter Human Rights Policy: Political Idealism and Realpolitik." In Rosenbaum, Herbert D., and Alexej Ugrinsky, eds., *Jimmy Carter: Foreign Policy and Post-Presidential Years.* Westport, CT: Greenwood Press, 1994, pp. 103–13.

Weissman, Stephen R. *American Foreign Policy in the Congo, 1960–1964.* Ithaca, NY: Cornell University Press, 1974.

Weissman, Stephen R. "CIA Covert Action in Zaire and Angola." *Political Science Quarterly* 44 (Summer 1979): 263–86.

Wells, Tom. *The War Within: America's Battle over Vietnam.* Berkeley: University of California Press, 1994.

Williams, William Appleman. *The Tragedy of American Diplomacy.* New York: Dell, 1972.

Williams, William Appleman, et al. *America in Vietnam: A Documentary History.* Garden City, NY: Anchor Press/Doubleday, 1985.

Woods, Randall B. *Fulbright: A Biography*. New York: Cambridge University Press, 1995.

Woods, Randall B., ed. *Vietnam and the American Political Tradition: The Politics of Dissent*. New York: Cambridge University Press, 2003.

X [George Kennan]. "The Sources of Soviet Conduct." *Foreign Affairs* 25 (1947): 566–82.

Yergin, Daniel. *The Prize: The Epic Quest for Oil, Money, and Power*. New York: Simon and Schuster, 1991.

Young, Marilyn. *The Vietnam Wars, 1945–1990*. New York: HarperCollins, 1991.

Zakaria, Fareed. *The Future of Freedom: Illiberal Democracy at Home and Abroad*. New York: Norton, 2003.

Index